Caring for Older People in the Community

Third Edition

Caring for Older People in the Community

Third Edition

Professor E Idris Williams, OBE

with contributions from Hana Hermanova,
Laurence Z Rubenstein and Darryl Wieland

Foreword by Professor J C Brocklehurst

Radcliffe Medical Press • Oxford and New York

Radcliffe Medical Press Ltd
18 Marcham Road, Abingdon, Oxon, OX14 1AA, UK

Radcliffe Medical Press, Inc
141 Fifth Avenue, New York, NY 10010, USA

British Library Cataloguing in Publication Data.

A catalogue record for this book is available from the British Library.

Library of Congress Cataloging-in-Publication Data is available.

ISBN 1 85775 025 X

Typeset by Creative Associates
Printed and bound in Great Britain by Biddles Ltd, Guildford & King's Lynn

Contents

Foreword

The last few years have seen huge changes in the face of medicine in the United Kingdom – not least in general practice. Continuing emphasis on cost containment has led to ever shortening periods of stay in hospitals and increases in day admissions. The care in the community philosophy has increased the numbers of physically and mentally disabled people who are now looked after at home, or sometimes in prison, or on the streets. As hospital geriatric departments have had their continuing care beds gradually whittled away, an increasing number of older peple are cared for in private residential and nursing homes. The medical management of these disabled people is now being transferred from geriatricians and their staff to general practitioners. All of this is happening against a background of increasing human lifespan. The numbers of nonegenarians and centenarians in our population are growing exponentially.

All of this has focused the role of general practice, increasing the scope and volume of its work. Primary medical care has responded to these responsibilities by organizational changes, the introduction of practice managers and practice nurses, and state-of-the-art methods of data handling.

The scientific basis of medical practice also changes year by year. New diseases, new investigational techniques and new therapeutic regimes have to be absorbed by doctors – in itself an exciting and challenging, but none the less arduous, task.

It is the role of the medical textbook to provide an immediately available source of up-to-date knowledge and information. It should be presented clearly, easy to access and well referenced to give leads for more intensive study of particular topics. A national textbook should also take account of parallel developments in other major medical systems abroad.

For general practitioners, Professor Idris Williams's text is now well established as a major work on old age, fulfilling all the criteria of an excellent medical textbook. This new edition maintains its pre-eminence in the field.

J C BROCKLEHURST CBE, MD, FRCP,
PROFESSOR EMERITUS
UNIVERSITY OF MANCHESTER

January 1995

Acknowledgements

I have had enormous help from many people in writing this third edition and I would like to express my very grateful thanks.

Frank Higgins, Tony Ruffell, John Bendall, Bob Tattersall, Nick Galloway, Kevin Gibbin, Rob Jones, Nori Graham, Christine Hopton, Paul Wallace, Joanna Hocknell and Helen Laverty have all helped me by reading chapters and making significant changes and contributions. I am very indebted to them for making this book relevant and up to date. I must also acknowledge the contribution of Charles Barker and Karen Kniveton for allowing me to use their section in the over-75s training package of 'social aspects'.

It is a particular pleasure the thank my friends Larry Rubenstein, Darryl Wieland and Hana Hermanova for contributing two chapters. These have put the subject in an international perspective.

I am very pleased also to be able to thank Age Concern England for permission to reproduce material from their Facts Sheets and the Alzheimer's Disease Society for permission to reproduce the excellent guidelines for GPs on the management of dementia and particularly to acknowledge the permission of the authors, Professor Andy Haines and Professor C Katona, and the Royal College of General Practitioners, who first published the guidelines in their Occasional Paper 58.

I would also like to thank my partners Drs Carole Brown, Elizabeth Phillipson, Peter Barrett, Nicholas Buckell, Jean Madeley and Christine Johnson for allowing me to include an audit of our care for the 75-year and over patients, and in particular, for the generous way in which they have supported my interest in older people.

My special thanks goes to my secretary, Greta Stone, for keeping me organized and the excellence of her word processing and other skills. Rose Henson and Maureen McGowan have also contributed significantly to the secretarial work. Lindsay Groom has done much of the researching and her proof-reading expertise has made the book more readable and coherent.

Finally, I would like to thank my wife for her tolerance of my working long hours at weekends when the time would perhaps have been better spent walking the Cumbrian fells.

The author and publishers also wish to thank the following for permission to use copyright material.

British Medical Journal, Cambridge University Press, Churchill Livingstone, Edward Arnold, Haymarket Medical Limited, Her Majesty's Stationery Office

(Central Statistical Office and Office of Population Censuses and Surveys), Oxford University Press, Routledge, Royal Society of Medicine Services Ltd, Taylor & Francis, The British Journal of General Practice and The Gerontological Society of America.

Every effort has been made to trace all the copyright holders, but if any have been inadvertently overlooked, the publishers will be pleased to make the necessary arrangements at the first opportunity.

1
Introduction

The need to produce a further edition of this book arose from the enormous changes which have taken place in the organization of community health and social services over the last few years. They represent part of a larger reorganization of the National Health Service and personal social services provided by local authorities. Three important White Papers prepared the ground for these changes. These were: *Promoting better health* (1987)[1], *Working for patients* (1988)[2], and *Caring for people* (1989)[3]. These form the basis of the National Health Service and Community Care Act (1990). This Act came into effect for the National Health Service in April 1991 and for the Community Social Services in April 1993.

These changes represented a new philosophy towards the provision of caring services; many of them have affected the lives of older people, who, of course, are major consumers of such services. The management and delivery of health and social care services have been reorganized and a new preventive care service has been introduced into the community. Hospital and community units, together with fundholding general practices, have brought new financial considerations into the planning of care and the mechanisms of priority setting. All these changes, and others which will be described in this book, have had an impact on the care delivered to older people. These changes were being forecast in the 1989 edition of this book, but now the full effects can be described more comprehensively and comments made about the experience of the first few years.

The layout of the book is basically the same. I have taken the opportunity to update basic information and introduce data from the 1991 census. Some reordering of the chapters has taken place to reflect a more logical sequence and many chapters have been largely rewritten. I have included a chapter on medical audit, which has been an important consequence of the National Health Service reforms. It is relevant to the care of older people; they are a group of people who are vulnerable to ineffective services.

The need to provide effective community care for older people is now a widely recognized international priority. Individual nations have different arrangements and I am fortunate to be able to include contributions from doctors working outside the UK. Dr Laurence Z. Rubenstein, the Director of the Geriatric Research, Education and Clinical Center, Veterans' Affairs Medical Center, Sepulveda, California, and Darryl Wieland, a Senior Researcher in that unit, provide a description of community care in the United States of America. Dr Hana Hermanova, Regional Adviser for Elderly, Disability and Rehabilitation to WHO, Europe, describes the situation in Europe.

The general philosophy of the book remains intact. It is based upon a positive approach to looking after older people. The general outlook for healthy living in old age is optimistic; older people are generally in good effective health and are able to function independently in their own homes, but they do have some specific needs that we must understand and to which we must respond. The first edition of the book was written in the summer of 1978 and the second in 1988. Out of interest I have included, as a postscript, the preface and conclusions of both the first and the second editions. They demonstrate the changes that have occurred in the past 16 years. No doubt still more changes are yet to come.

Finally, and very significantly, the community care of older people is an issue that is of considerable importance, not only to industrialized countries but also to all developing countries. Although the book contains details of the British scene and methods of delivery of health and social care, the basic characteristics of life in older age are common to all nations and the general principles of care detailed in this book are of relevance world-wide.

References

1. Secretaries of State for Health and Social Services, Wales, Northern Ireland and Scotland. (1987) *Promoting better health: the Government's programme for improving primary health care* (Cmnd 249) HMSO, London.

2. Secretaries of State for Health and Social Services, Wales, Northern Ireland and Scotland. (1988) *Working for patients.* (Cmnd 555) HMSO, London.

3. Secretaries of State for Health, Social Security, Wales and Scotland. (1989) *Caring for people: community care in the next decade and beyond.* (Cmnd 849) HMSO, London.

2
Community Care for Older People in the United States of America: An Overview

Laurence Z Rubenstein and Darryl Wieland

In this brief chapter, we describe trends in community geriatric care in the USA for the British reader. In past years, most comparative studies of British and American approaches to health care of older patients have focused on what the latter could learn from the former[1,2]. More recently, however, fundamental changes in both systems are making them more similar. On the British side, the new policy focus in health care cost containment (shared with the Americans) has led to changes in the NHS towards increased privatization and 'managed competition', strategies touted as keys to health reform in the USA[3-5]. On the American side, in addition to retaining emphasis on 'consumer choice', competition and private involvement, cost concerns are leading to global budgeting and financing reforms that will inevitably increase governmental responsibility for health care quality, availability and access[6]. British commentaries on new or anticipated health care problems[7-10] reflect concerns that have been longstanding among American geriatricians and primary care physicians of older patients: difficulties with continuity and quality of care, development of outcome standards for quality of life, service incentives leading to inappropriate utilization, problems of adequacy and availability of medical and rehabilitative services in poor areas and populations, and development of a *de facto* 'two tiered' service structure with inadequate access for many older people and others. Perhaps the time is ripe to learn even more from trans-Atlantic comparisons.

Demography and Health Status of Older Americans

In 1990, about 13% of Americans (roughly 32 million) were aged 65 or more, compared with over 15% of the UK population. While both proportions have been growing since 1900, the UK has had about a 2% larger proportion since 1940. Projections show that these proportions will converge above 16% in 2020, rising sharply to over 19% in 2030[11]. It is of particular relevance to geriatric care throughout the industrial West that the ageing of populations has been accompanied by 'ageing of the old' people. In the USA, the 'oldest older' segment (persons 85 years and older) is growing faster than other older age groups, and will itself comprise over 17% of elderly Americans in 2010[12]. While the health status of the old is extremely variable, these Americans live with a greater burden of disease and disability. As elsewhere, the problem for formal geriatric care is not merely one of treating chronic disease, but of buttressing declining sources of informal familial support: the substantial differential life expectancy at 60 and 80 years between men and women in both the USA and UK will increase the ratio of older women to older men, particularly among the oldest (Table 2.1). As our community geriatric patients age, they are, increasingly, as widowed women living alone.

Table 2.1: Life expectancy (years): USA and UK.

Age	1960		1987		Increase	
	USA	UK	USA	UK	USA	UK
Females						
60	19.6	19.3	22.5	21.2	2.9	1.9
80	6.8	6.3[a]	8.8	7.8	2.0	1.5
Males						
60	15.9	15.3	18.2	16.8	2.3	1.5
80	6.0	5.2[a]	6.9	6.0	0.9	0.8

Source: Based on data for Organization for Economic Cooperation and Development, 1990[23].
[a] 1961 data.

The ageing population in the USA is also becoming more ethnically diverse. While ethnic minorities comprised about 13% of elderly Americans in 1990, the proportion is expected to grow to over 21% in 2020, and to over 30% by mid-century (Figure 2.1).

In the 1990–2050 interval, the number of older African–Americans will grow 3.7 times to 9.6 million, older Hispanic people will multiply over seven times to 7.9 million, and other older minorities will grow over eight times to 5 million[13].

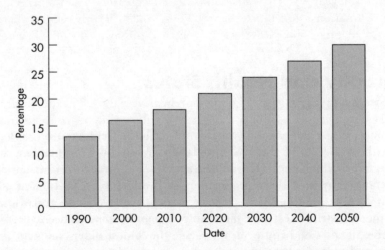

Figure 2.1: Growth of the USA minority elderly population: proportion of the population aged 65 and over who belong to minority groups. Source: Based on data from the US Senate Special Committee on Ageing, 1987[30].

The growing diversity will become increasingly important in the development of community as well as institutional geriatric care and in the primary ambulatory care of older patients. Aside from issues of access to culturally acceptable services, older minority populations may bear a greater burden of disability than older white people (Table 2.2[14]).

Table 2.2: Health status of older Americans: population ≥ 75 years by sex and race.

	Self-assessed health ≥ very good (%)	Unable/limited in major activity (%)
Females		
White	36.4	29.3
Black	24.6	44.5
Males		
White	35.4	20.1
Black	27.3	27.6

Source: Based on data from National Center for Health Statistics, 1986[14].

Financing of Health Services

The USA spends more on health services than any other nation, at about twice the average of other developed countries. Despite the relative youth of its population, it spent 2.8 times more per capita than the UK in 1989 ($2354 versus $836). The spending differential is not simply a reflection of relative national wealth. USA health expenditures accounted for almost 12% of the gross domestic product (GDP) in that year, which is also considerably greater than the average of other developed nations, and more than twice the 5.8% health related share of the UK's GDP. Unlike other developed countries, the majority of USA health expenditures (58%) were private[15].

In the USA health care financing involves a complex mix of public payers (federal, state and local governments) as well as private, out of pocket spending and health insurance. While there is no comprehensive national health insurance system, most employed individuals and their families obtain group insurance through their place of employment; older and disabled individuals are entitled to Medicare, the major public health insurance programme, and many poor Americans rely on Medicaid, the public health programme for the 'medically indigent'. (Medicare is health insurance provided universally to persons over the age of 65. Medicaid, which grew out of the welfare system, is available only to certain low income individuals and families of all ages who meet various means tests.) Unfortunately, public and private financing programmes are not systematically co-ordinated, and nearly 35 million, mostly younger Americans (14% of the population) are as yet neither privately nor publicly covered[16,17]. (These uninsured are comprised of many persons who are self-employed or whose employers do not provide insurance benefits, together with poor persons who do not qualify for Medicaid.)

In 1991, about two-thirds of older Americans had, in addition to their Medicare coverage, supplemental private health insurance. About half of the remainder had only Medicare, and the other half were insured both by Medicare and Medicaid programmes[18]. Here, too, coverages are associated with ethnic minority status: where almost 70% of white elderly Americans have both Medicare and private health insurance, less than 30% of both African–American and Latino people had this higher level of coverage. About 25% of older blacks and Latinos, but only 7% of whites, had Medicaid as well as Medicare coverage.

Organization and Delivery of Community Health Services

Given the diversity of the non-institutionalized older American population, the nature of community geriatric care is varied, and can include preventive, therapeutic, restorative or supportive services. Care of older non-institutionalized patients includes the services of family, friends and neighbours (informal care givers) as well as paid (formal) carers, ranging from unskilled and semiskilled aides to well trained professionals. However, it is clear that most community care given to older people is informal (unpaid), familial and supportive, consisting of assistance with basic and instrumental activities, as well as providing psychosocial support[19]. The role of formal community based preventive, therapeutic and restorative care is more limited in that it depends upon availability and access; the financing organizations for personal health services in the USA do not encourage their use[20].

Professional, formal health services in the USA have historically been orientated towards hospital based management of acute illnesses, and are provided through a loosely organized delivery system responsive to market and regulatory forces, with outpatient primary care provided largely by independent fee for service (FFS) physicians in solo or group practices. Hospitals, most of which are private non-profit institutions, open or close depending on local market demands and community resources and preferences. There is no nation-wide health planning, and planning by the individual states varies from nothing to strict control of hospital and nursing home construction. Physicians are free to specialize and practice where they wish, and thus many areas, namely poor inner city and remote rural areas, do not have sufficient numbers of primary care physicians. There are governmental programmes that attempt to provide some primary care to underserved populations in these areas. Most American FFS physicians see their patients in their surgeries and admit them to hospitals where they can continue to serve them[21].

In 1988, there were 2.3 active physicians per 1000 USA population, which is the average physician availability for the developed nations, and greater than the UK rate of 1.4 per 1000[14]. Nevertheless, important problems exist in the geographical and specialty distribution of American physicians. For example, the active physician to population ratio in rural USA averages 0.9/1000[23]. The 1986 physician contact rate of 5.3 visits per capita was not much greater than the UK rate of 4.5[23]. Of practising physicians, 66% are specialists (most of whom individuals can access directly), and only one-third are in primary care fields (family practice, paediatrics, internal medicine). This is a ratio that reflects physician income incentives favouring specialists and reverses the distribution typical of developed countries, leading to concerns about the adequacy of primary and community-based care for older as well as other Americans[24,25].

Exacerbating the problems of inadequate primary care availability for older Americans is the persistent shortage of geriatric medicine practitioners[26,27]. In great part, the dearth of both primary care physicians and geriatricians has been due to the predominant FFS physician payment mechanism that disproportionately rewards 'high-tech' procedural medicine, and discourages the more labour intensive, team based assessment and treatment necessary for the care of our complicated older patients. Recent reforms have led to a resource based, relative value schedule governing public reimbursement among specialties[28].

Public reimbursement (via the Medicaid and Medicare programmes) is largely responsible for the emergence of both nursing homes and home care in the USA. Nursing homes have also come to play a particularly prominent role in American geriatric care. Since 1950, the number of Americans living in nursing homes has grown more than fivefold, from under 300 000 in 1950 to over 15 000 000 in 1990[29,30]. More recently, there has been a tremendous growth in the number of Medicare certified home health agencies, from fewer than 3000 in 1980 to over 8100 in 1989[31,32]. Although nursing homes and home care agencies play some role in the variety of care older persons receive, reimbursement and regulatory policies, and as well as being responsible for their growth, give them their predominant shape[20,33]. From the viewpoint of Medicare reimbursed physician involvement in nursing homes and home care, relatively short-term, post-acute therapeutic and restorative care has an emphasis in both settings. Medical care for other purposes (e.g. ongoing primary care) in these settings is otherwise sharply limited.

As is common in other developed countries, long-term care services in the USA are not well integrated with the acute and primary ambulatory care systems. There have been few incentives to overcome this separation of services, because 'long' long-term care – whether provided at home or in nursing homes – is financed and secured mostly privately by individuals and their families. The major exception is the Medicaid program, which will pay for nursing home care for poor older residents or those who have spent most of their assets down to a specified minimum. Otherwise, the various levels of governmental pay for long-term and home care is only in certain cases; few individuals have private long-term care insurance benefits. In general, long-term care insurance is not affordable for the high-risk groups needing it, and not perceived as needed by the low-risk groups who can afford it.

Recently, however, both nursing home and home care providers in the USA have become involved in rehabilitative and what has been called 'short-term' long-term care, as policymakers look for ways to contain costs of extensive, expensive hospital care. Medicare, private insurance supplemental to Medicare, and Medicare reimbursed health maintenance organizations (HMOs) have begun to reimburse and provide limited care in these settings. Thus, home care programmes and nursing homes have become dynamically interrelated with the acute care sector, but usually without the true co-ordination conducive to quality, continuity of care, and cost containment[20,34]. Social and health services have been integrated effectively only in a few federally funded demonstration projects. The dominant public and private financing programmes effectively limit physician involvement in nursing home and home care.

In summary, typical medical care for the older American in the community consists of episodic, patient initiated surgery contacts with specialist or primary care physicians, and, for acute illnesses, short-term, 'high-tech' hospitalizations (*see* Figure 2.2[35]). These hospitalizations may lead to discharge to full service nursing homes, which their physicians may or may not visit (depending on rehabilitation goals and reimbursement considerations), or a return to the community for follow-up and ongoing primary care in the physicians' surgeries. There is little scope for physician–patient contact in the way of day hospitals or home care.

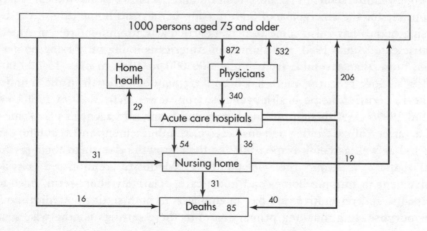

Figure 2.2: Annual movement of the USA population aged 75 and over through the health care system. Adapted from Denson, 1991[35]. Estimated numbers do not sum precisely due to rounding error, use of multiple sources to estimate different parts of the flowchart, and elimination of less utilized institutions (eg chronic disease and rehabilitation hospitals, inpatient mental health facilities) for which flow estimates do not exist.

Developing Trends

While it is likely there will be a continued growth of community geriatric care needs and services in the USA, predicting the development of health services is fraught with difficulty. Demographic, social and employment trends indicate that the nature of the American family's participation in the informal care of older members will undergo transformation. Women, many of whom have been increasing their participation in the paid workforce and have been having fewer children, are facing new demands as primary informal care-givers to dependent parents, spouses, and in-laws[36,37]. While, in general, families are extraordinarily adaptable in meeting these kinds of reciprocal obligations, formal community systems will probably be increasingly needed, but the nature and level of these services cannot be precisely determined until patterns and problems in emergent informal geriatric care can be identified.

We can certainly say with confidence that the community will continue to be the setting for the most American geriatric care in the near future. Since the first flourishing of the nursing home industry in the late 1960s and through the 1970s, nursing homes have not been built at rates that would even maintain their availability at past levels, when it was estimated that three to four frail older people resided in the community for every one in a nursing home[38]. In the mid-1980s, a major change in the law regarding hospital reimbursement by Medicare for older patients resulted in prospectively set payment depending on diagnosis. While evaluative studies have disagreed on the impact of this reform on health outcomes[39,40], lengths of stay of older patients in acute hospitals have been substantially reduced, but at the cost of increases in dependency and aftercare needs at discharge. Thus, pressures on community geriatric care resources (including nursing homes) have been further increased by decreased availability of extended hospital care.

As we have mentioned, the future organization of all American personal health services, not simply community geriatric care, is now unresolved. As we write, the nature and fate of President Clinton's health care reforms have not been revealed. Even if health care reform were to bring an environment supportive of well integrated, available, non-institutional geriatric care, including a mix of preventive, therapeutic, restorative, and supportive services, it would take many years and a major investment of resources in modifying research patterns and professional school curricula to supply sufficient staff for these programmes. In redirecting physician education towards primary and ambulatory care, a high priority will be to educate these and other health practitioners in the basics of geriatric care, including the need for screening and assessment, and identification of criteria for referral to work with specialty teams.

Institution of a variety of specialized geriatric assessment and treatment programmes is increasing in the USA. These programmes use a multidimensional, usually interdisciplinary, approach to evaluate an older individual's medical, psychosocial, and functional capabilities and problems, with the intention of arriving at a comprehensive plan for therapy and long-term follow-up. Controlled trials have documented that patients benefit significantly in several ways, including improved diagnostic accuracy, reductions in prescribed medications, greater access to rehabilitation services, improvements in functional and mental status, reductions in hospital and nursing home utilization, lower health care costs, and improved survival[41-43]. A recent meta-analysis of comprehensive geriatric assessment trials confirmed many of these benefits, and highlighted the particular efficacy of bed units among hospital programmes, and home assessments among community based services[44].

To date, these types of geriatric assessment and management programmes have been more common in the UK and northern Europe than in the USA. Due in part to the encouraging research results, inpatient and outpatient assessment services are being increasingly established, but these tend to be concentrated in limited prepaid delivery systems, such as the military veterans' health system, or some Medicare health maintenance organizations[45]. Some hospital based programmes have been established outside these systems, but, lacking a reimbursement base, they have grown slowly[46,47]. It seems clear that, only if health care reform in the USA goes beyond the currently championed formulae for managed competition and other cost containment nostrums, and establishes a system that is truly accountable for long-term outcomes of geriatric and other health care, will we be able to develop both a sufficient primary care work-force and an equitable system of effective geriatric assessment and care. While the USA has certainly become a world leader in high-technology medical care and research, with an abundance of excellent geriatric services and facilities in many regions, we have yet to develop and implement the systematic regionalized approach to universal health care that has long characterized services in the UK.

References

1. Kayser-Jones JS. (1990) *Old, alone and neglected: care of the aged in the United States and Scotland.* 2nd edn. University of California Press, Berkeley.

2. Barker WH. (1987) *Adding life to years: organised geriatrics services in Great Britain and implications for the United States.* Johns Hopkins University Press, Baltimore.

3. Day P, Klein R. (1989) The politics of modernisation: Britain's National Health Service in the 1980s. *Milbank* 67:1–34.

4. Day P, Klein R. (1991) Britain's health care experiment. *Health Affairs* 10(3): 39–59.

5. Enthoven AC. (1993) The history and principles of managed competition. *Health Affairs* 12(Suppl): 24–48.

6. Starr P, Zelman WA. (1993) Bridge to compromise: competition under a budget. *Health Affairs* 12(Suppl): 7–23.

7. Millard P, Higgs P, Rochon P. (1989) Ageing: should it be left to chance? *Br Med J* 298: 1020–21.

8. MacLennan W. (1988) Private nursing home care: the middle way. *Br Med J* 296: 732.

9. Lock S. (1989) Steaming through the NHS. *Br Med J* 298: 619–20.

10. Robinson R. (1989) New health care market (NHS Review). *Br Med J* 298: 437–9.

11. Organization for Economic Cooperation and Development. (1988) *Ageing populations: the social policy implications.* OECD, Paris.

12. Rabin DL, Stockton P. (1987) *Long-term care for the elderly: a factbook.* Oxford University Press, New York.

13. Taeuber C. (1990) Diversity: the dramatic reality. In: Bass S, Kutza E, Torres-Gil F, editors. *Diversity in ageing.* Scott Foresman, Glenview, Illinois, 1–45.

14. National Center for Health Statistics. (1986) *Health statistics on older persons: United States, 1986.* (Analytical and epidemiology studies, Series 3, No. 25). NCHS, Washington, DC.

15. Schieber G, Poullier J, Greenwald L. (1991) Health care systems in twenty-four countries. *Health Affairs* 10(3): 22–38.

16. US Bureau of the Census. (1990) *Health insurance coverage: the haves and have-nots.* (Statistical Brief, SB-9-90) USBC, Washington, DC.

17. Robert Wood Johnson Foundation. (1992) 34.6 million uninsured. *Updata* 3(1): 1–2.

18. Chulis G, Eppig F, Hogan M *et al.* (1993) Health insurance and the elderly. *Health Affairs* 12(1): 111–8.

19. Stone R, Cafferata G, Sangl J. (1987) Caregivers of the frail elderly: a national profile. *Gerontologist* 27: 616–26.

20. Wieland D, Ferrell B, Rubenstein LZ. (1991) Geriatric home health care: conceptual and demographic considerations. *Clin Geriatr Med* 7: 645–64.

21. De Lew N, Greenburg G, Kinchen K. (1992) A layman's guide to the US health care system. *Health Care Finance Rev* 14: 151–69.

22. Office of Technology Assessment. (1990) *Health care in rural America.* US Government Printing Office, Washington, DC.

23. Organization for Economic Cooperation and Development. (1990) *Health care systems in transition: the search for efficiency.* (Social policy studies, No 7) OECD, Paris.

24. Politzer R, Harris D, Gatson M, *et al.* (1991) Primary care physician supply and the medically underserved. *JAMA* 226: 104–9.

25. Rosenblatt R. (1992) Specialists or generalists: on whom should we base the American health care system? *JAMA* 267: 1665–7.

26. Siu A, Ke G, Beck J. (1989) Geriatric medicine in the United States: the current activities of former trainees. *J Am Geriatr Soc* 37: 272–6.

27. Rubenstein L, Wieland D. (1991) Geriatric medicine in the United States. *Année Gerontol* 5: 303–9.

28. Butler R, Hyer K. (1989) Reimbursement reform for the frail elderly. *J Am Geriatr Soc* 37: 1097–8.

29. Scanlon W, Feder J. (1985) The long-term care marketplace: an overview. In: Healthcare Financial Management Association. *Long-term care: challenges and opportunities.* HFMA, Oak Brook, Illinois.

30. US Senate Special Committee on Ageing. (1987) *Ageing America: trends and projections.* (LR 3377-188-D12198) US Department of Health and Human Services, Washington, DC.

31. American Medical Association. (1989) *Physician guide to home health care.* AMA, Chicago, Illinois.

32. Johnson C, Grant L. (1985) *The nursing home in American society.* Johns Hopkins University Press, Baltimore.

33. Marion Laboratories. (1989) *Long-term care digest: home health edition.* Marion Laboratories, Kansas City, Missouri.

34. Rubenstein L, Ouslander J, Wieland D. (1988) Dynamics and clinical implications of the nursing home–hospital interface. *Clin Geriatr Med* **4**: 471–91.

35. Denson P. (1991) *Tracing the elderly through the health care system*. Agency for Health Care Policy Research, Washington, DC.

36. Brody E. (1981) Women in the middle and family help to older people. *Gerontologist* **21**: 471–80.

37. Brody E, Schoonover C. (1986) Pattern of parent-care when adult daughters work and when they do not. *Gerontologist* **26**: 372–81.

38. Kane R, Kane R. (1987) *Long-term care: principles, programs and policies*. Springer, New York.

39. Fitzgerald J, Moore S, Dittus R. (1988) The care of elderly patients with hip fracture: changes since the implementation of the prospective payment system. *N Engl J Med* **319**: 1392–6.

40. Kahn K, Rubenstein L, Draper D, *et al.* (1990) The effects of the DRG-based prospective payment system on the quality of care for hospitalized Medicare patients: an introduction to the series. *JAMA* **264**: 1953–5.

41. Rubenstein L, Josephson K, Wieland D, *et al.* (1984) Effectiveness of a geriatric evaluation unit: a radomised clinical trial. *N Engl J Med* **311**: 1664–70.

42. Hendriksen C, Lund E, Stromgard E. (1984) Consequences of assessment and intervention among elderly people: a three-year randomised controlled trial. *Br Med J* **289**: 1522–4.

43. Vetter NJ, Jones DA, Victor CR. (1984) Effect of health visitors working with elderly patients in general practice: a randomised controlled trial. *Br Med J* **288**: 369–72.

44. Stuck A, Siu A, Wieland D, *et al.* (1993) Effects of comprehensive geriatric assessment; a meta-analysis of controlled trials. *Lancet* **342**: 1032–6.

45. Rubenstein L, Wieland D. (1991) Geriatric assessment and prospective payment systems. In: Romeis J, Coe R. *Quality and cost containment in care of the elderly: health services research perspectives*. Springer, New York, 99–119.

46. Epstein A, Hall J, Besdine R, *et al.* (1987) The emergence of geriatric assessment units: the 'new technology of geriatrics.' *Ann Intern Med* **106**: 229–303.

47. Lavizzo-Mourey R, Hillman A, Diserens D, *et al.* (1993) Hospitals' motivations in establishing or closing geriatric evaluation and management units: diffusion of a new patient-care technology in a changing health care environment. *J Gerontol Med Sci* **48**: M78–M83.

3
Healthy Ageing in Europe

Hana Hermanova

Ageing is the most important factor of current population change in Europe, affecting every individual and every society, its economy, social structure and health care system. It is, therefore, not surprising that it is receiving increasing government attention in most European countries. Life expectancy at birth varies throughout Europe, both between countries and between groups within countries. The most recent figures reported in the 1991 *Health for all* evaluation show a life expectancy range of 65.5–78.2 years (both sexes) across the different member states. The achievement of an overall life expectancy of 75 years by the year 2000 depends particularly on progress in Central, Eastern and Southern Europe[1].

In 1960, 14.4% of the European population were aged over 60. By 1980 this proportion increased to 16.9% and it should rise to 20.2% by the year 2000. The group most rapidly increasing comprises people aged 80 years or more. The increase is predicted to rise from 16 million to 21 million between 1980 and the year 2000. These demographic changes will have profound implications for the future of health policies and services, especially long-term care. If the needs of older people are to be met effectively within the boundaries of sustainable cost, it is important to adopt policies and programmes that will support them in remaining active and healthy for as long as possible[2].

Improvements in care and the increased survival of the sick have led to a shift in emphasis from prolonging life expectancy to increasing disability-free life or active life expectancy and exploring the quality of life in older age. Although reduced functional capacity is correlated with advancing age, it is not clear what percentage of reduced function is due to preventable loss of fitness and/or social contacts. Many ageing people do not show symptoms of mental or physical decline; on the contrary they tend to enjoy a level of health that permits them to lead socially and economically healthy lives. Seven out of 10 people in the age group 70–80 years need no assistance in caring for themselves. The emerging evidence suggests that, in the future, those under the age of 75 will be healthier, but those aged 85 and over will be increasingly frail and disabled, placing a heavier strain on health and social services.

Morbidity in older people is characterized by multiple pathology, non-specific presentation and a high incidence of secondary complications from disease and treatment. Only 20% of those aged 60 or above are free of any disease-related condition; the remaining 80% report a number of conditions or symptoms. Among the most prominent factors that compromise active life expectancy and detract from healthy ageing are arthritis, diminished hearing and visual acuity, dementia, depression, sleep disturbance, loss of balance, social isolation and institutionalization. These problems must receive priority, action and research in order to achieve a strategy for healthy ageing[1].

During this century, the average educational level and socio-economic conditions of older people have improved. These changes have contributed to better health status which means that older people are better informed, more politically involved and able to participate more actively in community life.

However, new problems are emerging because of migration of younger generations, high divorce rates, increased entry of women into the work force, and a greater complexity of everyday life; leading to a more complex situation when these populations age. For example, these changes lead to further social isolation among the elderly. Informal care givers are less available, thereby generating a need for more formal care arrangements. This has already happened in Europe, a fact often ignored by health and social services.

Historically, ageing and health tend to be given less priority in the government policies of most European countries. Community structures for care have not been instigated in most areas. Further effort is needed to improve the accessibility of housing, transport and community activity for older people, as well as strengthening social support, and in the modernization of health care delivery[1].

Ageing Differences in Europe

As mentioned already, there are differences between European countries in life expectancy, morbidity and disability levels. (For instance, Nordic countries have the longest life expectancy in Europe.) Therefore, another issue to be addressed is that of a perceived 'right' to reach old age in good health. A prerequisite for this is good health throughout the overall lifespan[1].

It is expected that the health and functional ability of people below the age of 75 will improve and that they will look for better opportunities to remain active in society. At the same time, governments are likely to be seeking a balance between early retirement (to ease the job market) and late retirement (to reduce the cost of pensions). Meanwhile a large increase in the number of people aged 85 or over will also create a further demand for personal care and help with the tasks of daily life.

Older People in European Union Countries

Following the 'European Year of Older People and Solidarity between Generations 1993', the issues of ageing and care of older people are now receiving high priority in government policies[3,4]. These include:

• giving more attention to the consequences of ageing in societies

- comparisons of different methods in handling ageing

- proposed action at a European level, taking into account the complex nature of the problem

- older people themselves are organized in non-governmental groups that very often create lobbies, and thus become partners in decision-making in pluralistic societies

- needs for legislation to become more protective towards the ageing population.

Most European health care systems have now incorporated care of older people as an integral part of their health service. Countries take different approaches to the medical care of older people, for instance, with their integration into the overall care system, or with the development of a specialized geriatric medicine service. There can be a mixture of these, and in Europe there are certain examples.

In Finland, the strategies to reform the services for the elderly have been the following:

- Amendment of provision for the system of fees to be paid for social welfare and health services. This was preceded by an experiment on home service fees, which was important from the viewpoint of caring for elderly people at home.

- Municipality-based continuation and expansion of organizations of multiprofessional services based on a principle of population responsibility.

- Promotion of informal care at legislation level and experiments with various working models related to it.

- Adjusting systems of various service providers (welfare mix) to provide individual care by means of a service and care plan practice.

- Development of cross-sectoral co-operation in municipalities regarding issues that are important for the elderly: environment, public services and housing, and co-operation on research and educational issues with the medical faculties of universities.

- Experimental and developmental projects have been initiated in co-operation with municipalities. The purpose is to develop local strategies as well as to train workers to analyse drawbacks and adjust their working methods themselves.

- Integrating voluntary work into the service for the elderly and increasing solidarity between generations.

- Medical faculties of universities have carried out many studies and prepared publications related to geriatrics. A factor of great importance to the practical work is the establishment of small units with the necessary expertise to care for older people suffering from dementia, as well as specific small group homes, day centres, nursing homes and hospital beds.

The main trends would seem to be as follows:

- the costs and benefits are attributed to a mixture of the state, voluntary and private sector

- the formal and informal sectors are encouraged to collaborate; carers must be supported

- the right balance between social goals and economic constraints should help to attain cost-effectiveness; most countries are seeking this balance

- services should be flexible and tailored to the needs of older people; key words such as care-packaging and case-management help to direct planning

- ethical issues are high on the agenda.

Older People in Central and Eastern European Countries

More than five years have elapsed since the 1989 revolutions, and the countries of Central and Eastern Europe are in the midst of enormous transformation. The current reforms have brought extensive change to society as a whole, felt also by the older members of these populations.

Ageing and health tend to be given less priority in the government policies of most Central and Eastern European countries. Health promotion and disease prevention programmes geared to the needs of older people are not well developed. This applies to issues such as physical activity, appropriate eating, reduction of alcohol use, control of drug prescriptions, and maintenance of social networks and security. Community structures for care are slowly being put into place. There is a need for further effort to improve the accessibility of housing, transport and community activity for older people, as well as strengthening social support. Older people are increasingly aware of their political power but their organizations are still weak in lobbying power.

In general, life expectancy is higher in the European Community countries than in Central and Eastern European countries. This confirms that certain lifestyles are conducive to health (good nutrition, physical exercise, less stress, healthier environments). Assessment of the contribution of health care systems to positive health status development is very difficult. The populations of Central and Eastern European countries have been exposed to long-term stress; its impact on health has never been adequately studied and assessed. A deeper analysis of this impact, based on comparable data, is needed.

The most important changes in health care, based on the introduction of health insurance plans, only became effective from two years ago; this is currently affecting geriatric care, resulting in cuts or abolition of services. On the social side, the decline of the purchasing power of pensions (through the raising of rents in municipal housing, cost of living etc.) has affected the health of older people by influencing their lifestyles. There is now evidence however, of new social programmes for older people, which are very often a welfare mix (public and private). At present, no evaluation has been made.

The solution to the problem is a continuous process and will include:

- creating awareness of the situation; to decrease inequalities which exist between the North/West and South/East. This will happen only when the socioeconomic conditions improve in Central and Eastern European countries

- presenting models of good research and good practice in the care of older people in the industrialized countries of Western and Northern Europe

- the introduction of a pluralistic system of care involving the state, volunteers and the private sector

- expanding geriatric services within a given economic framework

- older people will need to understand their role in society and the part they can play in decision-making

- promotion of self-help and self-care and the strengthening of rehabilitation.

Implications for Different Levels of Care

In most European countries, major reforms in health care systems are under way. The main objective is containment of health care costs and reduction of public spending. Provision of appropriate care for older people becomes an important social choice in terms of resource allocation if equity in access to high quality care for all population groups is envisaged.

Ageing is a particular challenge. European countries are responding in quite different ways. There are wide variations in institutionalization practices; Germany and France quite often provide long-term care in hospitals, while Sweden and the United Kingdom have developed strong home care programmes.

Countries also show wide variations in terms of financial coverage. The public/private mix differs significantly; for example, in the United Kingdom long-term care relies much more on the public sector than in Belgium and Germany. The public/private mix is now also emerging in Central and Eastern European countries[3,4].

There is a lack of economic studies on the various approaches and options in health care for older people. It is not possible to prove that home care is 'the most economic approach for society'; on the contrary, home care of a severely disabled older person could be more costly, and even less humane, than good institutional care.

The role of rehabilitation in the long-term care of older people is often neglected. Countries do not usually report the impact of rehabilitation or the decreasing indirect costs of health and social care. As hospitalizations are becoming shorter in most European countries, the role of community based services, particularly community based rehabilitation, will need re-evaluation and strengthening. The provision of community care for older people is a process of negotiation. Conflicting interests have to be resolved and very often no-one may be completely satisfied. The shift from institutional to home care is not an administrative process only. It is also a shift in attitude from decision/provider-led provision to a partnership with the users. The hospital/institution orientated countries of Central and Eastern Europe will need particular assistance in this area.

The role of prevention, particularly of the disabling consequences of chronic diseases or injuries, is not sufficiently emphasized. Investments in prevention could be rather expensive, but could pay off, for example: control of blood pressure to prevent strokes; vaccination against pneumococcal infections; control of diabetes to prevent disabling complications; reasonable physical activities to prevent or postpone the onset of osteoporosis or arthritis; prevention of accidents through simple environmental adaptations (eg removal of loose rugs, lights at both ends of staircases).

The methodology that would enable comparisons of health care expenditure in different countries, with regard to the needs and demands of the older population, is also lacking. It is difficult to measure quality of care and consumer satisfaction and relate these to differences in salaries of health care workers, costs of energy, maintenance, costs of drugs etc.

Whereas in the past most countries developed services for older people as part of their general systems of care for all members of society, it is now apparent that processes of ageing, particularly when considered in conjunction with the rapid changes in environment and living conditions, call for special arrangements, services and priorities within these care systems.

Conclusions

Ageing and care of older people are growing issues but they are still neglected.

The emphasis of policy and strategy for care of older people should be on the prevention of ill health and the promotion of good health. Caring for dependent older people is of great importance; models of affordable and accessible care have to be developed in all countries. There needs to be a balance between home care and institutional care, allowing for movement in both directions.

Education and training in care of older people plays a key role in reaching the above-mentioned objectives. Once the general public has the basic information about ageing and the role that older people could play in contributing to the development of a society, their attitudes towards them are likely to change; they will not be seen purely as consumers, but also as contributors. This will have a positive effect on policy making, particularly in the area of distribution of resources.

All professionals need to view ageing and older people in a different way: as all other age groups, they have the same rights to participate in society, and the same rights of access to affordable and good quality services, if there is a need.

Their care should be incorporated into the teaching programmes of all categories of personnel, both undergraduate and postgraduate. It is up to governments to decide whether they integrate these programmes into other disciplines (eg each medical discipline – with the exception of paediatrics and obstetrics – has its geriatrics) or whether they create separate specialties. Existence of centres of expertise in the care of older people promote the issue.

These challenges have been widely recognized by the WHO Regional Offices in Europe, who are responding by new approaches to healthy ageing. A specific policy goal is to provide opportunities and encouragement for those aged over 65 to remain active participants in the social and cultural life of the communities to which they belong. Instead of labelling older people as old fashioned or incompetent and reducing them to just a medical and/or social problem, they should be recognized for possessing life experience and wisdom, which can be passed on to their communities, and also for providing a social resource that is of value to the whole of society.

References

1. *Healthy ageing*. (1990) Technical Discussions for the Fortieth Session of the Regional Committee Europe. (EUR/RC40/Tech.Disc./1) E,F,G,R. WHO Regional Office for Europe, Copenhagen.

2. *Add life to years*. Report on Regional Office activities in health care of the elderly (update). (EUR/ICP/RHB 016A Rev. 1). WHO Regional Office for Europe, Copenhagen.

3. Hermanova HM. (1989) EUROLINK AGE: *Older people in the European Community – some basic facts*. Age Concern England, Mitcham, Surrey.

4. Fondation Ipsen (Automne 1990). *Les personnes agées dans la Communauté Européenne: present et avenir*. Dossier réalisé par la Fondation Ipsen, France.

4
Demographic Change in the United Kingdom

As indicated in the previous chapters, the demography of older age is changing in most countries of the world and it is important for those planning and providing health and social care to understand these changes. There are also enormous economic consequences resulting from increasing numbers of older and much older people. Census returns in this country over the last century indicate that the population of over 65- and over 75-year-old people has increased dramatically, both in actual numbers and in proportion to the total population (*see* Table 4.1 and Figure 4.1).

Table 4.1: Population trends since 1851 (England and Wales).

	1851 n millions (%)	1901 n millions (%)	1931 n millions (%)	1971 n millions (%)	1981 n millions (%)	1991 n millions (%)
Age (years)						
65+	0.65 (3.60)	1.50 (4.60)	3.00 (7.50)	6.35 (12.96)	7.27 (14.84)	8.04 (16.12)
75+	0.15 (0.83)	0.50 (1.53)	0.90 (2.25)	2.35 (4.80)	2.79 (5.69)	3.54 (7.09)
Total population	18	33	40	49	49	50

Data from censuses for 1851–1981, with additional data from OPCS, 1993[3].

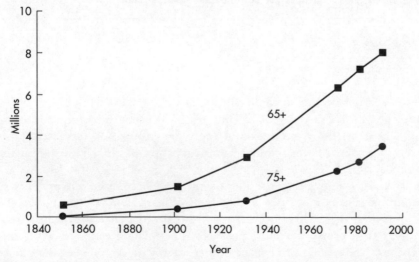

Figure 4.1: Population trends since 1851 for those over 65 years and over 75 years.

This increase is essentially due to both mortality and fertility factors. Declining infant and child mortality rates have resulted in larger proportions of the cohorts now surviving to adulthood going on to become elderly. Although the life expectancy in 1987 at the age of 60 was not radically different from that in 1900 the proportion of any cohort reaching 60 years is now much higher, so the life expectancy figure at birth is much improved. The life expectancy at birth at various times over the past century is shown in Table 4.2. Life expectancy at

Table 4.2: Trends in life expectancy.

Census year	Men (years)	Women (years)
1901	45.5	49.0
1931	58.4	62.4
1961	67.9	73.8
1981	70.8	76.8
1991	73.2	78.8
2001	74.5	79.9

Source: Central Statistical Office, 1992[5].

older ages has also shown some increase, more in women than men. At the age of 60 years, male life expectancy has increased by approximately four years, and female by seven years. Similarly, at the age of 70 years, male life expectancy has increased by two years, and female by almost five years. The expectation of life is forecast to continue to rise. For example, by 2001 it is expected to have increased by about one year for both men and women at the ages of 60 and 70. The life expectancies of older men and women are shown in Table 4.3[1].

Table 4.3: Life expectancy of older people (years).

	A person aged 60 years	A person aged 70 years	A person aged 80 years
Male	78	81	87
Female	82	84	88

Source: Department of Health, 1992[1].

There was a major decline in the birth rate in England and Wales in the period between the 1870s and the 1930s. Thus, with declining birth input into the demographic system, the relative size of the older group was increased. This explains the increase in both numbers and proportion of elderly people in the population today.

The 1991 census shows that the number of people counted as residents in Great Britain on census night was 54 888 844[3]. This was 0.4% lower than the corresponding total in 1981. However, it is considered that more people were missed in 1991 than previously and a provisional population estimate taking this into account now shows a small increase over the past 10 years. There were more births than deaths during the decade. People aged 65 years and over made up 16% of the population of Great Britain in 1991, an increase of 0.8% since 1981 (Table 4.4). The proportion of men and women who were aged 75 and over increased respectively by 0.5% and 0.8% between 1981 and 1991. The proportion who were aged 85 years and over increased by 0.5% in the inter-census period[2]. The number of people reaching 100 years of age has also increased; in the 1991 census this was 7159 of which 6104 were women and 1055 were men. This compares with total numbers of 200 in 1952 and 1750 in 1982. Despite the recent changes, the relatively small numbers in the population who are over the age of 85 years is still noteworthy; to reach this age and beyond is still an achievement.

Table 4.4: Percentage of population of Great Britain in older age groups on census night 1991.

	65–74 years	75–84 years	85+ years
Percentage	9.0	5.5	1.5

Source: OPCS, 1993[3].

Table 4.5 shows the relative numbers of men and women in each age band[3]. As age advances, the proportion of women increases. For people aged 75 years and over the ratio of women to men was 2:1 and for people aged 85 and over this rises to 3:1.

Table 4.5: Numbers of men and women in older age groups in Great Britain on census night 1991.

	65–74 years	75–84 years	85+ years
Men (%)	2 214 424 (44.8)	1 117 042 (36.8)	204 208 (24.6)
Women (%)	2 730 870 (55.2)	1 918 216 (63.2)	626 470 (75.4)
Total	4 945 294	3 035 258	830 678

Source: OPCS, 1993[3].

Studies of the marital status of older people show that very few are separated or divorced. Widowhood, however, is common. In the over 75-year age group, 64% of women are widowed, whereas 62% of men are still married[3] (*see* Table 4.6).

Table 4.6: Marital status of men and women over 65 years on census night 1991.

Age (years)	Single (%)	Married (%)	Widowed (%)	Divorced (%)
Men 65–74	7.7	77.4	11.3	3.7
Women 65–74	7.5	53.0	35.4	4.1
Men 75+	6.7	62.1	29.3	1.9
Women 75+	10.9	22.8	64.4	1.9

Source: OPCS, 1993[3].

It is debatable whether one can place old people in a social class, as previous occupations do not necessarily equate with present circumstances and living standards. From the numbers quoted in the 1990 General Household Survey[4], there seems to be little difference in socio-economic group between men in the older age groups and men in the rest of the population. It is evident, though, that younger women are more likely to be found in the professional, employers and managers socio-economic groups than are older women. Older women are more likely than younger women to be found in the semi-skilled or unskilled manual groups (*see* Table 4.7).

Table 4.7: Socio-economic group (%).

	Professional	Employers and managers	Intermediate and junior non-manual	Skilled manual and own-account non-professional	Semi-skilled manual and personal service	Unskilled manual
All men	7	19	18	36	15	4
Men						
65—74 years	7	19	17	35	15	7
Men 75+ years	7	23	16	33	17	5
All women[a]	6	18	25	29	18	5
Women						
65—74 years[a]	5	15	25	24	22	9
Women						
75+ years[a]	2	11	29	19	28	10

[a]Married women classified according to their husband's occupation.
Source: OPCS, 1992[4].

Ethnic minority groups have a markedly different age structure to that of the white population (*see* Table 4.8). In the 1991 census, one in six of the white population was aged 65 or over, compared with one in 30 of the ethnic minority population[3]. Correspondingly, children under 16 years formed a smaller proportion of the white population than of the ethnic minority population. The numbers of ethnic minority elders, however, is likely to increase[5].

Table 4.8: Ethnic groups in Great Britain on census night in 1991(%).

	Under 65 years	65–74 years	75+ years
White	93.7	98.5	99.4
Black Caribbean	1.0	0.5	0.15
Black other	0.8	0.1	0.04
Indian/Pakistani/Bangladeshi	3.1	0.7	0.3
Chinese	0.3	0.07	0.04
Other	1.0	0.2	0.1

Source: OPCS, 1993[3].

One of the most remarkable demographic contrasts in the world today is the variation between countries in the proportion of people aged 65 years or more. At one extreme, in Sweden they account for 17% of the population, at the other, in Kuwait, only 1%. The main contrast is between the developed countries and those which are less well developed. In 1985, Europe, with 13%, was the continent with the highest percentage of elderly people, followed by North America (12%), USSR (10%), Asia (4%) and Africa (3%). These percentages are expected to increase, in some cases dramatically, over the next 30 years[6].

As well as regional and national differences, there are local variations in each country. It would seem for instance to be a characteristic of many cities, especially in developed countries, that there is a higher proportion of elderly people in the inner areas. The experience in the UK is that there is an understandable movement of younger people to the suburbs, but economic forces often prevent older people from doing the same; social restraints can also contribute to this. Only a small proportion of those in the retirement age group migrate and most movers go only short distances[7]. Despite this, there have developed clusters of older people in certain desirable retirement areas, for instance on the south coast, and in some parts of North Wales.

At the local level, a doctor's list of say 2200 patients would expect to have 328 over 65-year-olds, of which 131 would be male and 197 would be female. Within this group there would be 125 over 75-year-olds (41 male and 84 female) and 23 over 85-year-olds (5 male and 18 female). Again, there are variations depending on locality and region, but the national average of people above retirement age is running at about the level of 18%.

The future trends in the population numbers of older people are interesting and represent a change from what has hitherto been happening. Jean Thompson[8], arguing from the position as it was in 1985, suggests that the number of people in the third age (60 years and over) should show little change relative to the total by the end of the century. Within this relative stability, numbers at the younger and older ends of the age range will change quite differently (see Figure 4.2). Over the short-term, the numbers of persons in their 60s will show a decline, these people being the survivors of the low numbers born in the 1920s and 1930s. At the same time, the number of persons aged 80 years and over is projected to increase rapidly. The effect will be to have both an increased proportion and actual number of much older people. The prevalence of disability (see Table 5.3) in private households shows that it is the over 75-year-old age group that has the highest level of disability[9]. The effects, therefore, of the increasing numbers of this age group with high levels of disability will be to produce an increased load on both the health and social services. These, however, are projections. Changes in economic circumstances, average age of retirement (for instance an equalling out of retirement age for men and women) and changing levels of disability because of a fitter population may all affect what happens in the next three decades. Other unknown factors, such as outbreaks of war or epidemics, may also be significant.

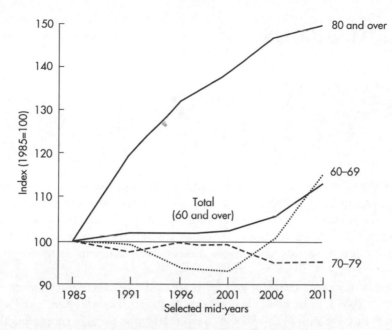

Figure 4.2: Persons aged 60 years and over, 1985–2011, Great Britain.

References

1. Department of Health. (1992) *The health of elderly people: an epidemiological overview*. (Central Health Monitoring Unit, Epidemiological Overview Series, Vol. 1) HMSO, London.

2. Office of Population Censuses and Surveys. (1992) *1991 Census: Great Britain*. (National Monitor CEN 91 CM 56.) Government Statistical Service, London.

3. Office of Population Censuses and Surveys. (1993) *1991 Census Report for Great Britain* (Part 1) Vol. 1. HMSO, London.

4. Office of Population, Censuses and Surveys, Social Survey Division. (1992) *General household survey* 1990. (Series GHS no. 21) HMSO, London.

5. Central Statistical Office (1992). *Social Trends 22*. HMSO, London.

6. Clarke JI. (1987) Ageing in Europe: introductory remarks. *Espace Populations Societés* 1987 **1**: 23–8.

7. Grundy E. (1987) Retirement migration and its consequences in England and Wales. *Ageing Soc* **7**: 57–82.

8. Thompson J. (1987) Ageing of the population: contemporary trends and issues. *Popul Trends* **50**: 18–22.

9. Martin J, Meltzer H, Elliot D. (1988) *Prevalence of disability among adults*. (OPCS surveys of disability in Great Britain, Report 1) HMSO, London.

5
Health Status

Although there is agreement that the health status of individuals aged 65 and over is gradually improving and the general health of the older population is good, it is difficult to produce clear evidence of this. Mortality statistics are sometimes used as a guide, but it is important to recognize that health is not reflected by levels of mortality. Nonetheless, it is interesting to observe the trends.

The main causes of death at age 55 years and over are shown for men and women in Table 5.1. In men, disorders of the circulatory system predominate throughout this age group, followed by respiratory disease and neoplasms. In the 55–64 age group in women, cancer is, however, the most frequent cause of death[1]. The frequency of deaths due to neoplasm drops gradually in women after this age, from around 50% between 55 and 65 years to 11% in those aged 85 and over.

Table 5.1: Main causes of death in men and women over 55 years: England and Wales, 1991.

	Age group (years)			
	55–64	65–74	75–84	85+
Men				
Circulatory system (%)	47	48	49	46
Respiratory system (%)	6	9	13	20
Neoplasms (%)	36	33	25	17
Other (%)	11	9	13	18
Total deaths	34 853	77 227	95 815	39 341
% of all deaths of men over 55 years	14	31	39	16
Women				
Circulatory system (%)	31	43	53	51
Respiratory system (%)	7	9	10	16
Neoplasms (%)	49	35	21	11
Other (%)	13	13	17	21
Total deaths	21 303	54 156	103 268	95 727
% of all deaths of women over 55 years	8	20	38	35

Sources: Office of Population, Censuses and Surveys, 1992[1]. Department of Health Central Health Monitoring Unit, 1992[2].

Mortality from coronary heart disease has fallen in the past five years, particularly in the younger age groups. By comparison, mortality from stroke has declined in all age groups in both men and women over the period 1969–91, falling by about half amongst those aged under 75 years.

Death rates from chronic airway obstruction has declined markedly in men aged under 75 years. For women, mortality rates are much lower than for men at all ages; after falling during the 1970s they have shown evidence, however, of a rise in recent years, particularly in the age group 65–74 years. This may reflect cohort smoking effects which are shown again in death rates from lung cancer[2].

Information on health and older people is available from a number of sources. The 1981/2 study of morbidity statistics carried out by the Royal College of General Practitioners showed that the main reason for consultation with general practitioners (GPs) included diseases of the circulatory, respiratory and musculoskeletal systems and the category of 'symptoms, signs and ill-defined conditions'[3].

Questions are included in the General Household Survey about general health and the presence of long-standing illness. At all ages over 65 most people reported their health being good or fairly good. There was a gradual increase in the number of those feeling not good as age advanced, and by the age of 85 years and over a total 27% of men and 33% of women were not feeling well[4].

As would be expected, the proportions of people with long-standing illness were higher in those aged 75 years and over in both men and women, particularly so in women. These proportions have been increasing in recent years; reasons for this include the increase in the number of much older people in the 75-year and over age group. This might also reflect changes in general attitude to illness, which has increased reporting, or may actually be a true increase in morbidity[2].

In 1990, 69% of people aged 75 years and over had a long-standing illness compared with 34% of all age groups. Not all long-standing illness is, however, so limiting that it reduces functional ability. About one-half of the oldest age group had a limiting long-standing disease[5].

Table 5.2 shows the causes of long-standing illness by age group and sex, as shown by the 1988 General Household Survey[6]. Musculoskeletal problems (excluding back trouble) and hearing and eyesight difficulties show a particular increase with age. This survey also reports that older people experience a higher prevalence of mental disorders than younger people. For people aged 65–74 and 75 and over, the prevalence is 29/1000 and 25/1000 respectively, compared with 17/1000 for the whole population. Mental health problems would appear to be under-reported[4]. The General Household Survey 1985[7], reported that 97% of people aged 65 and over wore glasses and 10% wore a hearing aid. Over the years there has been a slight reduction in the number of old people with no natural teeth. In 1988 it was around 80% for women of 75 years and over and about 75% for men of the same age[8].

Table 5.3 shows the prevalence of disability in older age groups reported in the OPCS survey of disability[9] and illustrates the increasing level in the population as age advances. As Figure 5.1 shows, the proportion of those with *severe* disability also rises with age. Figure 5.2 shows the high prevalence of disability resulting from hearing, sight and mobility problems. The increase in the number

Table 5.2: Selected causes of long-standing illness in older age groups: Great Britain, 1988 (rate per thousand population).

	Men		Women	
	65–74 years	75+ years	65–74 years	75+ years
Arthritis and rheumatism	131	141	242	306
Back problems	39	26	41	28
Other bone and joint problems	66	84	47	96
Hypertension	69	31	101	81
Heart attack	75	82	67	66
Stroke	39	38	24	30
Other heart problems	54	53	46	84
Other blood vessel/ embolic disorders	48	52	30	62
Asthma	20	14	31	19
Bronchitis and emphysema	52	65	25	35
Digestive system	75	86	69	95
Eye complaints	43	77	52	115
Ear complaints	39	76	30	77
Nervous system	33	33	43	30

Source: Office of Population, Censuses and Surveys, 1990[6].

Table 5.3: Estimates of the prevalence of disability among adults in older age groups in Great Britain.

	50–59 years	60–69 years	70–79 years	80+ years
%	13.3	24.0	40.8	71.4

Source: Martin et al., 1988[9].

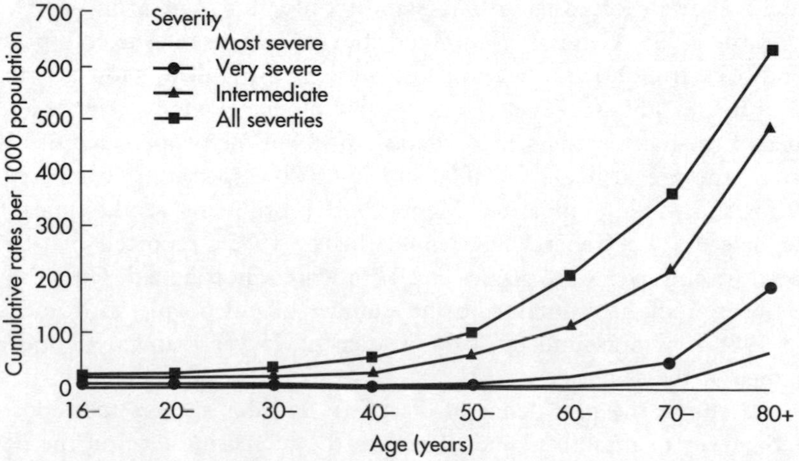

Figure 5.1: The prevalence of disability in Great Britain (private households). Source: Modified from Martin et al., 1988[9].

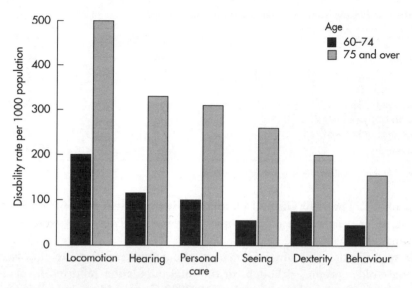

Figure 5.2: Estimates of prevalence of disability by type of disability and age, Great Britain, 1985/86. Source: Department of Health Central Monitoring Unit, 1992[2].

and proportion of much older people has been described in Chapter 4 (*see* Figure 4.2). The presence of a long-standing disability increases the risk of dependency. That is the need for an older person to be looked after because the disability prevents that person from looking after him/herself and attending to the basic activities of daily living. Long-standing disability does not necessarily lead to dependency but nevertheless the risk is there. Levels of dependency in older people are important when planning health and social services and their significance will be developed in subsequent chapters. The number of dependent older people is likely to increase with the increase in the number of the much older (ie those over 85 years). The aim of health and social care is, however, to reduce the number of 'dependent' years; if successful, this may reduce the number of dependent older people. This is important to the economic management of services and is integral to the quality of life years (QUALY) debate. Increasing longevity is not in itself the main objective; more important is increasing the quality of life in older age.

Data are available about some health related events and behaviour in older age. Home accidents surveillance data collected from a sample of accident and emergency attendances show that most accidents occur in or around the house, and that the proportion that occur within the house increases with age. Accidental deaths increase with age and falls are the major problem; burns are also a significant major cause of fatal home accidents in those aged 65 and over[10] (*see* Table 5.4).

The 1990 General Household Survey found that people aged 60 and over (24% of men and 20% of women) were less likely to smoke cigarettes than adults as a whole[5]. A study of alcohol consumption in 1987 and 1989 shows a decline with age, both in the percentage of those who drink and the average consumption

Table 5.4: Deaths from home accidents in older people.

Type of accident	65–74 years	75+ years
Fracture (%)	47	69
Poisoning/suspected poisoning (%)	19	9
Burn/scald (%)	8	6
Concussion (%)	7	5
Foreign body (%)	9	3
Other and unknown (%)	10	7
Total deaths	547	2502

Source: Home Accidents Deaths Database, 1992[10].

of alcohol[11]. The 1990 General Household Survey[5] gives information about exercise in older people. The older people were, the less likely they were to take part in sporting activities.

It is difficult to obtain information about how much acute illness there is amongst older people, although, in the total population reported levels of acute sickness have remained fairly stable. The 1990 General Household Survey reported that 12% of males and 15% of females had restricted activities due to illness or injury in the two weeks before interview, but no figures are given for the older group[5]. The average number of NHS GP consultations per year in 1991 was five, with the highest levels being amongst children and older people[12]. The average number of consultations with a GP for men and women over the age of 75 is seven and six per year respectively. There has been little change in this number over the past decade (*see* Table 5.5). After the age of 65 one-quarter of consultations occur in the home[5]. Older people can be expected to use the hospital

Table 5.5: Trends in consultations with an NHS GP: average number of NHS GP consultations per person per year.

	1972	1976	1979	1983	1987	1991
Men						
65–74 years	4	4	5	5	6	5
75+ years	7	5	5	7	7	7
Women						
65–74 years	5	4	5	6	6	6
75+ years	7	5	8	7	7	6
Total Population	4	3	4	4	5	5

Source: Office of Population, Censuses and Surveys, 1993[12].

services more than the younger group and the highest users are those over 75 years; this is also true of admissions to mental hospitals. Contact with other health and social services shows a general increase with all agencies as age advances[4]. Of those aged 85 and over, in the month before interview 36% had had contact with home helps, 20% with district nurses, 11% with 'meals on wheels', 19% with a chiropodist and 45% with a doctor.

The main case-finding studies that have been carried out over the past 20 years have almost always confirmed high levels of morbidity in much older people. Care must be taken, however, in the interpretation of these findings, as the mere presence of impairment is not necessarily a guide to health. Studies which have looked at the self-rating of health by older people provide a much more optimistic picture. Luker and Perkins[13], found that over 90% of older people in a survey in Manchester rated their health as being fair to good. It is therefore important to understand how older people see themselves and not rely on the experience and beliefs of younger people about health status in older age.

References

1. Office of Population, Censuses and Surveys. (1992) *OPCS Monitor DH2 92/2.* HMSO, London.

2. Department of Health Central Health Monitoring Unit. (1992) *The health of elderly people: and epidemiological overview.* (Epidemiological Overview Series Vol. 1.) HMSO London.

3. Royal College of General Practitioners, Office of Population, Censuses and Surveys, Department of Health and Social Security. (1986) *Morbidity statistics from general practice 1981/2, 3rd national study.* HMSO, London.

4. Office of Population, Censuses and Surveys, Social Survey Division. (1986) *General household survey 1984.* (Series GHS No. 14.) HMSO, London.

5. Office of Population, Censuses and Surveys, Social Survey Division. (1992) *General household survey 1990.* (Series GHS No. 21.) HMSO, London.

6. Office of Population, Censuses and Surveys, Social Survey Division. (1990) *General household survey 1988.* (Series GHS No. 19.) HMSO, London.

7. Office of Population, Censuses and Surveys, Social Survey Division. (1986) *General household survey 1985.* (Series GHS No. 16.) HMSO, London.

8. Office of Population, Censuses and Surveys. (1988) *Adult dental survey.* HMSO London.

9. Martin J, Meltzer H, Elliot D. (1988) *The prevalence of disability among adults.* (OPCS Surveys of disability in·Great Britain, Report 1.) HMSO, London.

10. Home Accidents Deaths Database. (1992) Quoted in: Department of Health. *The health of elderly people: an epidemiological overview.* (Epidemiological Overview Series Vol. 1.) HMSO, London.

11. Office of Population, Censuses and Surveys. (1991) *Drinking in England and Wales in the late 1980s.* HMSO, London.

12. Office of Population, Censuses and Surveys. (1993) *General household survey 1991.* (Series GHS No. 22.) HMSO, London.

13. Luker K, Perkins E. (1987) The elderly at home: service needs and provisions. *J R Coll Gen Pract* 37: 248–50.

6
Financial Status

Retirement marks the point when most people stop earning and come to depend upon pensions and benefits, either from state or private schemes to which they have been contributing during their working lives. Some also depend upon savings to some extent. In assessing the economic position of pensioners, it is necessary to take account of these aspects and also the changes that have occurred both in the actual levels of financial provision for older people and how these have changed relative to the rest of the population.

Before the 1908 Old Age Pension Act, older people had to rely on the Poor Law for financial assistance if they had no resources of their own. This Act marked the beginning of the state provision of pensions. This provision was meagre to start with and only those aged 70 and over who were of good character and of proven need were entitled to receive it. Things improved with the 1925 Widows, Orphans and Old Age Contributory Pensions Act, but it was the Beveridge Report of 1942 that paved the way for the almost universal provision of pensions for older people that was included in the series of Acts passed after 1945. These measures have been of major benefit, but even so large numbers of older people have needed the pension to be augmented by supplementary benefits, or, since 1988, Income Support.

Sources of Income

There are four main sources of income for persons in later life: state pensions, occupational pensions, earnings and investment income. The number of people in employment after pensionable age has decreased; to work beyond the age of 65 years is now uncommon. For those whose income falls below a defined level, Income Support is available. The relative sources of income have changed over time and this can be seen in Figure 6.1. Income from employment has declined and there has been an increase in occupational pensions. The proportion of persons aged 65 and over in receipt of pensions from their employer increased from 29% in 1974 to 38% in 1987[1,2]. These trends are likely to have continued. The state, however, remains the main source of income for older people and the level at which the state pension is fixed is crucial to their living standards[3].

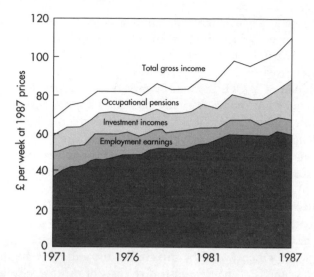

Figure 6.1: Income of pensioners.
Source: Central Statistical Office, 1991[4].

Level of Disposable Income

There is little data about the amount of disposable income available to pensioners or the range of income received. The 1990 *Family expenditure survey* showed that in both single and two-person families, income distribution amongst retired people is concentrated at the lower end of the income range (less than £100 per week) in comparison with non-retired households[5].

In the 1980s there was discussion about whether pensions had kept up with the increase in disposable income and living standards achieved by the rest of the population[6,7]. Differing views emerged and these depended upon the viewpoints of those analysing them. Although pensioners' share of total personal income had increased continuously over the previous 30 years, this overall trend obscured the plight of a subgroup who, for one reason or another, were disadvantaged. Although always likely to fluctuate, pensioners' disposable income is at about 70% that of non-pensioners.

In answer to a parliamentary question on the 9 February 1988, Mr Nicholas Scott stated that a pensioner's income grew on average by 2.7% a year in real terms between 1979 and 1985: 18% over the whole period. This rate of increase was more than twice as fast as that for the population as a whole. How much of this was due to state pension schemes and how much to private pension schemes was not stated.

The number of retirement pensioners increased by 9% between 1980 and 1986 and a further 1% yearly increase was likely thereafter. Retirement pension easily represents the largest single item of Social Security expenditure.

It is unwise to treat the older population as a homogenous economic subgroup of the total population. Evandrou and Victor have shown that there is considerable inequality amongst pensioners and, although older people as a whole may or may not have become a relatively more affluent group, there are striking differences in income distribution between them[7]. The term WOOPIE (well off older persons) has been used to describe affluent older people. Falkingham and Victor traced the evolution of WOOPIEs and described them as most likely to be male, aged under 75, and from the professional classes[3]. They are characterized by high rates of home ownership (in particular outright ownership), higher than average access to consumer durables and high levels of car and telephone ownership. Receipt of income from assets and occupational pensions were significant factors. Numerically, the number of WOOPIES is small, probably in the region of 200 000–300 000. Other acronyms that are sometimes used to describe this group are OPAL (older people with affluent life style) and JOLLIES (jet setting oldies with loads of loot).

Discussion has taken place about the possibility of introducing means testing for certain benefits, which would be directed at the elderly rich who are seen as not needing state support. The administrative costs of this exercise would be high and it is a fact that WOOPIES tend to be healthier and utilize public/social services less than other groups of old people. Thus those who can afford to pay for care are not necessarily the ones who need it.

Occupational Pension Schemes

Occupational schemes form an important part of the financial resources of older people. The 1990 *General household survey* asked questions to determine the proportion of the population who have retired from a job and were in receipt of such a pension[9]. Of interest was the number who had retired before or after the usual age and the reason for doing so.

Although there have been fluctuations over time, the proportion of employees who are members of their employers' pension schemes has remained at about 60% since 1975. The proportion of men (63%) has been higher than women (55%). There were variations, however, in membership of such schemes, depending upon age, occupation, and length of time in a job. One-tenth of all adults interviewed for the *General household survey* in 1990 were receiving an occupational pension. Men were about three times as likely as women to be drawing such a pension (17% compared with 6%). This proportion rose sharply after retirement age. The proportion of men receiving a pension from an employer rose from 39% among those aged 60–64, to 69% in those aged 65–69; there was a similar level at age 70 and over. The position was different for women; the proportion drawing a pension fell after the age of 69, from 25% of women aged 65–69 to only 13% of those aged 70 and over. This is probably because women aged 70 or over were less likely than younger women either to have joined an occupational pension scheme or to have continued working in full-time employment after marriage and/or the birth of their children, and were therefore less likely to have maintained occupational pension rights. About one-fifth of those drawing an occupational pension were not classified as retired, the majority of these respondents were still working. The likelihood of a respondent working while drawing an occupational pension from the previous job decreased with age. Among men, 29% of those aged 60–64 who were receiving a pension were currently working compared with only 9% of those aged 65–69. The earlier a pension was first drawn in relation to state retirement age the more likely the individual was still to be working.

Almost as many people had taken their pension early as had done so at the usual age for their scheme; among men the two proportions were the same at 45%. Among women, 49% had retired at the usual age for their pension scheme and only 35% had retired early. Although the proportion of all informants who first drew their pension after the usual age was small, only 6%, a larger proportion of women than of men, took their pensions late.

The largest proportion of informants, however, first drew their occupational pension at state retirement age; 46% of women were aged 60 and 32% of men were aged 65 when they first drew their pension. Probably because of the difference in state retirement ages, men were much less likely than women to have retired after the state retirement age; 3% of men who were receiving a pension compared with 19% of women had done so. The fact that women are more likely than men to have drawn their pension after state retirement age also suggests that some schemes had a fixed age of retirement that was nearer to the state retirement age for men. These findings would provide some support for the equalization of the retirement date for both men and women.

The most common reason informants gave for drawing their pension early was their own ill health. A larger proportion of women than of men gave ill health as a reason for taking their pension early: 41% compared with 31%. For both men and women, their own ill health was more likely to be given as a reason for drawing their occupational pension early by those who first drew their pension before the age of 55 than those who drew their pension at a later age. For those who first drew their pension after the age of 55, the offer of 'good terms' by their employer, particularly amongst men, was the reason cited most often for deciding to draw their pension before the usual age of the scheme. The third most frequently given reason for receiving an occupational pension early was redundancy. This was mentioned by about one-fifth of those who drew their pension early and fluctuated little in relation to when the pension was first drawn.

Pattern of Household Expenditure

Recent figures (*see* Table 6.1) show the pattern of household expenditure in pensioner households and the levels of income spent on various items. The low income pensioner households would appear to spend more on food and fuel than the higher income pensioner households, but compared with all households, pensioners tended to spend more proportionately on food, housing, light and fuel, but less on alcohol, tobacco, durable goods and, in particular, transport and vehicles[10].

Table 6.1: Patterns of household expenditure. Pensioner households are defined as those households where at least 75% of the income of the household comes from people of pensionable age. Source: Central Statistical Office, 1990[10].

	Percentage of reported expenditure									Average total expenditure (£ per week)
	Food	Housing	Fuel and light	Alcohol	Tobacco	Clothing and footwear	Durable household goods	Transport and vehicles	Other goods services miscellaneous	
Low income pensioner households	27.2	19.7	14.4	2.3	3.1	4.4	4.9	4.3	19.7	53.12
Other pensioner households	24.6	21.9	9.3	3.1	2.6	5.2	3.9	10.1	19.3	102.01
All households	19.0	16.1	5.6	4.6	2.5	7.0	7.0	15.0	23.0	188.21

Benefit Entitlement of Older Persons

In the years following World War II, a great number of welfare entitlements were made available to older people. Since the arrival of the Welfare State, they have consistently been by far the largest group of consumers of benefits. Despite this, there is no doubt that many older people fail to claim all the benefits to which they are entitled. There are several reasons for this: the large number of benefits is confusing and there has been poor publicity in the past; there are prevailing attitudes of benefits being 'charity'; and the pride that most people take in being financially independent has deterred some from claiming. Again, general practitioners, who are often the only source of advice to older people have themselves been ignorant of benefits and have sometimes been resistant to giving certificates of illness and disability. For this reason it is essential for health and social workers to have an idea of the benefits available. Unfortunately, these often change both in level and type, making it difficult to provide up to date information. The broad categories can, however, be summarized.

Retirement Pensions

Basic State Pension

The basic state pension, which is taxable, is paid to women at the age of 60 and men at 65, provided they have satisfied the National Insurance contribution conditions. This is paid only if the person has retired from regular work, but five years after the retirement age the basic pension is paid whether or not the person is working. Retirement pension is paid to a married woman on her husband's contributions when he retires, providing that she is aged over 60 and has retired from regular work, or has reached the age of 65. If a woman qualifies for a pension in her own right as well as her husband's, she receives whichever pension is the higher. Four months before a man's sixty-fifth birthday and a woman's sixtieth birthday, the Department of Social Security sends out a form to allow individuals to claim their pension. Pensions are normally paid weekly by an order book, which is cashed at a post office, but pensions can be paid directly into a bank or building society account. For housebound people, a neighbour or relative can cash a pension on their behalf. The value of the pension is reviewed and usually increased yearly. If the person has insufficient contributions a reduced pension may be paid. Divorced or widowed people may be able to use their former spouse's record to get a pension, or increase benefits. An additional pension is also available in special circumstances.

Additional Pension

On 6 April 1978, the State Earnings-Related Pension Scheme (SERPS) was started. This additional pension is based on earnings since April 1978. Where pensions are derived from state or employer superannuation schemes the individual may be 'contracted out' of SERPS. Anyone not contracted out who retired after the 6 April 1979 may qualify for an additional state pension, although as the scheme takes 20 years to reach maturity, no-one will receive a full additional pension until 1998. The additional pension is index related to earnings from April 1978. Employees on a contracted out pension scheme receive a guaranteed minimum pension in place of the state additional pension.

Graduated Pension

A graduated pension is also available in certain circumstances. This is a taxable pension scheme that ended in April 1975, but those who received such a pension at that time still normally have it paid with the basic retirement pension. Anyone who paid graduated contributions will have this extra pension paid with their basic retirement pension when they retire. The amount of money received depends on how much was paid into the graduated scheme before 1975.

Over Eighties Pension

When someone reaches 80 years, an extra £0.25 is added to any retirement pension. There is also a special pension (of at least £33.70 at 1993) for people who are aged 80 or over, but not entitled to a basic pension. This does not depend on contributions, but the recipient normally needs to have lived in Great Britain for ten years or more since the age of 60.

Help for People with Low Income

Income Support

This is a Social Security benefit aimed at helping people who do not have enough money to live on; it is intended to meet regular weekly needs. People who may get help from this benefit include people aged 60 and over, and those staying at home to look after a disabled relative. People can get help from Income Support even if they have savings up to £8000. If someone who claims has a partner to whom they are married, or with whom they live as if they were married to them, they have their partner's savings counted as well. If the savings are worth up to £3000 it will make no difference to the Income Support they get. Savings between £3000 and £8000 will make a difference, each £250 or part of £250 will be treated as if it was bringing in £1 per week.

The Social Fund

The following Social Fund payments may be able to provide lump sum cash payments to cover extra expenses that people find difficult to meet from their weekly income.

• Funeral payments can help with cost of arranging a funeral.

• Cold weather payments are automatically awarded for weeks when the weather is especially cold, to people aged 60 or over who are receiving Income Support.

- Community care grants help people live independently at home. They can be used for things such as beds, cookers, removal costs or help with certain travel costs.

- Budgeting loans can help with an item that the older person cannot afford, but these have to be repaid from the weekly Income Support.

- Crisis loans may be available in an emergency. These also have to be repaid.

Social Fund payments depend on the amount of the recipient's savings. Normally when someone is aged 60 or more, savings of more than £1000 are taken into account, but this savings limit does not apply for cold weather payments. Generally, to receive a Social Fund payment the recipient must be entitled to Income Support, but funeral payments are also paid to people receiving Housing Benefit or Council Tax Benefit and it is not necessary to be receiving Income Support to apply for a crisis loan.

Housing Benefit and Council Tax Benefit
Housing Benefit can provide help towards rent (including certain service charges). There are two types of Council Tax Benefit: the 'Main Council Tax Benefit' and the 'second adult rebate'. Both can reduce the amount of Council Tax payable. A person cannot receive either Housing Benefit or Main Council Tax Benefit if they have more than £16 000 savings. Savings of £3000 to £16 000 will affect the benefit. If Income Support is payable there will also be normal entitlement to these benefits. If the income is too high for Income Support it may be possible to receive some Housing Benefit and/or Council Tax Benefit. Whether any help is received and the amount payable, depends on a number of other factors, including income and savings, number of people in the family, age, whether the person is disabled and how much has to be paid in rent or Council Tax. The Second Adult Rebate Scheme can help some people who cannot get benefit on their own income and savings, but live with one or more people with a low income. If application is made for Income Support, a claim form for Housing Benefit and Council Tax Benefit will also be sent, otherwise it is necessary to contact the local council for an application form.

Help with House Repairs
Local councils can give grants towards the costs of certain repairs or improvements to the home. Obtaining the grant will depend on a number of factors including the type of work that needs to be done and an assessment of income and savings. If Income Support is being received it might be possible to get a community care grant or budgeting loan to help with the costs of minor repairs or redecoration. If a loan is taken out it may be possible to get an extra amount of Income Support to cover the interest on the loan.

Fuel Bills and Other Costs
The Income Support levels are intended to cover all essential weekly expenses and there are no extra Social Security payments to cover costs such as fuel bills, water

rates or telephone charges. Age Concern has facts sheets on heating and telephone costs which inform about possible help. For example there may be grants for insulation and draught proofing, which could help to reduce fuel bills, whereas some people can get assistance from the Social Services for telephone charges.

Help with Health Costs

Although most treatment under the National Health Service is free there are some things for which people may have to pay some or all the costs. These include: prescriptions, dental charges, eye tests, glasses and elastic stockings. Prescriptions are free to men aged 65 or over and women aged 60 or more. Help with NHS costs is also available to people on a low income. Those on Income Support can get free prescriptions, dental treatment, travel costs to hospital and sight tests, and also help towards the cost of glasses. Those not on Income Support may get some help towards these costs by filling in Form AG1. Dentists, opticians and pharmacists are able to provide this form.

Benefits for Carers and People with Disabilities

Attendance Allowance

This is a benefit for people who are physically or mentally disabled and need help with personal care or who need supervision from someone else; for example, they may qualify if help is needed with dressing, personal hygiene or moving around. There is no upper age limit for attendance allowance, but for a person under 65 years a disability living allowance should be claimed instead. It does not depend on National Insurance contributions and is not affected by savings or income. There are two weekly rates; the lower rate is for if help is needed in the day or the night, and a higher rate is for if help is needed both day and night. It is possible for someone to claim if they are living alone or with another person. What matters is that help is needed, not whether help is being received. Normally a person must meet the conditions for at least six months, but there are special rules for people who are terminally ill.

Disability Living Allowance

This is for people who become disabled before the age of 65 and who claim before they are 66. There are two parts: a mobility part (which replaced mobility allowance) and a care part (which replaced attendance allowance for those aged under 65). The mobility part is for people who cannot walk, have great difficulty walking, or who need someone with them when walking outdoors. Again it is paid at varying rates; the mobility part is paid at two rates and the care part is paid at three rates. The rules for the top two rates are the same as for attendance allowance; the lower care level is given to some people who are not disabled enough to qualify for one of the higher levels.

Invalid Care Allowance

Invalid care allowance is paid to people who are unable to work full time because they are caring for someone receiving payments from the care part of the disability living allowance, or attendance allowance. The recipient must be aged under 65 when first claiming and not earning more than £50 per week. If another benefit or pension is being received it may not be possible to also get an invalid care allowance.

Invalidity Benefit

This is paid to someone who has been unable to work for at least 28 weeks because they are sick or disabled. It depends on National Insurance Contributions. It may also be possible to receive an invalidity allowance based on the age of becoming unable to work and/or additional pension based on earnings. People who are receiving invalidity benefit when they reach pensionable age can choose whether to draw the pension or stay on invalidity benefit until the age of 65 for women and 70 for men.

Severe Disablement Allowance

This is an allowance for severely disabled people who are unable to work, but who have not paid enough contributions to get invalidity benefit. Certain medical conditions must be fulfilled and it is necessary to be under 65 years when the first claim is made.

Independent Living Fund

This fund previously made payments to severely disabled people who needed to pay for care or household tasks in order to remain living at home. No new applications were accepted after 25 November 1992, although payments will continue for those already receiving help. The Independent Living (1993) Fund has been set up for people who need help after April 1993; although it will provide more limited support it will only be available to people aged 16 to 65.

Help with Residential or Nursing Home Fees

The type of financial assistance that can be received towards residential or nursing home care will depend on whether the person entered the home before or after 1 April 1993. If the person was in a home before 1 April 1993 and has no more than £8000 savings, then special levels of income support towards the fees can be claimed. For those entering a home after 1 April 1993, and in need of financial support, then the local authority should be contacted. They will assess need for care and may agree to arrange a place in a home. A means test will be carried out to see how much will be needed to pay towards the fees. If a person has more than £8000 savings they will have to pay the full costs.

Other Benefits for People Who are Ill or Disabled

In addition to benefits mentioned above there are:

• Sickness Benefit and Statutory Sick Pay for people unable to work for up to 28 weeks

• Disability Working Allowance: a benefit related to income and savings that can top up low earnings

• Industrial Injury Benefit for people who have had an industrial accident or who have an occupational illness

• war pensions for people disabled during a war, or when serving in the forces.

People who are registered blind can get a reduction of £1.25 on the cost of their television licence. There are also concessionary licence fees of £5 for some elderly people who live in residential or nursing homes or certain council or housing association accommodation with a warden.

Travel concessions are sometimes available. Some councils offer free or reduced bus fares to older people. These vary, however, in different parts of the country. British Rail gives reductions on many train fares to people aged 60 and over who buy a 'senior citizens railcard', whilst coach companies and airlines may also offer reduced fares.

Other concessions vary, but people over a certain age may be able to get price reductions for admission to leisure centres, swimming pools, museums or other places of interest. Reduced fees for joining adult education classes may also be available.

Further Information

Age Concern England produces an annual publication called *Your rights*, which gives more information about pensions, benefits and other kinds of financial help. The 1993/94 edition costs £2.50 (including postage) and is available from the Publications Department, Age Concern England, 1268 London Road, London SW16 4ER. The factsheet on money benefits is updated frequently and there are a large number of other factsheets that give more detail about individual money benefits.

The Department of Social Security also has many leaflets; these are available free from local benefits agencies or by writing to the DSS Leaflets Unit, PO Box 21, Stanmore, Middlesex, HA7 1AY. For general information about social security benefits it is possible to telephone Freeline Social Security on 01800 666 555. For information about disability benefits it is possible to ring the free Benefits Enquiry Line on 01800 882 200. There may be a local agency in the area, such as an Age Concern group or a Citizens Advice Bureau, which can give further information or help with a problem related to a pension or social security benefit. The local library should have information about advice agencies in an area.

Acknowledgement

Information contained in this section of the book is derived largely from the Age Concern Fact Sheet, *A brief guide to money benefits* (April 1993). Permission to quote from this document from Age Concern England is gratefully acknowledged.

References

1. Office of Population, Censuses and Surveys, Social Survey Division. (1977) *General household survey* 1974. HMSO, London.

2. Office of Population, Censuses and Surveys, Social Survey Division. (1989) *General household survey* 1987. (Series GHS No. 17.) HMSO, London.

3. Falkingham J, Victor C. (1991) *The myth of the Woopie?: incomes, the elderly and targeting welfare.* Suntory-Toyota International Centre for Economics and Related Disciplines, London School of Economics, London.

4   Central Statistical Office. (1991) *Social Trends 21.* HMSO, London.

5. Central Statistical Office. (1990) F*amily expenditure survey.* HMSO, London.

6. Abrams M. (1983) Changes in the lifestyles of the elderly 1959–1982. In: Central Statistical Office. *Social trends 14.* HMSO, London, 11 16.

7. Fiegehen GC. (1986) Income after retirement. In: Central Statistical Office. *Social trends 16.* HMSO, London, 13–18.

8. Evandrou M, Victor C. (1988) *Differentiation in later life: social class and housing tenure cleavages.* Suntory-Toyota International Centre for Economics and Related Disciplines, London School of Economics, London.

9. Office of Population, Censuses and Surveys, Social Survey Division. (1992) *General household survey* 1990. (Series GHS No. 21.) HMSO, London.

10. Central Statistical Office. (1990) *Social trends 20.* HMSO, London.

7
Social Status

The social status of older people in the UK is well documented; from it a picture can be gained about how they live in the community. It has been possible to discern changes over the past two decades; the trends are often relevant to care provision.

Older People Living Alone

A growing proportion of older people live alone. These changes are indicated in Figure 7.1[1]. In 1962, 22% of people aged 65 and over in Great Britain lived alone, by 1989 it was 36%. The number of old people who lived only with a spouse has remained fairly constant at about 45%, but the percentage who lived with other people, which usually means in a two-generation family, has dropped from 44% in 1962 to 18% in 1989. This latter change seems to have taken place

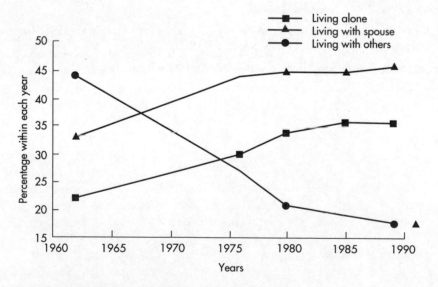

Figure 7.1: Household circumstances of people aged 65 years and over: percentage within years 1962–1989. Source: General Household Surveys, 1980, 1986 and 1989 (unpublished data). Data for 1962 and 1976 from Dale *et al.*, 1987[1].

partly because of the greater availability of accommodation, but mainly because of changes in family structure and family mobility.

Older people live on their own much more often than people in other age groups. In particular 29% of men aged 75 and over live alone and 57% of women (Table 7.1).

Table 7.1: Percentage living alone by age and sex: all persons aged 16 or over, Great Britain, 1990.

| | Percentage who lived alone | | |
	Men	Women	Total
Age (years)			
16–24	4	4	4
25–44	10	5	7
45–64	9	12	11
65–74	18	37	28
75 or over	29	57	47
All aged 16 or over	11	16	13
All persons[a]	8	13	11

[a]Including children.
Source: *General household survey*, 1990[5].

Although not shown in Table 7.1, it is probable that numbers for the 85-year-old and over group are slightly lower, because of an increased proportion of people in this group being in residential nursing homes. The high proportion of older people living alone has implications for social services; they will require more support in daily living, more support when illness occurs and more support if long standing disability is present.

However, living alone does not always mean than an older person is socially isolated and that they have little contact with neighbours and relatives. Indeed the reverse is often true, particularly if an old person has lived in the same area for most of his or her life. Many older people live alone by choice; they nevertheless enjoy an active social life. A distinction therefore, has to be drawn between those living alone and the section within this group who may be called 'isolates'. These are people who do not have any contact with friends or relatives and may often be found in a miserable or neglected state. The main members of this group are the unmarried and those who have never had children. Older people are also more at risk of being socially isolated if they have had sons and not daughters. Young men are more easily drawn into their wives' families and may lose contact with their own parents and other relatives. Fathers tend to have weaker ties with children and old men living alone are liable to have little contact with their off-spring. This may be a class related phenomenon; middle-class sons tend to have stronger ties with their fathers than those in working class families.

Loneliness may occur even if an old person is living with a large family. By contrast, some who live in extreme isolation maintain that they are never lonely and obviously have inner resources to help them. This is aided by their previous life-style; if they are used to writing letters and using the telephone they can maintain communications with their families and friends. There are, however, special situations that help to produce social isolation and these will be discussed later in Chapter 9, which is on social vulnerability. People living alone are subject to many hazards, one of which is poor nutrition.

Residential and Family Structure

Details of the housing tenure and amenities for elderly people are shown in Table 7.2. People aged 65 and over are more likely to own their houses outright, although those living alone include the highest proportion of any group renting accommodation either privately or from the council. In 1985, older people living alone were less likely to have a telephone (69%), central heating (59%), or the use of a car (12%), than those living in other types of household. These proportions are likely now to be much lower.

Table 7.2: Housing tenure and amenities for older people, Great Britain 1985.

	Type of household (%)			
	Elderly person living with spouse only	Elderly person living alone	Elderly person in other kinds of household	Households containing no elderly persons
Tenure				
Owner occupied, owned outright	55	40	43	15
Owner occupied, with mortgage	4	1	15	50
Rented from local authority or new town	33	47	34	27
Rented privately	8	12	8	9
Amenities				
Availability of WC	99	97	98	99
Availability of bath/shower	99	97	98	100
Central heating	68	59	62	72
Car	56	12	58	72
Telephone	87	69	80	83

Source: General household survey, 1986 (Table 12.4)[4].

Older people also live in residential homes and there has been a dramatic increase in the role of private residential homes; the numbers of residents rose between 1977 and 1990 by 420% and the share of total provision of residential homes (both private and local authority) rose from 15% to 51%. Figure 7.2 shows graphically the change in the roles of the various providers of residential care. There has in particular been a large increase in the proportion of people aged 85 and over in homes. Between 1980 and 1990 the number aged 85 and over increased from 59 000 to 115 000. This age group also accounted for a higher percentage of the residents of such homes, increasing from 37% in 1980 to 49% in 1990.

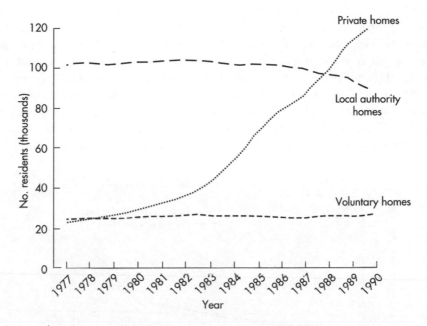

Figure 7.2: Residents aged 65 years and over, in homes for elderly people by type of home, England 1977–90. Source: Department of Health, 1992[2].

Although there has been a considerable reduction in the number of older people living with people other than a spouse, this group nevertheless accounts for about one-fifth of the total. Sometimes considerable role adjustments need to be made, particularly by the women. When the shared house is the original family house, the mother's authority is usually maintained. When a daughter-in-law is involved there may be friction and there is danger that the older woman may become a subordinate housekeeper and be marginalized within the family. This is one reason why older people prefer to live alone. It is sometimes easier when there are young children living in the house because an older person can feel valued by being, for instance, an important babysitter. Three generation households are becoming less common.

Most older people see friends or relatives fairly frequently. There is, however, an age-related reduction in the proportion of older people visited once a week or more. Single and divorced older people are less likely to have contacts with either relatives or friends. As age advances, older people tend less often to use public transport while unaccompanied. This is often because of ill health or disability. Overall, 28% of those aged 65 years and over who did not have a car did not use public transport either[2].

Surveys on disability in Great Britain that were conducted by the Office of Population Censuses and Surveys in 1985/6 showed that 6% of the disabled aged

65 to 74, and 18% of those aged 75 years and over, who were living at home, were housebound. The percentage reporting they were housebound increased with age and disability[2].

Information is available on the inability to perform selected household tasks independently. Figure 7.3 illustrates the trends for selected activities. The percentage of people unable to perform household tasks independently shows a general increase with age and this accelerates after the age of 80 years. For most tasks and at all ages the proportion of women reporting that they were unable to do them independently is greater than the proportion of men. The question on which the data was based, however, used reported abilities rather than tested abilities. The apparent sex differential may reflect differences in attitude on reporting, rather than true sex differences. People living alone may be more aware of their limitations than those living with a partner, and more women live alone.

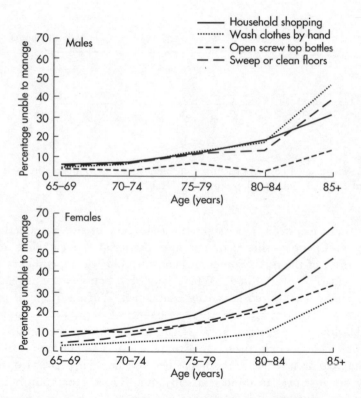

Figure 7.3: Household tasks: inability to manage independently by sex and age, Great Britain 1985. Source: Department of Health, 1992[2].

The 1976 survey of the elderly at home[3] showed that 73% of those aged 85 and over could cook a main meal, 60% could wash clothes, and 50% do light jobs in the garden. A substantial proportion of this age group suffered from a loss of mobility which limited their ability to do household shopping; 16% of men and 20% of women were permanently bedfast or housebound, and a further 16% of men and 30% of women could go out only with help. The sex difference in this case may reflect the greater proportion of women among those aged 85 years or more.

Information is available from the *General household survey 1985*[4] on self-care, which includes tasks such as having a bath, cutting toe nails and feeding. Figure 7.4 illustrates the change with age in the inability to perform selected self-care tasks. For most activities, including walking outdoors, the percentage of women reporting that they were unable to do a task is greater than that of men. In part this is explained by the greater proportion of much older women in the 75 years and over age group.

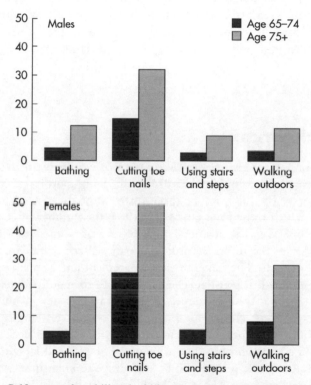

Figure 7.4: Self-care and mobility: inability to manage independently, by sex and age, Great Britain, 1985. Source: Department of Health, 1992[2].

Areas of Residence

Most older people continue to live in the family home throughout their retirement. People may, however, move house when they retire and there are several reasons for this. They may wish to move to a pleasanter environment and this usually means a migration to coastal areas, particularly in the south east, Cornwall and parts of North Wales. They often plan these moves well before retirement and already know the area well. They may lose social and family contacts, however, and this can make life difficult if illness occurs. Many post-retirement moves are only for a short distance, and are brought about by a need to move to housing that suits their new circumstances. They may look for a smaller, more convenient house, still near family and friends. Sometimes an older couple will move longer distances just to be near children who have moved away. Inner cities have in the past been places where large numbers of older people lived, having been there most of their lives. This may be changing due to urban renewal programmes. Better pensions and earlier retirement mean that both the opportunities and resources for moving are greater. The large number of people already in popular retirement areas may deter some, and staying in well established situations may well be seen to have attractions. There is another peak of movement at around the age of 75 where older people cannot manage in the family house and have to move to either residential or sheltered accommodation.

Work/Employment

There have been important changes in the pattern of employment over the past 20 years, which have resulted in a marked decline in the proportion of economically active older people. By 1984, under three-quarters of those aged 55–59 were working and only half of those aged 60–64. By 1989, the number of economically active men of 65 and over had dropped to 9%, and of women to 2%[5]. These proportions may vary in the future according to national economic circumstances, but probably not by much. The move to early retirement and a much more widespread availability of personal pension schemes for both men and women will continue to work in favour of reduced levels of economic activity in older people. There are some exceptions: clergy, high court judges and self-employed people can continue working. Some people wish to continue to work and need the status, money, interest and companionship that it brings. The reduced labour force may mean that in the future older people will be encouraged to continue working and even to return to previous jobs. The most likely result will be an increase in part-time work amongst pensioners. There are competing forces in society. There is a contradiction, however, because the strong pressure for early retirement because of high unemployment levels, particularly amongst young people, will remain. At the end of the day most people value retirement and see it as a new phase in life. It is probable therefore that low economic activity amongst pensioners will continue.

Attitudinal Issues in Society

As well as structural aspects in the social status of older people, there are also attitudinal issues which affect their lives and their need for health and social care. These include ageism, gender, race and ethnicity, and poverty.

Ageism

Butler[6] coined the word ageism to describe prejudice against older people. Ageism is a 'process of systematic stereotyping of, and discrimination against, older people because they are old'[6]. Older people are the victims of myths and stereotypes. These influence the attitudes of the young and middle-aged in relation to older people, and to their own experience of ageing. Ageism allows younger generations to see older people as different from themselves, thus they subtly decline to identify with their elders as human beings. It is the negative attitudes of individuals towards older people, and the reinforcement by our culture and institutions of such attitudes, that perpetuates ageism and allows it to flourish. The possibility of ageism and ageist practices in the health and social services needs to be confronted and challenged, especially by those working with older people.

Whenever a group experiences discrimination, prejudgements not based on actual experience are justified by stereotypes, which are usually negative. The consequence is that all members of a particular group are seen to have the same characteristics (older people, the disabled). A person's individuality is lost as he or she becomes subsumed under the group label. Differences in the experience of being older or disabled, for women and men, and for members of different racial groups and social classes, are ignored.

It is increasingly recognized that we live in an ageist society. Numerous surveys have attempted to measure attitudes towards ageing and older people. Stereotypes include views that older people are not sexually engaged, and are frail, forgetful and confused, cantankerous, dithering and withdrawn. Ageist attitudes permeate society and research is showing that older people are more likely to be handicapped by negative attitudes than by their own physical disabilities.

The language used when addressing older people is significant: 'old boy', 'old girl', 'old dear' are patronizing and infantalizing, and convey images of passivity and dependence. Within the NHS older people are referred to as geriatric patients regardless of their illness, being seen as a homogeneous group rather than as individuals with individual needs. Similarly social services departments provide residential care in 'old people's homes', now often called 'older people's homes'. The language changes in an attempt to avoid stereotyping, but the care accommodation is still restricted to one age band.

It has been argued that the health needs of older people receive low priority and that discrimination leads to older people becoming excluded from certain screening programmes and surgical procedures[7].

Ageist generalizations focus on the decline of physical abilities and mental faculties which allows the health and social services to make assumptions about the quality of life older people can expect. The introduction of assessment and screening for people aged 75 years and over provides an opportunity to address such institutional ageism in a positive way.

Gender

There is a numerical imbalance in later life; women form an increasing majority as age advances. There are at present three times more women than men aged over 85, leading to the feminization of later life[8]. Females now comprise the majority of older people in almost all societies, a fact that is sometimes ignored in studies on ageing.

The losses older women suffer are well documented. Most health and social service workers are aware of children leaving home, husbands dying, deaths of other relatives and friends and loss of health, but painful feelings of loss are also caused by the surface signs of ageing. This is because, while one stereotype of women is as sexual objects, a second is of women as homemakers and carers. Indeed many women perceive their identity as closely dependent on serving others, as wives, as mothers, and as daughters. Older women therefore risk being seen and, perhaps more importantly, risk seeing themselves as obsolete, because they not longer contribute to society through the identities assigned to them. Because of this, some older women may find it difficult to admit failing health and disability that prevent them from performing caring and household tasks. Importantly, workers in the health and social services often expect women to do caring and household tasks despite their health problems but do not have the same expectations of older men.

Far more women than men need care and support in order to remain living at home and they are the most reliant on state services. As has been mentioned earlier, older women have higher levels of physical incapacity than men and are more likely to suffer non-life threatening disabilities. A recent British survey[9] found that twice as many women as men aged over 75 were housebound (22% compared with 11%) and 36% of older men were medically assessed as 'fit' compared with 25% of older women. Gender differences in disability increase with age; twice as many women as men aged over 80 suffer 'severe' disabilities. Women have an advantage in longevity over men but suffer more total years of disablement, a consequence being that older women have a far greater chance of spending their later years in residential care.

Race and Ethnicity

Members of ethnic minority communities do not have all their needs met by the health and social services in Britain. It is now widely recognized that the services have failed adequately to address the problem, although a few authorities are making attempts to do so.

The services have little knowledge of the needs of people from ethnic minority communities, (ie communities of people who share a common identity or culture). Health workers often know little about diseases specific to non-white people and often do not understand how those from different cultures respond to illness and death. Research and training have failed to solve the problem. Consequently, hospitals and local authority residential homes ignore, or do not adequately address, the needs of black people and people whose culture differs from the dominant (white, male) culture[10,11].

This is particularly apparent in the area of mental health, where many black people have been labelled 'mentally ill' by psychiatrists who failed to acknowledge and understand the cultural context of the person's behaviour. A further signifi-cant barrier can be the attitudes of the workers themselves; stereotypes and myths lead to discrimination against people from ethnic minority communities. The term 'triple jeopardy' was coined by Alison Norman[10] to describe older black people in Britain; they are seen to suffer discrimination because of their age and physical condition, because of racism and because services are not accessible to them.

The role of community based health staff appears to be little understood, and contact by some staff (eg community nurses) with older people from ethnic minority communities[11] is virtually non-existent. Alison Norman[10] outlines a model which may prove to be a useful starting point. She argues that there is a strong case for taking services to people; advice sessions and talks on general health education can be given in the clubs, day centres, temples and churches where ethnic minority older people can be found.

Poverty

Few people over 65 years of age are economically active. A characteristic of insti-tutional ageism is the age barriers on employment. Such policies contribute to the view that older people are incapable, useless and dependent. The majority of older people are therefore dependent on fixed incomes. These fixed incomes reflect a person's life position. If people are relatively poor when they are younger, they will be poor when they are older. The result is that manual work-ers, people who have experienced long periods of unemployment, women, and people from ethnic minority communities, are more likely to experience poverty in later years. Studies have found that there are social class inequalities in later life. For example, mortality and poor health is higher for older working-class men than for older middle-class men. Class as defined here is the Registrar General's scale and therefore is closely related to income.

Some older people will be entirely dependent on state pensions; this applies to older women particularly and is a consequence of a lifetime of low earnings, intermittent work patterns (often due to caring responsibilities), part-time work-ing and dependency on men. Lack of money for some older people is a major problem, which is often exacerbated by poor living conditions. Some older people then will be confined to their homes because of lack of money and will suffer the effects of a poor quality environment. Living alone will make the situation less tolerable. Furthermore, many older people have very few visitors and often rely on health and social service workers (community nurses and home care workers) for contact with the outside world.

Poverty for many older people, then, is not just about lack of money; income is also associated with other material advantages, for example a car and those household goods which enable a comfortable life. Poor older people are more likely to rely on public transport to take them to increasingly centralized services (eg shops and health centres). A more accurate definition of poverty is the 'lack of access to a range of resources which are crucial for well-being, participation in society, autonomy and life satisfaction: these include, in addition to income, basic services such as health care, education, transport and decent housing'[8]. A key element is money but other elements flow from it; in effect, lack of money leads to the marginalization of many older people.

Acknowledgement

This section is taken from the background reading associated with the Radcliffe Medical Press Course, Over 75[12]. The original was prepared by Charles Barker and Karen Kniveton from Tameside Metropolitan Borough Social Services Department.

References

1. Dale A, Evandrou M, Arber S. (1987) Household structure for the elderly in Britain. *Ageing Soc* 7: 37–56.

2. Department of Health. (1992) *The health of elderly people: an epidemiological overview.* (Central Health Monitoring Unit, Epidemiological Overview Series Vol. 1.) HMSO, London.

3. Hunt A. (1978) *The elderly at home.* (Office of Population Censuses and Surveys, Social Survey Division) HMSO, London.

4. Office of Population Censuses and Surveys, Social Survey Division. (1989) *General household survey 1985.* (Series GHS No. 16.) HMSO, London.

5. Office of Population Censuses and Surveys, Social Survey Division. (1992) *General household survey 1990.* (Series GHS No. 21.) HMSO, London.

6. Butler R. (1985) *Why survive? Being old in America.* Macmillan, London.

7. Henwood M. (1989) No sense of urgency: age discrimination in health care. In: McEwan E, editor. *Age: the unrecognised discrimination in health care.* Age Concern England, Mitcham, Surrey.

8. Arbour S, Ginn J. (1991) *Gender and later life.* Sage, London.

9. Hall R, Channing D. (1990) Age: pattern of consultation and functional disability in elderly patients in one general practice. *Br Med J* 301: 424–8.

10. Norman A. (1985) *Triple jeopardy: growing old in a second home land.* (Policy studies on ageing, No. 3.) Centre for Policy on Ageing, London.

11. National Institute for Social Work. (1988) *Residential care: a positive choice*. Report of the independent review of residential care. HMSO, London.

12. Williams EI. (1992) *Over 75*: a course for health and social workers. Radcliffe Medical Press, Oxford.

8
Dynamics of Health and Ageing

Natural ageing is a subtle and little understood process. There is no point in time when a particular person becomes 'old' and yet the differences between a 40-year-old and an 80-year-old are quite clear. Little is known about the mechanism of ageing, but it is clearly important to get some understanding of the process and especially its relationship to disease. Aspects of ageing include not only physical and mental changes, but also social interactions.

Normal Ageing

Old age and the wish to prolong life have long had a fascination. The psalmist talked about a natural life length of three-score years and ten; ever since then people have desired to prolong this period. An increase in life expectancy has already occurred and the 70-year-old point is being reached by many more people. Whether there has been an increase in life span – namely the total possible time that an individual can live – is, however, debatable. This may not be achievable and the realistic aim must be to gain an increase in health expectancy so that full function is maintained for as long as possible. This is the basis of much modern thinking. Bernard Isaacs and his colleagues described in *The survival of the unfittest*[1], how, in 1972, people with high levels of disability were kept alive for long periods in institutions. This situation is less acceptable nowadays and the aim is to ensure that most people live for most of their lives in good functional health with a minimal period of high disability and dependency.

The natural ageing process has been termed senescence and shows itself, as Comfort[2] pointed out, as 'an increasing probability of death with chronological age'. This implies that changes take place in the body as time goes by in the absence of recognized disease. Very often, however, the process of senescence may also be accompanied by disease and one may well affect the other. It is still unclear what is the nature of the effect that these two processes have on each other and indeed, whether there do exist two quite separate ageing processes, one normal and the other abnormal.

Direct observations of the way in which people 'age' give some clue. It is sometimes noted that an older person just 'fades away', and, although disease is the likely reason, it does hint that natural ageing is also at work. The time scale of ageing is also variable, and it is well known that people can appear much older than their chronological age would suggest, and, similarly many old people act and look much younger than their years. There is, therefore, often a difference between biological age and chronological age and in a person's life, this may alter as time progresses. Ageing is not only a feature of external appearance but also of internal environment. Internal organs age at different rates. People of the same age group are often compared to determine features of actual ageing, but this cross-sectional approach only confirms the variability of physiological responses with the passage of time and different life-styles.

Longitudinal studies of cohorts may reveal more information about how vitality is lost. Comfort makes the point that, if we kept the vitality throughout life that we had at the age of twelve, about half of us would still be alive in seven hundred years' time[2]. We should be dying off, like radioactive atoms, at a random rate, and would have no specific age beyond which we knew that we were unlikely to live.

Many theories of ageing have been proposed to explain the process of natural senescence. No really convincing explanation has yet emerged, which is hardly surprising considering the complexity of the subject and the difficulties of experimentation. Some theories are, however, intriguing. Hippocrates thought that old age was due to loss of body heat. The anatomist, Theodore Swann, considered that a vital life material was gradually lost and this contributed to ageing. Observations that social class can affect longevity supported a view that environment can affect the rate of ageing. In experimental animals, exposure to radiation and overfeeding can both lead to premature death[3]. Genetic influences can affect the likelihood of attaining extreme old age, as the study of certain family pedigrees shows. Members of the well known Trevellyan family, for instance, constantly reach great ages. Different species have different life spans; for example, elephants live longer than mice. Is this because of different rates of cell division or an inherently slower rate of ageing or both? The idea of lethal genes which evolutionarily slipped through the net of natural selection because they were late acting and so beyond the normal reproducing people, was advanced by Medawar[3].

These theories, based to some extent on observation, do not, however, deepen our understanding of the process; nor do other theories based more on conjecture. For instance, the 'programme theory', where senescence is regarded as an inevitable stage in the sequence that begins with fertilization and carries on through fetal life, birth, childhood, youth and on to maturity, is again unlikely, because the relatively small variation in the age at which developing organisms attain each specific stage in development contrasts with the wide variations in the age of onset of many of the features of old age. For instance, the appearance of an occasional grey hair before normal growth is finished is hardly consistent with the programme theory. The consistent age of onset of the menopause on the other hand is supportive evidence. Furthermore, the toxic theory that argues that poisonous substances accumulate in the organism and produce dysfunction and death, fails to account for the anatomical specificity of many age-dependent changes. The wear and tear theory likens old age to machine failure, but it is impossible to apply this idea to such conditions as greying of hair and arcus senilis.

The theories described so far are basically non-biological. In an attempt to introduce biological principles, interest has centred on so-called error theories, and there are several of these. Evidence is seen of ageing in various microscopic elements in the body. Extracellular connective tissue may show changes in structure and cells themselves may become defective. On a widespread scale, as with the loss or greying of hair, numerous cells develop defects more or less simultaneously. Burch considers that many of these macroscopic manifestations of ageing reflect errors of synthesis of recognition proteins that occur in one, or sometimes several, central, growth-control cells, and the mutant products of the descendent cells attack target cells that bear complementary recognition proteins[4]. The macrocytic consequences of the attack are observed in the target cells, which, in some instances, are distributed at many anatomical sites. This points to a controlling central factor which may be the hypothalamus. Two rather similar theories have been proposed along these lines: the autoimmune and the autoaggressive theories. Both these are complex, but basically the idea of the autoimmune theory is that mutations occur that produce immunological intolerance resulting in self-impairment of cells and, in certain situations, cell death. The autoaggressive theory is more fundamental and postulates mutation, not in the system that controls the normal immune response to particular antigens, but in the system that normally controls the size and growth of target tissues throughout the body.

These ideas are important and obviously open up the way to more fundamental research. It is still difficult, however, to see a clear distinction between normal ageing or senescence and that associated with disease. Possibly ageing consists in the main of a constellation of specific age dependent, autoaggressive disorders that encompass both physiological and pathological ageing. The reader is referred to an excellent discussion of the subject by Evans for further information[5].

Despite the conjectures, in recent years considerable attention has focused on the modification of those aspects of ageing previously thought to be normal and unalterable[6]. This has proved to have very practical implications. When considering age-related losses in both mental and physical capacity, the substantial heterogeneity of older persons has sometimes been forgotten. Although wide variation of some biological parameters is a mark of ageing, there is evidence that the role of age in such losses has been overstated and that a major component of many so-called age associated reductions can be explained in terms of life-style, habit, diet and an array of psychosocial variables. The concept of 'normal' ageing arose when considering evidence of the effects of age on such clinically relevant entities as hearing, vision, renal function, glucose tolerance, systolic blood pressure, bone density and immune function. It appeared that there were inevitable changes present that were time related, although not necessarily due to time.

This idea of normal ageing can lead to negativism as it gives the impression that the decline is inevitable, and indeed harmless, and so inhibits attempts at its modification. To counteract this, it is necessary to distinguish between usual ageing and successful ageing. This allows a more positive approach, and, by studying successful ageing, the factors involved in this can then be elucidated. There is evidence, for instance, that suggests that much of the observed carbohydrate intolerance in older people may be caused by factors other than biological ageing, and that modification of the diet and the taking of exercise may substantially reduce the rate of these changes. Similarly, it is possible to modify the development of osteoporosis with age by, for instance, instituting moderate exercise programmes. Where mental impairment is present, attention and motivation may improve with appropriate intervention. Psychological factors are also relevant and autonomy is important to the wellbeing of an older person. The extent to which such autonomy is encouraged or denied may be a major determinant in whether ageing is usual or successful. Social support is also necessary in successful ageing and may work by mitigating some of the ill effects of changing circumstances sometimes seen in later life.

These ideas linking usual ageing, successful ageing and the effects of disease when considering the natural history of old age are important and have implications for care. The possibility of modifying the process of ageing by such vehicles as diet, exercise, life-style, social support and maintenance of personal autonomy, need to be accepted as part of a philosophy of health promotion in old age.

Changes in Specific Systems in Old Age

The effects of usual ageing sometimes merge with the abnormal and it is important to recognize what is controllable and what is uncontrollable. Some physical changes are obvious. Height is reduced and the body becomes smaller due to loss of body mass. Very often there is thoracic kyphosis, particularly in women. The hair becomes grey and may be lost in both men and women. Muscle power for sustained effort is reduced and the grip may become poor. Teeth are lost, or at least the gums retract, giving the so-called 'long in the tooth' appearance. Control of body temperature is harder to achieve and older people easily become cold. Patterns of sleep alter and night cramps occur with greater frequency. The voice changes and may grow thin due to loss of elasticity of the laryngeal cartilage and muscle. A full account of changes associated with ageing is given in textbooks of geriatric medicine. Some practical points are, however, given here.

Nervous System

There is a decline in neurological function with increasing age. Tendon and superficial reflexes are sometimes absent in older people, particularly the ankle jerks. Anderson found abdominal reflexes to be absent in about 20% of men and over 50% of women in older people examined at his Rutherglen Clinic[7].

Sensory perception may be reduced in old age, particularly in the legs and feet. The normal pattern is for reduced sensory discrimination, particularly in the ability to perceive changes in temperature. The decreased sensory perception that occurs is not necessarily neurological in origin. Light touch, for example, can be affected by the presence of oedema, which may make sensory testing extremely difficult. Although vibration sense is commonly lost in the lower extremities it is rather unusual for it to be accompanied by a loss of position sense, if the latter is tested for properly. Obviously patient compliance influences to a large degree the testing for position sense.

Most doctors would regard true loss of position sense as being pathological. Indeed, it must never be accepted that changes are necessarily due to ageing alone and consideration must be given to the possibility of disease. The brain shows some cell loss, but less than previously assumed, and not all types of brain cell are affected. There are also changes in neurotransmitter systems. Changes in the connecting dendrites may be more significant than in the main bodies of the cells themselves.

Special Senses

Herbst and Humphrey, using pure tone audiometry, assessed the prevalence of hearing impairment in a sample of people aged 70 or more, living at home[8]. They found that 60% of the sample were deaf; this is a higher proportion than previously assumed. Undoubtedly there has been a serious underestimate of the prevalence. There are, of course, possible pathological causes, and these are discussed in Chapter 18.

Eyesight deteriorates as age advances and becomes symptomatic by the mid-forties. Drooping of the upper eye lids is common in older people. The lens becomes increasingly opaque and less elastic, which results in decreased accommodation range and eventual loss of accommodation power. The pupillary reflexes become slower and the diameter of the pupil decreases. Recovery from glare takes longer and there is a deterioration in dark adaption and colour vision.

Digestive System

Deterioration in the digestive system is not particularly marked in old age. Diseases of the liver and gall bladder, however, become more common with increasing age. Gastrointestinal disturbances may increase and there is a tendency towards constipation.

Respiratory System

Respiratory efficiency is reduced along with the total lung volume. Oxygen absorption is the lungs may be impaired and its utilization by the tissues is less efficient. The respiratory reserve capacity is reduced, probably partly due to impaired movement of the rib cage.

Cardiovascular System

Blood pressure does not necessarily rise with age. Williams recorded the blood pressures of 270 unselected patients of 75 years and over (86 men and 184 women)[9]. The means of the readings in the various groups are shown in Table 8.1. These findings indicate that levels do not increase, even amongst much older people, although the wide standard deviation may indicate that variability is the main feature. There was little difference between the sexes. Survival seems to be more likely if the blood pressure is not too high or too low. These people probably represent a special group in the population where blood pressure was stable.

Table 8.1: Mean level of blood pressure (with standard deviations) for men and women over 75 years old.

Age group	Mean systolic and standard deviation (mmHg)	Mean diastolic and standard deviation (mmHg)
Male		
75–79	155 ± 24.77	86 ± 10.9
80–84	162 ± 24.80	87 ± 11.53
85–89	171 ± 31.37	90 ± 12.14
90+	142 ± 26.39	81 ± 14.72
All ages 75+	159 ± 26.25	86 ± 11.28
Female		
75–79	163 ± 23.64	91 ± 8.84
80–84	158 ± 23.24	90 ± 13.63
85–89	159 ± 25.34	90 ± 12.65
90+	156 ± 11.40	88 ± 4.47
All ages 75+	160 ± 23.57	90 ± 11.48

Sample: n = 270 (86 men; 184 women)
Source: Williams, 1973[9].

One of the problems with looking at the relationship between arterial pressure and age is that most studies, like the one quoted, are cross-sectional and not longitudinal. It may be that many of the patients in whom high blood pressure has produced damage to key organs, such as brain or kidney, will have already died by the time they reach 75 years, so the group reported above represents the survivors.

The arteries in old age become thickened and hard, probably due to an increase in arterial collagen. The collagen that is laid down in old age may be less elastic due to more molecular cross-linking. This results in the arteries themselves being less compliant. Veins are less affected by ageing. Thoracic kyphosis often displaces the apex beat of the heart and this may also be masked by emphysema. As many as two-thirds of patients aged 70 and over have systolic ejection murmurs over the aortic area.

Haemoglobin

Williams et al.[10] estimated haemoglobin levels in 286 patients over 75 year of age. A histogram of the distribution is shown in the Figure 8.1. The differences in haemoglobin levels between the sexes in ages up to 75 years has frequently been commented upon. From the study quoted, it would appear that this influence extends well beyond this age.

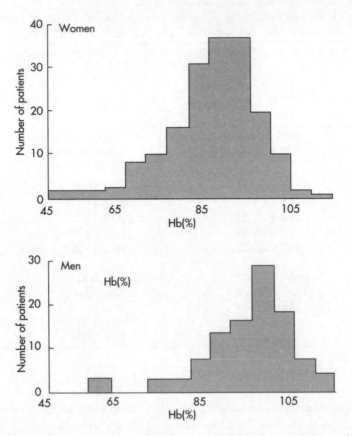

Figure 8.1: Haemoglobin values (100% = 14.8g/dl) in a population aged 75 and over. Source: Williams *et al.*, 1972[10].

Endocrine System

It is difficult to assess the precise effects of ageing on the various endocrine glands. This is partly due to the fact that routine measurement of endocrine function in elderly people is done as a one-off test at a particular time and dynamic serial tests of function are rarely carried out. Thyroid function is thought to decrease with age, but there is no clear evidence for this. There is some evidence that the stress response in the pituitary–adrenal axis is diminished in older people, though under non-stress conditions cortisone measurements are normal. Secretion of sex hormones declines with age and this affects secondary sex features, such as the breasts, which tend to atrophy.

Renal System

Changes do occur in renal function. There is evidence of a decline in glomerular filtration and renal blood flow. The acid/base balance is hard to maintain in old age.

Skin

Changes in the skin are very noticeable. Environmental factors can affect these changes and prolonged exposure to sunlight can accelerate the process. Skin ageing also varies from person to person, and it is possible that some hereditary influence is at work. The changes consist mainly of atrophy of the epidermis with an increase in pigmentation and degenerative changes in the collagenous and elastic fibres of the dermis. Pigmented areas are seen more frequently and there is a high incidence of small papillomata. The skin looks thinner, shows more wrinkles and appears lax and dry. The subcutaneous fat may be reduced and the skin sometimes has a loose, hanging appearance. The nails grow at a slower rate and may be more brittle. There may be a reduction in sweat due to atrophy of the sweat glands. Hair follicles are reduced in density and the hair is markedly thinner, but curiously rarely completely absent. Greying of the hair due to loss of melanin pigment is almost universal and the process can start at an early age.

Psychological Aspects of Ageing

As well as physical changes, old age brings with it an alteration in psychological outlook. This is variable, but certain characteristics are recognizable and these probably arise from the cumulative effects of psychological adaption in earlier stages of life. The pathway from early adulthood through middle adulthood to the pre-retirement phase of 60 to 65 years usually consists of a complex series of events that contribute to psychological ageing. Sex differences are apparent in this process, but probably less so now when increasing numbers of women have careers. Women do, however, tend to live longer than men, and the psychosocial transition can be different. Both men and women have to adjust to the eventual departure of children to live their own independent lives. Retirement needs coping with and, for women especially there is the prospect of widowhood. Social class differences are also present. Manual workers reach the summit of their working lives early, whereas professional workers do not reach their maximum working capacity until much later. Successful psychological reassessment in middle age can have a bearing on attitudes in old age. Realization that some ambitions will not be fulfilled and the adoption of realistic aims for the remaining time available are important in middle age and lead to a more contented old age. Many adjustments are necessary.

Some men despair of their physical decline in middle age, whereas others are proud of their relative youth. Women, too, become more aware of their husband's health and think of the possibilities of his dying. They rehearse for widowhood, and sometimes plan along these lines. For instance, they may want to move into a smaller, more convenient house and look to their own financial security. These may of course be merely sensible arrangements taken in response to changing circumstances. It is hoped that adjustments will be made to these problems before the major hurdle of retirement is reached. There is a risk at this time that disengagement may occur and newly retired people might withdraw from the mainstream of life. Ideally this should not happen and old people should maintain their interest and activity, certainly in what has become to be known as 'young old age' from 65 to 75 years. Eventually a stage is reached when an older person cannot cope with the demands of everyday living and becomes dependent on others. Some adapt to this, whereas others resent the whole concept of ageing and fear having to rely on others for help. In some cases, role reversal takes place with the individual's children adopting the parental role, while the older person takes the dependent child role. This often causes problems for the children as well as for the older individual. People living by themselves, particularly if their personality was originally introverted, gradually withdraw from social contact and become isolated.

When depression is present or physical neglect occurs, these people can become quite desolate and may cut themselves off from help. Intelligence itself does not show much decline with ageing, but the capacity to solve new problems deteriorates. Faced with the fear that they may no longer be able to solve problems, some older people may tend to become apathetic and often do not seek help even when this is readily available. Nevertheless there are many positive psychological features of ageing, especially today. The provision of an adequate pension with resultant financial security has allowed many to use this freedom to enable late development and the opportunity to fulfil ambitions previously denied by the demands of a working life.

Changing Characteristics of Illness in Old Age

Probably the first thing to say about any illness in old age is that it needs to be looked at in physical, mental and social terms. The relationship between the patient's environment and his or her mental and physical state is often crucially important. Illness may often be due to a combination of problems and management must take into account all these factors. Many pathological conditions are, of course more common in older people and there is a general increase in morbidity. Some diseases are age related; generalized arteriosclerosis and osteoporosis are two examples. Not surprisingly, multiple disability is so common as to be almost the rule. Thomas, in running a clinic for older people, found that more than 80% of this group had multiple disability[11]; numerous other surveys have supported this finding.

Many of the disabling conditions found are degenerative, but some are amenable to treatment. Many are minor, but the problem is that the presence of several of these can set up a vicious circle, resulting in a reduction in a person's functional capacity; severe disability ensues. An example of conditions interacting in this way is obesity affecting osteoarthritic knees, producing reduced mobility. The presence of anaemia may also affect adversely the course of many conditions.

Multiple symptomatology is also a common finding. This often causes problems for those taking a history from an older person. Some symptoms impair health more than others. In the author's survey of over 75-year-olds, dizziness or giddiness was a common symptom, occurring more frequently in patients in poor effective health. Forgetfulness is another distressing symptom of old age. Symptoms must be interpreted appropriately. Ferguson Anderson, for example, attaches the same significance to confusion in an older person as is given to convulsions in a baby; that is, it might be produced by a number of causes, including anything that increases the temperature[7]. Older people may have a different threshold of pain and may complain of it less frequently. They also do not seem to appreciate thirst so acutely. Temperature changes may also be unnoticed. Physical signs of illness in the aged require appropriate assessment. The changes already described that occur with natural ageing, influence, for instance, the measurement of heart size and position.

Illnesses in old age may have unusual clinical presentations. Infections often progress insidiously and may only be discovered at an advanced stage. In some infections the temperature does not necessarily rise and the white cell count remains normal. Tuberculosis sometimes presents as no more than general weakness and tiredness. Non-specific failure to thrive can be due to bacteraemia. Older patients with thyroid over- or underactivity may present with atypical symptoms.

Heart disease, too, has various presentations. Angina is relatively uncommon; myocardial infarction occurs but is difficult to diagnose clinically, as pain only occurs in about one-quarter of such patients and the attack may be asymptomatic. Confusion and restlessness are usually present in an acute heart attack and most forms of heart failure. Diabetes mellitus can also present atypically and may first be noticed as bed-wetting or incontinence. An illness in older patients can be complicated by such factors as hypothermia, sensitivity to drugs and subnutrition. Dehydration easily occurs and can cloud the picture.

Old age also brings with it some changes in attitude and behaviour. An important example is the phenomenon of non-reporting of symptoms or problems. This was first described by Williamson et al., and will be more fully commented upon in later chapters, as it is an important cause of loss of functional ability[12].

References

1. Isaacs B, Livingstone M, Neville Y. (1972) *The survival of the unfittest*. Routledge and Kegan Paul, London.

2. Comfort A. (1964) *Ageing: the biology of senescence*. Routledge and Kegan Paul, London.

3. Medawar PB. (1952) *An unsolved problem of biology*. HK Lewis, London.

4. Burch PRJ. (1974) The biological nature of ageing. In: Cape RTD, editor. *Symposia of Geriatric Medicine, 3*: 1973 Oct 20. West Midlands Institute of Geriatric Medicine and Gerontology, Birmingham, 3–14.

5. Evans JG. (1988) Ageing and disease. In: Evered D, Whelan J, editors. *Research and the ageing population*. Wiley, Chichester, 38–57.

6. Rowe JW, Kahn RL. (1987) Human ageing: usual and successful. *Science* **237**: 143–9.

7. Anderson WF. (1971) *Practical management of the elderly*. Blackwell Scientific, Oxford.

8. Herbst KG, Humphrey C. (1981) Prevalence of hearing impairment in the elderly living at home. *J R Coll Gen Pract* **31**: 155–60.

9. Williams EI. (1973) *A socio-medical study of patients over 75 years in an urban general practice* [thesis]. Manchester University, Manchester.

10. Williams EI, Bennett FM, Nixon JV, *et al.* (1972) Socio-medical study of patients over 75 in general practice. *Br Med J* ii: 445–8.

11. Thomas P. (1968) Experience of two preventative clinics for the elderly. *Br Med J* ii: 357–60.

12. Williamson J, Stokoe IH, Gray S *et al.* (1964) Old people at home: their unreported needs. *Lancet* i: 1117–20.

9
Social Vulnerability

The social status of older people within the community has already been considered in some detail in Chapter 7. It is necessary also to look at the implications of an individual's social state for his or her overall health. The word 'social' has come by usage to include a number of diverse aspects of life and this makes it difficult to use the term in a precise way when describing an older person's circumstances.

A person's social state can include *environment* (housing, household amenities, area of residence, heating, sanitation); *family structure* (living alone, with disabled spouse, three generation household); *integration* (with family, friends, the local community); *communication* (use of language, getting help in an emergency, use of the telephone, the cultural convention about with whom they communicate, what may be communicated, and what is private); ability to undertake *activities of daily living* (ADL) (pleasure pursuits, ability to work in the house, ability to self-care). The latter are concerned with functional ability. There is a convention that uses ADL to describe personal tasks and instrumental activities of daily living (IADL) to describe household tasks and social events.

Most people, including those who are older, aim to lead an independent life. To achieve this, some basic requirements and skills for day to day living are needed. These include the ability to perform personal and domestic tasks and to undertake social activities. Some external requirements are also required. These include shelter, access to food, clothes to wear, warmth, toilet facilities, cleanliness and safety. There is also the need for privacy, which older people in particular find very important, and the ability to express and receive personal warmth. Most also have a need to maintain status, either in the family or the neighbourhood, and a range of interests to be able to gain personal satisfaction and enjoyment.

Fortunately, these requirements are usually present in later life, together with the skills to undertake the basic activities, and most older people are able to live independently. When older people themselves are unable to undertake essential activities, relatives, neighbours and friends are usually able to provide the help needed. As a result, most live contentedly in the community in a state of social equilibrium, although this is sometimes only maintained with difficulty and personal cost to carers and friends. The fragility of this social equilibrium and the vulnerability of older people to its possible breakdown is the subject of this chapter.

Activities of Daily Living

Although aspects of social state such as environment, family structure, integration and communication are important in older age, ADL have a special relevance when looking at how a person functions in his or her environment. ADL can be divided into three types:

* Sociability: how the person relates to the outside world in leisure and social activities (eg visiting friends, going to the cinema)

* Domestic: how the person keeps the household going (eg cooking, cleaning, laundering, attending to household repairs, keeping the house safe)

* Personal: how the person attends to personal needs (eg bathing, cutting toe nails, dressing, toileting).

An important point to note in the domestic area is that some of the activities are influenced by conventional sex roles. For example, it is traditional for women to be associated with cooking and men with household repairs. It is important to ascertain which tasks are usually undertaken. If difficulty is being experienced in one task it is necessary to ask about others. There may be difficulties with these too and the full extent of the deterioration may not be perceived unless this is recognized.

The issue of habilitation (as distinct from rehabilitation) is important when it comes to skills. Many people avoid acquiring certain skills early in life and compensate for them later by buying them in. An example would be that of an older man who cannot do his own laundry, not because he has lost the ability but because he never needed to do this, having had either his wife or a laundry service to do it for him. As old age brings impoverishment, buying in or other alternative strategies are sometimes no longer possible. Skills then have to be acquired, almost in a remedial way, late in life.

Williams' Rings

Although it is possible to look separately at the three levels of ADL, there is a dynamic link between them. With the passage of time, function deterioration tends to occur first in sociability, then in performance of domestic tasks, and finally in personal tasks. If these three types of activity are seen as three concentric rings around the person, the outer ring represents sociability, the middle ring domestic tasks and the inner ring personal tasks[1] (Figure 9.1).

The outer ring contains the largest number of possible activities; it is not expected that an older person does all these things, but they fall into the same domain. To function adequately, an older person needs to be able to perform activities at each level; for independent living each ring needs to remain intact. Changes in abilities at each level are important. For example a person may be observed to cease attending a social club or place of worship or to stop taking holidays, but may still be able to undertake domestic and personal tasks. The

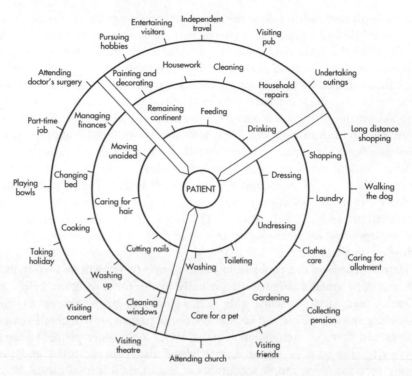

Figure 9.1: A model of social performance levels in older people. Source: Williams, 1986[1].

changes in activities in the outer ring are likely to herald the beginning of social decline.

Ageing is not only a physical and mental process but also a social process. The natural progression of social ageing is a deterioration in abilities to perform activities of daily living. In terms of the model, the process tends to take place from the outer ring inwards. It would appear from watching older people in the community that there are long periods of stability and a plateau of good functional ability can be present for a number of years. Deterioration tends to be stepwise and is often associated with some event. Rapid change in abilities of daily living usually occurs with acute illness or injury, for example acute chest infection or a broken limb. The illness may be physical or mental. In an acute situation, loss of ability at each stage is usually reversible and this is of great importance. Treatment of the illness, together with the provision of social support, facilitates this reversal. When a problem producing loss of ability to perform occurs to an otherwise able individual, treatment itself may reverse this problem, often fairly rapidly, and no social input will be necessary.

Most chronic illnesses, for instance dementia or a neurological disease, produce loss of function more gradually and this may not be noticed as easily. The decline may not be so readily reversed as in acute situations and social help and other support may be necessary to restore equilibrium.

The fact that deterioration in the ability to undertake certain tasks is often due to illness means that a change in behaviour should be regarded as a possible presenting symptom and indicates that an underlying problem is present. The change may be subtle and a high level of suspicion is necessary. The process of decline is usually from the outer ring inwards, but sometimes breakdown occurs at all levels at the same time. A good example is the development of a back problem. This can cause difficulties with stepping onto a bus, bathing and toe nail cutting. All these tasks require some back flexibility. Studies of patients in nursing homes have shown that there is a sequence of loss of personal abilities. Early to be affected are the abilities to bath and dress, but later losses include abilities to wash and toilet unaided. The capacity to feed oneself is the final ability to fail[2].

It is possible to construct a complementary series of concentric rings to describe the types of input appropriate at each level. Thus it is possible to help problems that are developing at the outer ring by seeking aid from voluntary organizations and self-help groups. The informal network of helpers and carers can be supported by arranging some respite care, or a supportive visit by a health visitor or doctor.

Help when there is a problem in the two inner rings will be mainly from social services departments (Figure 9.2), usually in the form of home help, 'Meals on Wheels', and perhaps some aids and appliances or adaptions to the home. Voluntary organizations and social services departments are able to provide day centres and services such as lunch clubs, which help older people to remain both physically and socially active. Lunch clubs also provide relief and periods of respite care for older people's households and other informal carers. Problems at the inner ring will additionally require nursing help, a sitting service, sheltered accommodation and, sometimes, nursing home or hospital admission.

The concept of effective health is considered in Chapter 12, where it is noted that those who were in good effective health had all the ability rings intact. Those

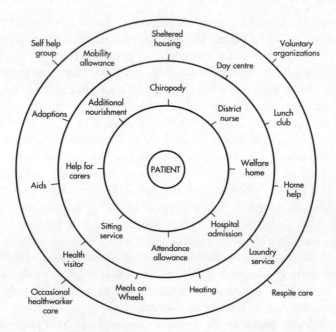

Figure 9.2: A model of services available to older people. Source: Williams, 1986[1].

in effective health group 2 had problems in the outer ring, were developing these in the middle ring also and were becoming essentially housefast. Those in effective health group 3 had problems in the inner ring and were likely to be chairfast, or bedfast. It was noted that of those aged 75 and over, about 60% were likely to be in good, 36% in medium, and 4% in bad effective health. This will, however, change with changing demography.

The importance of carers cannot be stated too often. When people have informal care, their ability to function socially in ordinary ways and at a reasonable level is critical to their carers. More will be said about carers later, but the relevance here is that most have tolerance limits. Many of the factors which precipitate breakdown are associated with a dependent's abilities at the inner ring. Carers find it difficult to tolerate incontinence or inability to move, feed and toilet independently (Table 9.1)[3]. The presence of these problems in the inner ring should alert professional carers to the risk of care breakdown.

Table 9.1: Tolerance factors.

	Frequency (% of cases)	Tolerance (% of supporters able to tolerate problem)
Sleep disturbance	62	16
Night wandering	24	24
Micturition	24	17
Shouting	10	20
Incontinence of faeces	56	43
Incontinence of urine	54	81
Falls	58	52
Inability to get out of bed unaided	52	35
Inability to get into bed unaided	50	40
Inability to get on commode unaided	36	22
Inability to get off commode unaided	38	21
Dangerous irresponsible behaviour	32	38
Inability to walk at all	16	13
Personality conflicts	26	54
Physically aggressive behaviour	18	44
Inability to dress unaided	44	77
Inability to wash and/or shave unaided	54	93
Inability to communicate	16	50
Daytime wandering	12	33
Inability to manage stairs unaided	10	60
Inabilty to feed unaided	12	67
Blindness	2	0

Source: Sanford, 1975[3].

Discussion of causes of functional decline have been limited so far to discussing the ageing process and the effects of illness and injury. There are other catalysts to the process that relate to the basic requirements for daily living. These can be gathered together under the term 'social detriment' and include psychological factors, economic circumstances, the environment, loneliness and institutionalization. Lack of privacy and opportunities to express personal warmth, or a perceived loss of status, can all interfere with the psychological balance of an older person and affect the will to self-care. Life satisfaction is reduced and motivation falters. Poor environmental conditions, such as inadequate housing, poor heating, lack of safety and defensible space, can also adversely affect the morale of an older person. Loneliness is a difficult condition to evaluate. Not all who live alone are lonely, and, conversely, even when there are people around, loneliness can still exist. Many of these factors contribute to the state of institutionalization. This can occur at home when a housefast person lacks stimulation or interest.

There is also the problem of personal administration. When some older people can no longer manage their personal finances they become socially vulnerable. Older people are among the commonest victims of burglary and aggravated assault, partly because they are perceived as unable to defend themselves but, more importantly, because they often prefer to use cash. More old people come into contact with social services departments initially for reasons directly related to personal finance than for any other reason.

The rings model is useful because it identifies the three underlying causes of functional decline: the ageing process, illness or accident, and social detriment. All three of these are interdependent and it is not always easy to distinguish the relevance and the importance of each in any particular situation. The possibility of the presence of one or more of the catalysts already mentioned also needs to be considered.

The model can also provide a check-list for each of the three levels of daily living function and take account of the dynamic relationship which exists between them. It emphasizes the importance of early recognition of functional decline and the fact that this can be restored by treatment and other support. It helps with the early identification of problems and can indicate what functional abilities should be asked about when undertaking health checks. For carers it is useful in enabling a better understanding of the levels of function and the point at which tolerance is at its limit. Finally, it underlines the fundamental objective in support for older people, that is to maintain independent living.

The model can therefore be used as the framework for thinking about the functional state of an old person: in acute situations identifying the degree of deficit, in continuing care by monitoring change, in anticipatory care by allowing early identification and forecasting possible breakdown. The limits of carer tolerance can also be judged.

Daily Life in Old Age

An interesting view of life in old age has been presented in research carried out in Berlin[4]. Baltes and her colleagues gathered data of the everyday behavioural repertoire of older people living independently. Forty-nine people with an average age of 72.7 years were recruited, 86% being women and 16% being married. The subjects were asked to complete diaries over seven consecutive days, six times within a seven-month period. Participants were asked to record on a standard form all activities in which they engaged during the day, their duration and the order in which they happened. This was from waking until going to sleep at night. Who they were with and what was the location were also recorded. There were 11 aggregated categories broadly divided into the obligatory activities (for example, ADL, medical treatment, transportation and resting), and leisure activities (which included physical activities, mental activities, media consumption, socializing, volunteer social engagements, religious activities and other leisure activities). These are detailed in Table 9.2.

Table 9.2: The everyday activity of old people: aggregated activities and original coding categories.

Aggregated categories		Original coding categories
Obligatory activities		
Activities of daily living (ADL) and Instrumental ADL	(1)	Self-care
	(2)	Eating
	(3)	Other
	(4)	Shopping
	(5)	Light housework
	(6)	Heavy housework
	(7)	Needlework
	(8)	Other
	(9)	Financial affairs
	(10)	Legal affairs
	(11)	Postal affairs
	(12)	Other
Medical treatment	(13)	Self-administered treatment
	(14)	Other administered treatment
Transportation	(15)	Use of public transportation
	(16)	Other
Resting activities (during the day)	(17)	Taking a nap
	(18)	Other
Leisure activities		
Physical activities	(19)	Taking a walk
	(20)	Gardening
	(21)	Making short trips
	(22)	Sports
Mental activities	(23)	Cultural activities
	(24)	Continuing education
	(25)	Creative activities
	(26)	Reading
	(27)	Writing
	(28)	Playing games
Media consumption	(29)	Listening to radio
	(30)	Watching TV
Socializing	(31)	Face to face conversation
	(32)	Phone conversation
	(33)	Visiting
Volunteer social engagement	(34)	Helping family members
	(35)	Helping others
Religious activities	(36)	Religious activities
Other leisure type activities	(37)	Other leisure type activities

Source: Baltes, Wahl and Schmid-Furstoss, 1990[4].

The results for the frequency of distribution of activities, companionship and location are shown in Figure 9.3. A large part of an older person's waking life is spent on things that have more to do with obligatory activities (61%) than on leisure activities (39%), and most of the time is spent at home and alone.

Baltes and her colleagues asked why older people still engage so frequently in obligatory activities, even though work, education, and family activities are no longer central features of their everyday life and social pressure, and expectations to be involved in them are reduced. They make some suggestions. Firstly, old age is a period during the life span in which the balance of starting new activities and losing old ones tends more and more towards the losses. It could be argued that losses produce a vacuum. Obligatory activities, such as household activities, may be easy ways to fill the gap. Secondly, they argue that this is an effect of the general slowing considered typical in older age, which also could affect the pace of everyday activities. Obligatory activities, although automated habits, may take more time to complete. A third reason would be that obligatory activities function as opportunities to secure social contacts, for instance shopping increases the likelihood of meeting and talking to people.

The most usual context of activities is shown to be the home, where older people most often engage in these alone. Older people appear to be restricted in what activities they can choose to do and with whom they choose to share these activities. The relationship between health and activity level and between both of these and personal control is clearly important to an understanding of the effects of illness on an older person's life and the factors which may influence the need for both health and social input. More research is required to understand these issues so that more effective provision of health and social care can be made.

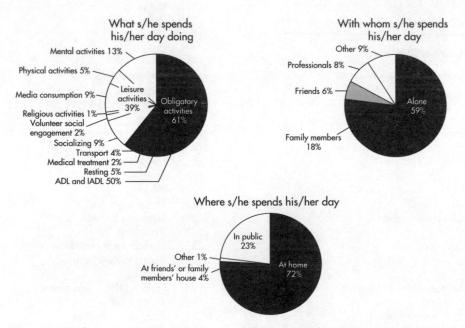

Figure 9.3: Frequency distributions in percentages of activities, companionship, and locations.
Source: Baltes, Wahl and Schmid-Furstoss, 1990[4].

Social Problems in Old Age

Problems occur quite frequently in the community which are largely 'social' in origin, but which nevertheless have some health components and both social and health workers are inevitably involved. Some present acutely as a crisis and these will be discussed later, but others arise gradually, and often their subtle nature makes it difficult for the family both to identify and solve them.

It may not be easy to perceive that older people are not keeping up with changing economic circumstances and are failing to assimilate new information. They need to keep abreast, for example, of changes in licensing fees for television, VAT rates, and interest on savings.

Economic distress occurs in old age and this may not only be due to lack of money, but also to spending more than they need. The house, for instance, may be too large and a burden to maintain. Some older people have financial commitments to relatives that are obviously unfair and cause a considerable amount of stress and worry. Alternatively, the present generation of older people comes from a thrifty generation who have always been taught to save for a 'rainy day' and old habits die hard. In extreme old age, they still feel a need to save or at least not to spend 'extravagantly', even though it seems obvious to other people that this frugality is quite unnecessary. They are reluctant to buy clothes and fuel for heating, even although they have enough money to do this. Savings may preclude help from the state and it is sometimes hard for relatives to persuade older people to spend more of their reserve money on the basic necessities of life.

Retirement may bring problems. It is hard to adjust to being constantly in the house after a lifetime at work. The retired person's spouse may find it hard to adjust to their presence. Marriages which were hitherto stable may become very strained when a couple spend all their time together. Emotional, if not actual, divorce may ensue. Quarrels may occur and result in rifts, not only between the older couple, but also within the extended family, with long lasting repercussions for their future care. It is well known that as age advances some older people become extremely unreasonable. Difficult character traits that were perhaps accepted in earlier years become exaggerated. Particular likes and dislikes can be taken to relatives and neighbours. Sometimes an older person may be in a position to make life extremely difficult for these people. The result is a lack of sympathy for the older person, who may then fail to receive the necessary help from those who seem best placed to provide it.

Minor mental deterioration may not be recognized and early behavioural changes may pass unnoticed until they become serious problems. A good example of this is a tendency to hoard. In the early stages this may amount to nothing more than an exaggeration of a natural instinct to gather supplies of food, or an older man's eccentric hobby of collecting newspapers or periodicals, but, once the house becomes a fantastic jumble of items, which to an outsider would appear irrelevant, it is clear that things have gone too far and the situation is abnormal.

Sexual problems sometimes arise and an older man may become very demanding to his now unsympathetic wife. His attention is perhaps turned on other women in the immediate circle and, although this is often regarded as playfulness and treated as a joke, it can be embarrassing and unwelcome. Although the family tends to cover up the real nature of the problem in these circumstances, a reassuring and positive response by health and social workers to a call for help is very necessary.

The phenomenon of the captive spouse is also seen. As time goes on, one member of the marital pair is likely to become ill and in need of care. This involves the other partner in a considerable additional burden. Not only are there the normal household duties, but also extra commitments of caring physically for a sick partner. This creates the situation where the well partner has to withdraw from all previous outside activities and care becomes a full-time occupation. There are times in late older age when a man or woman may be working harder than at any other time in earlier life; although the situation may appear to an outsider to be very well managed it is happening at great cost. Social as well as physical help is often desperately needed. Particularly tragic is the plight of older parents with a physically or mentally handicapped son or daughter living with them. The offspring is often ageing as well and needing more and not less help.

These are examples of social problems that are often part of a gradual decline. The process is slow. It may take years before it is realized how far standards have fallen. As with illness, many such problems are unreported and often multiple. Some are quite intractable and these have to be accepted. Trigger events of a relatively minor nature sometimes plunge the situation into crisis, and it is necessary to watch for these. Tension between an older person and a carer can mean withdrawal of care. In the three-generation household, where overcrowding exists and there is no privacy for children, problems can develop at school. If this occurs, resentment can arise across the generations, which may lead to reduced care for the older people.

Environmental problems are usually associated with housing. Property may physically deteriorate leading for example, to a leaking roof. Living in inner cities may bring its own problems. If there are derelict buildings nearby vermin may be attracted to uninhabited houses, particularly if these are dirty and poorly maintained. Deprived areas are happy hunting grounds for vandals and older people living in inner cities can be harassed and disturbed. Eviction may be a possibility when financial resources are low; threats to deprive someone of shelter can be extremely distressing. The misplaced pride of the older people, when faced with demands on slender means can reach the point of confabulation. Recent problems in relation to arrears of community charges are a case in point. It is possible that some older people do not fully understand the progression from rates to community charge to council tax. Older persons living with relatives may sometimes find themselves homeless when the family has to move to a smaller house with no spare room.

Acute Social Crises

Acute social crises occur when for some reason there is a breakdown in the provision of basic care. The precise nature of the breakdown depends on specific circumstances, for example, whether the person was previously able to self-care or needed some specific help. Whether the person lives alone or with relatives and carers is also an important factor.

Each of the gradually developing social problems described above can result in acute care breakdown. Isaacs and Neville, writing in 1972[5], identified three categories of vulnerable older people. The first is the *protected*, in which the older person who is unable to care for him/herself is in an institution and therefore protected from social problems. The second is the *defended*, in which the older person is cared for by a relative or carer and is therefore in a state of social equilibrium, and defended from the problems associated with care. The third is the *defeated* category; this is where an older person in a deteriorating social situation fails to receive any sort or care, or where relatives are suffering an intolerable strain in providing it. The concept is helpful, for, if defended situations are identified, then steps can be taken to ensure that the defence is maintained. In a defeated situation urgent steps need to be taken to restore equilibrium and this often means admission to sheltered accommodation. It is with defeated situations that health and social workers are often confronted. They are most commonly of two types - although there can be a mixture of both. These are client/patient related or carer/helper related.

Client/Patient Related

With client or patient related problems it is usually illness or injury which precipitates the crisis, but where the person is dependent upon a carer, the dependent's behaviour pattern and the effect that it has on the carer can also precipitate the breakdown.

As mentioned earlier in this chapter Sanford[3], looking at reasons for patients being admitted to hospital, found that 12% of all geriatric admissions were due to friends and carers being unable to cope any further. It was found that carers have tolerance limits, some situations being better tolerated than others. By far the largest group were associated with dependents' behavioural problems (80% of the total). The analysis is given in Table 9.1. Sleep disturbance and faecal incontinence were poorly tolerated, as might be expected, but, surprisingly, urinary incontinence and inability to wash and dress were coped with reasonably well.

Carer/Helper Related

An acute social emergency can also arise when help ceases because of supporters' own limitations. This may be due to illness, either physical or mental in the helper, or when there are other commitments, such as nursing a sick child or dealing with other family matters. Sometimes the helper has to move away from the area due to a change in occupation or in the spouse's occupation. Help may then stop altogether for the older person living alone. Even when a grandmother is living with a younger family, the arrival of a new baby may make it impossible, perhaps because of the shortage of space, for this to continue. The age of the helper may be important. Sometimes the supplier of basic care is also older and is unable to continue carrying the burden. In all situations, sometimes enough is enough, and, particularly where a patient has mental illness, the carers can come to the end of their tether and withdraw or demand immediate help.

Instances are found where the basic care provided is insufficient despite a family presence in the area. Isaacs and his co-authors in their book *Survival of the unfittest*[6] examine 39 examples of this type in some detail. The reasons why the social conditions of older people were allowed to deteriorate, despite the presence of available family, were divided into four groups: preoccupation, dilemma, refusal and rejection.

Preoccupation

This was considered to be the reason why 17 of the 39 patients with children in the area failed to receive adequate care and is a circumstance that will be well understood by anyone having to deal with older people. The relatives provided as much care as they could and were anxious to give more, but were prevented from doing so by prior commitments from which they were quite unable to free themselves, or by an impediment that they could not overcome. These causes included the health of the helper or care of another dependant.

Dilemma

This is where significant basic care is withheld because relatives, although capable and willing to give more help than they did, were forced to accept a different course in the interest of their own families. The dilemma of a son and daughter in these circumstances is whether to give prior consideration to the needs of the parent or to those of their own family. Often an attempt is made to do both, but even so, the parent still receives insufficient care. These situations are often full of anguish and feelings of guilt on the part of the offspring, and recrimination on the part of the older person. They are a rich source of family dispute and friction.

Refusal

This is where adequate care is absent because the older person is unwilling to receive it. In the series quoted by Isaacs *et al.*, they were almost all men and they were usually of an aggressive independent type, attracting very little love towards themselves and tending not to give any in return. These patients would not accept that they needed help and did not like to put themselves in the situation of being obliged to anyone else. They were often in dreadful social circumstances and, even when discovered by social workers, were extremely difficult to help.

Rejection

This is where the patient seems to have been rejected by his or her children. This rejection was frequently difficult to understand on first impression, but, after further enquiry, reasons were often found. Sometimes there was a family quarrel that went back for years and the rejection might initially have been on the parental side. Examples included a daughter thought not to have made a suitable marriage and a son who in the past had gone against parental wishes. Maybe the parents were ashamed of some event in the lives of their children, as in the case of one son who had been to prison. Alcoholism in the parent or long-standing quarrels about money might drive children away. Second marriages sometimes caused problems. Initially, this might have seemed a good idea, but once one partner had become ill, the other one might feel aggrieved at having responsibilities of care after so short a time. Children may have disapproved of the second marriage and subsequently may have proved unwilling to share in the care of a stepmother or stepfather. First marriages can also run into this sort of difficulty. Daughters may have problems; a daughter may have quarrelled with her mother to such a degree that she finds it impossible to meet her parents as a couple, despite the fact that she loves her father and would help him. Perhaps, when a daughter has been sexually abused by her father she may find it impossible to meet him in his old age when she is herself middle-aged, despite a desire to support her mother. This desire may be quite profound. Many abused girls think of themselves as sharing their mother's 'burdens', a carefully chosen word.

Older people do not like to be in another person's debt, even if these people are their own children. The presence of grandchildren is often good in overcoming these difficulties because of opportunities to reciprocate. If these are absent it might mean that the older couple become reluctant to ask for help and so a situation of neglect arises.

Co-operation Problems

Crisis situations may occur when there is a failure of communication between the caring services. This may happen particularly when a hospital fails to inform the community social, medical and nursing services of an older person's discharge from hospital. These difficulties may soon become less frequent in the light of new arrangements for discharge and the duty on social services departments to assess generically, which are contained in the National Health Service and Community Care Act (1990). Liaison between hospital doctors, general practitioners and other health and social workers should be strengthened. Lack of co-ordination between the domiciliary workers themselves may be a source of trouble. Clear demarcation of the role of a doctor and a social worker in a particular situation is sometimes not obvious and can only be overcome by person to person discussion about individual cases.

Compulsory Admission

There are circumstances where severe social breakdown has occurred and where for reasons of safety an older person needs to be moved to a place of care, even against their will. Powers exist under the National Assistance Act 1948 for the local authority to arrange compulsory removal to a hospital or other institution of a person who is unwilling to go voluntarily. Examples of the type of situation where this could happen is where a person is suffering from a chronic disease or is physically and mentally incapacitated and living in insanitary conditions and unable to care for him or herself. Another circumstance would be where the person does not receive proper care and attention from others. The procedure is that a 'proper officer' (usually a public health doctor) and another registered medical practitioner (usually the patient's general practitioner) must certify that such removal is in the interests of the patient, or that it would prevent injury to the health of, or serious nuisance to, other people. It is necessary at that point to make application to a magistrate's court and for the patient to be given seven days' notice.

In 1951 an incident exposed a weakness in the procedure and highlighted the need for more immediate intervention. An older person fell, refused to go into hospital, and rejected other help. Her pressure sores became infected and she subsequently died from tetanus. The local member of parliament was appalled by the affair and introduced a Private Member's Bill, which became the National Assistance (Amendment) Act 1951 and introduced an emergency procedure permitting the two doctors mentioned above to make an application to a magistrate for the patient to be removed to a place of care for a period of three weeks[7].

References

1. Williams EI. (1986) A model to describe social performance levels in elderly people. *J R Coll Gen Pract* **36**: 422–3.

2. Williams EI, Savage SA, McDonald PS, *et al.* (1992) Residents of private nursing homes and their care. *Br J Gen Pract* **42**: 477–81.

3. Sanford JRA. (1975) Tolerance of debility in elderly dependants by supporters at home: its significance for hospital practice. *Br Med J* **3**: 471–3.

4. Baltes MM, Wahl H-W, Schmid-Furstoss U. (1990) The daily life of elderly Germans: activity patterns, personal control and functional health. *J Gerontol* **45**: 173–9.

5. Isaacs B, Neville Y. (1972) *The measurement of need in old people*. Scottish Home and Health Department, Edinburgh.

6. Isaacs B, Livingstone M, Neville Y. (1972) *Survival of the unfittest*. Routledge and Kegan Paul, London.

7. Donaldson RJ, Donaldson LJ. (1993) *Essential public health medicine*. Kluwer, Dordrecht.

10
Health Care Resources in the Community

Introduction

Earlier editions (1979, 1989) of this book began the chapter on health care provision in the community by describing a 'real life' situation that was considered to be typical when providing such care for older people. The purpose was to highlight some of the difficulties experienced by health care workers and to open a discussion about how these might be helped and perhaps even resolved.

The story concerned a doctor who was called to see an older man late on a Friday afternoon. On his arrival, the patient, who was in his late seventies, was found to be suffering from bronchitis and had been ill for several weeks. He lived alone in poor social circumstances. The doctor was received aggressively by relatives who had just called to see the patient; they were disturbed by the situation, but, because of other commitments, felt unable to give adequate care. Despite the fact that nobody had bothered to do anything about the patient's plight they demanded that something be done, which in effect meant hospital admission. The problem was compounded by the fact that neither the doctor nor anyone else in the primary health team had previous knowledge of the situation. The doctor's task was difficult: the bronchitis could have been treated at home if there had been someone to look after the patient; ideally social help or a nursing home place would have been available, but a community care assessment would have taken time to arrange.

When contacted, the hospital was difficult; no beds were available and the weekend lay ahead. The relatives were still reluctant to stay. Eventually the hospital did admit the patient, but not without a great deal of persuasion and fairly universal frustration.

Anyone who has worked in the community for some time will recognize the situation and confirm that it contains no exaggerations. When quoted in 1989 the position was easier because of more readily available geriatric beds in most parts of the country, due to the growth of long stay accommodation provided by private residential and nursing homes, but the story illustrates the type of problem encountered during the past two decades in providing community care for old people. Many GPs had little interest in older people and most lacked specific geriatric training. Resettlement of patients discharged from hospital was poor and this deficiency was reinforced by inadequate communication between doctors, nurses and social workers working in the community. Hospital geriatric services were inundated with calls for help without really having the resources to meet them. The tripartite management of the community services by district health, family health and local government authorities made sensible planning difficult. Society's attitudes had changed over the years, particularly towards care for older people, and families were expecting higher standards of professional care; this led to demands on both health and social workers that were sometimes impossible to satisfy.

Change was therefore necessary, and since 1989 there has been a major reorganization of the National Health Service, and, since 1993, also in the way personal social services have been provided in the community. Improvement, from the point of view of caring for older people, will have to be measured against the background of the illustrative case described and some of the issues raised.

Triangle of Care

A basic feature of care in the community remains. That is, when a person needs care there are three possible places where this can be given. These are in the patient's home, supervised accommodation, or hospital. Supervised accommodation can be in local authority or privately owned residential or nursing homes, or in sheltered housing. The most appropriate place for the patient depends on the balance between the medical, nursing, and social need. It is important that these three places of care should be used appropriately; they form a triangle with, ideally, free flow of patients from one to the other (*see* Figure 10.1). Thus a patient may be admitted to hospital for acute care, but may return to the community and his/her home via the halfway stage of residential or nursing home if social and nursing problems need resolving. Alternatively, patients may be discharged directly to their own homes, with community social and nursing care arranged. Several possibilities therefore exist. The hospital at home concept, where intensive nursing and social help is provided in the patient's home for a limited period, has to prove to be an important contribution to effective community care.

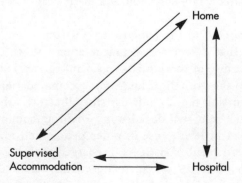

Figure 10.1: Triangle of care.

Overall Aim of Community Health Care for Older People

The provision of comprehensive care for older people in the community involves all aspects of good primary care and inevitably means health and social services working in close harmony. Not only does this concern the saving of lives and the reduction of suffering, but also improvement in the quality of life. This means an integrated and comprehensive service, which includes acute and continuing care, as well as preventive care. These are clearly linked; for example, a very important aspect of preventive care is good acute care.

The principal aim is to keep an older person in as good effective health as possible in the environment of their choice. To do this requires a wide range of services. The following list of objectives for good health and social care gives an idea of the scope of the services that should be available to older people.

1. To establish, when illness occurs, an accurate diagnosis on which logical treatment and accurate prognosis can be based: This implies good day to day care of older people and effective management of acute illness. Similarly, when social crises occur, effective assessment and response are needed. Often there are health *and* social components in an acute episode.

2. To identify the social and environmental needs of older people and refer appropriately to social and environmental services.

3. To improve, and if this is not possible, to maintain an older person's functional performance: cure may not always be possible, but an attempt should always be made to maximize effective health.

4. To provide effective continuing care for those with long term medical problems and chronic illness: this would include maintenance therapy, surveillance and rehabilitation.

5. To provide adequate resettlement for patients who are discharged from hospital back into the community: proper reception of patients is crucial to their continuing care.

6. To provide adequate care for dying patients, especially when they wish to die at home.

7. To give support and relief to informal carers who are looking after older people.

8. To be prepared to be an older person's advocate in situations of difficulty.

9. To enable older people to be outward looking and to accept responsibility for caring for themselves: in this sense the provision of care itself is not the prime aim of the community worker; it is rather, by education and encouragement, to facilitate self-care amongst older people.

10. To recognize 'at risk' situations: examples of these are patients living alone, the housefast, the over 75-year-olds, the bereaved, and those recently discharged from hospital. Special care is needed for these people.

11. To provide information and education for older people in a neighbourhood.

12. To foster a team approach to the provision of care: this should involve both health and social workers, who should form a community care team. It is no longer acceptable that a doctor should be involved solely in the medical aspects of old age, and a social worker only in the social care. Health and social problems are inevitably linked and both need attention if the overall situation is to be improved. This has long been a principle of care in the hospital where doctors, nurses and medical social workers worked in close co-operation. In the community such co-operation is no less essential.

13. To establish good relationships between the community care team for older patients and those providing care in hospitals or other institutions.

14. To provide a responsive service, both in social support and health care, with sufficient flexibility to provide high intensity care, where necessary, as in the 'hospital at home' schemes.

15. To assess the needs of the older people in the local community, so that effective services can be provided.

16. To provide adequate education and training for health and social workers in matters relating to good primary care of older people.

17. To carry out medical audit on care programmes for older people and be aware of quality control requirements.

The first two objectives are concerned with effective acute care, objectives 3–8 with continuing care and objectives 9–12 with health promotion and education. The final five deal with organizational matters. Some of these are being fulfilled very effectively. Acute care is of a high standard in most developed countries. However, good preventive care, teamwork and continuity of care have developed significantly in the last five years.

Resources in the Community

There is a wide range of health resources, both formal and informal, available to older people in the community. These are now frequently delivered by a team that consists of general practitioners, nurses, health visitors, practice staff members, therapists of various kinds, counsellors and many others. Voluntary services make very important contributions and, most significantly, carers provide a huge amount of essential day to day support without which it would be impossible for formal services to manage. Secondary care services are also important to the community. Apart from the need for inpatient hospital help, specialist services also outreach into the community in many important ways.

New Administrative Arrangements

In 1989, the Government introduced a White Paper *Working for patients*, which set out plans to reform and strengthen the National Health Service. The basic principles of the service were to remain intact; it would be open to all regardless of income and would be financed mainly out of taxation. Nevertheless, major changes were heralded. These concerned both hospital and general practitioner services. There were several key measures: more delegation of responsibilities to local level, self governing hospitals, new funding arrangements so that money for treating patients could cross administrative boundaries, additional consultants, GP practice budgets, reformed management bodies, and better audit arrangements. These proposals were incorporated into the National Health Service and Community Care Act 1990 and came into effect in April 1991.

Basic Changes Resulting from the 1990 Reforms

Administration

A significant change has been the introduction of a new management structure into the National Health Service. Responsibility for strategy now lies with the NHS Policy Board chaired by the Secretary of State, with operational responsibility in the hands of the NHS Executive chaired by a chief executive. The framework of Regional Health Authorities and District Health Authorities has remained, although with a reorganized membership and management structure.

However, new authorities, the Family Health Services Authorities (FHSAs), were created to replace the Family Practitioner Committees. These had been directly responsible to the Department of Health, but, under the new arrangements, they are responsible to the Regional Health Authorities. FHSAs have more managerial functions than Family Practitioner Committees, but fewer members. The chairman is appointed by the Secretary of State. The Regional Health Authority appoints five lay members and the four professional members (a doctor in general practice, a dentist, a community pharmacist, and a nurse with experience in community care) in a personal, not a representative, capacity. These members, together with the chief executive, (who is appointed by the chairman) and the lay members, make up the FHSA. The changes were intended to bring responsibility for primary health care and hospital services together at a strategic level. Local planning and integration could, it was thought, be better achieved, especially when comprehensive initiatives spanning both services were being contemplated.

NHS Function and Manpower Review

As the internal market of the National Health Service developed it became clear that the roles and functions of Regional Health Authorities, District Health Authorities and FHSAs needed review and realignment.

While Regional Health Authorities have been required to focus on monitoring the development of 'purchasing', their role had been mirrored by 'outposts' of the NHS Executive in monitoring the performance of the new trusts. This separation of monitoring functions had been seen to be essential in the early days to ensure that trusts were able to demonstrate their freedom of action from historical management lines. However, as time progressed it became clear that two such monitoring bodies were unnecessary. Ministers therefore proposed that legislation be enacted to:

- reduce the overall number of regions from 14 to 8

- merge the functions of the Regional Health Authorities and the outposts

- model the new organizations on the role of the outposts, thus making the statutory role of the Regional Health Authority redundant.

Also, within the first three years, most District Health Authorities had lost management responsibility for their hospital and community units as these units became trusts. This concentrated their function on purchasing, but, at the same time, the explosion in the number of GP fundholders and the latter's accountability to FHSAs called into question the separation of these two local health authorities. Although fundamentally different in style and process from the purchasing carried out by District Health Authorities, nonetheless the strengthening of FHSA purchasing powers over their contractors further diminished the case for separate purchasing authorities for primary and secondary care. Hence the review also recommended the merger of District Health Authorities and FHSAs.

Legislation for changes to statutory authorities is not planned until 1996 but management change in line with this philosophy has been pushed forward in the interim.

The Hospital Service

Underlying the changes in the hospital services was the belief that there was scope for delegating decision-making from District Health Authorities to hospital and other similar management units. Financial accountability was also involved in this initiative and has resulted in the introduction of a purchaser/provider split. An important objective was to create an organization in which those who are actually providing the services would also be responsible for day to day operational decisions. The important division of responsibility was that District Health Authorities would concentrate on: assessing what were the health needs of the local population; ensuring that there were effective services for the prevention and control of diseases and the promotion of health; ensuring that the population had access to a comprehensive range of high quality services; and the setting of targets for improvement in health and monitoring of performance against those targets. The District Health Authorities were seen as the purchaser and the hospital and community health services were seen as the providers. Although it was possible to put into effect these principles under the existing system, where District Health Authorities had direct management responsibilities for hospital units, the introduction of self governing units or trusts has allowed it to become more complete. Permission needs to be obtained from the Secretary of State for a hospital to become a trust, but once achieved it can run its own affairs whilst remaining in the National Health Service. By April 1994 the vast majority of hospitals, community units and ambulance services had become trusts. They have, in effect, become self-determining organizations and it will be interesting to see the long term effect upon patient care and services.

General Practice

The 1990 Act brought in a new contract for general practice and a year later the introduction of fundholding practices. Both of these have produced significant changes. Some changes had already been heralded in the White Paper *Promoting health* (1987) and these were built on in the subsequent White Paper *Working for patients* (1989). Many changes were introduced with the new contract and a description is inevitably complex. They concern, however, remuneration, introduction of new services, more intensive practice management, and changes in continuing medical education.

We shall look at remuneration and general changes first. The government was of the view that GPs would have stronger incentive to satisfy their patients' needs if a greater proportion of their income was attributable to the number of patients on their lists. Hitherto, capitation fees had formed an overage of 46% of a GP's income, and this was changed to at least 60%, with a corresponding reduction in the basic practice allowance paid to each doctor as a fixed sum, which was designed to cover expenses. There was concern about the possibility that this change would result in a return to large list sizes and a 'fight' to recruit additional patients. It has long been accepted that a smaller list size resulted in a higher standard of care. The effect of this change has yet to be evaluated and its consequences in the care of older people will be discussed later, but there has been no evidence to date of a marked shift in patient registration.

To achieve a full basic practice allowance a doctor is required to be available for patient contact for 26 hours per week; these should be equally spread through the week. Doctors providing less than the full contact time qualify for reduced allowances. It is generally accepted that 10 or more hours of the required availability will be spent on house visits. The idea behind these changes was that patients would have better access to the GP because of increased availability. Items of service payments were, however, retained, but they often depended upon achievement of targets, and again these will be described later. A special increased capitation was introduced for patients aged 75 years and over (as distinct from patients aged 65 years and over previously) to recognize the increased work-load associated with this group and also as a payment for the newly introduced health checks.

Special fee arrangements were also introduced for patients in deprived areas. A deprivation allowance is now available for doctors with patients living in electoral wards that demonstrate deprivation. This is calculated according to the Jarman index, which takes into account a number of factors such as single parent families and social class structure. This new fee reflects additional work-load.

A compulsory age of retirement of 70 years was introduced for GPs.

A more business-like approach became necessary as a result of the new contract. All practices must produce leaflets which give details of the doctors, their staff, clinics, services offered and so on. Practices must also review their leaflets each year. Most FHSAs ask practices to provide a business plan to document their plans for the development of the services and to itemize needs in order to determine future financial requirements. A practice report has to be published each year, giving details of basic services provided and practice activity. Many practices now employ a practice manager to deal with these matters and to assist in the organization of larger practice teams, providing a more diverse range of services. Special funds have been made available to practices to develop their information technology and computer capacity. Efforts have been made to provide practices with information about, for example, hospital waiting times. Patients can now change doctors more easily, so they have more choice.

The cost of drugs prescribed by GPs had been increasing over the previous decade, so that by 1989 the drug bill was the largest single element in the Family Practitioner Service budget: more than one-third of total expenditure. To promote more cost effective prescribing a new information system was introduced known as PACT (Prescribing Analysis and Costs), which provides good quality data on a regular basis and which enables doctors to compare their own prescribing habits with others locally and nationally. Under the 1990 Act doctors are also given indicative budgets for their prescribing costs. This gives GPs an indication of the budget that they should aim at and the outcome is monitored by the FHSA's medical and pharmaceutical advisers. Information about practice patient profiles and levels of morbidity are needed to indicate fairly what should be appropriate budgets and the result is that these are gradually being made more relevant to local situations.

A major objective of the new arrangements was to improve practice premises and services, especially in deprived areas. Increased financial support to doctors to improve their premises was introduced, for example, through increased improvement grants. 'Cost rent schemes', which gave financial support to doctors investing in premises or improvements were made more flexible and are now able to respond to local needs.

The commitment to developing primary care health teams through providing financial help to doctors employing ancillary staff was continued and extended. The type of staff and the overall maximum number who could be employed were no longer restricted, and the reimbursement scheme was extended. Applications for extra staff can now be made to the FHSA. This is normally included in the annual business plans made by GPs, which indicate proposed practice developments and the need for additional staff. The result has been a wider range of skills available to practices.

There is also in the new arrangements a requirement to look at ways of improving and monitoring quality in general practice. To this end a system of medical audit has been introduced. Each FHSA area has a Medical Audit Advisory Group (MAAG), which is an independent body with an elected chairman accountable to the FHSA. The principle is that audit should be peer led and based on audits done in the practice by GPs and other members of the practice team. The procedure is concerned with quality, but also has an important education function. The results of audit are confidential to the GPs and the MAAG. Many audits are, however, published and important improvements in care have resulted. The auditing of care for older people is detailed in Chapter 24.

New Services

Several new services have been introduced into general practice as a result of the new contract. Many of these are relevant to older people, but some of course are not. Important new health promotion services have been introduced. Health checks at the point of registration have proved successful. The three-year health check for all patients who have not seen the doctor in that time proved unpopular amongst GPs, and patients did not often take up the offer. Practices no longer have to offer this service. They do, however, have to provide such a check when requested. The introduction of target payments was initially seen as very threatening, but has been very successful, and for such services as cervical cytology and immunization has meant high uptake. Special health promotion clinics were introduced but have been superseded by health promotion payments. These are banded according to the content of three levels of health promotion activity or programme. The payment for GPs is complicated, but reflects the amount of work entailed and the relevance of the exercise. The health check for those aged 75 and over has been an important introduction. A description of this will be given in later chapters.

Other Services

The 1990 reforms also affected other services. Apart from GPs, the FHSA also has contracts with dentists, pharmacists and opticians.

Dental Services

Under the 1990 contract for NHS dental services, all patients, even those with only dentures, were encouraged to register with a general dental practitioner under a 'continuing care' contract. The contract included, amongst other things, free replacement of certain fillings and crowns, emergency help when the dentist's surgery was closed, and free denture repairs. Many dentists also provide home visits for people who are housebound and there is no extra charge for this under the NHS.

The importance of regular oral check-ups cannot be stressed too greatly. The overall burden and prognosis of oral cancer is similar to malignant melanoma and cervical cancer, both of which have greater public and professional awareness and are screened for as a matter of course. Many would like to see a reminder to register with, and attend, a dentist as a formal part of the routine annual assessment of older patients under the GP contract.

Gum disease is often painless; many people are not even aware that they have it. Some common signs are: gums which bleed when brushed, teeth which are loose, receding gums and bad breath, but not everyone will have all these signs.

Older people can get tooth decay because plaque also contains bacteria which can cause caries when combined with sugary foods and drinks. The necks of teeth exposed by gum disease are particularly prone to decay as they are not protected by enamel.

Older people are not automatically exempt from NHS dental charges, but those on Income Support may be entitled to full or partial exemption.

The success of the new 1990 contract in encouraging patients to register with a dentist, considerably distorted dentists' fees and income. This led to disputes between the government and the profession and the government commissioned a fundamental review of NHS dental services. The resulting 'Bloomfield' report has been published but the government has not yet responded.

Optical Services

Since April 1989, most adults are required to pay 'privately' for an eye examination, although the following groups of people are still able to obtain an NHS sight test, free of charge:

- diabetics
- glaucoma sufferers and their relatives over the age of 40
- registered blind or partially sighted
- those on income support.

While older people may not be automatically entitled to free NHS eye tests, it is still very important to have a regular check-up by an optometrist (optician) or ophthalmic medical practitioner, at least every two years.

As we grow older our eyes become more vulnerable to diseases and other disorders; hence the importance of regular check-ups. If housebound, the patient may be able to have a home visit, and if they would otherwise be entitled to an NHS sight test then the home visit will be free of charge too.

Most people must now pay for the full cost of their glasses, although most optometrists do have a low cost range, so cost should not be a barrier. Some people are able to get some help toward the cost of their glasses through an NHS voucher issued at the time of the sight test. Vouchers will vary in value according to individual circumstances, including the complexity of the lenses needed.

The normal healthy eye will need three times as much light at age 60 than at age 20. A good level of lighting is important, particularly for reading or close work, when direct illumination from an adjustable light shone from behind onto the book or work will prove helpful. Older people should also avoid areas of contrasting darkness. Good lighting at the top and bottom of stairs is vitally important.

People wishing to continue driving after the age of 70 years must renew their driving licence and make a declaration about their health. All drivers are required by law to notify the DVLA of the onset or worsening of a medical condition which might affect their ability to drive safely; this includes eyesight problems.

Pharmaceutical Services

Much confusion and concern has been engendered over the introduction of prescribing budgets for GPs in 1991. Considerable fear exists amongst many older people that they will no longer be entitled to their medication or that they will be labelled as 'expensive' patients and be thrown off their GP's list. There is no evidence of this happening but such misconceptions are extremely stressful for older people and must be refuted.

Certainly the NHS drugs bill was escalating almost 'out of control' and it still continues to rise well ahead of the rate of inflation. However, it is also true that GP prescribing costs varied dramatically and, in some cases, quite irrationally. The concept of introducing comparative budgets as a guide to GPs was intended to improve the rationality of prescribing as well as its cost effectiveness. The result has been that, while unjustified high cost prescribing has reduced, we have seen poorer prescribers actually increase their costs and make more rational use of new drugs as they have come onto the market.

No patient should ever be left with the impression that their age or infirmity will prejudice their access to NHS medical or pharmaceutical services. Older patients, men over 65 and women over 60 years of age, are entitled to exemption from prescription charges.

However, if there is a concern about the quality of medication supplied to patients it is when those drugs and appliances are supplied unnecessarily. Some patients, particularly those who are older, do tend to hoard supplies of drugs, which can then never be re-used; the consequent waste is colossal. The GP may not exercise adequate controls on repeat prescribing or patients may fail to inform their GP that they still have adequate supplies; both are issues that need to be addressed. Most pharmacists now keep patient medication records (PMRs) for patients on long-term medication who are of pensionable age (ie are exempt from charges), and others whom the pharmacist considers may have difficulty in understanding the nature and dosage of the drug supplied and the times at which it should be taken.

New contractual arrangements are being prepared for implementation in 1995, which will recognize efforts made by pharmacists to supply more information and advice to patients, to undertake health promotion activities and to tailor their services to reflect more effectively the needs of their patients.

Community NHS Trusts

Among the first wave of NHS trusts (April 1991) provider units responsible solely for community health services were underrepresented. However, subsequently it has been the policy of the National Health Service Executive to encourage providers of community and priority care services to apply for trust status independently of hospital units. This policy has been mainly a reflection of the increasing understanding that the implementation of *Care in the community* and the shift from secondary to primary care demand a strong infrastructure of community health service to work closely with GPs and with social services and voluntary agencies.

Most community health service trusts are responsible for providing a wide range of community based services, including those for mental health and learning disabilities and, usually, a range of day care domiciliary services for older people. The latter will include general community nursing and rehabilitation services. Where the size of population served is high, such as in large conurbations or shire counties, then several trusts may be involved in the provision of these services.

Management responsibility of the trusts is undertaken by a board comprising an appointed chairman and four non-executive directors. For trusts in university teaching areas, one extra non-executive member is appointed from the university. The board also has a chief executive and up to four executive directors. The latter must include financial, medical or dental and nursing representatives. The trusts are accountable to the Secretary of State through outposts of the National Health Service Management Executive. The business plans of the trust receive approval and are monitored by these management outposts.

The viability of an NHS trust depends upon it gaining contracts and income from these for the delivery of health services.

Contracts for Community Services

Historically, the quality of information on activity, costs and outcome of community health services has been limited. Most trusts therefore continue to agree block contracts with some broad indicative work-load figures for most of the services they manage. The major purchasers of community NHS trust services are the District Health Authorities. Increasingly, where there are now significant numbers of GP fundholders, the trusts are dependent for their income on contracts with these GPs. For purchase of community nursing services, GP fundholders are still required to agree contracts with community trusts or the few directly managed community units. They cannot purchase from the private sector or employ staff directly. Increasingly, District Health Authorities and FHSAs are jointly commissioning community services, recognizing the need to ensure co-ordinated provision and the most effective use of the total financial resources available.

Part Played by the FHSAs

The new FHSAs are very different from their predecessors, the Family Practitioner Committee. In mission statements they see their role as not only ensuring the appropriate provision of high quality primary health care, but also promoting health. This represents a much more proactive approach.

The new approach includes: providing advice, guidelines and information; being concerned about quality through identification of what constitutes good care and setting standards and monitoring performance; and developing services by identifying need and being willing to experiment and innovate. Resources are being increasingly managed with the result that a closer working relationship is being created gradually with health and social workers. Training and education is being provided and encouraged, in order to facilitate this change and help in development.

FHSAs have increased administrative budgets which reflect their increased management function. The essential core functions are retained, for example: patient registration, processing medical records, payments to practices, handling of complaints, office management, recruitment and training of staff, financial accounting, and management. Added to this is a range of new activities mainly concerned with service development, finance and information handling.

These changes have led to new management arrangements with the FHSA and a corresponding increase in staff numbers. Under a general manager or chief executive are divisions or directorates, such as training and personnel, finance and information, medical, nursing, planning and service development.

Changes are still occurring. As mentioned earlier, with the reduction in the responsibilities of District Health Authorities for the management of units, moves are being made to integrate their work with that of the FHSAs. The Secretary of State's functions and manpower review of the NHS management structure has led to proposals for legislation to allow mergers of District Health Authorities and FHSAs from 1 April 1996. However, it is likely that mergers will have taken place in practice before then.

Fundholding

The introduction of fundholding general practices was a major feature of the 1990 National Health Service and Community Care Act. The rationale concerned more appropriate use of funds, increased choice and improved quality. Before 1990, referral of patients to hospitals outside the district led to financial problems for these hospitals, and it was thought that allowing the money to 'follow the patient', would alleviate these difficulties. It was also felt that, if GPs controlled their own budgets, more choice would be available and hospitals would have the incentive to improve quality in order to attract custom.

At the start of the scheme, practices with lists of at least 9000 patients were invited to apply for their own budgets for a defined range of hospital services.

They could buy these services from either NHS or private sector hospitals. The services within these schemes included:

- outpatient services
- a defined group of inpatient and day care treatments (eg hip replacement and cataract removal)
- diagnostic tests (eg radiography and pathology).

Also included in the budgets were the cost of practice staff and prescribing costs. Since then, the list size has been reduced to 7000 patients and in some instances practices have come together for budget holding purposes. The result is that by April 1994 probably nearly 50% of the nation's population is served by a fundholding practice. Non-fundholding practices have their clinical budgets handled collectively by the District Health Authorities. Practices are, however, increasingly being involved in setting up wider groups or collectives to negotiate on behalf of non-fundholders. There has been concern that a two-tier system may evolve with different standards of care and treatment options. Eventually the system should even out, so that all patients have the same opportunities for effective hospital care. However, it must also be recognized that the NHS has always had many levels of service and access, dependent on where patients live. Recent announcements mean that fundholding will be extended to smaller practices, and the options available extended.

Effect of the Reforms on Older People

The new family practitioner services have been described above in some detail, as they affect most people. With the new emphasis of capitation fees in GP remuneration, there was concern that older people might not be popular additions to a list, because of the additional work-load generated, and therefore might find themselves without a doctor. The higher level of prescribing older people usually need might also have been a disincentive for doctors holding tight drug budgets to take them into their practices. However, it would seem that these fears were ill-founded and few reports have appeared describing discrimination against older patients. Undoubtedly, older people registered with fundholding practices have benefited from improvements in having hip replacements, cataracts, and other forms of surgery carried out quickly.

Certainly there have been benefits for older patients in all GP practices. There is now more information available about the practices, and there are better premises with good access, a more managed approach by a practice to services provided, more practice nurses who have had training in the problems of older age, and specific services such as physiotherapy, chiropody and minor surgery can now be accessed in the practice or health centre. The provision of health checks for those aged 75 years and over has been well received by older people themselves. Sometimes, however, expectations have been unfulfilled when services that were seen to be needed were not available.

In April 1993 the NHS reforms came into full effect with implementation of the community care proposals. It will take time for the impact of these changes on older people to be assessed but there should be benefit from the procedures of assessing health and social need both for individuals and populations, and in formulating a health and social care strategy. There is little published research of the effect on older people of the NHS reforms. Jones et al.[1] studied a random sample of 500 people aged 65 years and over, to examine any changes that had taken place between 1990 and 1992. Each of the participants was visited in 1990 and again in 1992. The proportion of patients receiving the services of a health visitor (5%) or day hospital (2%) remained similar, but numbers receiving district nursing fell from 13% in 1990 to 10% in 1992, and those receiving a chiropody service decreased from 29% to 26%. In both years 7% of respondents were waiting for hospital outpatients appointments; the mean waiting time increased from 3.9 months in 1990 to 4.9 months in 1992. There was an increase from 2% to 4% in those aged 75 and over who were waiting for day or inpatient treatment. There was an increase from 75% to 78% in patients aged 75 and over who had taken prescribed medication within the previous 24 hours. These changes in the early years of the reforms probably do not mean very much, but it is obviously necessary to continue the monitoring of services for older people so that changes can be made if necessary.

Specific Services

Medical Care

Medical care in the community is provided by GPs (family doctors). By the nature of their contract, GPs are considered to be self-employed. Their income is derived from a mixture of capitation fees, basic practice allowance and item of service fees. The extra work involved in caring for older people is recognized by increased capitation fees for patients aged 75 and over, and they are contractually obliged to offer a health check to patients in this age group. GPs are also able to earn additional income from outside appointments including part-time hospital posts and other sessional activities. There is, however, very little private practice in the community.

General practices have changed dramatically in the last two decades. There are now in the UK about 32 000 general practitioners; the average list of patients per doctor has decreased to around 1900 and is possibly still decreasing. The relative proportions of patients in the older age group is, however, increasing.

Most doctors (about 90%) now work in groups or partnerships. There is wide variation in practice sizes but typically a practice consists of three or four partners working together caring for about 8000 patients. The average age of a

GP is becoming lower, relatively few are now over 60 years old. The proportion of women is rising gradually (26% in 1992), but the proportion of doctors who have graduated at universities outside the UK or Eire is declining (around 20% in 1992). Doctors can work in health centres or private surgery premises. Most doctors now own their own modern surgery premises. The past 20 years have seen major changes in education in general practice. Nearly all undergraduate students now have periods of attachment to departments of general practice and spend time in practices.

Since 1982, approved training for general practice principals has become mandatory. To achieve principal status it is necessary to complete two years in approved hospital posts and one year as a trainee in general practice. About one in every four of all practices is a training practice.

Practice Staff
GPs are directly responsible for employing practice staff. In most circumstances 70% of the salary for ancillary workers is reimbursed by the FHSA to the general practitioner.

The numbers that can be employed are now unrestricted, although GPs must negotiate with the FHSA regarding how many a practice can actually employ. This number is related to the service needs of that practice. The members of the practice employed team include practice managers, medical secretaries, receptionists, practice nurses, nurse practitioners, and, sometimes, data handling secretaries and counsellors. There is now the opportunity to employ physiotherapists, health visitors and chiropodists. This group forms a very important part of the primary health care team and they often make the first contact with the patient. In a practice of 10 000 patients there could be one manager, six or seven full-time equivalent secretary/receptionists, and up to three practice nurses working from a treatment room. Nurse practitioners are not very common; they undertake more medical-type work and health promotion amongst older people.

In the last 10 years, the number of staff employed by GPs has more than doubled. Staff directly employed rose by 120% between 1982 and 1992 (from 24 530 to 54 019). Over the same period the number of practice nurses has increased more than six times to 9640. The largest category of practice staff is still, however, clerical staff, accounting for two thirds of the total in 1993.

Nursing Services
Nursing services are provided within the practice by practice nurses. He/she usually works from a treatment room and provides services that include injections, immunizations, dressings and blood sampling, and has involvement in health promotion sessions such as well-person clinics and clinics for patients with diabetes and hypertension. Many undertake first stage health checks on older people. Many practice nurses operate an open access service so that patients can bring problems directly to them.

Community nursing services are provided by the District Health Authorities through their community units which may also be trusts. These services include community nurses, community psychiatric nurses, nursing liaison teams, stoma nurses, and other specialized nurses. Often community nurses are attached to practices. This means that, although still employed by the community trusts, they devote their whole time to the patients of a practice or group of practices and integrate with other members of the primary care team. This has the advantage of allowing community based nurses to work in closer co-operation with the GP. There, in England, are around 9000 whole time equivalent community nurses and 6000 registered enrolled nurses assisting them. The number of nurses working in the community has increased over the years. Within this expansion there has, however, been a shift in the mix of skills and grades. The number of nurses with a district nurse qualification has decreased recently; nursing auxiliaries have, however, increased.

The important Cumberlege Report[2] highlighted some of the difficulties of nursing in the community. A series of weaknesses was found in the service provided, despite improved training and better knowledge. The report found that the needs of individual patients were not being identified systematically, nurses and GPs were not co-ordinating their activities, too much time was spent on collecting data, existing roles were difficult to change, and traditional working methods tended to prevail, resulting in services becoming poorly co-ordinated. There was also concern about the overlap and duplication that existed between specialist nurses, health visitors, GPs and social services departments. Cumberlege proposed the novel scheme of neighbourhood nursing services as a solution. This has advantages, but the proposals have been criticized because they would weaken the link between GPs and the nursing services, and thus would threaten the important principle of team care.

It was suggested by Williams and Wilson[3] that GPs could form parallel community medical groups, servicing the same population unit as the community nursing group; this would achieve a more united approach and maintain the team concept. Both these ideas would mean major changes in the system of providing community care; entrenched professional attitudes may turn out to be too much of a stumbling block. However, such schemes are beginning to develop in several areas of the country and may eventually become the norm. An alternative that is also finding favour is that nurses already employed in a practice should take over the role of community nurse. There is nothing to stop practices from doing this and it would solve many team and administrative problems, with consequent benefit to the patients. The autonomy of the nurse would, however, need to be carefully guarded. Certainly, as far as older persons are concerned, all the problems identified by Cumberlege are very pertinent; any improvement in the organization would be beneficial. More detailed discussions of the principles of nursing in the community are given in Chapter 21.

Health Visitor Services

Health visitors are also employed directly by the District Health Authority through their community trusts. Many are attached to practices in the same way as district nurses. The number of health visitors increased during the past two decades, but has started to decline recently. They have been traditionally concerned with health promotion and health education. Their work has been particularly directed towards children, especially the under five-year-olds. With a background of training in nursing and midwifery they have been effective in promoting child health care. Health visitors have for many years also held a brief for well older people, but they have mostly failed to give this age group a high priority[4]. The part played by health visitors in caring for older people has probably decreased in the last few years, and they do not appear to have become widely involved in a new anticipatory care programme for those aged 75 and over. In many ways this is unfortunate, as the skills of health visitors could be very effectively used in this age group.

Physiotherapists/Remedial Gymnast

Traditionally, physiotherapists worked in hospital rehabilitation units. Now, the importance of rehabilitation once the patient has returned home has been recognized, and these services are more widely available in the community. Physiotherapists are usually employed by community trusts or a hospital, but increasingly they are employed directly by GPs.

Their main concerns are with mobility, and they aim to prevent muscle deformity and wasting. Muscle usage is encouraged and loss of balance improved, to reduce poor co-ordination and enable the patient to walk unaided.

Occupational Therapists

These therapists are also employed by District Health Authorities and sometimes by local authority social services departments. They are concerned with enabling the patient to cope with such tasks as dressing, undressing, eating, drinking, shaving, cooking, cleaning, toileting and personal care. They have suffered in the past from being thought to be merely teachers of handicrafts that might relieve patients' boredom. They are, however, essential to recovery in many cases. This is achieved by teaching patients finer movements and skilled activities that enable them to function in their environment after an illness. Occupational therapy should start at the same time as physiotherapy and be part of the overall rehabilitation strategy.

Speech Therapists

Speech therapists are concerned with communication. The problem is often a difficult one; it involves not only speech problems but reading, writing and sign language. The sense of touch is also explored. The work is closely related to that of the other therapists and is of equal importance. Unfortunately, speech therapists are in relatively short supply and the help of voluntary organizations is sometimes needed to continue therapy on a long term basis.

The Primary Health Care Team

Although not always functioning effectively, the basic unit for the provision of care in the community is the primary health care team. The doctor no longer works in isolation, but is involved with other health workers and social workers. Possible members of this team have been described. There is some disillusionment about how effective teamwork has turned out to be. Ideally a team should work together to achieve previously agreed objectives. A football team's task is to win the game; at its simplest, the primary care team's task is to solve problems which affect people in the community. There is of course more to it than that. The problems need identifying, preventing and anticipating; some are not capable of being resolved and therefore continuing care is necessary. Despite criticism, primary care teams often do work well as a means of coping with problems.

There are in effect three different primary care teams. The first, sometimes called the megateam, consists of everyone concerned in any way with caring for people in the community. This can include pharmacists, chiropodists, dieticians, speech therapists, physiotherapists, teachers, policemen, priests and many others, as well as health and social service workers and practice staff. Within this group there is an important nucleus of health and social workers who are frequently presented with problems, and for this reason need to have close association with each other. These include the general practitioner, the district nurse, the midwife, the health visitor, the social worker and other key practice workers. This group is often called the macroteam. When faced with a problem, only two or three members of the macro- or megateams are usually involved. This is the crucial functional unit and is referred to as the miniteam.

Thus, when an older person suffers from an ulcerated leg, the GP, the district nurse and the social worker may be the key persons involved, forming the miniteam. When the situation is resolved this team disperses leaving perhaps one person behind to supervise continuing care. Often there is a key person who first recognizes the problem and brings the miniteam together. This person can be any member of the macroteam. This instigator usually takes up leadership of that particular miniteam. For example, in the case of an older person who is blind and having problems with prescriptions, the instigator might be the pharmacist and the miniteam might consist of the pharmacist, the GP and a social worker. Perhaps the district nurse may find an older person has deteriorating mobility, and may then need to bring in a physiotherapist, and perhaps even a social work-er, to form the miniteam to provide help to sort out this problem.

At the level of the miniteam, the concept of teamwork is very effective, espe-cially so with older people. It is essential that each member of the macroteam should understand this principle and the specific and contributory roles of each member of the team. Leadership tends to fall on the instigating member and each team should understand that the leadership function is to do with the nature of the problem and not seniority or position within the overall team.

Other Professional Resources

The primary care team in its widest sense also includes a number of other profes-sions. Gerontological dentistry is becoming increasingly important as people keep their teeth into old age. Careful and appropriate use and fitting of dentures is necessary, both for mastication and for cosmetic reasons. Many mouth and gum problems can also be helped by dentists. Examination of the mouth is an impor-tant part of screening.

Pharmacists often provide the first professional contact for older people on health matters, and are vital to ensuring that patients have an understanding of the medicines prescribed. Medication for older people is more fully discussed elsewhere. The importance of correct prescribing and dispensing for older people cannot be overstated.

Another crucial aspect of old age is to maintain mobility; this involves special attention to feet. Chiropody care is therefore essential. Again, screening should always involve foot examination and referral for appropriate care. The same applies to eye problems and the place of the optician in the care of older people is again important.

The role of teachers may appear to be minimal. However, it is becoming increasingly evident that older people need educational opportunities, not only with regard to health, but also in leisure activities, hobbies and other interests. Professional teaching advice and encouragement will be essential if the opportuni-ties in old age are to be maximized.

Ministers of religion continue to be valued by older people. This is particularly true during times of illness and bereavement. They are, however, involved in support at other times and are very helpful members of the primary care team.

Voluntary Services

A large number of voluntary organizations provide help for older people. Some are concerned with the overall issues of older age and others with its specific aspects. Of the former, Age Concern and Help the Aged are probably the best known. Their function is to campaign in the interests of older people, research into their needs and provide local and national services to help them. They have also become involved in raising public awareness of the problems and in furthering education and preventive activities. Other organizations concentrate on specific aspects, such as the Alzheimer's Disease Society and the Stroke Association.

Another significant group of voluntary organizations is self-help groups. There are several hundred of these groups in the UK; some are nationwide, others are local initiatives. Many are associated with problems experienced by older people. The aim is to provide opportunities for patients and carers to meet others with similar problems and foster mutual support activities. They fulfil a valuable service and community workers, including GPs, should be aware of the groups in a district. Helpful addresses are as follows:

Age Concern England
Astral House
1268 London Road
London SW16 4ER

Alzheimer's Disease Society
Second Floor, Gordon House
10 Greencoat Place
London SW1P 1PH

Help the Aged
16–18 St James's Walk
London EC1R 0BE

The Stroke Association
CHSA House
Whitecross Street
London EC1Y 8JJ

Prime Carers

The most important members of the caring team are the informal or prime carers. Usually, although not always, these carers are members of the family, and can include spouses, children, siblings or grandchildren. Sometimes the older person lives with relatives in a house that is not the original home. When an older person lives alone the family can be some distance away and the prime carer is then a neighbour or friend. Occasionally lodgers are the only help around. The part played by the family and others in the care of older people has come to be appreciated more and more since early research by Townsend and his co-workers in the 1960s first demonstrated their importance[5]. They found that these helpers undertook all aspects of care, including nursing, housework, cooking and shopping, even when acute illness was not present. A substantial proportion of carers also relied on help from other relatives, especially in times of their charge's illness. Townsend found too that there were limits to family care. Thirty per cent of old people were imposing significant strains on relatives. Amongst married couples, the wife or husband provided care for the sick partner, but this also produced considerable strain on the one providing the care. There is no reason to believe that the situation is any different today and could well be worse.

The nature of the help needed can add to the difficulty. Very often personal bodily care is required and an older person may be very modest in this respect. Some older people allow only their spouse to wash or bath them; this is especially true of men. It is thought improper for another female relative to attend to the bodily functions of an old man. Children may stop short of undertaking such tasks and this limits what the family can do. Older women are in a better position because it is often acceptable for daughters to attend to their needs, but sometimes this means that one member of the family is singled out for more than her fair share of the burden. This leads to an unequal distribution of responsibility for care and is the cause of breakdown. Often family help falters when personal needs are present. This may not always be perceived, as domestic tasks may continue to be undertaken very effectively.

Evidence of many of these difficulties experienced by carers has come from a study by Jones[6], which sought to explore the network of informal and formal care available to frail older people, to determine the problems suffered by carers themselves, particularly illness, when caring for dependent older people in the community, and to examine the implications of these problems for personal health and social services. The study suggests that families are caring for dependents at great cost to themselves and, furthermore, that most of them want to continue their caring role despite its demands. However, they need and would like more assistance from the formal community services in supporting their activities. The great majority of the carers studied were required to give personal assistance to their ageing relative and had to do this on their own. This entailed assisting with personal tasks, in particular, with incontinence. Disturbed nights and dangerous behaviour, particularly falling, were aspects of caring that caused most distress to carers. The study suggested that those caring for an older person cannot draw upon the large network of informal or formal carers that had previously been thought to exist. This was particularly so if the carer was living with the older person, in which case they had largely to bear the burden of care on their own with little support from services or other relatives.

One-quarter of the sample of carers perceived their health as being affected by their caring role, and one-quarter reported that their social life had been impaired as a result of acting as a carer. The lack of privacy and personal freedom affected their family life. One-quarter of the carers had not had a holiday for five years and one-tenth of the sample reported that they had ceased employment in order to care for their dependent relative. An unbearable amount of stress as a consequence of caring was reported by almost one-fifth of the sample. In general, daughters seemed to suffer more hardship than other carers. This is probably because caring for dependent people is only one of the many responsibilities facing mature women. Children and husbands also make demands on their time and emotions; this causes problems of priorities. Only a minority of the carers in the study were receiving the support of personal health and social services. For those that were, community nurses and home helps were the services most commonly visiting. Home helps and Meals on Wheels were much less likely to be available where a carer was living with the older dependent.

The study indicated that carers needed training in various aspects of caring and that health visitors may be the most suitable people to undertake this task. Many carers felt they needed advice on, for example, how to cope with incontinence, how to care for dependants after a stroke and how to lift them without risking their own health. Health visitors could also provide advice on benefits and an attendance allowance. There was an overwhelming need for respite or relief care for carers. The difficulty most often mentioned was the time and the unremitting nature of caring. Regular planned predictable breaks were what they reported needing most. Night disturbance caused a great deal of distress to carers and there was an obvious need for night sitters to provide a break for those carers to enable them at least to have some unbroken nights' sleep. The belief that voluntary agencies could provide the major source of support to carers and their dependents could not be substantiated by the study. The services they provided were very much valued and appreciated, but it was felt that they could in no way be seen as the focal point for future community care. Only a minority of carers estimated to be eligible for an attendance allowance had applied for it. Many carers did not know of its existence, or if they did, did not know of the appeals system.

It seems therefore that the idea of 'community care' has only a limited application and, in the majority of situations, the burden of care in this particular study fell heavily on one individual with very little support from other family members or community services. It is clear, therefore, that if families are going to continue to provide substantial support for the older population to enable them to live in the community rather than in institutions, they will need to be supported by community services in order to maintain a reasonable quality of life. Future policies concerning the care of older people need to be family orientated, not individual orientated; innovations are required to support the family as a whole.

The Association of Carers

The Association of Carers is a national body that concerns itself with the needs of carers. It encourages the formation of local groups where carers with mutual problems can provide each other with help and support. An advice service is available and information can be obtained very easily. As a national organization, it hopes to improve awareness of carers' contributions and, if necessary, to change the system. Full details can be obtained from: The National Association of Carers, Head Office, 20 Glasshouse Yard, London EC1A 4JN (Phone: 0171 490 8818).

Secondary Care

Secondary care is provided by hospital and consultant services under contract to the District Health Authorities or through hospital Trusts. These services reach out into the community in a number of different ways.

Outpatient Departments

These are important links between primary and secondary care and do not involve a patient being admitted to hospital. A patient's attendance at an out-patient department depends on the GP referring the patient to a consultant. The consultant may return the patient to GP care or continue to review the situation at the outpatient clinic. Often shared care is arranged between the two doctors. It is possible for the patient to receive other services within the hospital, for instance physiotherapy, speech therapy and certain special investigations that might be necessary. Rehabilitation after hospital inpatient treatment is often arranged in this way.

Domiciliary Visits

A consultant may undertake a visit to the patient's home for assessment and opinion. This is initiated by the GP, who ideally will also be present at the inter-view. It is used when a patient is not well enough to travel and also allows the consultant to see the patient at home and assess how he/she is coping there.

In these circumstances, the consultant becomes a member of the primary care team. Often hospital admission is avoided in these circumstances, with both the family and the GP being reassured.

Geriatric Community/Liaison Team

A team of hospital based nurses is available in some areas to visit patients in their own homes after discharge from hospital. They offer support and advice, particu-larly to relatives. Their function is essentially one of liaison between the hospital and carers in the community. Supervision of the rehabilitation and continuing care of patients is very much part of this work, which can also involve visits to those on a waiting list for admission to hospital.

Day Hospital

Most hospital geriatric services now provide day hospital facilities. The main pur-pose of this is to continue rehabilitation and maintain progress previously made in the hospital. The day hospital also provides services for patients who have not been in hospital. They spend most of their day there, and usually transport is arranged both there and back by ambulance. Relief is provided for the relatives in this way. Medical and nursing services are available on the spot and, if necessary, admission or readmission can be arranged. Early discharge from hospital is often facilitated. It is vital that the GP be fully informed about treatment, especially the drugs that are being prescribed, because it is the GP who is responsible for the patient when he or she is at home. There is a risk of mistakes being made when two doctors are responsible for the same patient. Treatment cards kept with the patient are important in these circumstances. Carer groups are a new and important development in day hospitals. It is very necessary for relatives and carers, who provide substantial care at home for day hospital patients, to have close understandings and communication with the professional carers at the hospital.

References

1. Jones D, Lester C, West R. Monitoring changes in health services for older people. In: Robinson R, Le Grande J, editors. *Evaluating the NHS reforms*. King's Fund, London, 130–54.

2. Department of Health and Social Security. (1986) *Neighbourhood nursing – a focus for care*. Report of the Community Nursing Review (The Cumberlege Report). HMSO, London.

3. Williams EI, Wilson AD. (1987) Health care units: an extended alternative to the Cumberlege proposals. *J R Coll Gen Pract* 37: 507 9.

4. Luker KA. (1987) Health visitor involvement with the elderly. In: Taylor RC, Buckley EG, editors. *Preventive care of the elderly: a review of current developments*. (Occasional Paper 35.) Royal College of General Practitioners, London, 42–4.

5. Townsend P, Wedderburn D. (1965) *The aged in the welfare state*. Bell, London.

6. Jones DA. (1986) *A survey of carers of elderly dependants living in the community*, final report. Research Team for the Care of the Elderly, University College of Wales College of Medicine, Cardiff.

11
Social Care Resources

Background

Most developed countries have community welfare services, but they can differ in form and emphasis. Many European countries, such as Denmark and Sweden, have a long history of social care and a wide variety of services. In the USA such care was started much later and was mainly centred on institutions. Self-help has always been a strong life philosophy in America, but recently community based services have been developed to help older people.

In the UK, before the Second World War, the provision of social services for older people was part of the package available under Poor Law provisions and was augmented by various voluntary organizations. The National Health Services Act of 1946 gave local authorities some powers to organize care for ill people and saw the development of home helps and some chiropody and laundry services. The 1948 National Assistance Act extended these powers. Welfare was promoted and older people benefited from some of these provisions, particularly the accommodation that was made available for people needing this care because of age or infirmity. This provision was in Part Three of the Act, hence the term 'Part Three accommodation' given to this type of welfare home. Part Two of the Act empowered housing authorities (now District or Metropolitan Councils) to establish sheltered house. Traditionally the gap between sheltered housing and local authority residential care has been a large one, but in recent years some housing authorities have set up a range of very sheltered housing, which merges into the type of provision made by social services authorities under Part Three of that Act. Such very sheltered housing is sometimes referred to as 'Part Three and a half'. Voluntary bodies were also active in providing long stay care.

These services were seen to be complementary to the services provided by the National Health Service. However, concern arose about the general lack of co-ordination of welfare services, with several departments in a local authority becoming involved in welfare provision. The result was a review, published in 1968 as the Seebohm Report[1], which recommended the establishment of a single social service department in each authority. The establishment of such departments took place in 1971, following the Local Authorities Social Services Act of 1970.

This was a major piece of reorganization and resulted in a much clearer understanding of the role of social services in providing care to specific client groups, including older people. It also demonstrated the need for adequate financing of the services and the need to have trained personnel to operate them.

The whole philosophy of the change was that there should be a comprehensive approach, including not only the ability to deal with crises, but also to assess needs and anticipate problems. A further local government reorganization, which occurred in 1974 brought in new authorities and delayed developments of some of these initiatives. In particular, the local authority personal services were not properly co-ordinated with the National Health Services; these were the responsibility of quite separate health authorities, outside the scope of local authorities. An important consequence of this was a failure to integrate social work components into primary care teams.

The responsibility of local authorities for services aimed at old people became much clearer. Thus domestic help, residential accommodation, Meals on Wheels and regulation of residential homes were all included. The new generic social workers had a role in providing general welfare support to older people as well as to other age groups in the community.

Problems, however, remained. Resources were not always adequate. Joint planning with health authorities was difficult to achieve, partly because the boundaries of the two types of authority did not coincide, although sometimes the failure was due to differences in objectives. At grass roots level, health workers failed to understand the new role of social workers and teamwork became ineffective. Expectations were not realized. The effect of limited resources meant that most of the social work effort went into child care work, which was seen to be a priority, and social support for older people was left to others. In the event, most of the contact with older persons was made by domestic services (home help organizers and social work assistants). The emphasis was on practical support, such as home help, aids and adaptions, Meals on Wheels and day care. Nevertheless, although there were national guidelines for levels of staff employment by local authority social services departments, there was great variation in the extent to which they met these guidelines. Some authorities exceeded the norm, but others fell far short.

The *General Household Survey 1986*[2] details the use of personal and social services by sex and age (*see* Table 11.1). It will be seen that the overall level of these services was not high. The uptake of home help, Meals on Wheels, lunch clubs and day centre places increased up to the age of 85. After 85 years, uptake of some services decreased. This is probably so today because this age group has their needs met either in residential homes or by active primary carers. The level of support services is influenced by the mental health of older persons, and this is especially so for chiropody, community nursing, home help and Meals on Wheels.

Throughout the 1980s a highly significant, although probably unplanned, change was taking place. The increasing numbers of older people meant an increasing need for long term residential care. This care was provided by local authorities, voluntary bodies and the private sector. The change which has taken place over the last decade is that, although the level of accommodation provided by the local authorities continued to be much the same, that provided by the private sector increased dramatically. In effect there has been a shift of provision of long term care for older people from the hospital sector to privately owned nursing and residential homes. Important was the removal in the 1970s of the

Table 11.1: Use of some personal social services by older people in the month before interview, by sex and age, persons aged 65 and over, Great Britain, 1984.

Personal social services	Age (years)					
	65–69	70–74	75–79	80–84	85 and over	All 65 and over
Home help(%)						
Men	2	4	9	14	25	6
Women	4	6	14	29	33	12
All older people	3	5	12	24	31	10
Meals on wheels (%)						
Men	1	1	4	10	6	3
Women	1	1	3	10	5	3
All older people	1	1	4	10	5	3
Lunch out[a] (%)						
Men	2	2	4	2	4	3
Women	8	2	4	11	7	4
All older people	2	2	4	8	6	4
Lunch provided[b] (%)						
Men	2	3	8	12	8	5
Women	3	3	7	17	12	7
All older people	3	3	7	15	11	6
Day centre (%)						
Men	2	2	5	4	3	3
Women	4	5	7	10	9	6
All older people	3	4	6	8	7	5
Bases = 100%						
Men	492	480	315	163	71	1521
Women	597	667	502	287	186	2239
All older people	1089	1147	817	450	257	3760

[a] At lunch club or day centre.
[b] Includes meals on wheels and lunch out.
Source: OPCS, 1986[2].

convalescent beds from the National Health Services; this was a factor in promoting the market for private facilities, particularly private nursing homes. The main reason for this increase in private provision was the availability of board and lodging payments to people who could not pay the fees, taking into account the older person's resources but not the level of disability. The Department of Health and Social Security made these payments without any built-in ceiling, so, with rising costs, the implications for the government were considerable. In practice the situation became untenable.

The Griffiths Report

These difficulties, in particular the rising costs of long term accommodation for older people, resulted in a number of influential reports. An Audit Commission report[3] argued for more effective community services, and particularly highlighted problems at hospital discharge and with residential care. As a result of these concerns Sir Roy Griffiths was asked to review the way in which public funds were used to support community care policy and advise on the options for action to improve the use of these funds for more effective community care. The Griffiths Report[4] made some clear proposals, which included:

- the appointment of a Minister for Community Care
- local social services to have the lead over planning and providing community care
- that packages of care be devised for individuals by a responsible case manager
- assessment for movement to residential homes where public funding is required
- ring-fencing of community care incomes
- a clear framework for co-ordinating health and social services.

The result was a White Paper, *Caring for people*[5]. This document acknowledged many of the problems identified in the Griffiths Report, and highlighted one in particular, the built-in bias contained in the government's funding arrangements towards residential care rather than services for people at home. The White Paper's aims were to:

- enable people to live as normal a life as possible in their own homes or in a homely environment in the local community
- to provide the right amount of care and support to help people achieve maximum possible independence
- to help them to achieve their full potential, by acquiring or reacquiring basic living skills.

It was also intended to give people a greater individual say in how they lived their lives and the services they needed to help them to do so. A 'homely environment in the local community' possibly meant rest or residential care home.
These are aims by which the service should be measured and to help this some very key specific objectives were included.
These were as follows:

- to promote the development of domiciliary day and respite services to enable people to live in their own homes where feasible and sensible
- to ensure that service providers make practical support for carers a high priority
- to make proper assessment of need and good care management the cornerstone of high quality care
- to promote the development of a flourishing independent sector alongside good quality public services
- to clarify the responsibilities of agencies and make it easier to hold them to account for their performance

- to secure better value for tax payers' money by introducing a new funding structure for social care.

These key proposals were included in the NHS and Community Care Act (1990). It took three years for this Act to be put into effect. The new arrangements started on the 1 April 1993. The Griffiths proposal for a Minister for Community Care was not acted upon, neither was assured ring-fencing for community care funds.

The Present Position

Local Authorities Social Services Committees now have a duty to produce annually updated community care plans for each area. These plans cover the development of services over a three-year period; authorities' performance will be assessed against them. These plans should be in keeping with the six key objectives of national policy mentioned above. Local authorities produce these plans in collaboration with health and (in theory) housing authorities, and consult with other organizations including service users and informal carers. The Act makes it clear that a community care plan should take a comprehensive view of all services that are needed to support people in the community. The effect has been to change dramatically the way in which social services are provided and funded.

Responsibility for paying for places in nursing and residential homes was transferred to the local authorities from the Department of Social Security from April 1993. The way that this was done meant that for the first time there was a ceiling on government commitment in this area. Social services departments must make new arrangements for assessing people who need services and then arrange, monitor and, where appropriate, pay for suitable services. This process is known as 'assessment and care management'. In doing this a social services department is required to make a clear distinction between the organizational responsibilities for assessment and care management (commissioning) and those for the management of the department's own services (provision). This is called the 'purchaser/provider split'.

The social services departments are expected to move away from providing most social care services themselves. Instead they should play an enabling role, encouraging the development of new services in the voluntary and independent sectors to create choice for people who need services. This process is called 'stimulating the mixed economy of care'. The social services departments are now accountable to people who use the services, and those who care for them, for the type and quality of the services that are provided. There are new arrangements for: inspecting all residential care homes, including local authority homes; dealing with complaints from service users; and monitoring and evaluating the effectiveness of the services provided in meeting service users' needs. An important provision of the 1990 Act is that the inspection of these services is at arm's length from the management of care provision. The inspection service has the duty to inspect its 'own' local authority provision against the same criteria used in the inspection of comparable provision in other districts.

Some of the changes were introduced before April 1993, such as arrangements for inspection and complaints. By April 1993, however, all areas in the country had agreed and detailed community care plans. Most include comprehensive objectives on the way in which care will be planned and provided. Strong emphasis is placed upon an individual's rights, preferences and opportunities for choice. These plans are made in partnership with other authorities, especially those concerned with health. They take note of the importance of care in the home or in a 'homely' environment. The needs of carers and those belonging to ethnic minorities are specially considered. A responsive and flexible service is the aim, providing equality of access, and a commitment to advocacy. The changes are probably driven by a need to keep down costs, but the policy of providing appropriate services is sensible, albeit by the use of assessment. The success of the change will in the end depend upon adequate funding and whether there are enough appropriately trained staff. It will probably take quite some time for this to be achieved. There will be gradual evolution rather than a 'big bang' start, but to show that the objectives have been achieved it will be necessary very quickly to demonstrate that resources are provided to match the needs.

Community Care for Older People

Older people are an important group of users of community services, although only a minority will need such support at any particular time. The general aim is to promote and sustain the ability of older persons to live independently. When they can no longer do so, dependence should be managed in ways which preserve dignity, choice and privacy. Older people should retain the same rights of choice as others, but when it is no longer possible to exercise those rights, their interests must be adequately safeguarded. Basically, community care services are concerned with abilities to self-care, undertake domestic tasks and maintain social relationships (see Williams' Rings Figure 9.1). Services are available to give support at these three levels.

There is no precise information about the numbers of older people needing support, but some idea can be gained from a succession of OPCS disability surveys published in a succession of general household surveys. It is known that, of those over 75 years of age, 50% have disability affecting mobility, about one-third have disability affecting personal care, one-third have difficulty with hearing, and one-quarter difficulty with seeing. In addition, 15% have problems with continence. Many people have more than one disability. It is estimated that between 10–15% of people over 65 years of age may be suffering from depression, and one-quarter of those over 85 years are likely to be demented.

The needs will be considerable and it is probable that services will not be able to match these needs. Local authorities are therefore likely to set priorities, usually in association with District Health Authorities and FHSAs. Priority groups could be older people:

- with profound and complex physical disabilities
- suffering from mental disorder
- whose carers are disabled
- who have severe relationship problems
- who are severely isolated
- who have acute short term problems due, perhaps, to accident, illness or bereavement.

Health workers should know what priorities are being made in their area as local authorities will differ in their plans and financial arrangements.

Local Authority Assessment

The assessment procedures which will be used initially by social services departments are likely to be flexible. They need to cater for other client groups apart from older people, for example, those with learning difficulties, mental health problems, physical or sensory disability, and HIV infection, and for people with alcohol or drug problems. The assessment procedure for older people is likely to be made in stages and there will be considerable variation in approach between different social services departments.

The processes that existed before the introduction of community care have continued to be the main sources of referral to social services. They include referrals from GPs, hospitals, community units, voluntary agencies, relatives, carers and many other people working in the community. Referers should have been informed of the mechanisms for referral and the forms to be used. When they are referred, a potential user of services will receive clear information about the assessment procedure. The assessments are important because providing the right services depends on a thorough appraisal of need. A common form of assessment of older people will concern examination of the need for residential care.

Where all that is needed is a single one-off service, or advice, no formal assessment will be needed. A simple assessment will be used where the resource is time limited. This would apply, for example, when an orange car badge is requested. A medical opinion may be necessary here and a fee may be charged.

A full assessment will be required for people who are physically or mentally unable to care for themselves unless they have the support of family or friends. These people will usually require constant attention and stress on carers is a factor for consideration. Other circumstances would be where people whose physical or mental state is such that they are considered to be at high risk or where they need daily support in order to continue to live in the community. People who need high levels of support from community services, because of their physical or mental state, will also have a social assessment.

Assessments will determine needs, but they will also determine whether eligibility criteria are being met. This is a relatively new introduction to the field of community care; it is based on the relationship between two factors. The first is the level of complexity of need, and the second is the availability of resources to meet that need. The idea of criteria undoubtedly conflicts with user choice, but the intention is that choice will be protected as far as possible, even if it is limited in practice. The criteria will apply only in situations where the social services departments are acting in the role of purchasers.

Matching needs to appropriate levels of service is likely to be a time consuming process if fairness and safety are to be ensured. At a simple level, where perhaps only limited assessment is needed, the eligibility criteria may be straightforward and may be concerned with practical assistance for clients who live in their own homes, such as Meals on Wheels, time limited help, car badges, installation of a telephone, a lunch club, an interpreter, help for those with hearing problems etc. A more complex assessment, however, will be required where intensive or very scarce services are required, or admission to a residential home or nursing home is being considered. Where scarce or expensive services are needed, assessors are likely to look very carefully at the possible options before deciding on the level of care that can be provided.

Throughout the whole of this assessment process the possibility of need being met by organizations other than social services departments will be considered. Examples of such outside help are voluntary day centres or lunch clubs, self-help groups, religious or cultural groups, day hospital, community care nursing, housing associations, district housing authority sheltered accommodation and long stay inpatient hospital care.

Details of assessment procedures, criteria of eligibility and possible care packages should be available from local social services departments. They are likely to be modified in the light of experience and systems will have to be flexible. The concern is that the additional administrative effort required to contain the vast increase in information gathering, documentation and interpretation that the Act requires, will absorb money that could be better spent on service provision.

Services Available

The changes described for the delivery of community care and the new procedures for assessment of need and priority setting have had far reaching implications for the actual provision of care. Taking this into account, the range of services available will now be detailed.

Home Care Service

Home help and home care services are among the most popular and effective services available through community care. About 12% of all over 65-year-old people, and 31% of those aged 75 and over, use this type of service[6]. The service entitles an older person to receive help of a domestic nature in the house, usually for two or three hours per day for any number of days in the week. The service has evolved over the past few years and a very flexible approach is now usually available. In some authorities, home helps are now termed 'community care assistants' in line with new national agreements on conditions of service and a new job description that includes personal care to clients. Very careful assessment is made of a patient's need and a note is made of the critical points of the day and night when help is required, and what type of help it should be. Within this flexibility it is the intention that the work undertaken is that which is beyond the capability of the older person. General cleaning, tidying, shopping and cooking are included. The visit also provides interesting company, which relieves loneliness and acts as a contact with the outside world, particularly with the social services department itself.

The availability of home help services is limited and is probably not enough to satisfy the needs of the population[7]. The allocation of time to individuals is quite low, rarely more than four hours per week, and does not appear to increase very significantly with greater dependence. The financial arrangements are flexible and vary from place to place. Some authorities provide a free service, on the grounds that the deserving will not then be afraid to ask. Other authorities make a charge based on a means test. The person's resources are assessed by the local home help organizer at the same time as the need for assistance.

Meals on Wheels

About 3% of people aged over 65 receive Meals on Wheels[2]. Over 26 million meals are delivered each year in England to older people in their own homes. Half of these are delivered by voluntary organizations. The highest proportion go to people of 80 years and over. The person usually receives a hot meal on two or three days a week; this is often not quite enough. The nutritional value of this meal is good and, although the older person has to pay, the service is subsidized, usually by the local authority. In some areas the service provides meals at other times of the day and at weekends. An emergency Meals on Wheels service is sometimes available.

Lunch Clubs

The number of meals served in lunch clubs decreased between 1976 and 1986 from 16 million to 13 million per year[8]. Lunches are often provided in community homes or church halls. The service is primarily used by older people who are sufficiently mobile to get out of the house and who can become involved in a little social activity. It has the advantage of efficiency because more people can be catered for. The meal is supervized by a responsible person who can also keep an eye on the group and detect any signs of deterioration.

Day Centres and Day Care

A day centre may be a meeting place where older people can see friends and engage in social activities. Hobbies can be catered for and there may be the opportunity for games and craft work. Sometimes the centre is in the form of a workshop where they can come for certain hours during the day and earn money.

A different type of centre is where day care is provided. Here, full care is available for the daytime and the centre is often associated with a residential home. Full supervision is present and meals are given. Persons attending are usually dependent on some form of care, particularly if they live alone or if the families are unable to provide care throughout the day. Transport is often provided for older people to get to and from these centres. This sort of care is also useful in providing an intermediate stage between residential accommodation and the patient's own home. It allows for flexibility between levels of care.

Residential Care

As has been indicated, Part Three of the National Assistance Act 1948 required local authorities to provide residential care for older people. Initially these homes were seen to be hotel-type lodgings for fit older people, but it is now regarded as preferable for this group to stay in their own home; permanent residential care is now provided only where somebody cannot manage at home or in the community, even with domiciliary support. There have been major changes in the provision of residential care and these will be more fully documented later in this chapter. Eligibility criteria have been laid down that have to be satisfied before admission; these also will be discussed later. On the whole, patients who are admitted to private or local authority residential homes are those who are reasonably well and mobile and do not need nursing care. The patient should be able to use a toilet, attend for meals, dress and have enough mobility to walk to the bedroom, albeit aided by a Zimmer frame. However, for some time now it has usually been those who are significantly frail who are admitted to residential care. Some degree of disability is usually present and some nursing attention may be required. There have always been people with mild degrees of mental impairment in residential homes, but it is wise that they do not constitute too high a proportion, since this may create an unfavourable environment for the more lucid residents. The population of patients with dementia in residential homes is increasing.

People are often admitted to residential homes from their own home, but a sizeable proportion, probably about half, are admitted directly from hospital. In either case, they will need to be assessed. In an emergency situation this may not be possible, but it will take place as soon as convenient. The decision to admit an older person to a home is taken by the local authority and is, in the first place, taken on grounds of social competence, but health status inevitably needs to be taken into account as well. The decision may be a difficult one to make. The degree of care needed must be weighed against the care that can be provided at home, and the best interests of the older person.

Short stay accommodation is often available too for older people who might have some temporary domestic difficulty. Holiday relief for relatives falls into this category. Sometimes an older person benefits from a short trial period at the home before admission; this enables him/her to test out the idea of permanent residence, and makes easier the, sometimes traumatic, transition from home to residential care. Similarly, patients transferred from hospital to a residential home will need special care and understanding in the first few weeks of adjustment.

As described earlier, the social services are now responsible for the financial support of older people in residential care who cannot afford the payments. These arrangements apply to those who enter homes after April 1993. The position is protected of those already in homes at that date and who are receiving the high level of Income Support. This is so even if the person is paying their own fees and resources become depleted after the new arrangements came into effect. The change did not affect social security benefits for people living in their own homes. There is a procedure for investigating complaints, particularly about decisions made about the help needed. Details of these procedures will be available through the social services department.

Before the new community care arrangements, private residential accommodation was governed by the 1984 Residential Homes Act, which was concerned with the regulation and inspection of such homes, and which also provided guidelines for the provision of trained staff, the procedures for control of medication, and the facilities available to residents. These arrangements stay in place, but have now become the responsibility of the social services departments. The relationship between the social services departments and the homes is that of purchaser/provider. Whether the cash limited nature of the social services' resources will allow for further growth and development of the private sector remains to be seen. A danger is that fees set by the social services department may turn out to be commercially insufficient and result in a reduction in the number of places available. GPs had hitherto provided the medical cover for private nursing homes and this continued. Sometimes patients come from a distance to take up residence in a home and have no GP. In these circumstances, it is possibly better that one GP looks after all the residents. Sometimes the home, a local practice, and the FHSA have to make special arrangements for this. The question arises about whether a GP should receive a retainer for duties carried out in a private nursing home. The General Medical Services Committee of the British Medical Association[9] has given guidelines on duties for which such payment can be accepted. They include advice on the general management of the home, involving such things as arrangements for storing drugs, disposal of clinical waste, patient record systems, confidentiality and medicolegal matters. Also included is advice regarding staff appointments and training, and the provision of an occupational health service. Residents who do not wish to receive NHS provision can be treated privately.

Sheltered Accommodation

Sheltered accommodation for older people has also developed in recent years. Accommodation is usually provided by local authority housing departments, but sometimes by housing associations or private companies. The units can be of a bungalow type or two or three storey blocks of flats. An average of about 36 dwellings constitutes a unit, together with a warden to supervise. Sometimes there are communal eating, meeting and laundering facilities. Living in these sheltered units can provide advantages such as cheap TV licence rates. Many have intercom and alarm bell systems. Units with these facilities are best used for less active older people. The warden's job is that of a good neighbour, who will summon the assistance of other services and relatives if necessary. He/she is not expected to do any nursing or give domestic help, but checks that individuals are coping and are not developing illnesses or being neglected.

On occasion, sheltered housing units have been built near a residential home, thus enabling the tenants to receive the benefit of support and attention from the qualified staff of the residential home and yet maintain a more satisfying state of independence. If increasing age brings about a general deterioration, then the move into the residential home can be easier.

Housing Associations

Housing associations or trusts were first established in the early part of this century as charitable bodies, to cater for those with special housing needs, including older people. Larger national associations, such as the Anchor Housing Association and the Hanover Housing Association, cater specially for the housing needs of older people. There are variations in the type of accommodation provided, some schemes involving groups of flats, or, as in the case of the Anchor Housing Association, the objective is to provide warden supported sheltered housing.

There is a growth of 'sheltered housing with extra care' schemes run by housing associations. These are built to special standards with extra care staff on the premises in addition to a warden. Some societies, such as Abbeyfield, aim to provide older people with their own rooms within the security and companionship of small households. All are registered charities and non-profit making. Legislation exists to promote and regulate the housing association movement.

Laundry Services

Most local authorities provide a laundry service to assist those caring for older people, particularly if incontinence is a problem. This is usually free. Special incontinence pads and equipment are also available through the community nursing services.

Extra Heating, Extra Diet, Help with Transport Fares

Local authorities through their social services departments may provide additional heating for an older person's house if this is considered necessary. Also, in some parts of the country, help is available for extra dietary needs and, in some cases, concessionary bus fares. Finance is usually arranged through the local authority. Sometimes financial help is available for telephones. Holidays, too, are occasionally arranged.

Adaptations of Houses

These can be arranged by social services departments. For example, help may be obtained in installing lifts or shower units, and in the widening of doorways to take a wheelchair.

Aids and Appliances

These are provided by social services departments and are specially helpful for rehabilitation (*see* Chapter 20).

Blind Register

Social services departments are particularly interested in blind people. They keep a register and offer special services for blind older people.

Social Casework

The nature and extent of social casework with older people can only briefly be touched upon here. It has been said that the social problems experienced by this group are practical rather than emotional, at least on the surface, and it is physical help that is needed rather than supportive casework. However, this is debatable and it is likely that older people experience the full range of emotional problems and they or their families may need help to manage these difficulties. Sometimes specific groups in a community, such as older people living in sheltered housing, may need social support to smooth out interpersonal differences. An obvious example when people live in a close community is rivalry for friendship or subgroup formation. Sometimes an older person may be excluded from social intercourse for reasons that are at first not clear. This type of problem involves careful analysis and attempts to restore social balance are often very time consuming. Long term support may be necessary; this can sometimes be achieved by using group activity, especially at day centres.

Social workers can also help to develop the community's awareness of the problems of older people. They can create 'good neighbour' schemes and identify trouble spots, where perhaps an area with a high proportion of older residents is being persistently vandalized. The aim in these circumstances is to make the community socially self-supporting. The work entails some subtlety and it is important to avoid segregating older people from the rest of the community. Integration is the principal objective.

Services to Carers

Much recent effort has been directed toward raising the profile of carers and enabling them to find their own voice. This has resulted in providers giving greater attention to the needs of carers, but there is probably some way to go before these needs are fully met. In some areas carer support workers have been established. The effectiveness of these initiatives needs to be evaluated. The new changes introduced in the Community Care Act may be confusing to carers and it will be necessary to ensure that full information is given and a quick response is made to carers' needs.

Role of General Practitioners in Assessment

Every social services department will work differently, and all GPs will need to be aware of the local arrangements when considering their roles in assessments of need and eligibility. Local agreements will have to be negotiated between representatives of GPs and the social services department if confusion is to be avoided.

There are some helpful national guidelines that have been issued by the British Medical Association. These are built on already existing concepts of good practice. It has long been understood that GPs and other members of the primary health care team are well placed to make the initial identification of need. This need is often due to a medical condition which affects an individual's ability to manage daily activities. It has been normal practice for GPs to refer cases requiring social help to social services departments using accepted local procedures.

The 1989 Act indicates that GPs now have a duty to refer to the Director of Social Services patients whom they believe to be in need of care in the community. There is no corresponding duty on the Director of Social Services to act upon the referral. Often GPs provide further information on request about a patient's health status to the social services department. The General Medical Services Council's document *General practitioners and community care: a guide to good practice*[9] clarifies the GP's responsibility in this respect. It is recommended that they provide social services departments with details of the reason for referral, the relevant medical problems and information about functional inability. It is important to have the patient's consent before giving confidential information. Referral information and health status information can be given to social services departments, providing the issue of confidentiality is observed and that GPs do this without charging a fee, as it is seen to be part of their normal terms of service. This applies both where the GP initiates the referral and when the GP responds to a request for further information. However, if GPs attend case conferences or conduct medical examinations then they can claim payment, normally through local authority/health authority collaborative arrangements.

References

1. Seebohm F, chairman. (1968) *Report of the committee on local authority and allied personal social services.* Presented to Parliament by the Secretary of State for the Home Department [*et al.*]. HMSO, London.

2. Office of Population Censuses and Surveys, Social Survey Division. (1989) *General household survey 1986.* HMSO, London.

3. Audit Commission. (1986) *Making a reality of community care.* HMSO, London.

4. Griffiths R. (1988) *Community care: agenda for action.* A report to the Secretary of State for Social Services. HMSO, London.

5. Parliamentary White Paper. (1989) *Caring for people: care in the next decade and beyond.* HMSO, London.

6. Martin J, Meltzer H, Elliott DM. (1988) *The prevalence of disability among adults.* (OPCS surveys of disability in Great Britain, Report 1.) HMSO, London.

7. Norman A. (1982) *Home helps: key issues in service provision.* Centre for Policy in Ageing, London.

8. Department of Health and Social Security. (1987) *Health and personal social services statistics for England,* HMSO, London.

9. British Medical Association. (1992) General practitioners and community care: a guide to good practice [letter]. General Medical Services Committee, BMA, London.

12
Preventive and Anticipatory Care: The Theory

Introduction

In the UK, medical care in the community has, over a long period, been provided by family doctors. In the past this care was usually initiated by the patients, either by attending the surgery or requesting a home visit. This is the so called 'reactive' form of response. The aim of the doctor was to respond promptly and relieve the acute situation, the emphasis being on cure. Thus, most GP care was episodic, but, because of the doctor's ready availability, it was generally successful in dealing with immediate problems.

This reactive response was also the norm when providing care for older people. It was, however, appreciated that there were limitations in concentrating on cure alone when dealing with older people and it was necessary to have an eye on long-term problems. The custom of regular visiting, therefore, developed, which was an acknowledgement of both this and the fact that older people needed surveillance if therapy was to be effectively monitored, deterioration detected early, and new problems identified. Unfortunately, the decision about which particular patients were to receive these visits, especially in pre-National Health Service days, was made in rather an arbitrary fashion, often depending on the patient's ability to pay. Such visits ran the risk of becoming merely social encounters with little medical content. Even so, these were doctor-initiated actions in the 'proactive' mode and were valuable in that interest was shown and contact made. They represented an early form of anticipatory care.

Despite the fact that house calls have been maintained as part of modern general practice and that over half the doctor–patient contacts in the over-85 years age group take place in the patient's home, it has been realized that it is often the wrong patients who were visited on a regular basis. Those in real need have not been accurately identified and, with an increased number of older people, the policy of visiting on a regular basis has become impractical. The average number of people of 75 years and over on an average GP's list is now about 125; this number is rising. A GP would need, therefore, to undertake about 30 visits per week to achieve a monthly visit for each patient. Furthermore, such visits in most cases would be unnecessary because most of this age group are well and many could attend the surgery. Nevertheless, the concept of keeping an eye on older patients was relevant and is still applicable. There has therefore developed over the past two decades a range of alternatives to the practice of regular visiting, an important feature of which has been the growing involvement of all members of the primary health care team.

The terminology used when discussing anticipatory care has unfortunately become confused and there is an overlap of meaning between some of the terms used. It is therefore necessary to make some definitions:

- *Primary prevention*: stopping disease before it has had the change to arise (eg immunization)

- *Secondary prevention:* the detection of disease when it is asymptomatic and often curable (eg cervical cytology)

- *Tertiary prevention*: early recognition and seeking out of established symptomatic disease or social detriment so that treatment and social support can be instituted to improve the quality of life and reduce the functional deficit produced

- *Anticipatory care:* a programme which looks ahead and aims to forestall any problems which may occur and thereby improve the quality of life; it includes all types of prevention and information about healthy life style and avoidance of hazard

- *Opportunistic anticipatory care:* the form of anticipatory care undertaken during normal contact with health workers, using, for instance, the opportunity presented by the patient/client seeking advice about other matters

- *Case finding:* coined to describe what happens when a health worker or social worker identifies a problem (or case) as part of a formal screening activity or when checking opportunistically; the problem could include physical, mental, social or family disease or dysfunction; further assessment is implied to work out solutions and formulate management plans

- *Health check:* the first stage of the 75 and over contractual assessment and a problem identifying exercise, which can lead to further assessment and management in primary care or, occasionally, full interdisciplinary assessments often using secondary care facilities

- *Assessment:* a broad term used when an older person is examined for specific purposes, such as to deal with incipient health or social breakdown, to deal with active breakdown, when there is a change in circumstance (eg discharge from hospital, move to residential care) and on an occasional basis to monitor long-term care; it includes both collection and evaluation of information. Social assessment is discussed in Chapter 11.

- *Effective health:* describes the health status of an older person, not by the presence or absence of disease, but by the ability to perform various activities of daily living.

The Development of Anticipatory Care Before 1990

The 1990 contract for GPs marked a watershed in the provision of anticipatory medical care for older people. Prior to this, only a minority of doctors undertook any form of preventive anticipatory care and the approach to this was only luke-warm. There were reasons for this, the main one being doubts about its effectiveness.

The early advocates of an anticipatory care approach were hospital geriatricians. Early pioneers like Cowan and Anderson[1], working in Rutherglen, assessed patients referred by GPs in an attempt to identify illness at an early stage. This was tertiary prevention, aimed, if possible, at effecting a cure but otherwise alleviation of the problem. However, it was James Williamson[2] and his colleagues who gave real impetus to this type of prevention by describing the phenomenon of 'unreported need'. Disturbed by the number of older people admitted to his hospital wards with late stage treatable illness, but who had not seen their GP for a considerable time, Williamson studied a sample of older people at home. He found that they had a significant amount of unreported medical need. Although not all studies have confirmed these findings, the majority have shown that unreported need was a feature of life in older age and is still present today.

Williamson's studies stimulated some GPs to introduce into their practices the comprehensive screen of older people. These early initiatives were important in gaining an understanding of the natural history of old age in the community and focused interest on the 75 and over age group. Williams[3] introduced the concept of 'effective health', which emphasized the importance of functional ability. These early studies gave the first clue that problems specifically associated with ageing often do not start until well beyond normal retirement age. Ageing was set into a highly variable longitudinal perspective and this underlined the value of primary care research.

By 1974, however, it became clear that comprehensive screening was impractical and doubt was cast upon its value. Follow-up studies in general practice showed that much time-consuming effort was being expended by the doctors without convincing evidence of a benefit to health, although some 'face value' benefit was demonstrated[4]. This led to a more selective approach. The point was made that some groups of elderly people were less likely to report illness and therefore might have high levels of unmet need. These might lead in turn to a reduction in the ability to self-care and function effectively. The most commonly identified vulnerable group was those who were much older that is, those people over the age of 80 years. Taylor and Ford[5], however, identified some other groups, which included the recently widowed, the never married, those living alone, the socially isolated, those without children, those in poor economic circumstances, those who had been recently discharged from hospital, those who had recently changed their dwelling, the divorced and separated, those in socio-economic group V and – one important extra group – those who had no effective prime carer.

Taylor and Ford studied the nature of the disadvantage experienced by individuals in these groups. They constructed a risk profile for each. This included the strengths and weaknesses in six domains of functioning (health, psychological state, activity, confidence, support and material well-being).

The most disadvantaged were found to be those recently moved, recently discharged from hospital, those divorced or separated, and much older people. The efficiency of using these predetermined at-risk groups to identify people likely to have unmet need was tested in selective case finding exercises; the conclusion was that they were not very efficient. The research also involved a detailed examination of groups based on age, sex and marital status, but, disappointingly this also failed to identify groups who could be specifically targeted. Some pragmatic lessons were, however, learned. If the screening were to be confined to the much older group, it was thought that it would be probably worthwhile, because there was an increased yield of unmet need. This fact in itself is helpful to anyone conducting screening projects. Similarly, those recently discharged from hospital are worth reviewing. If the present contractual arrangements for examining patients of 75 years and over is reviewed these findings may well provide an important pointer to the development of a selective approach.

An alternative approach to selective case finding was that of Barber and his colleagues in Glasgow[6]. They undertook extensive research and developed a programme of geriatric screening that depended on the use of an initial screening letter. This was used to identify those who were thought to require a comprehensive assessment. The initial screening was by a short nine-question postal questionnaire requiring simple 'yes' or 'no' answers. A 'yes' answer to any of the questions, or a non-reply to the letter indicated that the patient was in need of a more comprehensive assessment by a health visitor. The questions were designed to cover known areas of potential risk to the patient's physical, psychological and social state. The questionnaire consisted of the following nine questions:

1. Do you live on your own?

2. Are you in a position where you have no relative on whom you can rely for help?

3. Do you need regular help with housework or shopping?

4. Are there days when you are unable to prepare a hot meal for yourself?

5. Are you confined to your home through ill health?

6. Is there any difficulty or concern over your health which you have still to see about?

7. Do you have any problem with your eyes or eyesight?

8. Do you have any difficulty with hearing?

9. Have you been in hospital during the past year?

The screening letter was shown to be acceptable to older people. In Barber's experience over 80% completed and returned their questionnaire, and only 5% refused to have anything to do with it. Both the letter's sensitivity and specificity were satisfactory. Overall, it was assessed as correctly predicting a high proportion of 'cases'. Barber[7] has demonstrated that the use of the screening letter lowered doctors' work-load, but increased the work-load of health visitors and nurses.

There have been several refinements to these original nine questions. It was found that questions 3, 5, 6 and 8 succeeded in identifying 83% of all 'cases' at the expense of contacting or visiting only 30% of the population over the age of 65.

It is therefore possible that with fewer questions there should be fewer follow-up visits and, in turn, a further reduction in the total work-load. The age range of the patients contacted was clearly critical in these calculations. Undoubtedly the highest yields in terms of unmet need will be in the highest age range.

Another approach has been the use of opportunistic case finding. This means case finding which involves expeditious, but careful, screening during normal contact between patient and health worker. It is consultation based and, to be effective, it has to rely on a high proportion of older patients having contact with the practice during a period, perhaps of one year, in order to be certain that no one is slipping through the net. When considering the possibility and feasibility of this type of preventive activity it is necessary to ascertain what proportion of older patients are in fact seeing their doctors regularly.

To do this Williams[4] undertook a study to investigate what proportion of older people were seen during the course of a year. In two large practices, all face to face contacts with over 75-year-old patients were recorded. These included home visits by the doctor or deputizing services, surgery consultations, repeat prescriptions and contacts with the district nurse, health visitor and practice nurse. The doctors continued their normal practice of clinical care that did not involve any active screening programme (although some of the doctors undertook an occasional record review of their patients). Nearly 93% of the population of over 75-year-olds were seen in the course of a year. This supports the view that GPs see most of their patients reasonably often. This finding was confirmed later by Goldman[8]. Those patients who were not seen during the course of a year were identified and visited by a health visitor. Most of these patients were in good effective health. These findings were also confirmed by Ebrahim et al.[9], studying an over 65 years age group. They, together with Williams and Barley[10], confirmed these patients were a low risk group.

It appeared therefore that opportunistic screening of older persons, especially those aged over 65, was a practical possibility. As Freer[11] points out, in recent years awareness of self-care has increased amongst older people and they have become more involved in the management of their illnesses. It would seem, therefore, to be unrealistic to believe that doctors should bear all the responsibility for the detection of problems in their patients; a routine consultation could effectively be used to review with the patient anything which was causing a problem. The better informed the patient, of course, the greater the preventive potential of routine medical care. Freer[12] showed that opportunistic screening is both a feasible and a practical activity.

The work of Buckley and Runciman[13] shows that, generally, doctors are not good at screening. Their professional expectations are rarely satisfied by the apparently mundane nature of case finding, and they are uneasy about functional assessment. Milne et al.[14] showed that nurses could readily and effectively detect most of the major afflictions of old age. It therefore became clear that health visitors and nurses could play a very important part in undertaking case finding, although, as Karen Luker[15] has shown, health visitors may have problems fitting work amongst older people into the remainder of their duties. Nevertheless, in 1986 Goodwin[16] showed that health visitors were increasingly interested in becoming involved with older people, this being in keeping with their job definition as family visitors. Similarly, district nurses were becoming increasingly aware of, and wished to expand, the preventive side of their work[17].

Until the introduction of the new contract in 1990 there was still uncertainty about the value of comprehensive screening of older people. There were, however, some indications of its value and there were several different ways in which it could be carried out. These were:

• to do nothing except provide the normal service that is available for the rest of the population

• to rely on clinics for well older people provided by health authorities

• to undertake comprehensive screening of a total practice population of those aged over 65, over 70 or over 75

• to undertake a postal survey of all older patients, followed by health visitor or doctor contact if necessary

• to organize a case finding programme of home visits, by health visitors or nurses

• to carry out an opportunistic case finding exercise at a patient initiated contact.

The last four of these possibilities are basically case finding exercises. All patients need to be followed up by a fuller assessment of any problems identified.

The first option is basically to do nothing, and the argument used in favour of this is that the iceberg of illness is a myth, or at least minimal, that unreported need has not always been demonstrated and the level may be overstated in the literature. Some studies in general practice have indeed failed to confirm this amongst the patients and it is possible that in rural areas, for example, there are not the same problems. These questions were being actively discussed prior to the 1990 GP contract. John Fry[18] arguing the case against screening, asked the question: 'Checking the elderly – why should we bother?' He made the point that anticipatory care is a normal part of good community care. Others argued anecdotally that in old age things are best left alone, intervention only upsetting the equilibrium.

Added to this is the point that the uncritical transfer of research findings from the 1960s to the 1980s had led to an exaggeration of under-consultation amongst older people at the present time. The assumption that services must be provided for a group who will not take the initiative themselves has also been questioned. Doubt has been cast on the value of an approach that treats older people as having multiple problems until proved otherwise[19]. Arguments against screening have been advanced on the grounds that such a narrowing of perspective in focusing on problems does little to help older people to cope within the limitations of their life histories and environments, so denying older people both the recognition of their own individuality and the capacity to control their own lives as far as possible.

There is some truth in these arguments, but nevertheless, as Freer[12] asserted, the balance of the argument was strongly in favour of an anticipatory approach. It was against this background that the 1990 contract for general practice was introduced with its programme of health checks for those aged 75 years and over. It has been necessary since then to take a critical view of these arrangements and professionalize the programme to maximize its benefit.

Professional Attitudes

An important aspect of the professionalization of the process is the attitude of doctors towards an anticipatory approach. It is interesting to describe a study, which took place in 1983 and which puts the present situation into historical perspective. A postal survey of doctors who were members of the Royal College of General Practitioners in the North West of England[20] contained a question about screening older patients. There turned out to be considerable diversity of opinion about its value. Ten per cent of the doctors were already carrying out formal comprehensive screening sessions for older patients in their practices. Those who were not doing so were asked whether they would be prepared to undertake this type of screening and to state how strongly they felt about it (*see* Table 12.1). Only 11% were strongly in favour of screening, and 23% were strongly against. Comments included problems with work-load, time and finance. Several doctors pointed out that screening should be financed in the same way as contraceptive care, that is on a fee for service basis.

Table 12.1: Response of non-screening doctors to question of holding screening sessions for older people.

Response to question	Percentage
Strongly yes	11.5
Possibly	25.7
Don't know	24.8
Doubtful	15.0
Strongly no	23.0

Source: Williams, 1983[20].

Some recognized that there was a need for screening, but were unsure of their own commitment to it. Others needed to be convinced of its usefulness. When asked which methods they favoured for identifying problems, most preferred to do so during normal consulting times. The doctors also stressed the importance of sharing information gathered by other members of the primary care team, especially health visitors and district nurses. Recent work indicates that there may be changes in these attitudes and this will be described in Chapter 15.

The World Health Organization Convention

The convention of usage that is recommended by the World Health Organization[21] contains three definitions that are helpful when considering functional ability and are also helpful when understanding the concept of tertiary care. The convention can be summarized as follows: Impairment (the disease) gives rise to disability (the functional loss), which gives rise to handicap (the effect on lifestyle).

- *Impairment:* any loss or abnormality of psychological, physiological or anatomical structure or function
- *Disability:* any restrictional lack of ability (due to an impairment) to perform an activity in the manner or within the range considered normal for a person
- *Handicap:* a disadvantage resulting from an impairment or disability that limits or prevents the fulfilment of a role (the role may be related to age, sex, social, cultural or economic factors).

An example would be that an older person who has the impairment of arthritis suffers from the disability of being unable to walk unaided for more than 100 m, which produces the handicap of being unable to meet friends or go on holiday.

Preventive endeavours for older people are concerned with avoiding or reducing handicap. In old age it is often more important to ask about ability to perform rather than about symptoms. For example, a question about the ability to shop may give more information than merely enquiring about breathlessness on exertion.

Tertiary Prevention

Rationale

The idea of anticipatory care has evolved over the last 20 years and it is now established as an integral part of primary care itself. It is appropriate for all age groups and many specific situations. The importance of disease prevention, health promotion and ongoing surveillance cannot now be denied, and it is the basis of, for instance, the *Health of the nation* programme. The wider concept of anticipatory care will be discussed later, but an aspect of it which affects older people in particular is tertiary prevention. It has turned out to be a controversial topic, with perhaps only limited acceptance by members of the primary health care team. It is, however, a major constituent of an anticipatory care programme, and it is therefore necessary to clarify the rationale behind the activity.

Two age related phenomena are contributory factors: the tendency for older people to under-report medical and social problems, and the almost universal presence of multiple pathology. Added to this is the tendency for doctors to underdetect medical and social problems.

Recent studies confirm the presence of unreported illness[22-25]. The main reason for this is patient inertia, which can be due to a number of causes, such as fear of hospitalization and unpleasant investigations, the risk of a move to residential care, lack of information, and imagining that symptoms are not amenable to treatment. Health workers tend to collude with a patient and compound this inertia; 'it's your age' is a phrase often used, implying that nothing can be done.

Multiple pathology can be a major factor, but often many of the problems may not be individually life threatening (eg hallux valgus, varicose ulcers, osteoarthritis and obesity). The cumulative effect of several of these is loss of function, resulting in, for example, poor mobility.

An equation of diminishing function can therefore be written:

$$\text{Unreported need} + \text{multiple pathology} \longrightarrow \text{loss of function and reduction in quality of life}$$

The ageing process itself acts as a catalyst, but there are also other causal factors, including acute illness, injury, mental impairment, chronic disease, economic distress, loneliness and social stress. Functional ability is the most important aspect of health in older age, especially beyond the age of 75 years. These aspects have been discussed very fully in Chapter 9.

Aim

The aim of tertiary prevention in older people is to identify and alleviate established disease at an early stage in order to improve or maintain functional status. The important point is that it is usually possible to reduce disability and subsequent handicap, even if the impairment itself is not amenable to specific treatment. The preventive process is concerned with preventing disability and handicap, not impairment.

Effective Health

The concept of effective health[3] was based on the ability to perform various aspects of daily living and the presence or absence of disabling physical or mental illness. Three groups were identified:

- *Group 1:* patients who were able to do their own cooking, housework and shopping: they had normal mental states and no incapacitating illnesses

- *Group 2:* patients whose movements were restricted, often housefast, unable to do their own shopping, but who were able to cook and do some housework; mental deterioration may have been present but they were coping with the situation; these patients often had illness, but were able to deal with their problems

- *Group 3:* these were usually chair or bedfast patients; they were unable to cook, do their housework or shopping; there was often general restriction of movements; they may have had mental deterioration or incapacitating illness.

It was found that, of the patients of 75 years and over in one practice, 60% were in group 1, 36% in group 2 and 4% in group 3. Other workers have modified this concept over the years, but it is still found that the proportion of people in the three groups has remained essentially the same. The 60% in group 1 need no special help; those in group 2 do need some supervision and those in group 3 are often housefast or are in nursing or residential homes. It could be that, with the increasing numbers of much older people in the population, these proportions could change over the next 10 years.

Relationship Between Disability and Disease

The rationale depends upon a relationship between disease and disability. No epidemiological studies have been undertaken to demonstrate this relationship, despite the face value attraction of the concept. Ebrahim[26] has thrown light, however, on the complexity of the issue by producing a matrix (Table 12.2).

Table 12.2: Matrix of the effect of disease process on functional deficit[27].

	Disease process	
	Present	Absent
Functional deficit		
Present	A	B
Absent	C	D

It will be seen that linkage between disease and functional deficit allows for four possibilities:

A Disease is present and also functional decline. An example would be osteoarthritis of the hip or knee producing a reduction in mobility.

B Disease is absent, but nevertheless functional loss exists. Examples would include various external situational factors: isolation, loneliness, inappropriate housing, poverty; or personal factors such as poor motivation and psychological imbalance, which prevent a person from fulfilling important activities of daily living.

C Disease is present, but no disability is apparent. An example would be raised blood pressure, which might be present and be a serious health hazard and yet

no disability would be present. There are many other examples, such as controlled diabetes and asthma, which provide situations where patients need
long-term continuing care but are nevertheless capable of functioning adequately in the community.

D Disease is absent and there is no functional decline. This is the ideal situation
and is indeed a definition of health. Nevertheless, it is probable that most have
some minor problems which in themselves do not cause any inability to function. They are really on the borderline between D and A.

In the 75-years and over age group the numbers in each of the matrix cells is
probably unknown. It is also not known whether functional decline has a high
predictive value for mortality or use of services. Much research needs to be done
in this area.

The Wider Concept of Anticipatory Care

A primary health care unit needs to have a plan for the provision of its services,
and this includes services to older people. An important feature of this is an
anticipatory care programme. Although each unit must look to its own objectives
a suggested list would be as follows:

- to provide an opportunity to undertake a tertiary screening or case finding
  exercise designed to find unreported medical and social need with the aim of
  improving functional ability
- to identify special at-risk situations where specific follow-up arrangements can
  be made to maintain regular surveillance
- to review existing therapy and make arrangements for appropriate follow-up
- to review the social, financial and environmental situation of each old person
  (eg eligibility for Attendance Allowance, Invalid Care Benefit etc.)
- to note the functional status of an older person
- to alert other organizations (eg voluntary organizations) to older persons
  requiring their help
- to inform an older person about the services available in the community,
  especially those within the practice
- to provide health education and advice about self-help, so that personal autonomy is maintained and enhanced
- to update patients' records (eg telephone numbers and prime carers)
- to review any primary preventive needs (eg influenza immunization)
- to review the carer situation
- to create a disability register of older people in the practice.

The focus of much of an anticipatory care programme is the statutory health check for patients aged 75 years and over. A full comprehensive care approach, however, takes on more than is described in the contract. Tertiary prevention aims at identifying unmet need and, although this is important, it is only part of the programme. Other aspects include the creation of a data base, review of finance, medication and carer provision, follow-up of vulnerable groups, and the initiation of a continuing care arrangement where this is indicated. These aspects will be described later in the chapter on the practicalities of the health check (Chapter 13).

Dangers of an Anticipatory Care Programme

Looking at the objectives described above, it is clear that there are benefits in an anticipatory care programme, but there are also dangers:

- *Older age can become over medicalized* The idea that all adversity in older age is amenable to a quick medical fix is absurd and yet there may be a temptation to regard an anticipatory approach as being capable of being a cure all for all but the most irremediable circumstances.

- *Over treatment* This is linked to the above and, of course, should be avoided. A conservative approach to therapy is essential.

- *Raising expectations unrealistically* Again this is linked to the above. It is unfair to pretend that health and social workers have the answers to all problems, or the resources available to deal with them. Many difficult decisions about priorities, risks and the appropriate responses will have to be taken as a result of an anticipatory care programme.

- *Reducing patient autonomy and their need to be responsible for their own health* This is a real danger. A reactive approach puts responsibility firmly in the patient's hands. It gives them the initiative to secure medical and social help. With a proactive approach this responsibility is encroached upon. A hallmark of successful ageing is the ability to maintain autonomy and this should be encouraged.

- *Missing treatable illness* Any screening exercise must be capable of picking up the problem that it is seeking. In older age tertiary screening, the range of possible unmet need is so great that there is real danger of missing vital conditions. To avoid this pitfall a systematic and standardized approach is best.

- *Taking resources away from other aspects of care* Probably the most important preventive measure is to provide good acute care. Resources to deal effectively with acute episodes, both medical and social are essential.

- *Complacency amongst social and health staff* The idea of only doing health checks and leaving it at that is absurd. The necessary follow-up and continuing care arrangements are integral to the process.

- *Limiting interventions to merely filling in a check list* This could contribute to the above, but could also add to the danger of missing important needs.
- *Using inappropriately trained staff to do health checks* This could reduce the health check to a mere recording exercise without the possibility of interpreting the findings and understanding their significance. A positive finding inappropriately referred could be dangerous.

Ethical Issues

The above dangers raise awareness about the possible practical problems, but, as in other professionally led activities, anticipatory care programmes can also raise ethical issues. This is particularly true for tertiary prevention. A proactive programme therefore needs to be carefully thought out with a clearly stated rationale for the exercise.

A screening programme must be valid and resources must be available to deal with positive findings. In the case of tertiary screening this means that the reasons for doing it are sound, the effectiveness of the screening instrument is proven, and there is confidence that something can be done for the patient. With older people, the reason for undertaking tertiary prevention is unreported need; in good hands, the health check does identify this and in most cases something can be done to help the patient. The professions must insist that resources are available to deal with unmet needs. The fact that services are not available is not sufficient reason to abandon the principle of tertiary screening.

The health check is more than a screening exercise and encompasses continuing care, information giving and health education. All this must be acceptable to the patient. Evidence demonstrates that it is. It is also necessary to balance the dangers with the benefits. Health care workers must always be aware of any harmful results of intervention.

Confidentiality is an important issue and can take several forms. Occasionally conditions that the patient knows about, but does not wish to share with the family, are found at screening. For example, an older patient with an inoperable carcinoma of the breast may not want the family to know. There is also the issue of confidentiality within the team; would the patient agree to share medical information with a social worker, or someone in the local authority housing department? Sometimes problems with confidentiality can lead to collusion. How far does one collude with patients or relatives in difficult circumstances? Communication problems also arise. Patients must have the choice of refusing health checks and full information about the nature of the assessment must be given. Their views are important and must be respected. Decisions about what to do with the findings are sometimes difficult; for example, if a condition is found that is not dangerous and needs no treatment, is it always necessary to inform the patient? How far in a proactive situation does the mandate between doctor and patient go; is it merely to do an examination or does it imply full treatment and management of any condition discovered? Usually it does imply this, but sometimes a new mandate needs to be negotiated when differences of opinion appear between doctor and patient about how to deal with problems. The situation must always be looked at through the older person's eyes; a fragile equilibrium of functional ability may exist which it would be wrong to disturb. Doctors and other health workers may have to carry responsibility for non-action as well as action.

These ethical concerns apply to the whole team, but particularly to nurses. Interprofessional conflict may occur, for instance, when assessment depends upon information-sharing. Advice about nursing practice is given by the UKCC *Code of professional practice*, which states that registered nurses are accountable for their own practice and are therefore obliged to respect confidential patient information. The UKCC states that the responsibility for information being withheld or disclosed without the consent of the patient lies with the practitioner involved at the appropriate time and cannot be delegated.

In proactive screening, a practice nurse in primary care who has been mandated by the GP under the terms of the 1990 contract should be trained in assessment, observation and interviewing skills. Given this preparation, the nurse should be accountable for the standard and quality of the assessment, but there are potential difficulties between the professional code of conduct and the practice nurse's status as the doctor's employee. On this the UKCC states that the nurse is accountable for her actions regardless of who is her employer. It is therefore important that the relationship between the practice nurse and doctor allows free discussion of these potential areas of conflict and the development agreed practice policies.

Patient, nurse and doctor may have different sets of assumptions and expectations about the aim and scope of an assessment. It is important that these are clarified and negotiated between all three parties and that informed consent is obtained.

Similar issues are raised when social workers are involved in assessments. Careful guidelines need to be constructed for client/social worker encounters and communication with other community workers.

The Cost

Few attempts have been made to investigate the economic implications of health checks. The Department of Health will need to know the costs of the programme to the health service; additional capitation, additional ancillary staff funding and the costs associated with meeting any need must be identified.

At practice level additional costs are inevitable: nurse time, travelling expenses, receptionist/secretarial time, doctor time, telephone, postage, stationery etc. All this will need balancing against the increased capitation allowance for patients of 75 years and over, always bearing in mind that they will inevitably cause an additional work-load (*see* Audit of health checks, Chapter 24).

McEwan and Forster[27] have undertaken a helpful review of the costs and effectiveness of assessing older people in general practice. This has proved to be a difficult exercise because of lack of information in many of the published studies. Where information was available, however, the costs were high. They make the point that more cost-effective approaches should be encouraged and a monitoring group is needed to monitor this aspect of assessment programmes.

References

1. Cowan NR, Anderson WF. (1952) Experiences of a consultative health centre for old people. *Public Health* **74**: 377–82.

2. Williamson J, Stokoe IH, Gray S, *et al.* (1964) Old people at home: their unreported needs. *Lancet* **i**: 1117–20.

3. Williams EI, Bennett FM, Nixon JV, *et al.* (1972) A socio-medical study of patients over 75 in general practice. *Br Med J* **ii**: 445–8.

4. Williams EI. (1974) A follow-up of geriatric patients after socio-medical assessment. *J R Col Gen Pract* **24**: 341–6.

5. Taylor RC, Ford EG, Barber H. (1983) *Research perspectives on ageing: the elderly at risk*. Age Concern, London.

6. Barber JH, Wallis JB, McKeating E. (1980) A postal screening questionnaire in preventive geriatric care. *J R Coll Gen Pract* **30**: 49–51.

7. Barber JH, Wallis JB. (1982) The effects of a system of geriatric screening and assessment on general practice workload. *Health Bull* **40**: 125–132.

8. Goldman L. (1984) Characteristics of patients aged over 75 not seen during one year in general practice [letter]. *Br Med J* **288**: 645.

9. Ebrahim S, Hedley R, Sheldon M. (1984) Low levels of ill health among elderly non-consulters in general practice. *Br Med J* **289**: 1273–5.

10. Williams ES, Barley NH. (1985) Old people not known to the general practitioner: a low risk group. *Br Med J* **291**: 251–4.

11. Freer CB. (1985) Geriatric screening: a reappraisal of preventive strategies in the care of the elderly. *J R Coll Gen Pract* **35**: 288–90.

12. Freer CB (1987) Detecting hidden needs in the elderly: screening or case finding. In: *Preventive care of the elderly: a review of current developments*. Taylor RC, Buckley EG, editors. (Occasional Paper No. 35.) Royal College of General Practitioners, London, 26–9.

13. Buckley EG, Runciman PR. (1985) *Health assessment of the elderly at home* [report]. University of Edinburgh, Edinburgh.

14. Milne JS, Maule MM, Corbach S, *et al.* (1972) The design and testing of a questionnaire and examination to assess physical and mental health in older people using a staff nurse as an observer. *J Chronic Dis* **25**: 385–405.

15. Luker KA. (1987) Health visitor involvement with the elderly. Taylor RC, Buckley EG, editors. In: *Preventive care of the elderly: a review of current developments.* (Occasional Paper No. 35.) Royal College of General Practitioners, London, 42–4.

16. Goodwin S. (1986) Health visiting for the health of the aged. *Health Visitor* **59**: 319.

17. Lyne P. (1984) *'Just repairing the damage?': health education and the professions allied to medicine.* Health Education Council, London.

18. Fry J. (1984) Checking on the elderly – should we bother? *Update* **29**: 1029–31.

19. McDonald B, Rich C. (1983) *Look me in the eye: old women, ageing and ageism.* Womens' Press, London.

20. Williams EI. (1983) The general practitioner and the disabled. *J R Coll Gen Pract* **33**: 296–9.

21. World Health Organization. (1980) *International classification of impairments, disabilities and handicaps.* Geneva, WHO.

22. Herbst KJ, Humphrey C. (1981) Prevalence of hearing impairment in the elderly living at home. *JR Coll Gen Pract* **31**: 155–60.

23. Tobias B. (1988) Dental aspects of an elderly population. *Age Ageing* **17**: 103–10.

24. White EG, Mulley GP. (1989) Footcare for very elderly people: a community survey. *Age Ageing* **18**: 275–8.

25. Iliffe S, Haines A, Gallivan S, *et al.* (1991) Assessment of elderly people in general practice: 1. Social circumstances and mental state. *Br J Gen Pract* **41**: 9–12.

26. Bennett EJ, Ebrahim S. (1992) *The essentials of health care of the elderly.* Edward Arnold, London.

27. McEwan RT, Forster DP. (1993) A review of the costs and effectiveness of assessing the elderly in general practice. *Fam Pract* **10**: 55–62.

13
Health Checks:
The Practicalities

This chapter describes the practicalities of carrying out contractual health checks on patients aged 75 years and over. It will set out the organization necessary, and the flexibility in the system about where checks are carried out and by whom. Taking a history from an older person and the special features of examination in older age will be discussed, together with an account of special situations. The schedules for each of the three stages of the health check will be described in Chapter 14.

1990 Contract for General Practice

The 1990 contract obliged GPs to offer annual health checks to patients of 75 years and over. The relevant paragraphs are as follows. A GP will:

> Invite annually each patient on his/her list who has attained the age of 75 years to participate in a consultation; and make a domiciliary visit to each such patient for the purpose of assessing whether he or she needs to render personal medical services to that patient (para. 13D). Any consultation may take place in the course of a domiciliary visit; an invitation or an offer of a visit may be oral or in writing but must be confirmed in writing and recorded in the patient's notes together with the patient's response (para. 13B).

It was further stated that:

> When making an assessment following a consultation, the doctor must record in the patient's medical records the observations made on any matter which appears to be affecting the patient's general health. Included where appropriate will be sensory functions, mobility, mental condition, physical condition including continence, social environment and the use of medicines.

The Objectives of a Health Check Programme for Those of 75 Years and Over

The contract therefore places on GPs a responsibility to invite patients of 75 years and over to an annual consultation. It emphasizes the importance of the domiciliary visit and specifies the content of the check. Nothing is said, however, about the objectives or organization of such a programme; it is presumably left to the profession to determine these matters.

In Chapter 12 the purpose of the health check was described as the identification of impairments either currently producing, or which could produce in the future, a disability or handicap that might be eased or prevented by timely action. The overall aim is to preserve functional ability that will enable older patients to live in good effective health in the environment of their choice for as long as is practically possible. This fits in with basic primary care philosophy. Some realistic objectives are as follows:

- to identify health and social problems suffered by older people, in particular those which are unreported, and relate to disability (a wider view of 'problem identification' needs to be taken than is prescribed in the contract, but identification of the important disabilities associated with vision, hearing, mental state, mobility, continence and social environment and performance is of course essential)
- to provide an opportunity for health promotion and health education
- to review medication
- to provide an opportunity for primary and secondary prevention
- to review the needs of carers
- to construct a database of relevant patient information.

These objectives are similar to those underlying an anticipatory care programme.

Problems that are identified need to be interpreted in terms of their effect on patients' function and ability to live independently. This is an important process, which requires skill and experience.

The health check needs to be seen as part of an overall programme of care of older people. Time and energy should not be deflected away from other effective ways of improving health and functional ability, such as providing good acute care.

The Three-Stage Procedure

The contract's requirements are to offer to see patients who are 75 years and over and undertake certain observations on a yearly basis. Experience in practice has shown that the process has three stages.

Stage 1

This consists of the initial health check, the purpose of which is problem identification. If no problems are identified, general advice about health promotion, information about the practice and some guidance about health care can be given.

Stage 2

This is where a problem is identified and further assessment of that problem and necessary action takes place within the domain of primary care. This entails assessment related specifically to the problem identified. Most problems will be dealt with at this stage.

Stage 3

This is where further assessment is required because the problem is complex and more specialist help is needed. This entails a full comprehensive assessment (Figure 13.1).

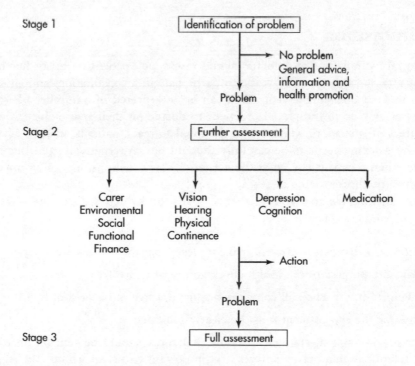

Figure 13.1: The three stages of the health check.

Tools for the Job

Practices may need to make changes in the way they keep their records to undertake a comprehensive health check programme for older people. These include:

- an up to date age/sex register so that patients aged 75 years and over can be easily identified; the FHSA can help to keep this updated; the register may be kept on cards or on a computer

- a record system to contain the extensive new information that will be collected on a yearly basis; several systems exist:

  - the records of patients of 75 years and over can be stored separately from those of younger patients

  - the records can be kept in the normal storage system with colour tagging for easy identification

  - the record system can be computerized.

Details of the health check, further assessment and action taken can be summarized and introduced into the note system or stored separately. Key facts must be available in the normal note system (eg patient's telephone number, prime carer, current problems and medication).

The Invitation

The contract stipulates that a doctor should invite each patient on his or her list, who has attained the age of 75 years, to participate in a consultation, and should offer to make a domiciliary visit. This can be interpreted in a number of ways and it is clearly up to individual practices to decide on their own policy. Many send letters of invitation, which are often timed to reach patients on their birthdays. The wording needs to be carefully thought out. Alternatively, an offer can be made when a patient is seen at the surgery. This usually results in an opportunistic health check.

When making the invitation either verbally or by letter there are several important points to consider:

- If a choice of location is offered, make it clear what the choices are.
- Explain the purpose of the health check and what it involves.
- It is helpful to say who will come (eg doctor, practice nurse or health visitor).
- A time for the appointment must be clearly indicated.
- If a reply is implied, state clearly how that reply should be sent (eg tear off slip, telephone number or letter). It is important to say to whom and where the reply should be sent.

Alternatively, it can be stated on the initial invitation letter that a nurse from the practice will come on a specified date and time unless communication is made to the practice that this is inconvenient. Above all, the reply system needs to be kept simple.

Note needs to be made in the patient's records (and also perhaps on a master list) of when the invitation was made and also the result. Poor response is often due to the method of invitation and its tone. Failure to respond may however indicate a problem and should be followed up. Examples of such problems include: wrong address, patient temporarily elsewhere, patient unable to understand. The much older, those living alone, and members of ethnic minorities are particularly likely not to respond.

A decision needs to be taken about people who actively refuse the invitation. They have the right to do this, although it is nevertheless possible that they have unmet needs. Whether to arrange an informal follow-up or respect the older person's opinion can be difficult to decide, but usually the practice knows of the background and this makes things easier. The uptake rate and reasons for refusal are important audits to make. The practice manager is probably the best person to organize identification of patients, the invitation and the making of appointments. An example of an invitation letter is shown in Figure 13.2. It should be noted that the print is considerably reduced for the purpose of the illustration; the actual letter should be in large print because of vision problems in old age.

Who Does the Check?

The contract states that it is the GP who is responsible for carrying out an assessment of patients aged 75 years and over. FHSAs however, have taken the view that doctors may delegate this to suitably qualified persons, for instance a practice nurse, or by agreement with the District Health Authority or community trust, to either an attached community nurse or health visitor. In the event, practice nurses are often involved in doing stage 1 health checks. Occupational therapists also have very relevant skills and experience for undertaking these checks and are sometimes employed by practices to do this.

What constitutes suitable qualification is debatable. A district nurse has valuable experience and training in home visits and a health visitor in health promotion. The experience of both is valuable. The Royal College of Nursing has issued an information pack for nurses in general practice which is very useful as background information[1,2].

The United Kingdom Central Council for Nursing, Midwifery and Health Visiting (UKCC)[3] has also issued a statement on practice nursing and aspects of the 1990 contract. Important points include:

• Relating to older people, the assessment should only be carried out with the informed consent of the patient or client; the nurse conducting the assessment should possess the necessary skills for performing it correctly.

The Manor Surgery
Middle Street
Beeston
Nottingham
NG9 1GA

Dear

During the course of the next few weeks we would like to invite you to have a general health check in your own home by one of our two practice nurses, Sister Sue Naylor or Sister Chris Wood. They will be able to discuss with you any of your needs or problems that you have at present or that you feel might develop in the future.

This invitation will be repeated yearly.

Could you please complete the slip below and return it to the surgery as soon as possible. Please tell us if there is any day on which it is not convenient to call.

Yours sincerely

SISTER SUE NAYLOR
....

NAME _____
ADDRESS _____
_____ TELEPHONE NUMBER _____
I WOULD/WOULD NOT LIKE TO HAVE A HEALTH CHECK
PLEASE DO NOT CALL ON _____
SIGNATURE _____

DRS BROWN, PHILLIPSON, BARRETT, BUCKELL,
MADELEY, JOHNSON and WILLIAMS

Figure 13.2: An example of a practice invitation letter to patients aged 75 and over.

- When considering accountability, the UKCC points out that nursing, midwifery and health visiting practitioners have an obligation to the Council to meet the requirements of its code of professional conduct. In this it requires such practitioners to acknowledge any limitations of competence; in such cases, they should refuse to accept delegated functions without first having received instruction in them and been assessed as competent.

These statements emphasize the responsibility for doctors and nurses alike to ensure competence in practice. In particular, nurses should not assume responsibilities for which they have not been adequately prepared. The Council stresses that the delegation of responsibility from a doctor to a nurse, and his/her acceptance of it, does not absolve the nurse from professional accountability. The nurse is accountable for his/her actions regardless of who is the employer. Doctors should consult their defence bodies regarding special arrangements for tasks delegated to nurses. Practice nurses should consult the Royal College of Nursing for the same purpose.

Doctors will therefore have to be satisfied that those undertaking screening tests are properly trained. All delegated schemes will naturally incorporate referral to a doctor at appropriate times. In the case of a confused patient, discussion with a GP and relatives is important.

The training a nurse needs to do a health check will depend on his or her experience and it will be necessary to identify an individual's particular needs. As a guide it could be expected that the nurse will have the following knowledge and skills:

- an understanding of the background to life in older age in the community and of the normal ageing process
- knowledge of the medical and social resources available in the community to care for older people in their own homes
- an understanding of the principles of anticipatory care for older people in the community
- the ability to undertake effectively the assessment procedures involved in health screening of older people
- an understanding of the purpose and extent of comprehensive screening of older people
- a knowledge of the organization of general practice
- a knowledge of the important medical, nursing and social problems associated with older age
- a knowledge of older people's needs
- positive attitudes to older people and their problems
- good interviewing and communication skills.

To satisfy these objectives, attendance at courses will be needed, together with a practical demonstration of examination and assessment techniques.

In a practice where the practice nurse does most of the assessments of patients aged 75 and over, a guide to working procedure would be as follows:

- An administrator will identify patients of 75 years and over, check the list of deaths and removals and issue written invitations before home visits are made.
- Nurses should interview patients using a first stage protocol as a guide.
- The findings should be reviewed and arrangements made for further assessment if indicated. The data should be stored within the record system and urgent problems referred to the GP immediately.

- The GP should review medication on the patient's next visit to the surgery or on a home visit and discuss this with the assessing nurse.

- A system should be arranged for reviewing the results of stage 2 and 3 assessment so that the results of these are incorporated into the record system and appropriate follow-up arrangements made.

Very importantly, the contract states that information gained during monitoring visits should be shared with the patient unless this is detrimental to their physical or mental health. It is appropriate for nurses to discuss with patients the summary of problems recorded as their contribution to this process. GPs should also take the opportunity of discussing this with patients during subsequent opportunistic contacts.

Lay Workers and Health Checks for People Aged 75 and Over: The Experience of the North Kensington Link Worker Project

Evidence from studies in Oxford, Gospel Oak, Winchester and Cirencester have indicated that assessment of older people may be carried out effectively by lay workers, providing they have the appropriate training and tools[4-11]. Based on these findings, the Link Worker Project was established in North Kensington around the development of an integrated service for elderly people (EPICS). Lay staff were recruited to work with local general practices and were given a one-month training course, based broadly on the areas of assessment specified by the 1990 GP contract. The course was organized through the Helen Hamlyn Research Unit in the Department of General Practice at St Mary's Hospital, Paddington, and a variety of medical and paramedical staff were involved in the teaching.

Following their training the link workers were supplied with a full assessment package, including a number of standardized items such as the Abbreviated Mental Test Score and the Hospital Anxiety and Depression Scale. In order to help with standardization and facilitate data collection, the assessment package was computerized and the link workers provided with light-weight portable personal computers.

Local practices were encouraged to employ the link workers on a pro rata basis to carry out the health checks for people aged 75 and over. The case-load of each link worker was estimated at 500 patients per annum and 70% of the cost of their employment were reimbursed by the FHSA. Uptake amongst local practices was high (around 70%), and the link workers proved to be very popular, not only with patients, achieving a response rate in excess of 65%, but also with practices who found that their skills developed considerably beyond assessment; in many cases the link workers became a key resource to the practices, providing information about services and financial entitlements for older people, and making referrals on behalf of the general practitioner. This is a very effective use of trained lay workers. It is inappropriate, however, to use unpaid and untrained volunteers to do the health checks[12]. The health check carries professional responsibility and to do it requires expertise and training. It would be unfair to older people to suggest that checks can be undertaken by an untrained person, and this would be against the spirit of the exercise.

Where Should Health Checks be Done?

The offer of a home visit is mandatory, but the check can be done in the surgery or health centre. Practices will vary in their approach to this. Time is the governing constraint and nurse visits to a patient's home can take up to an hour; it may therefore be difficult to work through an entire population of 75 year-old and over patients within the year. An opportunistic screen on the other hand can be done quickly and can be followed up by a much more specific nurse visit to the home to check for environmental hazards. Doing house calls entails travelling costs.

Opportunistic Health Checks

As described in Chapter 12, 90% of over 75-year-old patients are seen during a year either in the surgery or on a home visit. Before the introduction of the 1990 contract, the favoured way of undertaking tertiary prevention was at normal patient contact. This is still a very convenient option under the new arrangements. If a doctor or other health worker is actually visiting an older person and there is time available, the opportunity is obvious, but the basic health checks can also be performed during normal surgery activity provided an offer for a visit is made. Many practices are only able to see their patients of 75 years and over within the year by screening them opportunistically in this way. The way in which health checks are organized can therefore vary. Careful thought is necessary to determine the most convenient way for the practice. The programme needs continual review and audit.

Taking a History from an Older Person

When undertaking first stage health checks, interview and history-taking skills are all important. There are special reasons why obtaining information from an older person is sometimes difficult. The patient may suffer from memory failure, poor vision, deafness, or poor concentration, each of which hinders good communication. The assessor may not be sympathetic and may blame the patient for being vague and rambling. If the interview takes place in the surgery the patient may be overawed and feel threatened by the clinical environment. An interview at home may make a patient feel more comfortable by being on their own territory, but there may be a feeling of embarrassment or anxiety if the approach is too formal. A few general tips are useful.

The introduction at the beginning of the interview is often crucial to its success, because it sets the scene and, if done well, the person's trust is gained. A person's dignity must be maintained; using terms like 'grandpa' or resorting to first names should be avoided. An introduction should be friendly but relatively formal: a handshake helps, together with establishing eye contact. If the interviewer has never met the patient, it is important to say who they are and to explain their job and the purpose of the visit. Often the health worker and the patient know each other very well and a little 'chat' about previous events or shared interests breaks the ice. Much can be learned in the first moment of an encounter. Does the older person respond, not recognize you, or look perplexed? Some patients who are depressed or in the early stages of dementia may have such difficulties and poor response may be an early signal of change. Deafness also becomes obvious at an early stage and lack of effective mobility is easily recognised.

It is necessary for the interviewer to think about spatial positions in the room and sit near enough to the older person to show interest and be at the same level to make sure that the patient feels comfortable and is not strained. Possible distractions – the dog, the cat or a boiling kettle – need settling before the interview starts. The older person may want a relative present or even a neighbour who is in effect the carer. The presence of such a person is often very helpful, as information can be verified and uncertainties clarified. However, a third person can add to the difficulties. A health worker commented in the notes after an interview that the husband, who was also present, persisted in interrupting with comments and 'diversionary anecdotes'. It can be helpful if the older person is allowed to talk privately to the interviewer because sometimes on such occasions information is given about harassment or abuse.

The interviewer often knows the patient well and is aware of the medical history, which is often long and complicated by multiple pathology. When enquiring about problems, some symptoms may have been present for a long time and not be mentioned because they are considered to be normal, although they may be significant to the health worker. New symptoms may also be ignored for the same reason. Direct questioning is important, especially about functional ability. Older people may complain about symptoms but fail to mention the degree of disability caused. It is worth remembering that about 70% of people over 80 years old have some degree of disability, and in 20% this is likely to be severe.

Older people, having lived a long time, usually have quite a story to tell anyone prepared to listen. It is often a delicate task to bring the patient back to the purpose of the interview without being impolite. Occasionally the story can be used to test relevant areas of memory. It is not always necessary to follow the direct sequence of the check-list. However, firmness may be required to get back on track. It is important to allow enough time for the interview and not to appear hurried, but some discipline is needed to avoid too lengthy an interview. Older people get tired, as well as the interviewer.

During the course of a health check, it is necessary to ask some intimate questions, such as about continence. These should be left until late in the interview to allow rapport and trust to develop. The form of questioning will need to be sensitive. Direct enquiry, for instance, about continence may produce a negative reply: a more effective question is: 'Do you have trouble holding your water?'

Finally it is necessary to check the important points that have emerged at the end of the interview. This can be done with a friend or relative of the patient, but the interviewer needs to clarify with the patient that problems have been interpreted correctly and that where action is required this is understood. Most older people do have problems with disability; if none is found it is likely that they have been missed. It is helpful to have the 'geriatric giants' in mind: confusion, falls, immobility, incontinence and pressure sores. The major problems in old age are also sometimes described as the six 'Is': immobility, incontinence, instability, inability, insanity and iatrogenesis. A quick check through these may help to avoid missing something important.

Examination of an Older Person

Although a full examination is not part of the initial check it may be needed in stage 2. Some general points about how to examine an older person may however be helpful. Gentleness is all important. Older people bruise easily and often they are fragile. Everything must be done with care, and a full explanation about what is going to happen beforehand. An older person may be embarrassed by their unattractive body and watch carefully for any hint of distaste in the examiner. It is helpful to talk to patients during the examination, comment reassuringly and thank them for their co-operation. Getting patients to remove clothing is often difficult and time consuming. It is best if they do this themselves and it can give a useful clue to their abilities. Make sure the room is warm and that the person is protected by a blanket. It is often possible to do an effective examination by using a 'keyhole' technique, exposing different parts of the body separately and progressively. Many patients have aids (spectacles, hearing aids, dentures, walking sticks, wheelchairs etc.) and it is reasonable to examine these too. A hearing aid which is not working needs to be fixed. A walking stick with a worn ferrule may be dangerous on a wet pavement. Older people's footwear is often ill-fitting. Dentures may be old and functioning poorly.

As mentioned, a full examination is not necessary in a stage 1 health check, the important thing being history taking. Nevertheless, some examination is inevitable; the question is how much. Even when talking to a patient, one can observe demeanour, mobility, smell, turnout, cleanliness, breathlessness, ankle swelling, pallor, tremor, effects of previous illness such as weakness, weight loss, forgetfulness, and a patient's ability to see and hear. An older person offered a health check may expect a physical examination including a blood pressure reading and a urine test. Convention has it that these are routine and not to do them may disappoint and expose the health worker to charges of being perfunctory and uninterested. Most health workers do carry out a blood pressure check these days, although opinions differ about the relevance of a urine test. It is, however, easy to do and, because of the importance of identifying diabetes, it should be done. There is evidence that treating raised blood pressure in older people is of value up to the age of 80[13]. These are matters for individual decision. However, it is important to explain why, for instance, blood pressure and urine tests are not being carried out if this is the case. The time constraints on undertaking a health check need to be remembered. At most half an hour is usually the time that a health worker can spare and this is probably right for the patient too. Most of the time is best spent in obtaining a proper history.

Specific Situations Found as a Result of Health Checks

Patients who are Fit

A proportion of those eligible for health checks will be fit, living in good social circumstances, and have no problems under the active supervision, and so will not need extra help. What can be done for this type of patient? First, it is helpful to have it confirmed that all is well; it is usually reassuring that the practice is concerned about its older patients. A service may be needed at some time in the future, and further information about practice organization and personal contact with a member of the team who may not previously have been known to the patient is helpful. There is also the opportunity for health promotion and education.

Patients with Problems

This includes those already under active supervision by a doctor or district nurse, but who can have additional problems which are unknown to the practice. Despite evidence that patients not regularly seen by the doctor are in good general health, it cannot be safely assumed that they do not have unreported needs. Health checks of both of these types of patient cannot therefore be perfunctory.

The patient may not always perceive as a problem the same things that a health worker would perceive as a 'problem'. It is necessary to look at the situation through the older person's eyes. Some patients may have adapted to a particular difficulty and see no reason to involve services in an attempt to effect change. Health and social workers are good at perceiving the situation and judging when it is best to let things be. However, time spent listening to patients talking about these issues is usually time well spent. The purpose of the visit is not to undertake comprehensive assessment but to identify those areas where patients are experiencing problems so that further work can be done by a more appropriate person. This means the assessor should avoid probing in sensitive areas and encouraging the expression of emotional distress at an assessment designed for other purposes. The patients who are experiencing problems with relationships, self-esteem, loneliness, bereavement, anxiety or depression will need skilled help. The health check is intended to identify this need not to meet it.

Carers

It should not be assumed that everyone aged 75 and over has or needs a carer. Many patients will be fit and independent, but others do depend on carers and it will be important to obtain a clear picture of the carer's needs. Carers have tolerance limits and such factors as a patient's sleep disturbance, faecal incontinence and mental illness are poorly tolerated. They may also have their own problems such as illness and other commitments, or may experience feelings of frustration. It is important to give the older person an opportunity to speak to the assessor alone. Elder abuse is a topic of growing importance.

Residential Care

Patients in residential and nursing homes are not specifically excluded in the contact and are still patients on a GP's list. They should also receive health checks. Maintenance of effective health is no less important for residents of homes. If deterioration in function is gradual it is easy for staff who have constant contact with a person to miss it. However, the health checks will need to be modified and questions will have to be appropriate to the residential or nursing home environment. Questions relating to activities of daily living, medication, finance and lifestyle will need to be modified.

Vulnerable People

Inevitably, when seeing an older person, certain general situations become apparent. Some of these indicate that there are potential risks and they should be recorded. The risk is not necessarily associated with susceptibility to certain diseases (except perhaps hypothermia and malnutrition), but a vulnerability to poor quality of life because of impaired physical, social and mental functioning. These may result in inability to self-care and the person may need additional domiciliary help or admission to residential care. Defining at-risk groups is difficult because, even within certain categories, there is considerable variation. Living alone is often quoted as being an at-risk situation and yet many live alone surrounded by support systems which enable them to cope.

Ethnic Minorities

An important subgroup of older people are those belonging to the ethnic minorities. An increase in their number is predicted and little is known about their health needs. A survey of older people born in India and Pakistan showed that over half of those aged over 75 years were not fully independent in the basic activities of daily living[14]. Communication problems are likely to exist if the first language is not English and this probably contributes to the under-usage of services by this group[15]. Doctors will need to identify such patients on their list and liaise with community workers in meeting special needs, for instance for interpreters.

Some of the more important pitfalls include:

• assuming that the family will 'look after their own': despite widespread willingness to take on the responsibility, housing to take three generations is very expensive and many families cannot afford this.

• Offering services that are not flexible enough to cope with cultural variation, for example:

  – showers should be offered, not baths, for Asian patients

  – food which offends religious or cultural principles, or is simply unfamiliar; frail or sick people need food to be comforting and appealing

  – ignoring or disparaging self-medication within the cultural tradition.

Hospital–Community Interface

One advantage of undertaking health checks on over 75-year-old patients is that they allow a health and social disability database to be completed for each patient. Apart from recording medical conditions, services used and social circumstances, there is opportunity to note functional ability as measured by ability to perform the activities of daily living. A dynamic appreciation of changes in these aspects can then be gained by watching change year by year. Such information is also useful when patients move between care systems, such as in and out of hospital. More is now understood about the problems and dangers of older people at this interface, particularly at discharge (see Chapter 17). Although predischarge assessment takes place in hospital, problems still arise for patients being resettled, particularly with the ability to cope in their own environment. Failures also occur with formal services and the informal caring network. Information about pre-admission status, which is available from health check results, is likely to be valuable to hospital clinicians, occupational therapists and social workers. Communication of this information to secondary health workers should be considered.

Examples of basic data that could be available for 75-year and older patients on admission to hospital are:

- carer availability
- special at-risk situations
- existing medical problems
- medication
- services received before admission
- activities of daily living
- reasons for a postdischarge visit.

References

1. Royal College of Nursing. (1991) *Guidelines for assessment of elderly people*. RCN, London.

2. Royal College of Nursing. (1991) *Practice nursing – your questions answered*. RCN, London.

3. United Kingdom Central Council for Nursing, Midwifery and Health Visiting. (1990) *Practice nursing and the contract for general practice*. UKCC, London.

4. Donaldson C, Mooney G. (1991) Needs assessment, priority setting and contracts for health care: an economic view. *Br Med J* 303: 1529–30.

5. Jarman B. (1983) Identification of underprivileged areas. *Br Med J* 286: 1705–6.

6. Carpenter G, Demopoulos D. (1990) Screening in the elderly in the community: controlled trial of dependency surveillance using a questionnaire administered by volunteers. *Br Med J* 300: 1253–6.

7. Tulloch A, Moore V. (1979) A randomised controlled trial of geriatric screening and surveillance in general practice. *J R Coll Gen Pract* 29: 733–42.

8. Livingstone G, Thomas A, Graham N, *et al.* (1990) The Gospel Oak project: the use of health and social services by dependent elderly people in the community. *Health Trends* 22: 70–3.

9. Beales D, Hicks E. (1993) Staywell 75+: preventive home visits to people aged 75 and over with trained volunteers from within a group general practice. Phoenix Surgery, Cirencester.

10. Wallace PG. (1990) Linking up with the over 75s. *Br J Gen Pract* 40: 267–9.

11. Young E, Wallace P, Brewster S, *et al.* Linkworking: maximising the potential of health checks for people aged 75 and over by linking them to community care provision. In press.*

12. Williams EI, Carpenter GI, Victor C, *et al.* (1991) Screening the over 75s: are volunteers the answer? *Geriatr Med* 21 (9): 25–8.

* A full report of this project is available from the Department of General Practice and Primary Care, The Royal Free Hospital School of Medicine, Rowlands Hill Street, London NW3 2PF.

13. Beard K, Bulpitt C, Mascie-Taylor H, *et al.* (1992) Management of elderly patients with sustained hypertension. *Br Med J* **304**: 412–6.

14. Donaldson LJ. (1986) Health and social status of elderly Asians: a community survey. *Br Med J* **293**: 1079–82.

15. Kalsi N, Constantinides P. (1989) Working towards racial equality in health care: the Haringey experience. King's Fund, London.

14
Health Checks: The Procedures

When undertaking a health check on an older person, a health worker needs to have some structure on which to base the interview. Many checklists have been designed to assist this process; an example would be that modified from the RCGP Occasional Paper No. 45[1] as shown in Figure 14.1.

Ideally a check-list should be user friendly, capable of recording important data, and be comprehensive. Most do not, however, contain questions that will gather data reliably and provide a trigger for further assessment. A series of such questions has been designed for both stage 1 and stage 2 of the three-stage health check as detailed in Chapter 13. These are published in RCGP Occasional Paper No 59 and are included with permission[2]. The effect has been to make health

Name.. NHS No..........................
Address...
.... Postcode..........................
Phone.. D.O.B...........................
Lives alone/with..
If patient/has carer, who? .... Practice patient Yes ❑ No ❑

1 HOME

Problems with:
- Stairs ❑
- Access to bathroom ❑
- Access to toilet ❑
- Heating ❑
- Damp ❑
- Fumes ❑
- Too big ❑
- Too small ❑
- Repairs/adaptations ❑

2 ACTIVITIES OF DAILY LIVING

Problems with		Who helps?
Gardening	❑	
Cleaning	❑	
Minor repairs	❑	
Shopping (local)	❑	
Shopping (long distance)	❑	
Cooking	❑	
Washing clothes	❑	
Washing self – bath/shower	❑	
– strip wash	❑	
Dressing	❑	

3 CARER

	Yes	No
Is patient a carer?	❑	❑
Has patient a carer?	❑	❑
Carer present?	❑	❑
Care adequate?	❑	❑

Needs of carer – problem?
....
Health of carer – problem?
....

4 MOBILITY

Patient – goes out alone
- goes out with escort ❑
- confined to house ❑
- bedfast ❑

Problems with: Feet ❑
- Falls/loss of balance ❑
- Joints – swelling ❑
- – stiffness ❑
- – pain ❑
- Limbs – weakness ❑
- – wasting ❑
- – spasticity ❑
- – tremor ❑

Aids used : Walking stick ❑..................
Zimmer ❑..................
Wheelchair ❑..................
Gait observed...

5 HEARING AND SIGHT

Problems:
- Hearing – conversation ❑
- – whispered voice ❑
- With hearing aid? ❑
- Reading print? ❑
- Watching TV? ❑
- Spectacles OK? ❑
- Completely blind? ❑

At risk category: Recently moved ❑
Recently discharged ❑
Divorced/separated ❑

6 SOCIAL ASSESSMENT

Problems with:
- Communications – speech ❑
- – language ❑
- Use of telephone ❑
- Transport ❑
- Money ❑
- Contact with family ❑
- Loneliness ❑

	Yes	No
Has patient involvement with social groups?	❑	❑
Plans for emergencies	❑	❑
Recent bereavement	❑	❑

7 MENTAL STATE

Problems with:
- Depression ❑
- Anxiety ❑
- Sleeping ❑

Evidence of confusion ❑
Questionnaire score (if used)

8 GENERAL HEALTH

Problems with:
- Appetite ❑
- Indigestion ❑
- Teeth ❑
- Breathing ❑
- Unsteadiness ❑
- Swollen ankles ❑
- Headaches ❑
- Skin ❑
- Urinary continence ❑
- Faecal incontinence ❑
- Nutrition ❑
- Other
  - Blood pressure ❑
  - Urine ❑
  - Barthel Score ❑

9 MEDICATION

List prescribed/not prescribed:	Renewal date
....	....
....	....
....	....
....	....
....	....
....	....
....	....
....	....
....	....
....	....
....	....

Side effects?
....
....
....
....
....

Figure 14.1: Health check checklist.

checks simpler as the initial problem identification stage has been separated out from the second stage of further assessment and action.

In summary, stage 1 is the initial health check where problems are identified. Stage 2 follows if problems are encountered; if not, general advice, information and health promotion is given. Stage 2 is further assessment. Most problems are dealt with in primary care; if this is not possible, stage 3 is needed, where full assessment involving secondary health and other services is necessary.

Stage 1 Health Check Schedule

The stage 1 health check schedule is intended to be used by an appropriately trained health care worker. It can be used in a patient's home or in a surgery. The questions asked should be used as a guide and information gained recorded on a summary sheet for storage in patients' records (*see* Figure 14.1)[2]. It is recommended that these be filled in as each section is completed. Built into the questions and answers is an indication of the type of further assessment required. There are 10 sections in all. Each set of questions is designed to identify problems that should trigger further assessment. The stage 2 primary care assessment schedule (see later) sets out the recommended further primary care assessment sections that correspond to the stage 1 health check.

Social Assessment

1 Does someone else live at home with you?

.... If **Yes**

2 Do you generally look after him/her (I mean help to wash, dress, get around)?

Yes[a]

.... If **No**

3 Do you see relatives, friends or neighbours at least two or three times a week?

.... No[b]

4 Do you have a relative, neighbour or friend who you can call on for help when required?

.... No[b]

[a]Further carer and social assessment indicated.
[b]Further social assessment indicated.

Home Environment

1 In the last year, have you had difficulty keeping your home warm?

.... Yes[a]

2 In the last six months have you had any falls at home?

.... Yes[a]

3 Is there anything about your home that needs changing?

.... Yes[a]

Independent of subject's view, do you believe there is anything about his/her home environment that needs modification?

.... Yes[a]

[a]Further home assessment indicated.

Mobility

Do you, or could you if you had to:

1 Go up and down stairs and steps on your own (if necessary using a frame, tripod or stick)?

.... No[a]

2 Walk 50 yards down the road on your own (if necessary using a frame, tripod or stick)?

.... No[a]

[a]Further functional and home assessment indicated.

General Function

Do you, or could you if you had to:

1 Do the shopping by yourself?

.... No[a]

2 Do light housework or simple repairs by yourself?

.... No[a]

3 Cook a hot meal by yourself?

.... No[a]

4 Cut your own toenails?

.... No[a]

5 Wash all over on your own (including bathing or showering)?
.... No[a]

6 Dress yourself including zips and buttons?
.... No[a]

[a]Further functional/physical and home assessment indicated.

Senses

1 Do you have any difficulty hearing and understanding what a person says to you (even if you are wearing a hearing aid) in a quiet room if they speak normally to you?
.... Yes[a]

2 Do you have any difficulty in seeing newsprint, even when you are wearing your glasses?
.... Yes[b]

[a]Further hearing assessment indicated.
[b]Further visual assessment indicated.

Continence

1 Do you ever wet yourself if you are not able to get to the toilet as soon as you need to, when asleep, or if you cough or sneeze?
.... If Yes

2 Does this usually happen at least once a week?
.... Yes[a]

3 Do you ever soil or mess yourself?
.... Yes[a]

[a]Further continence and home assessment indicated.

Medication

1 Do you usually take any medication prescribed by your doctor?
.... If Yes

2 How many different ones? List:
.... (if > 3[a])

3 Do you have difficulty in remembering when to take them?

.... If **Yes**[a]

4 Are the medications on repeat prescription?

.... If **Yes**[a]

[a]Further medication review indicated.

Mental Function

Some practices may prefer to use the Geriatric Depression Scale and Abbreviated Mental Test Score to assess mental function in stage 1.

1 Do you feel sad, depressed or miserable?

.... Yes[a]

2 Do you have problems with your everyday memory?

.... Yes[a]

Does the older person's attitude or behaviour suggest agitation, depression or mental impairment?

.... Yes[a]

[a]Further mental assessment indicated.

Finances

1 Do you have any difficulty in making ends meet? I mean is it difficult to find the money to pay your bills?

.... Yes[a]

2 Do you have any difficulty in managing your own finances? I mean things like paying for bills, working out change, etc?

.... Yes[a]

[a]Refer to Department of Social Security.

Lifestyle

1 In general, how often do you have a drink of alcohol?

.... If every day[a]

2 Do you smoke cigarettes?

.... If **Yes**

About how many do you usually smoke in a day?

.... (> 10)[a]

[a]Further life-style review indicated.

This schedule includes more than is indicated in the GP contract, but presents a more comprehensive and useful review. The further assessments indicated for stage 2 are undertaken by a GP, social worker, health visitor, occupational therapist or nurse.

Some practices use the screening questionnaire for mental function and depression (Geriatric Depression Scale and Abbreviated Mental Test Score) at stage 1 as they are more reliable in identifying mental problems. The choice is, therefore, to do this or merely to use the two simple questions given above and respond accordingly.

A shortened form of the Geriatric Depression Scale screening questionnaire[3] can be used (each answer in capitals scores 1; scores >5 indicate probable depression); it includes the following questions:

- Are you basically satisfied with your life?   yes/NO
- Have you dropped many of your activities and interests?   YES/no
- Do you feel that your life is empty?   YES/no
- Do you often get bored?   YES/no
- Are you in good spirits most of the time?   yes/NO
- Are you afraid that something bad is going to happen to you?   YES/no
- Do you feel happy most of the time?   yes/NO
- Do you often feel helpless?   YES/no
- Do you prefer to stay at home, rather than going out and doing
  new things?   YES/no
- Do you feel you have more problems with memory than most?   YES/no
- Do you think it is wonderful to be alive now?   yes/NO
- Do you feel pretty worthless the way you are now?   YES/no
- Do you feel full of energy?   yes/NO
- Do you feel your situation is hopeless?   YES/no
- Do you think that most people are better off than you are?   YES/no

The screening questionnaire for the Abbreviated Mental Test Score[4] indicates probably cognitive impairment with a score of <8 (score 1 only for each correct answer). Questions asked are:

- What is your age?
- What is the time (to nearest hour)?
- Please remember this address (for example: '42 West Street')

- What year is it?
- What is your home address?
- Who are these two people (photographs of the Pope and the Queen – both of these must be identified correctly to score one point)?
- What is your date of birth?
- What year did the First World War start?
- What is the name of the present monarch?
- Please count backwards from 20 to 1.
- Please repeat the address I asked you to remember.

The question in the stage 1 schedule can easily be converted into a check-list format by a practice if this found to be more convenient to the interviewers. A check list would be similar to that indicated in Figure 14.1.

General Health

Apart from problems involving mobility, mental deterioration, sensory deprivation and incontinence, some other conditions are worth noting: a history of falls, poor appetite, indigestion, dental problems, breathlessness, ankle swelling, unsteadiness, skin irritation, foot problems, hernia and haemorrhoids. If present, these will need further appropriate assessment and action. It is now agreed that blood pressure should be measured and, as it is so easy to carry out, the urine should be tested. Some may want specifically to measure the quality of life.

Inspection of Aids and Appliances

It would be helpful to check these: for example, dentures, spectacles, walking sticks, Zimmer frame, other walking aids, hearing aid, wheel chair, bath aid and home appliances.

Health Promotion

If no problem is found at stage 1, it is recommended that certain health promotion aspects are discussed:

- immunization (eg influenza, tetanus, pneumonia)
- information about services
- sensible eating and alcohol consumption
- advice on smoking, weight control, exercise and accident avoidance
- preservation of autonomy and ability to self-care
- maintenance of social contacts.

Stage 2 Further Assessment in Primary Care

A proportion of the health checks will identify problems. Most of these will demand some further assessment, but nearly all will be handled within the sphere primary care. The further assessment will usually consist of a fuller history, some specific examinations and possibly some investigations. It will be followed by a plan of action that will include therapy and perhaps social action or referral. This assessment can take place at the same time as the initial health check, depending on who is doing it, where it is done and the time constraints. If the health check is done opportunistically by the GP, further management will be along normal clinical lines. However, if it is done by a nurse or a health visitor in a patient's home, it will be likely that most problems identified will be passed on to the GP or other primary care worker. Even so, many problems are dealt with by the nurse or health visitor.

Suggested General Protocols for Further Assessment

In the normal course of events, further assessment and action within primary care follows traditional lines, but it is helpful to have a general idea of appropriate further history taking and which examinations to undertake when presented with some specific problems. These will be described under the main headings of the health check: social, carer, home, functional/mobility, physical/continence, visual/hearing, mental, medication and finance. Some general guidelines for each section are given first with a fuller description of the schedule later.

Social Assessment

This section is concerned with the social network, communication, change in circumstance, social contacts, participation in social events and plans for emergencies. Most problems will be within the expertise of a health visitor or social worker. Sometimes referral to social services departments will be needed. Further assessment in this section entails questioning to gain more information.

Carer Assessment

Two possibilities exist here: problems with carer arrangements for the patient, or problems with the patient him/herself acting as carer. Often some social work is needed. Separate interviews with the carer and the patient are helpful.

Home Assessment

Two types of problems are possible here. The first concerns general problems in the house, such as stairs, access, toileting, damp, heating, cooking and laundry facilities; the second is concerned with accident hazards. Both types frequently require help from social services departments.

Functional Assessment

This concerns the ability to undertake the activities of daily living (ADL). Stage 1 assessment tests ADL at three levels: sociability, domestic and personal. If difficulty is found at any of these levels a search needs to be made for its cause. This means at least further physical, mental and environmental assessment. A measure of functional abilities can be made using the Barthel Index, which extends the concept to include mobility and continence. It is a validated scoring instrument and it has the advantage of being widely used in hospital practice and social services departments.

Physical Assessment

Further assessment of specific symptoms and signs usually follows conventional lines. Functional disability, a history of falls and poor mobility are common reasons for full history-taking and examination. Routine investigations including urine testing and blood pressure measurement come into play at this point. If not already noted, it is important to observe the gait of the patient and note the use of mechanical aids. Evidence of postural hypotension should also be sought.

Continence Assessment

Any hint of either faecal or urinary incontinence demands further assessment. The aim is to determine the degree and type of incontinence, the level of control achieved, and a possible cause.

Visual Assessment

In the primary care assessment of vision the use of a near vision chart and field of vision test will be sufficient. Most problems will require referral to an ophthalmologist.

Hearing Assessment

Further hearing assessment will involve a simple hearing test, perhaps by using a watch, and an examination of the ear for wax. If a hearing aid is used that also should be checked. If specific problems are found, referral to an ENT consultant is advisable.

Mental Assessment

If the abbreviated mental test and geriatric depression score have been used at the stage 1 health check, the presence or absence of the most important mental problems will have been ascertained. If these have not been used and there is a suspicion that mental problems exist, then tests must be undertaken as part of a further stage of the assessment. Dementia or depression may then be confirmed. Action depends upon degree. Both conditions can, in mild form, be diagnosed and managed in primary care, but more severe cases demand referral. It must be stressed again that, although formal tests are important, an impression from the history and examination must not be ignored.

Medication Review

Important points to note are any need for adjustments to existing therapies, clarifying arrangements for repeat prescriptions, and making sure that patients and carers understand the reasons for taking the medication. A list of current medication may help the patient in this respect. Consideration can also be given to the following points: appropriateness, dosage, compliance, over-medication, side-effects, suitability of containers, and whether over the counter medications and alternative remedies are used.

Financial Review

It will be necessary to find out whether the patient has all the financial help to which they are entitled. Tact will be needed to determine this. Details of available help will be included at this point. Sources of help include social security offices and citizens advice bureaux. Age Concern fact sheets are useful (Appendix 14.1).

Further Assessment Protocols

These protocols are intended to be a guide to the appropriate questions and investigations that may be used to clarify problems identified at initial assessment. The questions are intended to be a guide to general areas of enquiry. However, in the case of activities of daily living, cognitive function and depression, the use of specific, standardized scales (Barthel, AMTS and GDS) has demonstrable advantages and it is recommended that these should be used. The further assessments suggested at stage 2 may indicate the need for referral to specific agencies or specialists, but, for most problems, action will be confined to primary care.

Social Assessment
Aims

- to alert a practice to 'at-risk' situations for note in the record or computer system
- to identify the possibility of poor diet, which may need health visitor advice
- to identify isolation, which may need social worker help
- to identify problems with getting help in emergency, which may need social worker help
- to determine unsatisfactory social contacts which may need social worker help.

Suggested Areas for Enquiry and Examination

- details of social network (neighbours)
- loneliness
- communication problems (eg speech, language)
- recent bereavement
- recent change of address
- problem with diet
- nutritional state
- can person use telephone if available?
- transport availability
- contact with family and friends
- services used
- involvement with social groups
- plans for emergency.

Carer Assessment

Aims

- if the person is a carer, to identify stress which may herald the breakdown of care
- if the person is being cared for, to ascertain whether care is adequate.

This usually needs a separate interview. The following questions are a guide. If a social worker is involved, a fuller separate assessment scale may be needed.
If the person is a carer:

- Does their caring duty affect their:
  - health
  - free time
  - mobility
  - sleep
  - emotional state?
- Does the level of caring suggest that the person is:
  - coping
  - coming under pressure
  - at the end of their tether?
- Is additional help required?

If the person is being cared for:

- look at the carer and ask the three questions above
- is the caring adequate for needs of the person?
- is additional help required?

Home Assessment

Aims

- to identify problems with housing which could create problems for the older person
- to identify accident hazards.

Suggested Areas for Enquiry and Examination

- problems with
  - stairs
  - access to the bedroom
  - access to the toilet
  - heating
  - damp
- need for repairs or adaptions:
  - unsuitable position or size
  - difficulties with access
  - poor cooking facilities
  - accident hazards.

Functional Assessment

Aims

- to measure the extent of functional ability
- to identify the problems that may be amenable to intervention.

Suggested Areas for Enquiry and Examination

There is a range of ADL, which may be considered under three headings: sociability (activities outside the home), domestic activities and personal activities.

A number of aspects of sociability may already have been covered in the first section of the stage 2 check (social). Further aspects include:

- doing the shopping
- walking the dog
- attending place of worship
- visiting a theatre or concert
- taking a holiday
- pursuing a hobby.

Domestic activities to be assessed encompass:

- doing the washing
- housework
- household repairs
- gardening
- decorating
- doing the cooking
- washing up.

Personal ADL are the individual tasks of vital importance to each older person, including:

- mobility around the house
- transferring from bed to chair
- managing the stairs
- dressing
- grooming
- bathing
- using the toilet
- bladder control
- bowel control
- feeding.

The recommended instrument for further assessment of personal ADL is the Barthel Index (Table 14.1). This standardized instrument is widely used and has the advantage of a scoring system.

General Physical Assessment

Aim

- To discover causes for the functional disability found.

Suggested Areas for Enquiry and Examination

This should involve full physical examination by a doctor, perhaps with emphasis on a particular system (eg neurological, musculoskeletal), and would probably include urine test, blood pressure measurement and certain investigations.

Falls and poor mobility are the most common triggers to full physical examination. There are a large number of causes for both of these problems. Problems may be dealt with in primary care or they may need referral to appropriate specialists or full independent assessment.

Table 14.1: The Barthel ADL Index[5].

Function	Score	Description
Mobility – indoors	0	Immobile
	1	Wheelchair-independent
	2	Help of one untrained person
	3	Independent (may use aid)
Transfers	0	Unable – no sitting balance, two people to lift
	1	Major help: physical help from one strong or two normal people; can sit
	2	Minor help: one person easily or supervision for safety
	3	Independent
Stairs	0	Unable
	1	Needs help (verbal, physical, carrying aid)
	2	Independent up and down, carrying any walking aid
Dressing	0	Dependent
	1	Needs help but can do half unaided
	2	Independent including buttons, zips, laces etc.
Grooming	0	Needs help with personal care
	1	Independent; implements can be provided by helper; includes doing teeth, fitting false teeth, doing hair, shaving and washing
Bathing	0	Dependent
	1	Independent: bath – must get in and out unsupervised
Toilet use	0	Dependent
	1	Needs help but can do something (including wiping self)
	2	Can reach toilet/commode, undress sufficiently, clean self and leave
Bladder	0	Inconsistent or catheterized but unable to manage
	1	Occasional accident (maximum is once per 24 hours)
	2	Continent for over seven days
Bowels	0	Incontinent (or needs to be given enemas)
	1	Occasional accident (less than once a week); assess preceding week
	2	Continent for over seven days
Feeding	0	Unable
	1	Needs help in cutting up food, spreading butter etc. but feeds self
	2	Independent (food cooked, served and provided within reach but not cut up); normal food (not only soft food)
Score:	>12	Generally independent
	8–11	Moderate dependence
	5–8	Severe dependence
	<5	Total dependence

Urinary Continence Assessment

Aims

* to determine the degree and type of incontinence
* to determine the level of control achieved
* to search for any possible treatable cause.

Suggested Areas for Enquiry and Examination

Examination should include a search for possible causes, including urinary tract infection, vaginitis, faecal impaction, tumours, mechanical causes, diabetes, heart failure, medication problems, and central nervous system disease. The examination would include urine test, genital and rectal examination, and a review of the medication. A full history is needed of the timing, symptoms, degree of control, reaction to activity and the volume of urine passed. Incontinence of urine, particularly if short-term, may be reversible, for example, that due to diuretics, infection and psychological or iatrogenic causes. Long standing incontinence will need advice from appropriate specialists. Continence charting may be helpful.

Faecal Continence Assessment

Aims

* to determine the type of incontinence
* to search for any possible treatable cause.

Suggested Areas for Enquiry and Examination

A general examination as well as rectal examination should be carried out, as causes may not necessarily be local. A common cause is faecal impaction producing spurious diarrhoea. Short-term incontinence may be due to infection or dietary disturbance. Any serious illness may be associated with faecal incontinence and some drugs may also be responsible (eg antibiotics). Self-prescribed laxatives may be the cause. Recognition of carcinoma of the bowel is important.

Visual Assessment

Aims

* to determine whether vision can be improved
* to see if any problems present can be treated
* to determine whether new spectacles are needed
* to determine whether special aids are needed.

Suggested Areas for Enquiry and Examination

In primary care, an assessment of vision using a Snellen chart and a field of vision test would probably be all that is necessary. Problems associated with visual defect and field of vision should be referred to an ophthalmologist.

Hearing Assessment

Aims

- to ascertain whether hearing can be improved
- to determine whether wax is present in the ear
- where a hearing aid present, to ascertain whether it is working adequately.

Suggested Areas for Enquiry and Examination

This should involve a simple hearing test, such as a whisper test, examination of the ear for wax, and referral to an ENT surgeon if specific problems are discovered.

The six-inch whisper test[6] may be used:

- Stand behind the person at a distance of six inches.
- Take a deep breath in, breath right out and whisper '3A2'.
- Ask the person to repeat this.
- The test is passed if the sequence is repeated correctly.
- If they respond incorrectly or not at all, repeat the test once more using '1F3'.
- If the person fails, examine the ears.

Medication Review

Aims

- to make adjustments to medication as a result of the review
- to make realistic arrangements for repeat prescriptions
- to explain to the person and carer the reasons for the medication.

Suggested Areas for Enquiry and Examination

Consideration should be given to the following points:

- appropriateness
- dosage

- compliance
- understanding of purpose
- non-comprehension
- over-medication
- side-effects
- iatrogenic effects
- containers
- clarity of instructions
- over the counter drugs
- ethnic remedies
- repeat prescription schedule.

Resource: Pharmacy.

Financial Review
Aim

- to consider whether the patient has the full entitlement of financial help. Tact will be needed to make this sort of assessment.

Suggested Areas for Enquiry and Examination

- Are normal entitlements being received and what is the level of capital saving?
- Other sources of income, eg private pensions.
- Levels of commitment, eg responsibility for the care of another person.
- Assess specific entitlements, eg poll tax rebate, attendance allowance.
- If there are problems, refer to Social Security offices or Citizens Advice Bureau.

Resource: DSS Offices, Citizens Advice Bureau, Age Concern Fact Sheets.

Mental Function Assessment
Aim

- to identify the presence of mental problems particularly depression and dementia.

Tact is needed for this kind of assessment.

Identification of dementia or depression can be difficult, because many older people attempt to disguise the presence of these conditions. Ideally, a full present state examination should be carried out, but in practice this is likely to be beyond the scope of the health check.

A number of standardized scales have been developed for the detection of depression and dementia. These have the advantages of being brief and effective in identifying problems. It is recommended that the Geriatric Depression Scale (GDS)[3] and the Abbreviated Mental Test Score (AMTS)[4] be used for the detection of depression and dementia respectively. These may seem awkward to use at first, but, with a little practice, they can usually be administered without problems. The scales can be administered at interview, or given to the older person for self-completion.

It is important not to restrict assessment to the use of the scales, but to supplement the findings with information gained from further enquiry, observation of the person's attitude or behaviour, and, if possible, details provided by someone who knows them well, such as a spouse or carer.

Where depression is identified, the opinion of a psychiatrist may be sought, or alternatively treatment is instigated as appropriate with an antidepressant.

In the case of dementia, underlying causes for reduced cognitive function should be sought and it may be necessary to seek the opinion of a psychiatrist.

Further Review of Lifestyle

Aims

- to seek to promote a healthy life-style, especially with regard to diet and exercise/activity
- to explore aspects of life-style that may place the older person at risk, or may be causing problems, especially smoking, drinking and diet.

Suggested Areas for Enquiry and Examination

Diet

- fresh fruit
- vegetables
- cooked meals
- fibre.

Smoking

- number of cigarettes smoked
- attempts to stop
- smoking related disease/symptoms.

Alcohol

- frequency of consumption
- type and amount consumed on average each occasion
- evidence of alcohol related problems (sleep, dyspepsia, anxiety, memory loss etc.)
- evidence of concealed drinking (eg hidden bottles and cans).

Action and Possibilities

Health checks can identify problems that need attention, and can also provide an opportunity to review previously known conditions. In both situations it is often necessary to initiate a programme of continuing care so that the condition can be monitored. Consideration will have to be given to how often this should happen and who should be responsible. The decision will, of course, depend on circumstances but monitoring can often be undertaken by the practice nurse or health visitor, maybe in a special clinic.

Full discussion of health resources and social resources has taken place in Chapters 10 and 11. A list of possible actions following the stage two further assessment is as follows:

- note taken of 'at-risk' situations
- referral to GP for treatment and further assessment
- health visitor surveillance
- use of specific hospital services
- further investigation
- nursing services
- chiropody
- physiotherapy
- occupational therapy
- optician
- dentist
- speech therapy
- hearing aid clinic
- voluntary services
- re-housing
- community care assistants
- lunch clubs
- residential/nursing home
- Meals on Wheels
- holiday relief
- blind register
- day centre
- additional heating
- social case work
- laundry
- appliances
- financial aid
- mental health advice.

The Lisson Grove Benefits Program

The Lisson Grove Welfare Benefits Program is designed to help advisers determine entitlement to welfare benefits. Most means-tested and other benefits are covered, with explanatory material detailing the remainder. The program was developed at St Mary's Hospital Medical School, part of Imperial College in London. The project receives support from the Helen Hamlyn Foundation.

Each client is asked sufficient questions to determine their benefits entitlement. Guidance on using the program is available on-screen at all times. Answers to questions are checked for validity before being accepted. Results are not held over to the end of a consultation; each is shown as soon as possible.

Over 500 fully cross-referenced help screens provide relevant advice on answering questions, offer interpretation of results, and give guidance on the operation of the program. The help screens also contain general information on the welfare benefits system. A comprehensive manual accompanies the package.

The program incorporates a sophisticated review and recalculation feature, allowing for new calculations to be made at any time. If the user changes an answer, the data is recalculated. Any new questions that become necessary are asked, and irrelevant information is discarded. The program shows any changes to the results and ensures that each case remains consistent. This makes it possible to explore a range of options in just a few keystrokes, for example to show a client how entitlements change on retirement, or to demonstrate the effects of taking part-time work.

Comprehensive print-out facilities are also provided. Any result or help message can be printed while on screen. Summaries can be printed at any time, not just at the end of a case. Where answers have been changed and data recalculated, this is indicated on the print-out.

The program is currently used at over 800 sites in more than 500 organizations, including citizens advice bureaux, social services, health authorities and local authority welfare rights units. Regular updates follow each change in social security legislation. Copies of this program are available from Tim Blackwell or John Blackwell, Lisson Grove Health Centre, London, NW8 8EG. (Tel: 0171 724 0480).

Stage 3 Full Assessment

Following health checks, full assessment is required when an identified problem cannot be successfully resolved within primary care and the help of the secondary services is required. Usually this involves a situation where there is actual or potential breakdown in independent living. It is not a common occurrence. Other situations in general practice where such an assessment is needed include admission to residential care, discharge from hospital, where the carer requests urgent help, and in acute medical/social crises.

Because there are many causes of breakdown in independent living, full assessment needs to be comprehensive and multidisciplinary. It usually results in a detailed investigation of an individual's total situation in terms of physical and psychological state, functional state, formal and informal social support, and physical environment. The purpose of the assessment is to determine the needs of the older person and the carer. The place of assessment will vary according to the circumstances, but it could be in the patient's home, a nursing home, a health centre or a hospital, usually on an outpatient basis.

The composition of the assessment team will vary, but could include a GP, a nurse, a social worker (perhaps case manager), a hospital consultant (especially geriatrician or psychogeriatrician) and therapists (occupational, physiotherapy and speech). The team's task is to define problems and arrange an appropriate action plan, remembering that the aim is to maximize choice for the individual patient rather than to make decisions for them. The following list summarizes such an assessment:

- a complete medical check-up including history, physical examination and appropriate laboratory studies. Specific attention to state of vision, hearing, dentition, nutrition and medications, including information on accuracy of medication-taking

- mental assessment, including objective measures of memory and cognition, mood, evidence of alcohol or drug addiction

- functional assessment, which should include both actual performance and ability to perform personal ADL and domestic daily activities

- social history and social status should be examined, including the support network available; look at carers and evidence of emotional as well as physical support, financial status, coping ability and formal and informal services already being used

- environmental assessment including housing conditions, heating, cleanliness, telephone, safety hazards, neighbourhood suitability, availability of transportation and likelihood of relocation.

Note

The Royal College of Physicians Research Unit and the British Geriatric Society have produced a document with recommended schedules that links with Occasional Paper No 59[2]. It is entitled *Standardized assessment skills for elderly people*. It is a report of joint workshops of the Royal College of Physicians and the British Geriatric Society held in London in 1992, and can be obtained from the Royal College of Physicians of London, 11 St Andrew's Place, London NW1 4LE.

References

1. Williams EI, Buckley G, Freer C. (1990) *Care of old people: a framework for progress.* (Occasional Paper No. 45.) Royal College of General Practitioners, London.

2. Williams EI, Wallace P. (1993) *Health checks for people aged 75 and over.* (Occasional Paper No. 59.) Royal College of General Practitioners, London.

3. Shelk JI, Yesavage JA. (1986) Geriatric depression scale (GDS): recent evidence and development of a shorter version. In: Brink TL, editor. *Clinical gerontology: a guide to assessment and intervention.* Haworth, New York.

4. Hodkinson HM. (1972) Evaluation of a mental test score for assessment of mental impairment in the elderly. *Age Ageing* 1: 233–8.

5. Wade DT, Collin C. (1988) *The Barthel ADL index: a standard measure of disability.* *Int Disabil Stud* 10: 64–7.

6. Swan IRC, Browning GG. (1985) The whispered voice as a screening test for hearing impairment. *J R Coll Gen Pract* 35: 197.

Appendix 14.1

Age Concern England Produces the Following Information Fact Sheets

1. Help with heating
2. Sheltered housing for sale
3. Television licence concessions
4. Holidays for older people
5. Dental care in retirement
6. Finding help at home
7. Making your will
8. Rented accommodation for older people
9. Rented accommodation for older people in Greater London
10. Local authority charging procedures for residential and nursing home care
11. Preserved rights to Income Support for residential and nursing homes
12. Raising income or capital from your home
13. Older home owners: financial help with repairs
14. Probate: dealing with someone's estate
15. Income tax and older people
16. Income related benefits: income and capital
17. Housing Benefit and Council Tax Benefit
18. A brief guide to money benefits
19. Your state pension and carrying on working
20. National insurance contributions and qualifying for a pension
21. The Council Tax and older people
22. Legal arrangements for managing financial affairs
23. Help with incontinence
24. Housing schemes for older people where a capital sum is required
25. Income Support and the Social Fund
26. Travel information for older people
27. Arranging a funeral
28. Help with telephones
29. Finding residential and nursing home accommodation
30. Leisure education
31. Older workers
32. Disability and ageing: your rights to social services
33. Feeling safer at home and outside
34. Attendance Allowance and Disability Living Allowance

A maximum of five factsheets (whether a selection of different factsheets or multiple copies of one) will be sent free of charge from Age Concern England, Astral House, 1268 London Road, London SW16 4ER (Phone: 0181 679 8000; Fax: 0181 679 6069).

15
Health Checks: Do They Work?

It has been argued that health checks are a form of tertiary screening whose central purpose is to identify problems at an early stage so that they can be alleviated or contained. The rationale described earlier sounds sensible enough in theory but the important question is whether it works in practice. However, before reviewing published evidence on the effectiveness of health checks, an important point needs to be made. In the 30 years since screening was first introduced a change has taken place in the understanding of what can be achieved by tertiary screening. In the early days, doctors and health workers concentrated on looking for disease with the aim of cure or alleviation. The early lists of 'conditions found' illustrates this. Nowadays the emphasis is on identifying functional problems, such as poor mobility and vision failure, with the aim of preventing or reducing disability and handicap. This has made some of the earlier research, which focused solely on disease, less relevant.

When looking for evidence of effectiveness it is necessary first to confirm that unreported need does exist.

Evidence of Unreported Need

Evidence of the existence of unreported need has unfolded over a number of years and it is worth briefly reviewing some of the earlier work.

Williamson and his colleagues[1] were the first to recognize that amongst older people there was a high level of unmet need, as shown by the number of conditions unknown to health workers. They wrote:

> Most of the unknown disabilities were moderate to severe. This suggests that most old people do not report their complaints to their doctors until the condition is advanced. Thus a general practitioner service based on the self-reporting of illness is likely to be seriously handicapped in meeting the needs of old people. It might be argued that many of the unknown disabilities we detected are degenerative and progressive and therefore not amenable to curative measures. This is unjustifiably pessimistic: preventive medicine is at least as important in old age as it is in earlier life and there are few conditions in old people which medical and social measures will not help if applied soon enough. Indeed in many of these degenerative states further progress of disability can be arrested or at least slowed down.

Williams and colleagues[2] studied over 75-year-old patients in their practice; they confirmed unreported illness and showed that its importance was the effect it had on functional ability. They wrote: 'Most old people were active and enjoying life: 40% however were not in good effective health. The health visitor was invaluable in identifying these and some cases could be improved.'

Currie et al.[3] studying patients aged between 70 and 72 years, found a high number of disabilities – an average of 3.2 per patient – of which 20.5% were unreported to doctors. They wrote: 'Unreported disease in the elderly indicates failure to make contact and failure to ask the right question.'

Freedman et al.[4] screened the over 65-year-old patients in their practice and found a different picture. The degree of serious illness revealed was small but 2.8% of the patients needed to be referred to their GP for further investigation or for further treatment of conditions already diagnosed; 16.5% of patients needed more social care. Despite this it was concluded that wider use of such screening would not significantly improve the health of the population. The proportion of over 75-year-old patients was relatively low (women 34%; men 21%). Therefore the chances of detecting benefits might be expected to be lower than if the group had consisted entirely of over 75-year-olds.

Tulloch and Moore[5], as part of a randomized controlled trial of over 70-year-old patients, also studied their unreported needs. On screening and surveillance, 380 medical conditions were found among 295 patients (an average of one per patient); 144 (38%) of these were previously unrecognized. They wrote:

Unrecognized problems were found most often in the following systems: circulatory system (22%); musculoskeletal system (18%); nervous system and sense organs (13%). Conventional care initiated by the patient had not identified half of the circulatory conditions, 88% of the musculoskeletal disorders and 16% of problems with the nervous system and sense organs.

It is likely that the problem of deafness in older people is seriously underestimated. Herbst and Humphrey[6] found that 60% of a sample of over 70-year-old patients were partially deaf. They wrote: 'The problem lies rather in recognizing the existence of hearing problems where they are not spontaneously mentioned by the patient.'

Vetter et al.[7] studying the effects of health visitors working with older patients in general practice, found that a high number of referrals to services, including the GP, resulted.

Not only is medical need unreported, but also dental need. Tobias[8], investigating residents in sheltered accommodation, found a high need for dental treatment. She wrote:

Dental needs are often unreported. There is often a failure to recognize ill-fitting dentures and dental care is given low priority amongst elderly subjects compared with other social needs such as failing eyesight or chiropody.

White and Mulley[9], assessing foot problems in over 80-year-olds living at home, found that they were common. They wrote:

77% had difficulty cutting their toenails and 30% complained of pain in the feet. The most common foot problems were corns and calluses, abnormal nails, hallux valgus and other toe abnormalities.

McEwan *et al.*[10] investigated the effectiveness of a screening programme for people of 75 years and over. Although no comment was made about unreported need, their results were interesting in that they indicated the likely level of disability problems that occur in this age group. Examples included problems with teeth (14%), feet (18%), diet (12%), bladder (5%), vision (22%), hearing (20%) and bathing (19%).

Iliffe *et al.*[11] surveying patients aged 75 years and over, especially for social circumstances and mental state, showed that GPs under-diagnosed both dementia and depression. He wrote:

> The study showed that an annual assessment of elderly people as required by the new general practitioner contract would yield much new evidence of depression and dementia and assist in the identification of heavy drinkers. Up to 30% of patients aged 75 and over are likely to require further assessment on the basis of screening tests for depression and cognitive impairment.

Nevertheless, it remains unclear to what extent identification of these patients will lead to improvement in outcome for both them and their carers, and at what cost. It would appear then that we are beginning to get reliable information about the prevalence of disability amongst over 75-year-old persons and that there is non-reporting of problems by older people and under-diagnosis by GPs. The question still remains, however, of whether routine health checks make any difference.

Evidence of Effectiveness

A number of studies have been undertaken to determine the effectiveness of screening older people. The first three reported were descriptive, but the remainder have been randomized controlled studies.

Lowther *et al.*[12], in one of the first evaluations of early diagnostic services for older people were optimistic. They wrote:

> Clear evidence of improvement was found in half of the patients who carried out recommendations and this improvement was attributable to earlier diagnosis in 42% of cases. Including all patients examined, the proportion helped by early diagnosis at 18 to 30 months follow-up was 23%.

It was concluded that an offer of a routine examination to high risks groups is of benefit to older people and a form of medical practice that should be widely adopted.

Williams[13] followed up his screening of over 75-year-old patients and found that 20% were improved. He concluded that, 'The experience was worthwhile in that early detection reduced the period of suffering and without identification of disease, rational therapy could not be instituted.

Barber and Wallis[14], evaluating the benefits of continuing geriatric assessment, reported a comparison between a first and second survey carried out on the same population. They wrote:

Each patient had an average of 4.8 problems at the time of the second assessment. The number of active and unknown problems had fallen from 6.4 per patient at the initial assessment. The greatest improvements were found in such areas as clothing, bedding, heating, dentition, diet, vision and hearing, and the least in such aspects as dependency, home hazards and problems with a caring relative. We remain convinced that a continuing programme of geriatric assessment is valuable in general practice.

Tulloch and Moore[5], in their randomized controlled trial, found that the screening programme increased the use of social health services, but decreased the expected duration of a stay in hospital. They formed a firm impression that the screened patients were more comfortable and less disabled, although there was no unequivocal objective evidence of this. The patients, however, remained independent for longer.

Vetter et al.[7] studied the effect of health visitors working with older people in general practice and carried out a randomized controlled trial. The group studied were aged 70 years and over, who were patients from an urban practice and a rural practice. They wrote:

Independent assessments made at the beginning and end of the study showed that the health visitor in an urban practice had some impact on her case-load of patients. She provided more services for them, their mortality was reduced and their quality of life improved, although the last measure just failed to be statistically significant. The health visitor working in a rural practice had no such effect.

Carpenter and Demopoulos[15] wrote that:

Regular visiting of old people at home by non-professional volunteers completing a simple activities of daily living questionnaire is inexpensive, practical and has an impact on the population visited.

McKewan[10], commenting on a randomized controlled study of nurses undertaking a home visit to over 75-year-old patients, wrote: 'The main benefit of a screening process is that the special attention and education provided improves adaption to old age and an awareness of the support systems available.'

Hendriksen et al.[16], commenting on their randomized controlled study of regular visits from a health visitor, wrote:

Subjects in the intervention group benefited from the regular visits and the increased distribution of aids and modifications to their homes to which these led. The regular visits probably also produced an important increase in confidence.

Pathy et al.[17] carried out a randomized controlled study of case-finding and surveillance in patients aged 65 and over in general practice in South Wales. Problem identification was by postal questionnaire focusing on function. The study lasted three years. Mortality was significantly lower in the intervention group (18%) than in the controls (24%). The total number of hospital admissions did not differ between the intervention and the control groups, but duration of hospital stay was significantly shorter in the intervention group in the 65–74-year-old patients. Self-rated health status was superior in the intervention group. Pathy concluded that the use of a postal screening questionnaire with selective follow-up could favourably influence outcome and use of health care resources by older people living at home.

Stuck[18] and his colleagues reported a meta-analysis of controlled trials of comprehensive geriatric assessments. This was prompted by disagreement on the usefulness of such assessment in published individual trials. The analysis was carried out by pooling the results of 28 controlled trials comprising of 4959 subjects. The analysis did, however, suggest that comprehensive geriatric assessment programmes linking geriatric evaluation with strong long-term management are effective in improving survival and function in older persons. The most striking benefits accrued from hospital based studies, but the home visit health check programmes also showed some significant beneficial effects. Careful follow up is clearly important.

An important, but rather difficult randomized clinical trial was carried out in America. Rubenstein and his colleagues[19] assigned frail older inpatients with a high probability of nursing home placement to an innovative geriatric evalution unit intended to provide improved diagnostic assessment, therapy, rehabilitation, and placement. Patients randomly assigned to the experimental and control groups were equivalent at entry. At one year, patients who had been assigned to the geriatric assessment unit had much lower mortality than controls, and were less likely to have initially been discharged to a nursing home, or to have spent any time in a nursing home during the follow-up period. The control group of patients had substantially more acute care hospital days, nursing home days and acute care hospital readmissions. Patients in the assessment unit were significantly more likely to have improvement in functional status and morale than controls. Direct costs for institutional care were lower for the experimental group, especially after adjustment for survival. It was concluded that geriatric evaluation units could provide substantial benefits for appropriate groups of older patients over and above the benefits of traditional hospital approaches. This study is widely quoted as confirming the benefits of assessment.

The conclusions are therefore mixed. Some earlier studies did show health benefit, but these have not always been confirmed. Almost all comment on the improvement in quality of life. There have been variations in the type of screening procedures used. Often the initial screen has been undertaken by health visitors or nurses, who may differ in their experience and skill and it is difficult to compare individual studies. However, the evidence for patients' benefit from comprehensive geriatric assessment seems to be growing.

An influential study on screening was carried out by the South East London Screening Study group[20], which involved a controlled trial of multiphasic screening in middle age. Results failed to show any benefit and the study has been used to argue against screening in general, but it is irrelevant to older people, as they were excluded, the cut-off age being 65 years. The 75 years and over age group have a much higher risk of disease than the rest of the population, the result of which is that positive cases of disease are greatly in excess of 'false positives' in this age group, thus increasing the efficiency of screening.

What is it safe to conclude from these studies? The over 75 age group has within it a substantial level of disability, not all of it reported. The case for routine health checks on the basis of cure of specific disease is unproven, although no satisfactory study on a large enough scale has ever been undertaken to disprove the assertion. There is a case for health checks on the basis of early identification leading to a better quality of life. All studies point in this direction.

The health checks that have been introduced in the 1990 GP contract have not been formally evaluated. There is an urgent need to do this. In the meantime the checks need to be carried out properly and efficiently. Poorly conducted health checks will achieve nothing.

Other Considerations

The terms 'screening' and 'tertiary prevention' have in some senses clouded the issue of health checks. More is involved than just the prevention of handicap and disability. If this can be proved to be an outcome, so much the better, but it will be some time before definitive evidence is available. There are other clearly demonstrable advantages to regular health checks for older people, although the way the 1990 contract has defined what should be done has not helped to make this clear. In the field of prevention, regular contact provides opportunities for primary and secondary prevention. Immunization against influenza for old people is recommended[21] and it can be argued that tetanus immunization is as necessary in older age as in younger age groups.

It is also recommended that pneumococcal immunization be considered in older people who have been in hospital with chest conditions. It is recommended that both breast screening and cervical cytology should be available to women well beyond the age of 65[22,23].

Health education is also valuable. Older persons should be encouraged to self-care, preserve autonomy and maintain social contacts. Advice about smoking, alcohol intake, diet, exercise and avoidance of accidents are all important in older age.

Many problems suffered by older people arise because of lack of information. The opportunity presented by regular contact with them to give information about the practice, the services available in the community, financial services and social services, should be used to the full.

The health check can also be looked at as part of a continuing care programme. Many older people have long-term medical conditions, which, in the normal course of care, require periodic surveillance. Review of medication, blood checks and so on, may be necessary to monitor existing conditions that are already being managed by the primary care team.

These additional objectives of the health checks for those aged 75 and over make it difficult to apply conventional tests for effective screening. Nevertheless, it should be possible to show that the checks effectively identify problems and that functional benefit follows. The health check must be reliable, acceptable to patients and of reasonable cost. Resources needed must be available. An evaluation programme must take these into account, but other benefits must not be ignored.

We now have a good idea of the prevalence of disability amongst over 75-year-old people in the community. We can predict the approximate percentage who will have particular problems, for example, vision (20–30%), hearing (20%), mobility (10–15%), mood (20-30%), cognition (5–10%), continence (10–15%), dressing (2–5%), bathing (30%), social support (10%) and medication problems (20–30%). This enables an assessor, when reviewing a series of checks, to get an idea of the efficiency of the assessment procedure.

For most of the above disabilities, some form of treatment is usually available; incontinence and depression are two examples of conditions where substantial help can often be given. The debate between care and cure frequently surfaces when dealing with older patients. Cure, especially when dealing with degenerative diseases, is not often possible, yet good care can make the life of the patient more tolerable and worthwhile. Health checks may identify incurable disabilities, but allow a programme for continuing care to be initiated. Care is the benefit here, not cure. Evaluation studies must take this outcome into account.

New Evidence

Since the introduction of the new contract in 1990, anecdotal evidence from GPs about the effectiveness of health screening for older people has been mixed. Comments have ranged from 'useless' to 'helpful'. The health promotion programme for those aged 75 years and over has been better received than other similar programmes for younger people. On the grounds of equity at least, older people deserve the same health promotion interest as other sections of the community.

Two publications have documented early experience of the health check programme. Jill Tremellen[24] evaluated the assessment scheme for people aged 75 by examining data that were collected from individual practices. Questionnaires were sent to doctors and practice nurses undertaking assessments and to a sample of older patients in the Wiltshire Family Health Services Authority. A random 2% sample of older patients was selected to answer the questions on patient satisfaction. Sixty-four per cent of the patients accepted the assessment offer. Doctors carried out 8786 assessments and nurses 10 779 assessments. Sixty-one per cent were carried out in the home, with nurses doing most of these. Nurses with extra qualifications identified the highest number of unmet needs (400 per 1000 visits).

Sixty-eight per cent of the doctors thought assessments unnecessary, whereas 52% of the nurses thought them important. Ninety-three per cent of patients found assessments useful. The doctors who undertook the assessments mainly opportunistically picked up few new problems. It was clear that nurses were much more enthusiastic but required training to fit them to do home visits confidently. Patients who were assessed found it worthwhile.

Brown et al.[25] looked at what had happened in a structured random selection of 20 practices in a FHSA area. These practices were visited to collect information on how assessments were organized and carried out. Three practices had performed no health checks. There was considerable variation in the way that assessments were organized and few of the practices had completed an assessment on all their patients during this time. Altogether, a total of 43% of patients assessed had a new problem that required action. It was concluded that the need for annual assessment should be kept under review and that adequate resources should be made available for the needs discovered. Again, improved training for practice nurses was thought to be needed. Brown et al.'s study therefore reconfirmed the existence of unmet and unreported need.

Nurses may be more aware of the benefits of such an exercise than doctors, and tend to be the members of the team who carry them out. The need for specific training is clear. No sensible business organization would introduce changes on the shop floor without ensuring that staff had received the appropriate training! Well resourced educational packages are now available in a format suitable for all members of the primary care team including social workers[26]. A cohesive approach to assessment in the community is urgently required.

Chew et al.[27] reported on a study, describing how the requirement to offer annual assessment was being implemented, what role was played by the FHSAs, how GPs and practice nurses viewed the assessment, and the experience and view of older people. The organizational aspects of the 75 years and over assessments were similar to those found in Nottinghamshire, with a variety of methods being employed. More than two-thirds of the GPs reported no or very few refusals or non-responders to invitations. Seventy-one per cent of doctors estimated that practices had assessed over 60% of their older patients in the first year. Twenty-six per cent of GPs reported that more than half of the assessments were done opportunistically. Fifty per cent reported that half or more of the assessments were carried out by practice nurses and, where nurses were involved, more were done at home.

Chew and colleagues found some interesting facts about the age 75 and over health check programme. Thirty per cent of GP respondents said that the assessment picked up one or more of the problems suggested. Only a small minority of GPs felt that any particular problem was often identified, but only 3% of GPs felt that they never identified new problems. Almost two-thirds of respondents said they rarely or never identified new problems relating to mental conditions. Those practices that conducted more of their assessments opportunistically were significantly less likely to identify new problems. Those practices that used practice nurses to do substantial proportions of assessments were more likely to identify new problems, except in mental conditions and medication. Practices that conducted a higher proportion of assessments in the patients' homes identified new problems more commonly. An increase in referral to community based health and social services was reported as a direct result of assessments. Most GPs were willing to make individual and aggregated data available to other parties and one-third reported auditing the process of assessment of patients aged 75 and over.

The GPs were asked about their views on the value of routine assessment of older people. One-third of the practices gave this assessment a high priority, but only 7% felt it to be of great value in improving the overall health of older people; 56% thought that it was of little or no value. However, most GPs felt the assessments were a way of providing advice and reassurance to this group of patients. GPs in practices where nurses conducted a large proportion of assessments were more likely to perceive them as useful. The doctors' perceptions of the extent to which older people welcomed assessments were strongly related to the ways in which they organized assessments and their perceptions of their value. More than two-thirds of GPs said they would continue to offer routine assessments to selected groups of patients, even if the requirement to do so was removed from the terms of service, but only 28% would offer them to all older people.

Interviews also took place with practice nurses. The assessments carried out by them tended to be longer than those done by GPs. Only 36% of nurses had been offered any training and less than one-third had actually received training relating to age 75 and over assessments. Half the nurses had written guidelines to assist them when carrying out the assessments. More nurses than GPs reported often picking up new problems at assessment, but only one nurse reported identifying new problems of mental condition. The majority of nurses, however, felt that routine assessments of those aged 75 and over were useful in many respects; three-quarters of nurses felt that they were of value in improving the overall health of older people and 20% thought they were of great value.

This study looked at the views of consumers and it was clear that older people were very positive about the idea of annual health checks; those who experienced them were equally positive about the reality. They did, however, seem to have little understanding of what was involved and the likely value. They were grateful for the GP's interest in them and were largely uncritical of the service provided. Of concern, however, is the discrepancy that appeared to exist between GPs' accounts of their performance on assessment for older people and the accounts of older people themselves. This may be because some patients had forgotten having been offered an assessment and others may have received an opportunistic assessment of which they were unaware. However, it does point to the need for increased systematic data to be collected. FHSA managers in the study expressed some reservations but most thought that the requirements should not be dropped from the GP terms of service, at least without some rigorous and widespread evaluation of its effectiveness.

From all these studies it is clear that many doctors and nurses need education on the most effective way of undertaking assessments on older people. The fact that early mental illness does not seem to be picked up is of concern. There is also some evidence that suggests that even when mental disorders are identified little is done to help or further evaluate the situation[11].

There is unpublished evidence that second and third year checks fail to reveal the same level of unmet need. This is to be expected, but closer examination of the evidence shows that, although there is reduced yield in the younger members of the group, in the 85 years and over age group the yield is steady. If changes are to be made in the programme, it would be sensible to examine the younger group less frequently but maintain annual checks for those aged 85 and over. Perhaps some more specific targeting could also be introduced.

Professor Shah Ebrahim (1993, personal communication) has suggested that the effectiveness of health checks for older people should be examined under a series of different headings that take account of the variety of ways in which benefit might be measured. These are as follows:

- *Effectiveness:* Randomized controlled trials have demonstrated benefits, including a reduction in death rates, reduced hospital and long term care institutional bed use, improved morale and consumer satisfaction.

- *Efficiency:* Only one trial has attempted to evaluate the cost-effectiveness of screening and demonstrated that the savings in hospital bed use were more than sufficient to pay for the screening team[19].

- *Appropriateness:* Early detection of problems is an appropriate activity, since many so-called 'well' older people have treatable disabilities.

- *Satisfaction:* There is little doubt that patients like the attention given during a health check and it is rarely reviewed as an intrusion.

- *Equity:* Health promotion and screening programmes abound for 'well' women and men at ages when the incidence of serious disease is trivial compared with those in their 70s and 80s.

- *Empowerment:* The health checks provide a model of partnership between professional and patient, with the definition of problems and their solutions arrived at in a dialogue.

- *Education:* The need to ensure that those who do health checks for older people are properly trained is one of the best opportunities for post-qualification education that has ever occurred.

More work clearly needs to be done, but there is probably enough positive evidence to make it worthwhile continuing with a health check programme for older people. By the end of the century the care of those aged 75 years and over may present the nation's greatest health challenge[28].

References

1. Williamson J, Stokoe IH, Gray S, *et al.* (1964) Old people at home: their unreported needs. *Lancet* i: 1117–20.

2. Williams EI, Bennett FM, Nixon JV, *et al.* (1972) A socio-medial study of patients over 75 in general practice. *Br Med J* ii: 445–8.

3. Currie G, MacNeill RM, Walker JG, et al. (1974) Medical and social screening of patients aged 70 to 72 by an urban general practice health team. Br Med J ii: 108–11.

4. Freedman GR, Charlewood JE, Dodd PA. (1978) Screening the aged in general practice. J R Coll Gen Pract 28: 421–5.

5. Tulloch AJ, Moore V. (1979) A randomized controlled trial of geriatric screening and surveillance in general practice. J R Coll Gen Pract 29: 733–42.

6. Herbst KG, Humphrey C. (1981) Prevalence of hearing impairment in the elderly living at home. J R Coll Gen Pract 31: 155–60.

7. Vetter NJ, Jones DA, Victor CR. (1984) Effect of health visitors working with elderly patients in general practice: a randomized controlled trial. Br Med J 288: 369–72.

8. Tobias B. (1988) Dental aspects of an elderly population. Age Ageing 17: 103–10.

9. Mulley GP, White EG. (1989) Footcare for very elderly people: a community survey. Age Ageing 18: 275–8.

10. McEwan RT, Davison N, Forster DP, et al. (1990) Screening elderly people in primary care: a randomised controlled trial. Br J Gen Pract 40: 94–7.

11. Iliffe S, Haines A, Gallivan S, et al. (1991) Assessment of elderly people in general practice: 1. Social circumstances and mental state. Br J Gen Pract 41: 9–12.

12. Lowther CP, McLeod RDM, Williamson J. (1970) Evaluation of early diagnostic services for the elderly. Br Med J 3: 275–7.

13. Williams EI. (1974) A follow-up of geriatric patients after socio-medical assessment. J R Coll Gen Pract 24: 341–6.

14. Barber JH, Wallis JB. (1978) The benefits to an elderly population of continuing geriatric assessment. J R Coll Gen Pract 28: 428–33.

15. Carpenter GI, Demopoulos GR. (1990) Screening the elderly in the community: controlled trial of dependency surveillance using a questionnaire administered by volunteers. Br Med J 300: 1253–6.

16. Hendriksen C, Lund E, Stromgard E. (1984) Consequences of assessment and intervention among elderly people: a three year randomized controlled trial. Br Med J 289: 1522–4.

17. Pathy MSJ, Bayer A, Harding K, et al. (1992) Randomised trial of case finding and surveillance of elderly people at home. Lancet 340: 890–93.

18. Stuck AE, Siu AL, Wielland GD, et al. (1993) Comprehensive geriatric assessment: a meta-analysis of controlled trials. Lancet 342: 1032–6.

19. Rubenstein LZ, Josephson KR, Weilland GD, et al. (1984) Effectiveness of a geriatric evaluation unit. Eng J Med 311: 1664–70.

20. The South East London Screening Study Group. (1977) A controlled trial of multiplastic screening in middle age: results of the South East London Screening Study. Int J Epidemiol 6: 357–63.

21. Chief Medical Officer. (1989) Letter to Family Practitioner Committees for circulation to all general practitioners, regional medical officers and district medical officers, 19th September. PLCMO(89)6. Department of Health, London.

22. Forrest P, chairman. (1986) Breast cancer screening. Report to Health Ministers of England, Wales, Scotland and Northern Ireland by a working group. HMSO, London.

23. Fletcher A. (1990) Screening for cancer of the cervix in elderly women. *Lancet* **335**: 97–9.

24. Tremellen J. (1992) Assessment of patients aged 75 and over in general practice. *Br Med J* **305**: 621–4.

25. Brown K, Williams EI, Groom L. (1992) Health checks on patients 75 years and over in Nottinghamshire after the new GP contract. *Br Med J* **305**: 619–21.

26. Williams EI. (1992) *Over 75: care assessment and health promotion package*. Radcliffe Medical Press, Oxford.

27. Chew CA, Wilkin D, Glendenning C. (1994) Annual assessments of patients aged 75 years and over: general practitioners' and practice nurses' views and experiences. *Br J Gen Pract* **44**: 263–7.

28. Harris A. (1992) Health checks for people over 75 [editorial]. *Br Med J* **305**: 599–600.

16
The Older Person in Family Medicine

Community health care of older people in the UK largely takes place in health centres or in doctors' surgeries. In other countries there are variations, but the essential processes of care remain the same. For non-ambulant patients, care is available in their own homes or in nursing and residential homes. The high numbers of older people using these services make them an important component of primary care. This chapter will consider the patterns of care in the community and some clinical aspects of that care, and discuss organizational policies underlying the planning of such care for older people in the community.

Older people tend to present with a wide variety of problems and receive a diversity of treatments, investigations and referrals. A good deal is known about the management of patients in hospital and the treatment they receive, but there is relatively little information about the treatment that is received by patients in the community.

Patterns of Care

Drawing on data collected during a study in primary care carried out in Manchester, Wilkin and Williams[1] began to fill this gap. The research was based on information collected from 200 GPs from all consultations occurring on a representative sample of 15 working days. Data on some 90 000 consultations were analysed, of which 20 000 were with people over 65 years of age[2]. This analysis will now be discussed in some detail.

Distribution of Consultations by Age

The distribution of consultations by age was compared with the distribution of the total population of the study area, as indicated in the 1981 census; a predictable pattern was observed. The age group 0–14 years made up 20% of the total population, but only 17% of consultations. At the other end of the age spectrum, this was reversed, so that those aged 75 years or over made up 6% of the population, but 8% of consultations. However, there was a gradual increase from middle age to old age in numbers consulting GPs. There was no evidence of a sharp change at the age of 65. The overall pattern was similar to that reported in the National Morbidity Study for 1971/2, which showed a total of 17% of consultations with patients in the over-65 years age group, compared with 19% in the Manchester studies[1,2]. The fact that there was an increased proportion in the later investigation indicates that the contribution of older people to the work of the GP will increase as the number of such people in the population rises.

Disease Categories

Data were available from the study on the relative importance of different diagnostic categories; these changed sharply with age in the adult population (Table 16.1). Circulatory and musculoskeletal disorders became progressively more important with increasing age, whilst infectious disease, mental disease, genitourinary disease, skin disorders and accidents all decreased in proportion to the total case mix. Such change was even more pronounced than is suggested in the table, because the presentation concealed considerable variations within the broad International Classification of Diseases (ICD) categories[3]. Thus, not only was there an increase in the proportion of endocrine and metabolic diseases, but, within this category, the proportion of consultations for diabetes mellitus increased. For the 15–54 age group, 19% of diagnoses in the category 'endocrine and metabolic disorders' were for diabetes, but for the 75 years and over age group this figure rose to 54%. Although the relative importance of psychiatric disorders declines with age, GPs were dealing with more chronic mental problems in older people. Amongst the age 85+ group, 52% of psychiatric diagnoses were for dementia and only 22% for anxiety or depression. For respiratory

Table 16.1: Diagnostic categories by age group (%).

ICD category	Age group				Total
	15–54	55–64	65–74	75+	
Infectious and parasitic	7.7	3.4	2.9	2.3	5.7
Neoplasms	0.9	2.3	2.7	3.1	1.6
Endocrine, nutritional and metabolic	2.3	3.5	3.3	3.1	2.7
Blood	0.7	0.6	1.3	2.1	0.9
Mental	9.3	9.3	7.6	7.3	8.9
Central nervous system	6.1	6.6	6.9	7.1	6.4
Circulatory system	4.6	19.7	24.4	25.9	12.2
Respiratory system	14.5	15.7	15.2	12.0	14.5
Digestive system	4.9	5.7	5.1	5.0	5.1
Genitourinary	6.6	3.1	2.5	2.4	5.0
Skin	6.0	3.8	3.4	3.2	5.0
Musculoskeletal	7.6	13.0	12.6	13.3	9.8
Signs and symptoms	2.3	2.3	2.5	4.0	2.5
Accidents, injury, etc.	6.7	4.2	3.4	3.7	5.5
Supplementary	19.0	6.8	6.1	5.4	13.7
Total number (100%)	45 846	12 454	11 154	8278	77 732

Source: Wilkin and Williams, 1986[1].

disorders, minor respiratory tract infection became progressively less important with age, whilst acute and chronic bronchitis became more important. Bronchitis accounted for 14% of diagnoses in this category in the 15–54 age group, and 50% for the 75 years and over group. In the category of 'signs and symptoms', 36% of the over 75-year-olds were described as suffering from senility or senescence. Interestingly, the proportion of consultations for marital and social problems was low for all age groups. There was no evidence that GP recorded more social problems amongst older patients. The proportion of patients with more than one diagnosis increased from 14% in the 15–54 age group to 20% for those aged 55–64, 23% for the 65–74 age group and 24% for those aged over 75. Older patients were therefore more commonly presenting to GPs with a complex inter-action of health problems. The types of problems presented to the GP according to age revealed predictable patterns[2]. Coughs, colds and sore throats were 45% of all symptoms presented by young children (0–5 years), but only 14% of those presented by older people. In contrast, muscular aches and pains constituted less than 10% of symptoms amongst children and teenagers (0–17 years) but 23% amongst older people. Skin infections and irritation were most common amongst teenagers (15% of all symptoms) and least common in older people (5% of all symptoms). No only do these patterns reflect possible variations in the prevalence of these symptoms at different ages, they also reflect attitudes toward symptoms when they occur. Willingness to tolerate particular symptoms is dependent on a wide range of social factors and on expectations of what is normal; these turn out to be age-related. Thus parents are understandably concerned about the possible effects of coughs and colds in small children, although they may think nothing of the same symptoms in themselves. Older people who may be suffering from symptoms of long-term chronic illness would be less likely to go to the GP with apparently minor symptoms.

Patterns of Care

In the light of these changes in the case-mix mentioned previously, it is hardly surprising that differences were found in the pattern of care provided for different age groups (Table 16.2). The proportion of new consultations (patient initiated rather than doctor initiated) declined with age so that amongst much older

Table 16.2: The pattern of care as a percentage of all consultations in the study population in one year.

Age group	New cases	Home visits	Prescription	Lab test	Consultant referral	Other referral
15–54	55	5	67	5	7	2
55–64	39	8	74	3	6	1
65–74	37	20	80	3	6	2
75+	33	47	75	2	6	3

Source: Wilkin and Williams, 1986[1].

patients, two-thirds of all consultations were for follow-up care. However, this change did not occur sharply at the age of 65. There was a steady upward trend in the proportion of follow-up work done with increasing age. At the same time, the proportion of consultations conducted in the patients' home increased, but, in this case, there was a marked difference between the 55–64 age group and the 65–74 age group, and again for the 75+ age group. This continued into the 85+ age group, where two-thirds of consultations were home visits.

Older patients (age 55+) were more likely to receive a prescription than young adults, but this pattern did not continue into the 75+ age group. This may reflect an increase in the level of surveillance and follow-up for much older people, since such consultations often required no further treatment. Often complex multiple pharmacology amongst older patients might suggest a need for more investigation. It was therefore surprising to find that laboratory utilization declined from 5% of all consultations in the 15–54 age group, to 2% for the over 75 age group. Although older people are generally known to be heavy users of hospital services, there is no evidence of greater propensity for GPs to refer older patients. Indeed, referrals to consultants declined very slightly with age in contrast with referrals to district nurses and social services, which increased, but even amongst the 75+ age group, referrals to all other agencies combined amounted to only one-half the level of those to consultants.

Variations in Patterns of Care

There was an enormous variation between GPs. Figure 16.1 shows consultation rates and indicates the extent of this variation. The overall rate for older people was 4.6 consultations per year compared with 2.9 for those aged less than 65

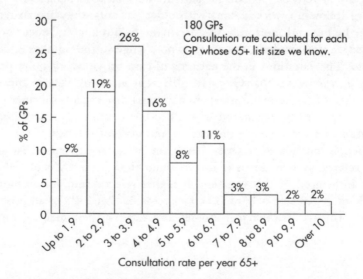

Figure 16.1: Consultation rate for patients of 65+ years.

years, but for more than one-quarter of GPs the consultation rate for older people was less than three contacts per year. A similar proportion saw their older
patients more than six times a year. Home visits were equally varied. Sixteen per
cent of the GPs did less than five home visits per week, whilst 15% did more
than 30. Referral rates also showed similar variation; the average rate was 6%, but
13% of the GPs had rates higher than 10% and a similar proportion had rates
below 2%.

Conclusions

Several important findings came out of this study. Whilst it is almost a truism to
say that older age does not begin at 65, the very fact that this administrative
dividing line is usually adopted for practical and research purposes tends to gen-
erate a perception of older age as a discrete phenomenon. Comparisons between
people of over 65 years and the rest of the population appear to reveal sharp differences, but the data from this study showed a more gradual transition, in which
the 55–64 age group has more in common with the 65–74 group than with the
younger adult population.

The general point can be made that ageing is a biological, psychological and
social process that is only turned into a discreet entity by administrative regula-
tions, for example, retirement age, additional payments for GPs for patients of
75 years and over, and specialist geriatric hospital services. Whilst there are
reasonable grounds for such arrangements, there is no necessity to reinforce the
negative stereotypes of older age that are all too common already. At least in primary care it should be possible to treat ageing as the variable process the
evidence clearly shows it to be, and treating patients as individuals in the wider
context of their lives.

However, the pattern of GP care for patients does clearly change with increasing age. More follow-up work is done with older patients; they are visited more
often in their homes and more referrals are made to nursing and social services.
Less investigative work is done, but there is no change in the number of referrals
to consultants. The variations in the patterns of care provided for older people is
very striking and indicates that GPs have different views of what is appropriate
for their patients. Older people can experience gross differences in primary health
care if they happen to be registered with different doctors. Not only does this
have implications for older people themselves, but also for the rest of the services.
Individual people do not necessarily have similar access to specialist services
through the referral system. Little is known about the effectiveness of GP care or
whether it is influenced by this variation. A higher referral rate, for example, may
not mean a higher standard of care. The fact remains that 94% of all people over
the age of 65 still live in their own homes and receive their medical care from
GPs.

Record Keeping

Good care of older people requires accurate and appropriate records. Some practices conduct a review of the records of patients when they reach their 75th birthday, discarding redundant documents and starting a new system in line with the health check programme for 75-year-olds and over. An age/sex register of patients over 65 years is essential in planning preventive and anticipatory care, for there is no reason why health checks should not also be done opportunistically in patients who are aged over 65. Indeed, the early detection of, for example, Alzheimer's disease, is valuable in planning care. Some practices also keep a register of the attendance of all older persons with doctor, nurse or health visitor and for repeat prescriptions, so that information is available about those who do not attend. It is likely that non-attenders will be in good health. Admissions and discharges of older people to hospital, welfare and nursing-homes can also be recorded in the register; this enables more effective care to be given during these periods.

It is also helpful to maintain a disease or disability register. This can be done for the over 65 year population or, indeed, for the whole practice. The number of different disabilities recorded may vary between 10 and 50, but it is probably wise to limit to a relatively small number of important conditions. This is so that the task does not become too daunting! Examples would include diabetes mellitus, dementia, vision problems, immobility due to arthritis, stroke and heart failure. These registers are particularly useful when undertaking an audit of care for particular diseases. It is interesting to consider what proportion of patients in a practice is disabled. In a questionnaire survey of GPs carried out in 1983, the author found that most of the responding doctors thought that it was less than 15% and that most of these disabled were in the over-65 age group[4]. The doctors were asked to state which type of patients they considered to be disabled. Table 16.3 lists these with the percentage of doctors mentioning each category. Included in

Table 16.3: Doctors' perception of disability: conditions mentioned spontaneously in response to the question, 'Which specific groups of patients do you regard as disabled?'

Disability	Extent of disability	Doctors (%)
Blindness	Complete or partial	77.3
Mental problem	Congenital or acquired incapacitating mental illness	76.6
Mobility problem	Arthritis of all types	76.6
Deafness	Complete or partial	64.1
Cardiovascular disease	Heart failure, angina, claudication	56.3
Respiratory disease	Obstructive airways disease, bronchitis	52.3
Children with congenital defect		50.8
Stroke		51.6
Neurological disease	Multiple sclerosis, parkinsonism	42.2
Amputation		33.6
Effects of trauma		21.1
Incontinence	Urinary or faecal	5.5
Other	Included diabetes, epilepsy, stoma, speech defect, social problems	39.8

Source: Williams, 1983[4].

the group 'other' was disability caused by social impairment, which included environmental, economic, cultural and education causes. The list gives some idea of the sort of categories that could be included in a disability register.

The record system used by most GPs is the 'Lloyd George' envelope. This is highly unsatisfactory but the move to A4 sized records has been slow and relatively few GPs have this system. The review at 75 years or earlier may be an opportunity for changing to A4 records so that older people in the practice have this type of record. Clearly, the letters and investigations need to be filed separately in the notes in date order. Problem lists, both active and inactive, are very useful. An up to date therapy list is also essential, especially when repeat prescriptions are being issued. Some practices have treatment cards that the patient holds; these have advantages especially where several health workers are involved. They do, however, need to be kept up to date and accurate. This is now frequently computerized. An important inclusion in the records is details of any assessments that have been carried out and a provision for updating these assessments. Who should have access to the note system is often debated and patients themselves also have rights in this matter. Most practices would expect key health workers to use and contribute to the records. The introduction of computers into practices had made many of these tasks easier.

Principles of Medication

Most doctors are aware of the risk of prescribing large numbers of drugs for older patients, but they are also aware of the high demand for these drugs to alleviate multiple symptomatology. The pressure on the doctor to give symptomatic treatment can be quite considerable. At the same time, most doctors, nurses and social workers have had the experience of finding an older person at home with a large number of bottles of tablets on the mantelpiece, only to discover, when moving into the kitchen or bathroom, an equally large number of bottles on shelves and in cabinets. The older person is all too often unaware of what these tablets are for; many of them have been in the house for a long time and their use is frequently quite irrational and haphazard. This is not confined to patients at home. When visiting residential or nursing homes, it is remarkable to see the long lists of drugs pinned up in the office. There is thus a situation where large quantities and types of medicines are prescribed for older people, and it is constantly necessary to review the medication being taken by them.

Cartwright and Smith[5] described a study that looked at the medicines prescribed for and taken by a nationally representative sample of older people. An increasing proportion of all prescribed medicines now goes to people aged over 65 (Figure 16.2). In 1985, the proportion of older people in the population was 18% and they received 39% of the prescription items dispensed. While the numbers of all prescription items for all ages increased by 8% between 1977 and 1984, there was a slight fall in the prescribing for the non-older age group. Larger changes were seen for medicines in certain therapeutic groups

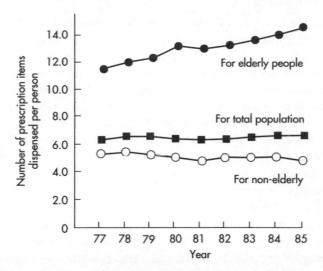

Figure 16.2: Recent trends in prescribing. Source: Cartwright and Smith, 1988[5].

Table 16.4: Some trends in prescribing by therapeutic class.

Therapeutic class	No. preparations dispensed			Proportional change (%)
	1977	1980	1984	1977–84
Sedatives and tranquillizers	20 836	18 920	13 622	−35
Hypnotics	14 015	13 626	13 471	−4
Analgesics–minor	17 578	17 409	17 958	+2
Antidepressants	6715	6263	6185	−8
Preparations acting on the heart	12 763	16 922	19 851	+56
Diuretics	15 549	19 538	21 700	+40
Antihypertensives	5603	6081	7972	+42
Preparations prescribed for rheumatism	13 595	15 839	17 915	+32
All other prescriptions	167 701	168 809	180 138	+7
All groups	295 656	303 334	320 543	+8

Source: Cartwright and Smith, 1988[5].

(Table 16.4). It is interesting to note that for all ages the number of prescriptions for sedatives and tranquillizers decreased substantially.

The study found that, on average, older people were taking just under two prescribed medicines; roughly one-third were taking none, one-third were taking one or two, and one-third took three or more. Encouragingly, nearly three-fifths of the study population regarded their health for their age as excellent or good. These older people understood at least something of the purpose of nearly all the prescribed medicines they were taking and said they found most of them very helpful. The majority, three-quarters, of the older people took their prescribed medicines as advised. However, the study did identify some discouraging features, particularly in the information that older people were given about their medicines; also, the record-keeping of doctors and the supervision that was given to the patients was not satisfactory. Labelling of the prescribed medicines was also found to be unsuitable in form. Cartwright and Smith[5] gave some specific recommendations that included the need to improve record-keeping and the desirability of greater involvement of pharmacists in increasing the effectiveness of prescribing. More education for trainee GPs and medical students was advocated. They concluded that labelling of medicines should be clearer and that it would be helpful if written information about their medicines was given to patients.

In older age, physiological changes occur that can affect the action of drugs in the body. Absorption normally takes place from the gastrointestinal tract and ageing may reduce the blood flow to these areas and also the number of absorbing cells. There is no direct evidence, however, that absorption is seriously reduced in older age. Drugs are normally metabolized in the liver, where they are broken down to inactive forms prior to excretion via the kidneys. Some drugs are excreted unchanged. In older age, the liver and kidneys become less efficient in undertaking these processes. This leads to slower elimination of drugs from the body; they therefore remain active for longer periods. This natural physiological ageing process can be augmented by disease. Renal and hepatic illness can reduce drug elimination, as can conditions such as heart failure or dehydration. Reduction in overall body size associated with older age may affect the distribution of drugs in the body. Tissues may alter in their response to certain drugs, a good example being barbiturates, where the sedative effect on the brain may be increased; fortunately these drugs are seldom used today. Older people, therefore, can be expected to be more sensitive to drugs and suffer more often from side-effects. Drug interactions may also be increased.

Despite these general considerations, it is hard in practice to determine whether physiological changes in an individual patient will have been enough to cause increased liability to side-effects or whether the cause is incorrect dosage. Chronological age may outstrip biological age and an older person may retain perfectly efficient physiological mechanisms. Nevertheless, the danger must be appreciated and a watch kept for possible overtreatment.

Not all drugs are affected by these changes. In general, preparations used as replacement therapy need to be given in normal doses and, indeed, there is sometimes the danger of undertreatment. For example, in thyroid deficiency it might be that too low a dose of thyroxine is being given to achieve the ideal therapeutic effect. Without being aware of these problems, the doctor is at risk of wrongly prescribing for his or her older patients; this can be made more difficult by self-prescribing. Sometimes large numbers of proprietary preparations are taken alongside prescribed medicines. There is even a chance that older people are given drugs by friends and relatives that were originally prescribed for other people! Members of ethnic groups have their own cultural remedies that are taken alongside medically prescribed preparations.

There is also the problem of whether older people take their prescribed treatment properly. Some do not understand the tablet-taking and, as a high proportion of older people are responsible for taking their own medicines, it is hardly surprising that many do not take their treatment as intended by the doctor. This is particularly true of patients living alone and who are not receiving any regular supervision.

Under these circumstances, problems with adverse drug reactions are not uncommon. This has been highlighted by Williamson[6] who carried out an investigation for the British Geriatrics Society into admission to 42 hospital geriatric departments. Of the admissions, 2.8% were necessitated solely by the adverse effects of drugs and 12.4% of the patients had adverse reactions of some kind. It appears that all doctors are faced with the problem, as Williamson found that the level of adverse reactions amongst the patients being referred to geriatric wards from other hospital departments was the same as in patients being admitted from their homes.

It is of course of prime importance to make an accurate diagnosis if effective treatment is to be given. Difficulties arise in older people because of the presence of several illnesses, which can often interact with each other. Some diseases are not amenable to treatment and some are perhaps better left alone. The doctor should have realistic aims when treating older people, and the effect of the drug given must be clear and have a purpose. This often means setting priorities so that perhaps only the most important conditions and those most likely to respond are treated. A minimum number of drugs should be used and, if more are necessary, they should be given for as short a time as possible. Other treatments, apart from pharmacological, are sometimes possible. Occasionally, changes in diet, attention to social difficulties and simple physiotherapy can be just as effective as drug treatment. Arranging twice-weekly visits to lunch centres can dramatically improve a lonely older person's outlook and appetite. Oedema can disappear once mobility is restored. Above all, the reassuring presence and attention of the doctor is often therapeutic.

The doctor should know the pharmacological action of the drugs used and should be aware also of the correct doses for an older person and the possible side-effects and interactions. It is useful to adjust the dose according to the patient's body weight, as with children. The use of placebos and the purely symptomatic treatment of illness is sometimes necessary, but this should be kept to a minimum and preferably used only for a limited period. Drugs that are likely to be beneficial should not be withheld just because a patient is older, but sometimes it is obvious that the effect of the drug on the patient is worse than the symptoms being treated, and then it is better to stop treatment. In practice, it is sometimes more important and beneficial to take patients off treatment than to start a new course of tablets.

Many problems would be alleviated by keeping to the general principles of prescribing just outlined, but there are also organizational difficulties, an obvious one being the practice of repeat prescribing. An older person on a drug needs reviewing at suitable intervals. Side-effects may arise that the patient him/herself will not report. Shaw and Opit[7] studying the medication of 127 randomly selected patients aged over 70, found that about half the patients were on long-term treatment, 19 had had no recorded contact with the family doctor for six months or longer, and examination of the patient by a nurse suggested that three might be suffering from drug toxicity. The concluded that reliance on self-referral of side-effects by older patients was unsafe. Periodic review of older patients on long-term treatment is therefore essential.

Drug compliance in older people can also be improved by education. Many devices have been recommended for improving patients' understanding of their medication. Instructions can be written down or transferred on to a calendar. A tablet-identification card is helpful to augment written instructions. Supervisors can give the patient a daily supply in a small box and check later to see if they have been taken. Special packaging can be used with tablets marked for each day. Pharmacists can be helpful in giving older patients specific and clear instructions. The habit of hoarding tablets can be reduced when the date of dispensing is noted on the label. A difficulty arises sometimes when patients are given tablets that have an unfamiliar appearance because they have been produced by a different drug manufacturer. The patient thinks this is a different drug and treats it with some suspicion; this is particularly true of patients discharged from hospital. Their treatment needs to be carefully reviewed by the doctor and a check made that the patient is taking the tablets as advised. The difference between approved generic names and proprietary names is also confusing for an older person. A co-operation card held by the patient, showing the current treatment is useful in co-ordinating advice and therapy. The patient should be asked directly about any other medicines or pills that he/she is taking. Simplicity of treatment is essential; if one tablet can take the place of three, so much the better.

It is helpful for doctors to check on their own trends in prescribing by an annual review of their prescribed drugs using PACT (Prescribing Analysis and Cost) data from the Department of Health.

Alternative Medicine

Sometimes patients use alternative or complementary help often with their doctor's knowledge and support. The general attitude of the medical profession has changed considerably towards these alternatives and many doctors now practise some form of alternative medicine themselves; others are ready to refer. This reflects a wider understanding and acceptance of the benefits of alternative forms of treatment. The range of possibilities is very wide. Older people most often use the services of an osteopath, a chiropractor, an acupuncturist and, occasionally, a hypnotist. The contribution of other healers to the collective well-being of older people is welcome too. The effectiveness of their work should, however, be evaluated so that this contribution can be documented.

Investigations

Despite the fact that GPs tend not to undertake many investigations in older people, it is nevertheless an important possible outcome of a consultation and it is necessary to have an understanding of the interpretation of the investigations performed.

Biochemistry

There has been a considerable increase in the number of biochemical tests available during the past decade, and it is now usual to receive a comprehensive profile of such tests as a routine. It was initially impossible to find details of the normal range of these values for older people. These are now available in textbooks of geriatric medicine. Variations may occur in local pathological departments and their norms should be consulted where necessary. Most of the differences associated with older age in the normal values of biochemical tests, if they occur at all, are not usually of practical importance. Serum albumin tends to fall with age but not by very much. The only range that is markedly different in older age is that of serum phosphate, which falls considerably in older men, so that the appropriate range is lower than for young men and, indeed, for older women. The blood urea level is not always indicative of renal function in older people. A substantial reduction of renal function can still give normal blood urea.

Although older age itself has only minor effects, there are a number of other factors that influence the levels. These include illness itself, renal impairment, the effects of multiple pathology and disturbances due to drugs. When interpreting results, account has to be taken of any of these conditions that happen to be present. It is useful to inform the biochemist of coexistent factors and to discuss the results. Many of the effects produced by these conditions are complicated. Another problem is the way in which diseases present. Sometimes diseases presenting atypically only come to light as a result of wide profile tests. Biochemical tests can, therefore, be used for screening, but, because of variability in norms, special care is needed. Consultation with the clinical pathologist is essential.

Laboratory data in normal older age, and in sick older people are summarized in Tables 16.5[8,9] and 16.6.

Table 16.5: Laboratory data in normal older age. (Modified from Hodkinson, 1992[8], in Farnsworth and Mulley, 1992[9]; reproduced with permission[9].)

Parameters decreased	Parameters unchanged	Parameters increased
Serum calcium (men)	Serum sodium	Blood urea
Serum phosphate (men)	Serum bicarbonate	Serum creatinine
Total thyroxine	Serum chloride	Serum potassium
Free thyroxine	Serum magnesium	Plasma glucose
Serum iron	Serum AST	Serum uric acid
TIBC	Serum ALT	Serum calcium (women)
Serum albumin	Serum 5'nucleotidase	Serum phosphate (women)
White blood cell count	Serum creatine kinase	Serum ALP
	Serum amylase	Serum globulins
	Haemoglobin	ESR
	Red cell indices	Plasma viscosity
	Coagulation indices	C-reactive protein
		Fibrinolytic activity

Table 16.6: Laboratory data in sick older people. (Modified from Hodkinson, 1992[8], in Farnsworth and Mulley, 1992[9]; reproduced with permission[9].)

Parameters decreased	Parameters increased
Serum sodium	Blood urea
Total thyroxine	Free thyroxine index
Tri-iodothyronine	Reverse T_3
Serum albumin	Serum albumin
	Globulins (eg TBG, transferrin)

Haematology

The quantity and quality of red cells do not change significantly with age, although the number of white blood cells may decrease, mainly due to a reduction in the lymphocyte count. It has been suggested that the erythrocyte sedimentation rate (ESR) increases with advancing age and that this is physiological. The range of normal values in older age is, however, uncertain. Perhaps a reason for this is the difficulty of identifying an unequivocally healthy older population. In a study of an age and sex matched sample of 200 subjects aged 60–89, Griffiths *et al.*[10] have found that an ESR exceeding 19 mm/h in men and 22 mm/h in women warrants further investigation. Anaemia of any kind may result in an increase in ESR and this needs to be taken into account. Importantly, an ESR of 100 mm/h or more is commonly associated with both giant cell arteritis and polymyalgia rheumatica.

The question arises of what should be the normal level of haemoglobin in older people of both sexes. There have, however, been a wide range of values found in surveys of older persons, but it is suggested that levels of 13 g/dl for males and 12 g/dl for females are the lower ranges of normal haemoglobin levels.

Microbiology and Virology

The most common bacteriological investigations undertaken in older people in general practice are on urine. The incidence of bacteriuria increases with advancing age and is more common in females, both young and old, but it is markedly more common in older males when compared with young males. Much of this bacteriuria is asymptomatic, although there are causes for its presence. For a full discussion of this important subject a textbook of geriatric medicine should be consulted.

Practice Policy Towards Care of Older People

Much of this book is concerned with the organization of services for older people in the community, particularly in primary health care units or general practices.

The objectives of such care have already been outlined (*see* Chapter 10). It is clear that care providers need to have a policy when planning how those objectives will be achieved. In other words, there is a need, as always, for a plan. This section will look at aspects of care which may be included in such a plan.

Overall Policy

The first essential is to accept a positive attitude towards older people. They present difficulties that challenge both health and social workers to the limit; there is a tendency, because of this, to become uninterested. Solving these problems can be very satisfying and this should be emphasized when advocating positive attitudes. It is impossible to categorize 'older people' as a single homogeneous group. In fact heterogeneity is the rule; chronological and biological age do not go hand in hand. Older people are people like everyone else and should not be treated differently just because of age. Nevertheless, older people do have special needs and these should be catered for in a practice plan. Examples would include higher levels of disability, more of them living alone than in other age groups, and a tendency to under-report illness and social problems.

There are many practical issues that need to be considered. The health centre or surgery building needs to be older person friendly; in particular, ease of access must be a priority. Ground floor consulting rooms and toilets need to be available; the toilets need to be usable by disabled persons. Surgery times need to be convenient for older people to attend, taking into account the timing of public transport. The waiting room needs to be free of hazards. Information about facilities offered needs to be available in easily readable practice leaflets (eg about the practice nurse, health visitor and district nurse). There should be a policy about home visits and also early appointments. Older people can have problems when making appointments and may find telephoning difficult. It might be that older people need longer appointments and these should be available. How continuing care is organized depends on whether the doctors see this as their responsibility or whether others, for instance the nursing care team, are involved. Certainly, direct access to practice nursing should be widely available. The health check systems have been described at length, but patients need to know the purpose of these and the benefits available. Practices should accept older people on to their lists if they move into the practice area. To remove an older person who is already on the list is despicable. Patient participation groups have not become established in general practice, but ways in which the opinions of older patients can be heard need to be explored.

Care of older people is helped by the employment of appropriate ancillary staff. Practice nurses, counsellors, physiotherapists, chiropodists, occupational therapists, dieticians and social workers are all extremely valuable members of the team when caring for older people. They should have sufficient office and treatment room accommodation, and access to the general resources within the practice. Close collaboration between team members is vital and can be helped by regular meetings. Continuing training of staff is necessary if full effectiveness is to be achieved.

References

1. Wilkin D, Williams EI. (1986) Patterns of care for the elderly in general practice. *J R Coll Gen Pract* **36**: 567–70.

2. Wilkin D, Metcalfe DHM, Hallam L, *et al*. (1984) Area variations in the process of care in urban general practice. *Br Med J* **289**: 229–32.

3. World Health Organization. (1978) *International classification of diseases*. 9th revision, WHO, Geneva.

4. Williams EI. (1983) The general practitioner and the disabled. *J R Coll Gen Pract* **33**: 296–9.

5. Cartwright A, Smith C. (1988) *Elderly people, their medicines and their doctors*. Routledge, London.

6. Williamson J. (1978) Prescribing problems in the elderly. *Practitioner* **220**: 749–55.

7. Shaw SM, Opit LJ. (1976) Need for supervision of the elderly receiving long term prescribed medication. *Br Med J* **i**: 505–7.

8. Hodkinson HM. (1992) Reference ranges for biological data in older persons. In: Evans JG, Williams TS, editors. *Oxford textbook of geriatric medicine*. Oxford University Press, Oxford, 725–7.

9. Farnsworth TA, Mulley GP. (1992) Diagnostic dilemmas in acutely ill elderly people. *Med Lab Sci* **49**: 326–33.

10. Griffiths RA, Good WR, Watson NP, *et al*. (1984) Normal erythrocyte sedimentation rate in the elderly. *Br Med J* **289**: 724–5.

17
The Hospital–Community Interface

The main division in the provision of health care for older people is between primary and secondary care. The movement of a patient across this interface in both directions is facilitated by the family doctor and other members of the primary care team. When movement is from the community to hospital, there are several pathways. The patient may be admitted, they may attend an outpatient department, or, if the patient is unable to travel to the hospital, a consultant may visit the patient at home, which is known as domiciliary consultation.

When admission is required, this is normally arranged by the patient's GP, although there are other possible methods. On discharge, the patient can be followed up at an outpatient department or at a day hospital. When discharge from hospital is followed by an outpatient appointment the GP and the team are once more completely responsible for the patient's care. When day hospital follow-up is arranged, then the care is shared.

Within this framework, however, problems develop. It sometimes takes many weeks to arrange an outpatient appointment, especially in such specialties as orthopaedics, where demand is high. The major initiatives to reduce waiting lists for both inpatient admission and outpatient consultation have helped this problem, but not solved it. The development of fundholding practices and hospital trusts has increased flexibility, but has sometimes meant that the quality of service a patient receives is dependent on the type of practice with which he or she is registered. The Patient's Charter now provides some clear guidelines about expected standards. Because of problems in the community, which can include non-availability of GPs, the normal admission processes are sometimes bypassed and patients are admitted by self-referral. However, the single most important difficulty at the interface has been the discharge of patients back into the community after hospital admission. Because of the importance of an older person's discharge from hospital and reception back into the community, this chapter is devoted mainly to this particular event. It will be concerned with describing research that has highlighted many of the difficulties and from which new guidelines have emerged to help with the successful resettlement of patients.

During the past 20 years there has been a regular flow of studies concerned with the process of discharging older patients from hospital; most have described difficulties in resettling such patients. One of the features mentioned has been readmission, especially in an emergency. Levels have varied, but it has been shown to be as high as 18% in the first year. Attempts have been made to identify factors that might lead to urgent readmission. Graham and Livesley[1], studying patients readmitted to a department of geriatric medicine, were able to define causes for readmission. These included unavoidable deterioration of the medical condition, inadequate medical treatment, non-compliance and poor rehabilitation. Victor and Vetter[2], studying readmission amongst a 4% sample of patients discharged from all specialties, found that 17% were readmitted within three months. They found no social or demographic characteristics that were associated with early readmission, but commented that it was due mainly to relapse of the original illness.

Early Unplanned Readmission

There is also evidence that a high proportion of urgent readmissions take place within 28 days. In a study carried out by Williams and Fitton[3-6], an examination was made of the process of discharge and emergency readmission within 28 days. It examined readmissions of older people discharged from hospital across the spectrum of specialties. From the study, valuable insights were gained about both the processes of admission to and discharge from hospital.

The study was undertaken in a district general hospital in 1985 and involved collecting details of all patients who were admitted and discharged from the hospital who were over 65 years of age during the course of that year. A random sample of patients who had been admitted as an emergency within 28 days of discharge was constructed (the 'study' group) together with a matched sample of patients who were not readmitted (the 'control' group). There were 133 patients in each of the study and control groups. The main source of data collection was from the patients and their principal informal carers. Interviews with hospital sisters also provided supporting data. With the patients' permission, their GPs were contacted by letter and a brief questionnaire was enclosed for completion. There were, therefore, four sources of information and the response rates were good.

By far the greatest proportion (76%) of patients were discharged on the first occasion to their place of residence. Sixteen per cent died during the admission and 6% had not been discharged at the end of data collection. Of those discharged, 6% were readmitted within 28 days as an emergency and 3% were admitted within 28 days as a planned readmission. Of the 266 patients who took part in the project, 64% were women and 36% were men. The most common age range for both sexes was between 70 and 80 years, the mean age of the group being 79.0. Because of matching for age, sex and marital status it was not possible to compare the study and control group for these variables. However, the sample was found to have the same distribution as for all patients aged over 65 admitted during the period of the study, so that it is unlikely that these variables had any effect on readmission. They do, however, provide a representative sample of the hospital population.

The way in which patients were admitted initially to hospital was recorded for both groups and for the study group also at the second admission (see Table 17.1). There were 11 methods by which patients were admitted to hospital: their own general practitioner or one from the same practice, a deputizing service

Table 17.1: Mode of admission of patients at first and second admission.

	Own GP	Deputizing service	Via district nurse/ social worker direct	Consultant comiciliary visit	Outpatient/ day hospital	Family/ patient direct	Hospital transfer/ carer relief	Total
First admission								
Study number	57	8	10	9	14	28	6	132 [a]
%	43	6	8	7	10	20	5	100
Control number	38	8	14	10	36	19	8	133
%	29	6	10	8	27	14	6	100
Second admission								
Study number	60	14	13	7	8	30	–	132 [a]
%	45	10	10	5	6	23	–	100

Source: Williams and Fitton, 1988[3].

[a] Insufficient information for one patient.

general practitioner, a district nurse direct, a social worker direct, following a domicilliary visit by a consultant, direct from an outpatient visit, direct from the day hospital, by the family or a friend direct, by the patient direct, transfer from another hospital and prearranged carer relief.

At their first admission, significantly more patients in the study group were admitted from the GP than in the control group. They were also more likely to be admitted direct to hospital by their families or because of self-referral than those in the control group. Control patients were far more likely to be admitted from outpatient departments or day hospitals. It is possible these findings indicate more serious illness in the study group and, as the difference is significant, they are pointers to the likelihood of readmission.

Proportions of modes of admission varied little between the first and second admission of the study patients. It is interesting to note that only 36% of the entire group were admitted via their own GP. Almost the same proportion of study patients were admitted via their GP on the first and second occasion. A surprisingly high proportion of patients were admitted by direct arrangements between the hospital and family or friends, or by self-referral. The proportions in this respect from the study group's first and second admissions were again very similar. Of those in the study group admitted the first time through the GP, 70% were admitted via the GP on the second admission; of those who were self- or family-admitted for the first admission, 44% were so again on the second admission.

Reasons for Readmission

All the 133 study patients were readmitted in an emergency. A review of each showed that, more often, several factors contributed to the readmission. In each instance it was, however, possible to identify one principal reason, although this was sometimes difficult because two factors seemed to be of nearly equal importance.

There were seven principal reasons for readmission (*see* Table 17.2). The most common was relapse of the initial medical condition. The criterion used was that the relapse produced a medical situation that necessitated readmission in its own right. The 'new problem' group consisted of 20 patients who developed a new condition that did not relate to the original problem.

Very many of the readmitted patients had carer problems, but in 19 cases it was thought that the reason for readmission was principally carer failure. In only five of these the carer was a spouse, in the remainder they were other relatives, except for two in which the carers were a lodger and a neighbour, both of whom were described as giving care, but they were clearly not reliable in being able to provide consistent and adequate support. Of the seven people who were readmitted because of a complication of the original illness, five were orthopaedic and two were surgical cases. Most were because of complications of surgery. Eight patients were readmitted for terminal care; all suffered from neoplastic disease. As would be expected, those who cared for them at home were under severe

Table 17.2: Principal reasons for unplanned readmission.

Reasons for readmission	n.	%	Mean age (yrs)	Sex		Lives alone		Interval between discharge and readmission (days)	
				m	f	N	%	Median	Range
Relapse of initial illness	67	51	79.9	26	41	30	45	11	1–27
New problem developed	20	15	74.3	5	15	6	30	9	1–20
Carer problems	19	14	79.5	4	15	9	47	7	1–27
Complications of initial illness	7	5	71.0	1	6	4	57	3	1–25
Terminal care	8	6	74.6	5	3	1	12	15	7–27
Medication problems	8	6	79.0	4	4	4	50	8	1–23
Problems with services	4	3	80.0	3	1	3	75	14	4–24
Whole group	133	100	76.9					9	1–27

Source: Williams and Fitton, 1988[3].

pressure. In six of these patients the carer was a husband or wife who was also older and in poor health. The next group was associated with medication failure. It had been expected that problems with medication might feature as a contributory factor rather than as a principal reason for readmission. However, in eight patients, medication problems directly caused the subsequent readmission. Finally, four patients were readmitted directly as a result of failure in formal services. All of these were due to district nurse failure because of communication breakdown between the hospital and community services.

Table 17.2 shows the principal reason for readmission in relation to age, sex and whether the patient lived alone, and also the median number of days between discharge and readmission. The median interim between discharge and readmission for the total group of 133 patients was nine days. This varied according to the reason for readmission. Complications, medication problems and carer problems resulted in quick readmission, whereas unplanned terminal care and problems with services took longer. Although the numbers were too few to make a definitive statement in this respect they may indicate a trend. The relationship between the patient's sex and the reason for readmission did not appear to be significant. There were high proportions of those living with others among patients who were readmitted with relapse, or a new problem or terminal care. Considering the varying specialties, there was no overall statistically significant difference between the readmission rates for each of these. There were relatively more geriatric medicine patients in the study group, but most of the specialties had nearly equal numbers of study and control patients. Orthopaedic surgery was, however, the exception, where there were 59% in the control group compared with 41% in the study group.

In nearly every study patient there were contributory factors that made readmission more likely. The seven principal reasons for readmission were identified, but each of these could also have been a contributory factor. For example, the prime cause could have been a medication problem, but relapse and carer difficulties may well have been strong contributory factors. Fifteen contributory factors were identified and are shown in Table 17.3. Carer difficulties stand out clearly as being the most significant in relation to readmission. The practical and emotional strain of caring for an older patient who has just been discharged from hospital was very apparent during interviews. Premature discharge, as assessed by study patients and

Table 17.3: Contributory factors in early unplanned readmission ($n = 133$ except where stated).

Contributory factors	Number	%
Carer problems ($n = 100$)	83	83
Discharge too soon		
– carer/patient opinion	77	58
– GP's opinion ($n = 83$)	26	31
Lack of information from hospital to GP ($n = 104$)	49	47
Living alone	57	43
Poor health on discharge (carer/patient opinion)	49	37
Inadequate preparation for discharge	49	37
Incontinence (urinary and faecal)	44	33
Medication problems	39	29
Problems with services	24	18
Relapse of initial illness	18	14
GP's failure to visit	15	11
Very confused (hospital/patient/carer opinion)	13	10
New problems developed	4	3
Discharged self	2	2
Complication of initial illness	1	1

Source: Williams and Fitton, 1988[3].

carers, was the second most common contributory factor. In 24 cases the GP was in agreement that the discharge was premature. Other causes for concern were the high level of medication problems, service failure, poor preparation for discharge in terms of assessment and advice, too short notice, failure of notification to GPs and/or their subsequent failure to visit patients when discharged. Confusion and incontinence, especially if both faecal and urinary, were also factors. Readmitted patients often had more than one contributory factor and sometimes had many (one patient had nine!). Problems were not, however, absent in the control group and only a very good carer presence prevented readmission. Some patients were readmitted in the fifth and sixth weeks following discharge for much the same reasons as those in the study group and they could easily have been classed as emergency early readmission. Problems were more common, however, in the study group and often significantly so, as is shown in Table 17.4.

Apart from direct and contributory reasons for readmission there were some other statistically significant differences between the study and control groups. These included:

Table 17.4: Comparison between study and control patients regarding factors that would contribute to readmission.

Problem	Study No.	%	Control No.	%	Significance		
Carer problems: (n = 193; Study = 100; Control = 93)							
Health affected	54	54	34	37	$\chi^2 = 5$	1df	p<0.05
Frustration and restriction	67	67	34	37	$\chi^2 = 16.7$	1df	p<0.0005
Difficulty with communication	31	31	13	14	$\chi^2 = 7$	1df	p<0.01
Too early discharge: GP opinion (n = 179; Study = 83; Control = 96)	26	31	11	12	$\chi^2 = 14.4$	1df	p<0.001
Poor health on discharge: ward sister opinion (n = 265; Study = 132; Control = 133)	13	10	5	4	$\chi^2 = 9.25$	2df	p<0.01
No advice given at discharge (n = 263; Study = 130; Control = 133)	66	51	43	32	$\chi^2 = 9.2$	1df	p=0.002
Incontinence (urinary or faecal) (n = 265; Study = 132; Control = 133)	22	17	16	12	$\chi^2 = 1.2$	1df	NS
Problems with medication after discharge (n = 266; Study = 133; Control = 133)	42	31	50	38	$\chi^2 = 1.1$	1df	NS
Problems with services after discharge (n = 266; Study = 133; Control = 133)	52	39	44	33	$\chi^2 = 1.0$	1df	NS
No GP visit after discharge (n = 260; Study = 128; Control = 132)	36	28	50	38	$\chi^2 = 3$	1df	NS
No discharge notice to GP (n = 207: Study = 101; Control = 106)	30	30	8	8	$\chi^2 = 15.4$	1df	p=0.0001

Source: Williams and Fitton, 1988[3].

- low income
- high level of previous admission
- where a district nurse or social worker was already visiting
- admission by their own GP
- carers who had concern about their own health
- carers who had a high frustration level
- carers engaged in personal tasks for the patient, for example, washing and dressing
- faecal incontinence
- communication problems between patient and carer
- poor mobility.

The following list shows factors for which statistical significance was nearly reached:

- admission to a department of geriatric medicine
- over five items of medication prescribed on discharge
- discharge late in the day
- no transport of the patient's own
- carers with longstanding illnesses
- carers who had to do the housework for the patient
- carers who were not spouses
- carers with family problems of their own
- carers who had experienced life problems in the previous year
- living in the present house for a relatively short time
- poor general health.

An assessment was made about whether readmission was preventable. It was noted that readmission was likely to have been avoided if more effective action had been taken in one or more of five areas. These were: preparation for and timing of the discharge, attention to the needs of the carer, timing and adequate information to the GP and subsequent action by the GP, sufficient and prompt nursing and social service support, and, finally, management of medication. It was considered that in about 60% of the cases, readmission would have been avoided if proper arrangements had been made in these areas.

The overall impression was that patients were receiving adequate services before the first admission[4]. The high level of these services indicated the vulnerability of the patients. In general, the study group had more help than the control group, probably because of the severity of illness. The range of services is shown in Table 17.5. A substantial number of patients had services organized for them on leaving hospital. These were not necessarily the same services that had been present before admission. Sometimes patients refused services at this time, mainly for financial reasons. Just over half of the study group had a district nurse arranged at discharge; half of these were new services and the remainder were reinstated. Just over one-third of control patients had a district nurse arranged, two-thirds of which were new services. The result was a net increase in district nursing for the whole group. The level of district nursing service increased significantly with age.

About half of the study group and slightly under half of the control group had a home help service, most of which was reinstated. The use of home help services also increased significantly with age and also with living alone and the absence of a carer. A social worker was arranged for about one-third of the study patients, but for very few of the control group. Other services were organized for relatively few patients. In all circumstances, those who were much older, lived alone, were in poor general health, were confused, had poor mobility or were incontinent were the most likely to have services arranged.

Table 17.5: Provision of services on first admission and after first discharge.

Service	Group	% of patients receiving service on first admission	% of patients receiving service on first discharge	increase/ decrease (%)
District nurse	Study	40	51	+11
	Control	25	39	+14
Social worker	Study	23	35	+12
	Control	10	16	+6
Meals on Wheels	Study	10	20	+10
	Control	9	16	+7
Day centre	Study	11	18	+7
	Control	8	17	+9
Home help	Study	35	40	+5
	Control	30	35	+5
Physiotherapy	Study	4	3	−1
	Control	3	6	+3
Health visitor	Study	18	14	−4
	Control	14	14	=
Chiropodist	Study	35	6	−29
	Control	41	18	−25

Source: Williams and Fitton, 1988[3].

There were, however, problems with the services. Excluding GP services, 36% of the total group complained of difficulties with community services. The variety of problems experienced was great and many patients seemed to have had more than one type of problem. These are shown in Table 17.6. There were more problems in the study group, but nevertheless, the level was not significantly different between that and the control group. The problems were basically of three types: no arrangements, delay in starting the service, and inadequate service to meet the needs. These occurred throughout the different services, but the most important failure was when nursing services were deficient. The most serious situation was when no health care worker visited the patient's home after discharge, and this was always due to communication failure. Also, administrative problems sometimes caused deficiencies. In 18% of the readmitted group, service failure was considered to be a strong contributory factor to readmission.

These experiences show that, despite reasonable levels of service provision, problems can still occur. Communication problems certainly need attention. It would seem that someone in the community should assess the needs of the patient as soon as discharge occurs. Delay in instituting services is very important to these patients, particularly when they live alone, and, of course, to their carers.

Notice of discharge, either by a discharge note or formal letter, was not received by the GP for 18% of the total group[5]. In some instances there was also delay in receiving notification. The GPs were made aware of the discharge within the first week in only 66% of cases. There was dissatisfaction among GPs about both the information received from the hospital and the delay in receiving such notice. Sixty-seven per cent of discharged patients received a visit from a GP at some stage, but post-discharge visits were most likely to have been initiated by the patients and their families. GPs were most likely to

Table 17.6: Problems with services.

	Study		Control	
	No.	%	No.	%
Inadequate provision of services				
(district nurse or social worker)	18	34	17	39
Delay in start after discharge:				
District nurse	10	19	5	11
Other (social worker, home help,				
Meals on Wheels, occupational therapist)	9	17	15	34
Inadequate hospital preparation and lack				
of arrangements	10	19	1	2
Personality clashes	3	6	1	2
Housing/finance	2	4	5	11
Total	52		44	

Source: Williams and Fitton, 1988[3].

visit patients who had informal carers or who were much older.

Patients were asked whether they were satisfied with their GP. Nearly three-quarters were, but some were very dissatisfied. The carers, when asked the same question, were more critical. Both volunteered information about doctors' handling of the discharge procedure. The main criticisms were when no follow-up visiting was arranged, especially to housebound patients. They also commented about some GPs' unsympathetic manner and sometimes poor management. Clearly, a code of practice is needed about informing the GP about the discharge of an older patient and the way in which GPs should respond to the discharge. Although it is realized that some discharged patients will not need a home visit, it is probable that some contact is still necessary from someone in the community to review needs and to discuss problems. The attitudes of professional carers towards patients who are older are clearly important in determining outcome and patient satisfaction.

During the study, some very interesting information was gathered about the carers of patients discharged from hospital[6]. It is possible that what was found was an indication of the difficulties experienced by carers of older people in general. Of the total group of patients, 18% had no identifiable carer and this in itself poses immediate problems in the community. The majority of carers were over 60 years old themselves, and some of them were very much older. One-third were men and two-thirds were women. One-quarter of the carers did not live with the patient for whom they were caring. The stress of caring for an older patient was very apparent. Nearly half of the total group said their health had been affected by the task. There was also a considerable amount of frustration. Many carers felt restricted and tied because of patients' continuing needs. Some carers said that their own family life had been destroyed at the expense of meeting the patients' needs and this happened especially when the carers did not live with the patients. The carers often felt depressed and fatigued and had experienced problems 'with their nerves'. They commented on the unremitting pressure on them and the time consuming nature of the job of attending to the patients' needs.

Carers also mentioned problems associated with the dissatisfaction with the hospital's management of the patient's medical condition and follow up support. They were frustrated by the differences between their perception of the severity of the patient's condition and the hospital staff's assessment. They felt the hospital were under-assessing the severity of the patient's condition and the result was that they felt they were deprived of much needed care and support. Carers were very often coping with personal tasks for patients, such as dressing, bathing and washing, and also, in many cases, were having to deal with household tasks. Some of this care had been going on for many years. The whole problem was often aggravated by incontinence, which was found to be a hard problem to tolerate. In a few cases the carers were concerned about the fact that the patients were neglecting themselves or were at risk of accidents or misuse of prescribed drugs. A few carers had to contend with irresponsible behaviour.

Carers are a very important group, with real needs in the community. They need information about the patient both from the hospital and the community workers. This must include details of the medical condition and treatment, what is a likely outcome and what is the general assessment of the patient's condition and abilities. Also, there must be an assessment of the carer's needs themselves. It is tempting to think that when there is a carer present, no additional help is needed, but perhaps additional home help is required. Sometimes, especially in the first few weeks after discharge, financial assistance may also be needed and an attendance allowance should be sought.

Nearly 85% of the total group went home on some medication and nearly 30% went home with more than four items[7]. The older the patient, the more likely it was that medication was given on discharge, although they were less likely to be given more than four items. Medication was used as directed in only 45% of cases. The largest proportion of prescriptions were drugs for the cardiovascular, respiratory and central nervous systems. About one-third of the group had problems with medication; these were of many types. Medication was sometimes inappropriate, as, for example, the patient who was kept on thyroxine despite coronary artery disease and severe asthma. Patient confusion was also a problem; several examples were seen of patients who were too confused to understand their medication. Patients were occasionally taking the tablets in the wrong doses despite verbal and written instructions. There were frequent examples of instances where neither patient nor carer understood why the tablets were prescribed. Some carers confessed to having tried tablets themselves to see if they could determine the effect. Sometimes instructions on the container did not agree with the verbal instructions given at the hospital, or, perhaps necessary drugs were not given at discharge or the wait for them to be dispensed was too long, so the patient was left without any supplies. There were also problems with patients' eyesight that made it difficult for them to see the labels and also to tell which were the different types of tablets. Patients were sometimes not confident that changes made by the hospital in relation to treatment that they had been previously taking were in fact correct, and so reverted to the previous dosage. Sometimes medication was too difficult to handle; for example, one patient found a salbutamol inhaler impossible to use. Some of these problems were serious and were factors in early readmission.

Medication Guidelines

The study highlights the fact that discharge from hospital can be associated with medication problems. There should be clear guidelines available to minimize these difficulties. These could include:

- counsel patients and carers before discharge about medication
- give appropriately labelled and easy to handle bottles and containers
- give a 10-day supply of a drug with instructions to let the GP know of the need for a repeat prescription at an early point
- give verbal and written instructions to carers, especially when patients are confused
- take account of the patient's health before dispensing so that problems associated with confusion, arthritis, immobility can be foreseen
- have a check-list to go through with the patient about important instructions
- give early notification to the general practitioner.

General Guidelines for Discharge

It is clear that at such an important point in a patient's life as a discharge from hospital, clear guidelines should be available about how this should be managed, both by the community and the hospital. The following are suggested for the hospital:

- assess home circumstances
- check that carers exist at home
- ascertain that discharge is appropriate
- assess the patient's ability to self-care at home
- give adequate warning to relatives and carers
- arrange transport so that the patient can get home during the daytime
- go through a drug check-list
- make sure that appropriate advice is understood
- confirm arrangements for services
- check that some professional in the community knows that the patient is being discharged
- ring the GP's surgery with brief details
- beware of special circumstances where early readmission is more likely; these would include:

- low income groups
- where the patient has been in hospital often before
- where the illness has been severe
- where the patient's general condition is poor, especially where confusion, immobility and incontinence occur
- where patients were admitted via the general practitioner
- where the carer is in poor health or has other commitments.

There is a helpful discussion in the Department of Health's publication *Discharge of patients from hospital*[8].

Discharge is only one aspect of the process; reception of patients back into the community is also important. No specific guidelines are generally available for the care of older people once they are discharged. One reason for this is the variability in the health and social status of such patients and their specific needs. It cannot be assumed that older patients are discharged with all their health problems solved and able to return to community life without help. Many can, but others need continuing medical nursing and social support. Identifying those who do need support is the key to a successful resettlement programme. Although recently discharged older people are seen to be an 'at risk' group, there are clearly those who are more at risk than others. It is an under-researched area.

There is a group of patients who clearly need specific help and these are the ones for whom nursing care is arranged by the hospital. This group will therefore have a link person who will communicate details of the patient's condition to the other members of the primary health care team. Those who do not have nursing care arranged can be more isolated. To investigate the state of health and the needs of such patients Williams *et al.*[9] looked at a random sample of 75-year-old and over patients who were discharged from hospital and not referred to the district nursing service. Nearly 500 patients were interviewed. Table 17.7 shows the specialties they were discharged from; it is interesting to note that, even though

Table 17.7: Specialty.

	Total	
	No.	%
General medicine[a]	81	17
Geriatrics/Medicine of the Elderly[a]	158	34
General surgery	134	29
ENT	8	2
Trauma/orthopaedics	13	3
Ophthalmology	61	13
Gynaecology	8	2
Other	7	1
Total	470	100

[a]During the study, one hospital changed its admission procedure so that all patients over 75 years referred to the Medical Department were admitted to Medicine of the Elderly.

more than half were from some type of surgical ward, no nursing after-care had been arranged. Most had received one or more services before admission and these were not always reinstated. Sixty-one per cent of the patients had been in contact with their GP since discharge.

The physical and mental status of each patient was measured. Looking at physical condition, 7% had no problems, 44% had moderate problems, 34% had moderately severe problems, and 16% had severe problems. Seventy-eight per cent of the group were in good mental condition, but 18% were poor and 4% were very poor. Forty-one per cent did not have disabilities, 29% had moderate disabilities and 30% were severely disabled. The picture presented was therefore one of marked variability, but with at least half the patients with significant physical problems and one-fifth with poor mental status. Disability, when examined in detail, demonstrated considerable variation in the tasks which people could do (Tables 17.8, 17.9, 17.10).

Table 17.8: Patients with severe problems on some physical status items (n=470).

	Severe or very severe problem	
	No.	%
Use of wheelchair	28	6
Getting in/out of bath	161	34
Impaired vision	64	14
Impaired hearing	37	8
Appetite	52	11
Difficulty chewing	15	3
Sleep problems	68	14
Breathing problems	74	16
Incontinence	47	10
Moving around on level	26	6

Table 17.9: Patients with severe problems on disability and self-care items (n=470).

	Cannot manage alone	
	No.	%
Climbing stairs	108	23
Heavy shopping	278	59
Heavy housework	293	62
Preparing hot meal	98	21
Taking object from overhead shelf	150	32
Tying knot	46	10
Cutting toenails	212	45
Bathing/washing all over	74	16
Catching buses	222	47
Washing hair	137	29
Dressing self	25	5
Putting on shoe/socks	37	8
Washing hands and face	10	2

Table 17.10: Patients with problems on some mental status items (n=470).

	Patients with problems	
	No.	%
Frequently or constantly depressed	56	12
Sometimes crying for no reason	97	21
Sometimes forgetting where they put things	226	48
Cannot control anxiety at all or only when occupied	148	31

As part of this study, an evaluation was made of a programme of timetabled visiting by health visitor assistants[10]. The actions taken by them were recorded. A total of eight visits per patient were made over the year. No overall benefit from this visiting programme was, however, found. As would be expected the number of actions taken was related to the patient's health status and sex: more actions were taken for those in poor health and for women. Age and whether the patient lived alone did not affect the number of actions taken.

These studies confirm the variability of the needs and health status of older patients being discharged from hospital. It may be difficult to justify the cost of a policy of routinely visiting all discharged older people. Some, however, do need continuing care. Poor health at discharge is the clear measure for continuing care and this is common sense. The GP, district nurse and health visitor together have a comprehensive knowledge of the vulnerable patients in the practice or area, and GPs now have contractual requirements to offer an annual assessment of all patients of 75 years and over. Practice based staff, particularly practice nurses, are more likely to be aware of potential difficulties than hospital based staff, especially when the patient has had a relatively short stay in hospital, was on a ward with a high turnover, or did not appear on medical evidence alone to need support after discharge. The most reliable safety net for vulnerable patients would be provided by ensuring that the hospital contacts the GP and the practice based community team promptly, ideally before discharge or otherwise on the day of discharge itself. Recent advances in technology can make this communication far more effective than in the past. In addition, if health visitors, GPs and practice nurses agree on an assessment scheme for post-discharge visits that covers areas of concern to all three professions, decisions on the best care for the most vulnerable patients could be based on a single visit to the patient's home or at the surgery.

References

1. Graham H, Livesley B. (1983) Can readmissions to a geriatric medical unit be prevented? *Lancet* i: 404–6.

2. Victor C, Vetter NJ. (1985) The early readmission of the elderly to hospital. *Age Ageing* 52: 79–84.

3. Williams EI, Fitton F. (1988) Factors affecting early unplanned readmission of elderly hospital patients. *Br Med J* 297: 784–7.

4. Williams EI, Fitton F. (1991) Use of nursing and social services by elderly patients discharged from hospital. *Br J Gen Pract* **41**: 72–75.

5. Williams EI, Fitton F. (1990) General practitioner response to elderly patients discharged from hospital. *Br Med J* **300**: 159–61.

6. Williams EI, Fitton F. (1991) Survey of carers of elderly patients discharged from hospital. *Br J Gen Pract* **41**: 105–8.

7. Williams EI. (1991) Keep taking the tablets: better guidelines needed on discharge. *Geriatr Med* **21(9)**: 13.

8. Department of Health. (1989) *Discharge of patients from hospital.* (Health Circular HC(89)5.) DoH, London.

9. Williams EI, Greenwell J, Groom LM. (1992) Characteristics of patients aged 75 years and over who are discharged from hospital without district nursing support. *J Pub Health Med* **14**: 321–7.

10. Williams EI, Greenwell J, Groom LM. The care of people over 75 years old after discharge from hospital: an evaluation of timetabled visiting by health visitor assistants. *J Public Health Med* **14**: 138–44.

18
Common Problems in Family Medicine

Introduction

It is necessary in family medicine, when dealing with older people, to widen the concept of diagnosis. Multiple pathology is the rule in older age and several diagnoses are possible at any given time. Often these are quite separate in themselves and involve different systems. Their treatment is usually distinct. However, they must also be considered collectively because several different pathologies can produce a cumulative effect on function, and relatively minor conditions often together produce a significant problem. Thus a 'diagnosis' could be an osteoarthritic hip in an overweight person who has a bunion on the right foot and who has a significant loss of mobility as a result of these conditions. This more fully describes the problem. The importance of loss of function makes it necessary to make a diagnosis, not only in terms of diseases present, but also of the effect these have on function. It is often necessary also to take account of a patient's environment and life-style, for instance, whether the older person cares for others or lives alone.

It is therefore impossible to consider individual diseases as separate entities when caring for older persons[1]. The principle of defining problems in terms of functional deficit and then seeking solutions that take these into account is very important.

The solutions are sometimes non-pharmacological and can include physiotherapy and various social inputs. This book is not concerned with the description of diseases of older age (there are excellent text books available that do this), but there are certain conditions that contribute significantly to functional impairment. Included in this group are stroke, diabetes mellitus, certain mental disorders, acute confusion, vision and hearing defects and arthritis. For some diseases, clinical guidelines for their management are becoming increasingly available. This is an encouraging and helpful development.

Stroke

Stroke is a common condition and is the main cause of death in the UK after heart disease and cancer. Each year nearly two in every 1000 of the population will suffer from stroke. Amongst older people, the incidence rises steeply. More than half of all patients with acute stroke are aged over 70 years. Strokes are responsible for considerable residual disability; 60% of patients are either dead or dependent in activities of daily living six months later. Their management is expensive and accounts for about 5% of NHS hospital costs. In the community it is important that prompt initial care should be given and that this should be followed by effective continuing care.

The term 'stroke' is applied to describe the clinical manifestation of two distinct happenings in the cerebrovascular system. These are blockage or haemorrhage. The former is usually by a clot or thrombus, but also can be caused by an embolus arising in the heart, or in the carotid or vertebral arteries. This blockage produces death of the part of the brain supplied by the affected artery. The area of destroyed tissue is called an infarction. Thus cerebral thrombosis or occlusion (blockage) produces cerebral infarction; it accounts for about 85% of strokes. The position and extent of the infarction determines the difference in clinical manifestation. These are referred to as acute ischaemic strokes. Haemorrhage from a cerebral artery causes bleeding into the surrounding brain tissue and causes damage in this way, as well as by cutting off or reducing the blood supply to the parts supplied by the artery. This accounts for about 15% of all strokes.

Transient Ischaemic Attacks

Within the group of cerebrovascular happenings are episodes known as transient ischaemic attacks (TIAs). The underlying disease is different and consists of a reduction in the blood supply to the brain that is only of short duration. This is due to temporary blockage of parts of the cerebral circulation by micro-emboli of dislodged platelets arising from atheromatous plaques situated at the branching of the common carotid artery, the vertebrobasilar artery, or, in some cases, the heart itself. Anaemia, and kidney and liver failure can also help to cause TIAs. Obstruction of the blood supply to the brain by cervical spondylosis may be contributory.

TIAs are important as they may herald a full cerebral thrombosis. They are treatable and it may be possible to take action to avoid more serious trouble. The clinical findings can vary and depend on the source of the micro-emboli. Those arising in the carotid artery may be associated with eye symptoms such as hemianopia or even complete blindness, and also with limb weakness, which is usually unilateral. Speech defects may also occur. Sometimes a murmur may be audible over the carotid artery. When the source of the micro-emboli is the vertebrobasilar arterial system, the symptoms include dizziness, double vision or sometimes complete loss of sight, limb weakness (which is often bilateral) and speech difficulty. Memory disturbances may also be a feature. Vertebrobasilar attacks are said to have a better prognosis and rarely proceed to full stroke. In practice, however, it is clinically often difficult to separate these two types. A careful examination of the heart may reveal disease, which may be the source of a micro-embolism from this organ. An ECG is certainly needed, though possibly not an Echocardiogram. Full recovery of the symptoms however, takes place within a few minutes and certainly within 24 hours, although the attacks may be recurrent.

Treatment of TIAs usually involves two or three days of rest and a gradual resumption of activity within a week. Any possible underlying cause, such as anaemia, drug misuse or hypoglycaemia, should be treated and this would mean doing investigations such as a full blood count, blood sugar level, chest radiograph and ECG. Temporal arteritis is sometimes a cause of TIA and an ESR or blood viscosity test should be done, as these levels are raised in these conditions.

Blood pressure should be monitored and the diastolic level kept below 100 mmHg by using antihypertensive agents if necessary. Treatment for hypertension should not, however, be given in the acute phase of the illness unless malignant hypertension is present. If hypertension persists for one week after the acute episode then patients under 80 years old should receive antihypertensive therapy. It is likely that the patients with TIA will derive benefit from this treatment since they have a greater absolute risk of subsequent serious vascular events when compared with asymptomatic people with hypertension in the general population. The currently accepted criterion for hypertension is a systolic pressure of over 160 mmHg and/or diastolic pressure over 90 mmHg.

There are arguments in favour of full hospital investigation of a patient who has suffered from a TIA, because it may be possible to prevent further episodes (particularly the onset of a full cerebral accident), by surgical procedures such as endarterectomy. There is evidence from clinical trials about the effectiveness of surgical intervention in patients with significant carotid stenosis. The question of anticoagulation on a long-term basis will also have to be considered. In much older patients, careful thought needs to be taken about whether this is worthwhile. However, if patient compliance can be guaranteed, particularly when atrial fibrillation is present, many would now advocate anticoagulation, otherwise aspirin is recommended at a dose of 150–300 mg daily, reduced to 75 mg daily if gastric symptoms occur. It would seem advisable to use an enteric-coated preparation of aspirin. If there is any doubt about the nature of the TIA and its underlying cause, it is always helpful to get the advice of a consultant geriatrician so that the situation can be fully explored.

Complete Stroke

The clinical presentation of a complete stroke can be complex and the effects can range from mild to severe. The World Health Organization's definition of a stroke is a condition with rapidly developing clinical signs of focal loss of cerebral function, with symptoms lasting more than 24 hours or leading to death with no apparent cause other than a problem of vascular origin. The diagnosis is purely clinical and therefore a careful clinical assessment is necessary for effective management. The patient may experience early symptoms of headache and unsteadiness, and sensations of weakness can be experienced. Later, these can often be remembered clearly and described dramatically. In the acute stage, the patient may lose consciousness and go into a deep coma; at other times the patient may remain lucid throughout the episode. A clear history of sudden onset of focal neurological deficit can, however, be obtained from the patient or relative. A whole range of neurological deficits can occur, but most commonly the person is left with a hemiplegia, together with weakness of the facial muscles and sometimes a speech defect. Other conditions may be present at the same time as a stroke, and some, such as hypertension or fibrillation may lead directly to the attack. It is often impossible to distinguish clearly between cerebral thrombosis and cerebral haemorrhage; the latter is most likely to be the underlying event if there is a pre-existing hypertension and is more likely to occur in a younger individual. In both haemorrhage and embolus, the onset of a stroke is likely to be sudden. If there is a gradual onset or progressive neurological signs, other causes for the symptoms and signs should be sought.

Several immediate actions may be needed when faced with a person suffering from a full cerebrovascular accident. Urgent first aid is often necessary and breathing difficulty may make it essential to ensure a clear airway. False teeth should be removed and the inhalation of vomit avoided by positioning the patient on his/her side. There is no treatment which should routinely be given immediately in the majority of patients with acute strokes. There is usually little doubt about the diagnosis, but if the doctor is early on the scene there may be difficulty in deciding whether the patient has suffered from a full stroke or a TIA. Sometimes the problem is solved by rapid improvement of symptoms, but, if the general condition of the patient is satisfactory, the doctor can reasonably wait a little before making a final diagnosis.

Sometimes patients present with increased intracranial pressure as demonstrated by the presence of papilloedema. Other conditions apart from cerebrovascular accident may produce raised pressure and the doctor should enquire for a history of injury and consider the possibility of a resulting subdural haematoma. A history of headache, especially in the presence of papilloedema, may indicate the presence of a cerebral tumour. Infection may also produce a similar clinical picture and note should be taken of a raised temperature and neck stiffness to exclude the presence of meningitis. Many other conditions can also mimic cerebrovascular accident in older age; these can include epilepsy, migraine, cardiac conditions, Stokes–Adams attacks and hypoglycaemia.

The doctor should bear all these possibilities in mind when making a full assessment, but then it will be necessary to make the often difficult decision about whether to admit the patient to hospital. In patients with TIAs, most GPs would be prepared to treat the condition at home, but with complete stroke, the decision is not as clear. Some will say that all stroke patients should be admitted to hospital and, although this may be theoretically correct, there are others who are prepared to treat mild cases at home. There are several factors to be considered. The patient's clinical condition is often all-important. Mild hemiplegias with rapidly recovering movement may be suitable for home care. Sometimes in a much older patient, where detailed investigation is not really sensible, it is better to keep him/her at home and thus avoid the stresses, both mental and physical, of being transferred by ambulance to the new environment of a hospital. Extension of a stroke can indeed sometimes be precipitated by such movement. If death is imminent and the condition is obviously terminal, it is more humane to nurse the patient at home.

Hospital admission, however, is necessary for selected patients to clarify the diagnosis, undertake investigations into the possible cause, and provide specific medical treatment. The nature and extent of extracerebral disease also needs assessing and, when such conditions as heart failure and bronchopneumonia are also present, this will indicate hospital admission. A previous history or stroke may indicate admission, as is also the case when there is impaired consciousness.

Another important consideration is whether adequate nursing is available at home. Will the relatives be able to look after the patient and are there suitable bedroom facilities? Family reaction to strokes can vary; some insist that the patient be admitted to hospital and some insist on the reverse. Hospital admission becomes essential, however, when constant and heavy nursing is likely to be necessary. Doubt may sometimes exist about whether the condition is due to thrombosis or to a treatable haemorrhage. In these patients, full investigation is indicated, including examination of the cerebrovascular fluid and, if available, a computed tomography (CT) scan. The latter investigation is particularly relevant if a patient is likely to require anticoagulation or aspirin. Neurosurgical treatment is available for cerebrovascular episodes due to haemorrhage and this is, of course, the argument for hospital admission of all patients with stroke, so that full investigations can be carried out. This really is more important for younger subjects suffering from stroke caused by a possible subarachnoid haemorrhage, which is a special type of brain haemorrhage that can be helped surgically. In older people, however, the possibility of such neurosurgical intervention occurs much less frequently. There are regional variations in the facilities for investigation and only certain areas have special stroke units. When these are available, a fine balance of judgement is necessary when considering the question of whether to admit an older person to hospital or to proceed with home care. There is really no reliable data on outcome of patients with stroke who are treated at home compared with those who are treated in hospital; research needs to be done to clarify these issues.

Management of an established stroke at home involves three things: medical care, nursing care and rehabilitation. In skilled hands anticoagulants at home can be introduced and monitored. There is also the problem of whether to treat raised blood pressure. The patient may already be on treatment and this should be continued, but in the early stages of stroke it is probably unwise to reduce a raised blood pressure.

Nursing care will involve the usual attention to such things as general washing, cleaning, toileting, maintenance of adequate fluid levels and dietary advice. Lifting paralysed patients up and down the bed requires care to avoid shoulder subluxation and is usually a two-handed task. The head should be elevated to reduce cerebral oedema. The period of bed rest should be reduced to as short a time as possible in order to reduce the risk of thrombosis in the veins of the calf muscles, hypostatic pneumonia, joint contractures and pressure sores. The prevention of venous thrombo-embolism is important as deep venous thrombosis occurs in about half of patients with hemiparesis. Physical methods of prevention include graded compression stockings, which should be used in all immobile patients with stroke.

Rehabilitation is vitally necessary if the patient is to make a good functional recovery and should start at the beginning of the illness. The stages of rehabilitation are described in Chapter 20. It might be that physiotherapy fails to influence the neurological outcome, but nevertheless, the patient's ability to cope with daily living can probably be improved by exercises that improve general fitness and enable other working muscles to compensate. The success of this type of rehabilitation may be better at home than in hospital.

When the acute stage has passed, the aim of management must be not only to enable the patient to make as full a functional recovery as possible, but also to avoid a recurrence of further strokes. This latter will probably mean investigations on the lines suggested for TIAs. Full recovery cannot be expected in all cases of stroke and the health care team is left with patients in whom residual damage is present, who were either managed at home in the first place or have been discharged from hospital.

The full resources of rehabilitation services are necessary to enable this type of patient to adjust to the disability and the inevitability of a restricted life-style. The patient's psychological adjustment to this situation also needs attention and the family's attitude needs to be discussed, particularly as considerable social adaptation will be needed. Help from all members of the primary health care team should be forthcoming, particularly to reassure the patient that he/she has not been forgotten once the initial episode has been successfully overcome. There are many severely handicapped people with hemiplegia who have benefited from successful rehabilitation in the early stages, but who regress once this is finally withdrawn. Support for the family under these circumstances is of vital importance because they are left with most of the responsibility and they continue to need help, particularly when speech has been affected and communication with a patient is difficult. Supportive home visits by members of the primary health care team are very important. Voluntary organizations such as Age Concern and appropriate self-help groups can also be extremely useful in these circumstances. Sometimes adaptations are needed to the house to enable a patient to move about more effectively. There is also a wide range of aids available and help from social workers is valuable to assess the needs for these. Wheelchairs are also useful. An application should also be made for an attendance allowance.

Finally, how possible is it to prevent stroke or recurrence of stroke in older people? This is not always possible, but some precursor conditions, such as diabetes, obesity and heart failure, can be treated effectively and should be identified. As mentioned earlier, the treatment of raised blood pressure in patients up to the age of at least 80 is worthwhile. The place of long-term anticoagulants and arterial surgery in older age remain, however, still speculative. The use of aspirin after ischaemic strokes is considered now to be useful in doses similar to that recommended for TIAs. Patients who might benefit from long-term antiplatelet therapy should have an early CT scan to exclude haemorrhage before starting treatment.

An up to date account of the management of acute stroke is given by Sandercock and Lindley[2].

Common Conditions Affecting Mental Function

Dementia

Background

On average, around 7% of patients on GPs' lists are aged 75 or over; of these, about 10% are likely to be demented to a significant degree. The proportion rises with age and may reach 20% over the age of 85. The majority of cases of dementia in the UK (around 50%) are probably caused purely by Alzheimer's disease. The second most common cause is multi-infarct dementia (20%), which reflects areas of brain infarction and is generally secondary to hypertension and/or atherosclerosis. A further 15–20% show evidence of both conditions.

Alcohol related dementia accounts for a small proportion of cases in older people, but is frequently underdiagnosed. Potentially reversible causes of dementia in older people include normal pressure hydrocephalus, hypothyroidism, vitamin B_{12} deficiency, frontal meningioma and neurosyphilis. Unfortunately, with the exception of normal pressure hydrocephalus and frontal meningioma, treatment of these conditions rarely has any perceptible effect on cognitive function.

Dementia can also affect younger people. In the age group 40–65 the prevalence has been estimated to be 0.1%.

Recognition

Dementia needs to be distinguished from normal forgetfulness. As people get older, they worry about forgetting, for example names or items that they have intended to purchase or activities they intend to undertake. However, they retain the ability to remember associated details, for example, of the person whose name they have forgotten. In dementia not, only the name, but the context appears irretrievable.

It is important to distinguish dementia from delirium (acute confusional state) and depression. Delirium usually indicates an underlying physical cause, such as infection or intoxication, which may be drug induced. The history is usually acute, with deterioration over a few days or weeks, and it may of course be superimposed on pre-existing dementia. The characteristic presenting feature is a fluctuating level of consciousness. Other features which suggest delirium rather than dementia include hallucinations and intense fearfulness. Dementia does not in itself cause clouding of consciousness.

Depression should be considered particularly where there is a short history (weeks or months) and in patients who are withdrawn or apathetic and who appear indifferent to the assessment process. Depression is important to diagnose because of the likelihood of response to treatment. It may coexist with dementia in its early stages, in which case there may be a fairly clear onset over a long period, which is characteristic of Alzheimer's disease alone.

Inconsistent responses to cognitive testing are common in depression, which does not cause problems with language (dysphasia) or parietal lobe symptoms such as disorders of motor skills (apraxia). Transient cerebral ischaemic episodes, hypertension, focal neurological signs or symptoms, and fluctuations in the level of functioning suggest multi-infarct dementia, which is more likely in cigarette smokers. Dysphasic and apraxic errors may occur both in Alzheimer's disease and multi-infarct dementia.

Initial Assessment

The functions of the initial assessment are:

- to achieve a clear diagnosis
- to identify treatable causes of cognitive impairment and other treatable pathology
- to clarify the care needs of the patient and of the carer(s).

Documentation of a full history from an informant is essential to clarify the onset and course of the cognitive impairment, the degree of functional incapacity (for example, continence, dressing, feeding, ability to handle financial affairs) and the current network of informal and statutory support. Specific deficiencies in care and areas of carer stress can also be identified. Examination of the mental state requires a high index of suspicion for depression and for acute organic states as well as the need to look out for dysphasia, dyspraxia and agnosia.

Abnormal behaviour may be observed directly as well as being reported by an informant. A suitable screening instrument for cognitive impairment is the Mini-Mental State Examination[3] (*see* Chapter 14). This instrument can be administered during the annual check-up of older patients (75 and over) required under the GP contract. Initial physical examination will seek evidence for associated treatable conditions (eg anaemia due to B_{12} deficiency, myxoedema). Normal pressure hydrocephalus is suggested by an early onset of gait disorder and inappropriate micturition. Focal neurological signs, evidence of generalized atheroma (especially carotid bruits) and hypertension suggest multi-infarct dementia. However, the ability of clinical science and the presence of specific symptoms to discriminate between Alzheimer's disease and multi-infarct dementia is relatively poor. If at all possible the initial assessment should take place in the home setting, since this often reveals problems in functioning that are not apparent in the sheltered environment of the surgery. This is particularly important in the case of demented patients living alone.

Investigations by a General Practitioner

Physical examination should be undertaken with particular reference to cardiovascular and neurological disease. Routine blood screening to exclude treatable causes of dementia includes full blood count (and serum vitamin B_{12} and serum and RBC folate levels if there is a macrocytosis) and thyroid function tests. Some would also include testing for syphilis. Gamma-glutamyl transferase may be raised in heavy drinkers. Urine should be tested for glucose and protein and sent for culture and sensitivity, particularly if there is evidence of urinary incontinence. A random (or preferably a post prandial) blood glucose is a more sensitive test for diabetes than urine testing. Patients with delirium need full and urgent investigation to identify and treat the underlying cause. Plain chest radiographs may be useful in identifying neoplasia or tuberculosis.

Possible investigations by GPs include:

- Full blood count
- Serum vitamin B_{12}
- Serum and RBC folate
- Thyroid-stimulating hormone
- Gamma-glutamyl transferase
- Syphilis test
- Midstream urine
- Chest radiograph

Specialist Investigations

A CT scan is helpful in confirming normal pressure hydrocephalus and contributes to making the distinction between Alzheimer's disease and multi-infarct dementia, as well as clearly showing subdural haematomas. Except where normal pressure hydrocephalus or subdural haematoma is suspected on clinical grounds, the CT scan is unlikely to alter management and, in view of its expense, is not routinely indicated in patients aged 75 and over in whom the clinical picture is unequivocally that of dementia.

Younger patients in their fifties or early sixties should be referred to a neurologist who may decide on more specialist investigations. These may include a CT scan and possible genetic testing if there is a family history of dementia.

Prognostic Factors

In general, patients with Alzheimer's disease have a slightly better prognosis than those with multi-infarct dementia. Community surveys suggest a mean survival time of six to eight years from survey detection in the former and five years in the latter. In Alzheimer's disease, the severity of the dementia correlates with prognosis. Patients whose onset of illness is relatively early often have a more malignant course, whereas those with an age at onset of 80 or over have little reduction of life expectancy. In multi-infarct dementia prognosis is not correlated with severity and, commonly, death is the result of a further cerebrovascular or cardiac event.

No specific treatment is currently available for Alzheimer's disease. In the case of multi-infarct dementia, however, control of risk factors (hypertension in which the blood pressure should be reduced to around 90 mmHg diastolic, smoking, obesity, diabetes) may improve cognitive functioning as well as reducing the risk of re-infarction. It is equally important to reduce these risk factors in patients liable to develop multi-infarct dementia. This particularly includes those with a history of either stroke or TIAs. In these patients, dementia develops as a decompensation once sufficient brain tissue has infarcted. As indicated earlier, unless there is a specific contraindication, a small dose of aspirin (for example, 300 mg daily or less) may appropriately be given to patients with TIAs or established multi-infarct dementia to reduce the risk of further infarction[4]. Recent evidence suggests that a dose of 75 mg may be adequate and lead to fewer adverse effects[5].

The mainstays of management in established dementia are:

• to identify specific problems (for example, incontinence progression – remember there may be other concurrent causes) and strategies to improve them

• to preserve existing functioning

• to provide adequate overall care for the patient and their network of informal support.

A full assessment should lead to the creation of an individually tailored 'care package', regularly reviewed to remain sensitive to changing needs. Drug treatment should be aimed mainly at controlling behaviour and treating causes of acute deterioration. Major tranquillizers (for example: chlorpromazine or thioridazine starting at 25 mg; haloperidol starting at 1.5 mg) may be useful to reduce disinhibition, aggression or wandering, but may cause considerable sedation, extrapyramidal movement disorder and increased confusion. In general, all drugs should be titrated against response to achieve the lowest effective dose and reviewed regularly. Polypharmacy is particularly likely to lead to adverse effects in demented patients and compliance is often a problem. Non-drug management consists mainly of appropriate service provision, apart from specific psychological approaches, such as reminiscence therapy and reality orientation, which may be available through the psychogeriatric services.

Although there is no specific treatment for the dementias, it is well recognized that patients can benefit from attention to factors such as swift treatment of infections, regular meals, avoiding changes of environment, prescribing as few drugs as possible and, above all, full support for carers.

Criteria for Referral

All demented patients may be referred to a psychogeriatrician or geriatrician, at least for initial assessment, after which they may be referred back to the care of the GP. This could create a considerable burden on services, however, if systematic screening is being undertaken as part of the annual check for patients aged 75 and over. Some GPs may prefer to keep the initial management and assessment in their own hands. Social factors are also a major consideration in the decision whether or not to refer a patient. For instance, those who live alone may need referral and admission even for minor and fairly short-lived infections or complications. If there is a specific indication for specialized continuing assessment, or therapeutic intervention focused on demented patients, themselves and/or their carers, they should be followed up by a multidisciplinary psychogeriatric team where available.

A sudden onset of confusion or sudden deterioration in the state of a demented person requires medical assessment to exclude causes such as urinary infection, faecal impaction, chest infection and side-effects of drugs. Failure to find a cause for the deterioration or failure of the patient to respond to treatment of the apparent cause are indications for referral.

A demand for respite care is another important indication for referral because of the need to prevent breakdown in the carer's ability to cope, which may in turn lead to long-term institutionalization. Admissions for respite care need to be planned well in advance; therefore early referral is recommended if respite care is likely to be needed. In general, hospital respite care is only available to those patients who are not suitable for residential care. If they are, respite care should be arranged through the social services.

Under the new *Care in the community* programme, from April 1993, GPs and other health care professionals have a key role in providing or validating relevant information where a health problem such as dementia contributes to a patient's overall needs. When dementia is involved it is necessary to pass on as full information as possible when making referrals.

Services

A wide variety of services may be available from health and local authorities, and increasingly from voluntary organizations and private agencies.

Assessment

Health service provision includes acute assessment and follow-up, which is preferably carried out by a multidisciplinary team and largely domiciliary based. Specific assessment functions include psychometric assessment (where diagnosis is in doubt or to define focal deficits) and assessment of functioning in everyday activities. Assessment may take place in a day hospital setting, which may require regular attendance for a period of weeks.

Domiciliary Support

There may be a district wide network of domicilary support from specialist, nursing-trained 'health advisers to older people'. In many areas a domiciliary sitting service will be provided by the voluntary or private sector.

Respite Care and Continuing Care

Limited respite care provision and continuing care facilities for patients with dementia are sometimes run locally by the geriatric services. They provide some residential care for demented patients with major physical illness and/or mobility problems, but the private and voluntary sectors are increasingly providing beds for these patients.

Local Authority Provision

Local authority provision is variable, but includes social workers, home helps, Meals on Wheels, laundry and incontinence services, good-neighbour schemes, and networks of long-term day centres. Residential care is also provided in warden-controlled flats and residential homes, the latter also providing some short-term respite care.

Under the new *Care in the community* programme, local authorities may commission voluntary or private agencies to provide these facilities. However, the local authority retains responsibility for such provision if no other agencies come forward.

From April 1993, patients seeking financial support for residential or nursing homes have had to apply to their local authority social services department. GPs need to establish close links with the authorities' care managers for this provision.

Voluntary Agencies

A variety of voluntary agencies also provide services, including carers' support groups and volunteers who visit demented patients and their carers. They may be contacted, for example, through the local branch of the Alzheimer's Disease Society or Age Concern.

Private Agencies

Private agencies are rapidly developing domiciliary care facilities for older people as well as nursing and residential establishments. Some of these agencies offer domiciliary care for people with dementia and their carers. At present there is no statutory requirement for the registration and inspection of such agencies. Rigorous local checks should be undertaken before carers or professionals involve them in supporting a family caring for a person with dementia.

Monitoring and Follow-up

Frequency of monitoring depends on the severity of the patient's condition, the presence or absence of carers (both professional and informal), and whether or not the patient attends a day centre or other facility.

Responsibility

The most crucial aspect of follow-up is determining who will take primary responsibility. The psychogeriatric department, the GP, the community psychiatric nurse, the nurse adviser for older people or the district nurse are all potential candidates in individual cases.

Surveillance

Surveillance of the older population is greatly facilitated by the use of an 'at risk' register, which can be compiled from the practice age/sex register.

Frequency

Frequency of follow-up might be four- to six-monthly in the case of a patient whose condition is stable and who has a well established support network. In the case of an isolated patient or one without adequate support, visits may need to be every two weeks or more often.

What to Monitor

Monitoring may include repeat testing of cognitive function using the Abbreviated Mental Test Score or other suitable instrument to determine whether deterioration is occurring. Routine questioning and examination as appropriate are indicated to detect intercurrent problems, particularly urinary and faecal incontinence or constipation, dehydration, evidence of inadequate nutrition, anaemia and cardiac failure. Regular functional assessment is valuable in determining whether the patient and carer need extra support. This includes asking whether patients need assistance with personal care routines such as washing and bathing, feeding, cutting of nails, toileting and dressing, as well as home care tasks such as cooking, cleaning, shopping, paying bills and collecting pensions. Knowledge of the patient's mobility is also vital. This includes whether the patient can get in and out of a chair, walk on the flat or climb stairs, and whether the patient wanders, or exhibits any other dangerous behaviour.

The Carer

Follow-up also provides an opportunity to assess the carer's response to changing circumstances. Evidence of depression or other psychiatric morbidity in the carer may be an indication for greater professional support.

Support for Carers

Support for carers is a crucial part of the management of dementia. Much of the burden of caring falls on relatives, friends and neighbours. They may be patients themselves and the GP is particularly well placed to assess problems as they affect the whole family. Carers often find the reality of their relative's dementia difficult to accept and they may experience denial and/or guilt. Symptoms of personality change, failure to recognize the carer, wandering and incontinence are particularly distressing. Carers should be encouraged to ventilate their feelings, and, if possible, to share them with other carers and members of the primary care team as well as with family and friends. They may have high levels of psychiatric morbidity, which may be reduced by improving support services or institutional care where appropriate[6]. Carers also need to be aware of the natural history of the disease and that sudden deterioration necessitates a medical assessment to determine the underlying cause.

Carers should be encouraged to join the Alzheimer's Disease Society, which aims to give support to families by linking them through membership and self-help groups. This society also provides a monthly newsletter and literature on the disease and related diseases, and provides information about services. It also aims to raise public awareness for the improvement of services available to carers. The Alzheimer's Disease Society has produced a publication *Caring for the person with dementia – a guide for families and other carers*; this can be obtained from the Society at: Gordon House, 10 Greencoat Place, London SW1P 1PH. Nancy Kohner's excellent *Caring at home* is published by the National Extension College, 188 Brooklands Avenue, Cambridge, CB2 2HN. The Dementia Services Development Centre publishes a book for trainee GPs: *Dementia touches everyone: a guide for trainers and trainees in general practice 1993*. This book is available from the Dementia Services Development Centre, University of Stirling, Stirling FK9 4LA.

Benefits for Carers

The care and mobility components of the Disability Living Allowance (DLA) and Attendance Allowance can be claimed by people who need help with personal care or need supervision to avoid danger. They are not means-tested. Many patients with dementia will be eligible. Patients will be eligible if they live alone, with family or friends or with other people.

People who make their first claim after the age of 65 can only claim Attendance Allowance, which is paid at two rates. People who put in their first claim before their 66th birthday can get the DLA care component. The DLA mobility component is payable at two rates.

Invalid Care Allowance is payable to carers who spend at least 35 hours a week looking after someone who gets Attendance Allowance or DLA care component at the higher or middle rate. It is not means-tested or dependent on the person's past working record.

People with dementia may qualify for an additional discount for council tax.

Further information on these benefits is available from social security offices and from the national office of the Alzheimer's Disease Society.

Ideas for Conducting Audits on Care for Dementia Sufferers

- proportion of patients aged 75 and over tested by a standard instrument for cognitive impairment
- evidence that depression and delirium have been excluded as causes of cognitive impairment
- appropriate investigations for potentially remediable causes of dementia
- information about carer(s) recorded in notes
- regular follow-up and monitoring.

The section on Dementia has been taken from *Management Dementia: Guidelines for GPs*, published by The Alzheimer's Disease Society which was itself based on *Chapter 13* (Professor Andrew Haines and Professor Cornelius Katona) in *Occasional Paper No 58*, Clinical Guidelines (edited by Haines and Hurwitz) Royal College of General Practitioners, London, 1992. The guidelines are not evidence based.

Acute Confusion

The sudden onset of confusion in an older person is not an uncommon occurrence and ranks as an emergency that needs considerable skill and patience to manage effectively. The term 'acute confusional state' or 'delirium' is usually given to these episodes. Confusion is a clinical syndrome and not a diagnosis. Dementia can predispose an individual to confusion, but there are many other possibilities and it is always necessary to search for an underlying cause and remember that there may be several of these present at once. The list is lengthy and a full account can be found in a textbook of geriatric medicine. A summary of the causes is, however, given in Table 18.1[7].

Table 18.1: Causes of acute confusional state.

Intracranial	Space-occupying lesion
	Low pressure encephalitis
	Infection
	Vascular episode
	Trauma
Toxic	Systemic infection
	Gangrene
	Alcohol
Endocrine	Thyroid disease
	Diabetes mellitus
Organ failure	Renal
	Hepatic
	Respiratory
	Anaemia
Vitamin deficiency	B group
Medication	Altered response in older age
	Withdrawal symptoms
	Polypharmacy
Mental	Presence of Alzheimer's Disease or multi-infarct dementia, especially when associated with chronic constipation, pain and discomfort
	Depression
Social stress	Acute worries regarding family ⎫
	Harassment ⎬ especially when dementia is
	Unfamiliar surroundings ⎭ present
	Change in residence

Source: Williams, 1988[7].

Some acute crisis situations can also occur when there is a rapid deterioration of subacute or chronic confusion. They produce a very practical problem for community health and social workers. There are also background causes that contribute to the development of the crisis, but are not the illness itself. These are usually concerned with the provision of basic care to the patient and occur when this care is unavailable or withdrawn. Inadequacy of the services may also precipitate an acute situation and this has sometimes been called the 'GP frustration crisis'. The doctor dealing with the situation finds him/herself getting little help

from either the hospital or social services, but is faced with continual representa-
tions from relatives, neighbours, shopkeepers and even town councillors to 'do
something about' an older person. A great deal of strain results and the doctor is
tempted to manipulate a crisis so that help can be obtained in a dramatic, but
perhaps not absolutely necessary, form; this usually means an attempt to seek
hospital admission. Sometimes this is, in effect, treatment for the doctor's problem! An example of this was the case of an older lady who regularly rang late
each evening confessing some serious crime that she had committed earlier that
day. She usually contacted the police as well, but was hurriedly told to get in
touch with her doctor! In this type of category comes also what Arie[8] calls the
'preventive crisis', which may also be referred to as the 'Friday afternoon crisis'.
Here, a doctor sees a potentially difficult problem late on a Friday afternoon and,
being anxious to have it resolved, seeks urgent hospital admission. This may be a
form of prevention and perhaps hospitals should recognize this; but equally, the
doctor should be quite willing to accept the patient back into his care once the
initial problem has been sorted out.

Acute confusional states usually have a rapid onset and often occur at night or
in the early morning. Consciousness is clouded and disorientation is a marked
feature. The mood is usually one of fear and anxiety, but occasionally the patient
can be incongruously jocular, oblivious to reality. Speech is often incoherent and
agitation with motor restlessness can be prominent. An important feature is the
fluctuation of mental state over time. The acute confusion is often an episode in a
more chronic situation in which the symptoms are suddenly exacerbated. In older
people, the state of subacute confusion is common. The episodes of acute confusion are usually short-lived with eventual recovery. This can depend on the
underlying cause. Death may, however, be a possible outcome.

It is of prime importance to make a diagnosis of the patient's condition. A very
careful history needs to be taken; here a GP is in a privileged position.
Knowledge of the background of previous illness, treatment currently being taken
and the possibility of family stress is invaluable. The time course of the condition
also needs to be known. Unfortunately, sometimes the GP is unaware of these
because the condition has been unreported. The overall health of the patient
needs assessing, including noting physical illness and making an appraisal of the
social and environmental circumstances. A very careful look needs to be taken for
underlying background and precipitating causes. For example, a special search
must be made for respiratory and urinary-tract infection.

Most psychiatry services for older people aim to provide an appropriately
prompt response to crises with a home assessment visit. A team member may
visit if really necessary on the same day as the referral, or as swiftly as the situation demands. Out of hours, the response will generally be from the 'on call'
team, which may also cover general adult psychiatry, but this will still bring
expert help. Co-operation and assistance from the social services department are
usually forthcoming; expert help on the spot can be very useful to the GP and it
often makes it possible to manage the situation at home by diffusing a difficult
situation and providing emergency care just at the right time.

Management of acute confusional state depends upon the underlying cause. In
many instances, hospital admission is necessary for investigation and treatment.

When the episode is clearly associated with dementia, however, management at home has advantages because a move to a hospital environment can deepen the confusion. Often the patient is known to be suffering from the condition and, if not, a careful history from relatives or neighbours will usually indicate previous significant mental changes. A full history and examination is still necessary because other underlying illnesses may be present and be the principal cause of the confusion. In general practice few investigations are possible in the home, but testing the urine for sugar and infection are helpful, together with a blood test for cell count, haemoglobin, sugar, ESR, urea and electrolytes. Estimation of serum calcium level may be important because it is realized that primary hyperparathyroidism presents with acute confusion in older women. It is necessary to remember that calcium is raised in osteoporosis, neoplasm, Paget's disease and thyrotoxicosis; therefore, a serum phosphate and a haematocrit are also necessary.

If it is decided to manage the patient at home, it is essential to seek the help of a psychogeriatrician. The advantages are that this allows confirmation of the diagnosis and makes sure that there are no underlying causes present or further investigations necessary. It also provides the opportunity for a realistic plan of management to be formulated and secures a link with the hospital, so there is knowledge of the patient's previous condition if eventual admission becomes necessary. Proper communication and consultation between all the necessary services involved and the carers is essential. Sometimes this may usefully take the form of a case conference at the patient's home, where the specialist, GP and the nursing and social work members of the team can all be present. At the case conference, apart from a physical examination and history, the following assessments must be made to determine the patient's needs and the resources that are available to satisfy them. A nursing assessment will include note of other conditions that are present, such as infections and skin ulcers, and problems that may occur with diet, medication and dealing with a bedfast situation. A social assessment should include noting any difficulties that will occur in feeding, dressing, toileting and bathing the patient, and with food preparation, laundry and cleaning of the house. Ensuring adequate heating will also be necessary. A suitable room for nursing the patient will be required; when assessing this, the needs of other people, especially children, in the household should be considered. Safety is important and account must be taken of the risk of fire, electricity and gas appliances, and the opportunities available for the patient to wander. The carers will need very careful support and it is necessary to assess how much help they can realistically give in providing 24-hour cover.

In acute confusional state, drugs should be used sparingly as they can make the situation worse. In a restless patient, sedation may be used, but the doses should be small and a careful watch be kept for reactions. There are several possibilities, but most general practitioners tend to use the one they know best. The three most useful are haloperidol, thioridazine and chlormethiazole. Haloperidol is effective and has the advantage of a decreased risk of hypotension. It should only be used for a short time because it may produce extrapyramidial side-effects. Anti-parkinsonian drugs should be avoided because of the risk of causing increased confusion. Thioridazine is also useful; it has a low incidence of parkinsonian side-effects, but can give rise to postural hypotension. Chlormethiazole is also used in patients with confusional agitation and is relatively free of side-effects at a low dose. For all these drugs it is essential in the young older person to start with about half the dose of the normal adult, and, in those who are older and those of low weight, with a quarter of the normal dose. Careful monitoring of the effects is essential, especially excessive drowsiness, which can lead to falls and incontinence. In some circumstances, if there has been any hint of poor nutrition, vitamin supplements may be helpful.

Particular problems arise where the patient lives alone; sometimes hospital admission is necessary just for this reason. Occasionally, when the mental problem is severe or the patient refuses to co-operate, serious difficulties of care result. Use of provisions under the Mental Health Act are sometimes necessary in these circumstances.

Long-term supervision is usually necessary once the initial crisis period is passed. Established nursing and social worker services need to be reassessed and placed on a maintenance basis. Short-term respite is needed for carers. Although not common in the UK, boarding out of mentally sick older people in foster homes is used in some countries to provide such care. Private residential nursing homes are now a prominent feature. They all to some extent deal with older people with dementia but some are specially registered to deal with the older mentally ill. The house in which the patient lives may be inappropriate and occasionally it is best to rehouse or make adaptations to the existing building. If this is impossible and the person lives alone, permanent admission to residential accommodation may be the only possibility.

An open mind needs to be kept on all the options and it might be that, at some future date, hospital admission may be necessary because of a rapidly changing clinical condition, or failure to respond to treatment. Day hospital care may sometimes be helpful, as it has the advantage of avoiding the difficulties associated with admission. The pressure on relatives is considerably relieved when this can be arranged and there is the added advantage of others being able to watch more closely the patient's response to treatment.

The preventive aspects of the community care team's work are important when considering confusional problems in older people. The aim should be to recognize intellectual impairment at an early stage. This can be done by having an alert attitude to older people presenting at the surgery. The importance of knowing what to look for at an early stage in the development of mental illness cannot be overstressed. Failure of recent memory, changing behaviour, alteration in emotional response and depression are features that should be noted.

There are also certain at-risk groups that are more likely to develop mental illness in its widest sense and they need special surveillance. They include people living alone, the recently bereaved and those with social problems, particularly of finance and housing. Patients recently discharged from hospital or welfare homes may well find difficulty in adapting to life in the community; they sometimes relapse, developing mental symptoms. The family doctor is in a special position to be able to recognize the early deterioration of a person's mental condition because of his/her knowledge of their previous personality. Despite this, it is possible that crises will occur, but with preventive action their frequency should be reduced.

Affective Disorders

Depression

Depression is common in older age and accounts for up to half the admissions to mental hospitals in the over 65 age group. Its prevalence is up to 10% in men and 15% in women[9]. The main feature is an alteration in mood. The individual presents with a weary air of overall depression and there is often an associated degree of apathy and retardation. Patients may be fearful for their own health and that of their relatives, and show hypochondriacal symptoms. They may worry even more about their own financial and housing difficulties. There may be physical components to the illness, including complaints of lack of sleep, poor appetite, headache and loss of energy. They lose interest in previous enjoyable pastimes and have a feeling of worthlessness. Anxiety is sometimes an accompaniment and this is exhibited by restlessness and unnecessary worry.

A small percentage, perhaps between 5% and 10% of these patients, exhibit the manic phase of the illness. These people are hyperexcitable, often agitated and highly talkative, going to great lengths to describe the importance of their achievements. Outrageous activities may be embarked upon, they may spend a large quantity of money on items such as a new car or quite unnecessary pieces of furniture.

Suicide is a real danger in a depressed older person, the incidence being higher than in younger age groups. They feel a sense of unworthiness and no longer want to live; they talk about 'doing away with themselves'. This is particularly likely to happen when they have recently lost a spouse or other relative. They often say they would be better off if they could join the lost loved one. Occasionally a depressed older person is able to camouflage the depression quite successfully by confining conversation to the past and being unwilling to talk about the problems of the present. By so doing, the feelings of sadness that are constantly present are blocked out by more pleasant memories of past life.

Good results are obtained with antidepressant treatment, although appropriate doses and patient compliance are necessary. A small dose should be given initially with gradual build-up. Standard treatment is to use the tricyclic group, with dothiepine, imipramine and amitriptyline being the most commonly used, probably because of their sedative effect. Note should be taken, however, of contra-indications and side-effects. Of importance is supportive psychotherapy and counselling. Patients need the opportunity to talk about their depression. This in itself may be the only treatment required. In older age drug treatment should be continued for at least 18 months. Some would say that it should be continued indefinitely. The relapse rate is high.

GPs are not good at recognizing depression[10,11]. The Geriatric Depression Scale[12] is recommended as a screening instrument (*see* Chapter 14). Once recognized, however, treatment or supportive counselling should be given. Patients who demonstrate suicidal tendencies, who are not responding to treatment, show delusions, or have manic depressive psychoses should be referred for specialist advice.

Paraphrenia

Sometimes patients present in older age with symptoms that are predominantly paranoid, most often manifest as a feeling of being watched or persecuted in some way. Anderson[13] describes the patient as 'classically a woman, often unmarried, and frequently affected by disorders of either vision or hearing'. Indeed, deafness is said to be very potent in producing these symptoms. Patients who might have had paranoid traits throughout life, develop delusions in older age, particularly about neighbours, whom they see as a threat. Others develop fantasy ideas about sex and imagine that they are being watched whilst undressing or have worries about being molested. Virtually all of these patients improve with antipsychotic medication and, providing they keep taking it, can manage to survive acceptably in the community.

Acute Anxiety State

This is also common in older age. Patients present with a worried and agitated demeanour. Bodily symptoms are common and the patient often complains of sweating, faintness, rapid pulse rate and headaches; indeed, physical symptoms may predominate. There are usually predisposing causes, such as financial and housing worries. Harassment may be a problem and older people, particularly those living alone, may be easily upset by the uncalled-for activity of certain neighbours. Particularly unpleasant cases occur when older women are attacked and even raped either in their own home or outside. Fear of this type of assault can easily induce an acute anxiety state. Anxiety and agitation are also common features of depressive illness. Depression therefore should be particularly looked for in such patients.

Behavioural Disorders and Personality Changes

It has been said that personality defects that are present in earlier life are exaggerated as one grows older and this can be seen quite commonly in the community. A person who has been a little on the ungenerous side can become, with age, positively mean and miserly. Similarly, one who has been occasionally short tempered can become extremely awkward and unpleasant in older age. A person who was constantly quarrelling with neighbours can take this to extremes as the years advance. Enemies created in earlier life can take on a more important and sinister aspect. This may apply to relatives. Sometimes there have been hidden jealousies between members of the same family and these come to the surface in older age. These personality changes lead to the patient becoming more inward-looking; the circle of friendships diminishes, and in the end the older person lives a hermit's life and can be quite unapproachable and difficult to help.

There is described amongst hospital inpatients a condition of institutional neurosis, in which they show apathy and loss of initiative. This is said to be one reason for keeping people out of hospital. It can, however, also happen at home and the neurosis can equally well occur when patients are 'institutionalized' in the confines of their own houses.

Although older people very rarely consult with sexual problems, the family may come to the doctor with stories of aberrant sexual behaviour. An older man may suddenly develop a preoccupation with sex and this may produce difficulties with female relatives or helpers. Sometimes indecent exposure is a problem and occasionally sexual advances may be made to any member of the opposite sex who happens to be present. These may even take the form of indecent assault on children. A sexual problem may also manifest itself in quite unrealistic jealousies and can result in physical violence.

Alcoholism is occasionally seen for the first time in older age and there may be associated features of anxiety or depression. It is necessary, when dealing with an acute episode of confusion, to bear in mind the possibility of this problem and look for the tell-tale evidence of large numbers of bottles scattered around the house or in dustbins.

Obsessive neurosis may also develop in older people and they can become completely dominated by such things as cleanliness and the position of various pieces of furniture around the house. The timing of meals will have to be exact, as perhaps will the amount of sleep taken. Sometimes, such obsessions concern physical health and the patient may become absolutely fixed on the idea that he/she has got a cancer and frequent visits are paid to the doctor complaining of a whole variety of symptoms. Many radiographs and consultants' opinions are demanded, and the patient, within a few months, can pass rapidly from one hospital department to another. Very little seems to be able to convince these people that they are, in fact, physically well. Again such features may be due to an underlying depressive illness, treatment for which may transform the situation.

The Law and Vulnerable Older People

Incapacity in older age brings with it the need on occasion for both protection and representation. The law is inevitably concerned with these issues and the subject is of some complexity. The Age Concern book, *The law and vulnerable elderly people*[14], gives an excellent account of the law as it stands and discusses some of the issues.

The law has changed regarding the power of attorney, which has improved the practical management of these situations. A power of attorney is the arrangement whereby a person gives authority to another or others to act on his/her behalf. It is used, for example, when the infirmity is physical and an older person has difficulty in writing a cheque. Since the Enduring Powers of Attorney Act (1985) came into force on 10 March 1986, there are now two forms of power: the power of attorney and the enduring power of attorney. The power of attorney enables some other person to sign documents in the name of the person who has given the power. Authority given to the donee is wide, but it can be limited to a particular purpose. Once the power has been executed, it can be produced to interested persons and the signature of the donee will then be accepted in place of that of the donor. The power of attorney should, however, only be used when the donor is of full mental capacity; if the older person's mental state deteriorates, the existing power will become invalid. This has caused problems in the past, and because of this the Enduring Powers of Attorney Act came into force. It followed the Law Commission's report, *The incapacitated principle*, which recommended that the law be changed so that certain powers of attorney could continue after the donor becomes mentally incapacitated. Enduring power of attorney is designed to ensure that the nature of the power is understood by the donor and the attorney. It has been of considerable benefit, both to the legal profession and to others dealing with older persons.

To deal with the problem of mental incapacity, the Enduring Powers of Attorney Act provides that a power of attorney executed under the provisions of that act does not expire when the donor of power becomes mentally incapable, but continues during the incapacity.

The enduring power of attorney is a fairly simple form. The attorney appointed can be either an individual or two persons jointly, and they can be given full authority to act or their authority can be limited to certain areas. It would be normal in most cases where the attorney is a close relative and probably an ultimate beneficiary of the donor's estate, for the person to be given general authority to deal with all the donor's property and affairs. Specific restrictions can, however, be inserted into the power but there is a crucial difference from the old powers; the donor states that, 'I intend that the power should continue even if I become mentally incapable.' The donor is required to state that he/she has read the notes in Part A of the form that set out full details of what the attorney can do, and in particular set out that the power will continue if the donor becomes mentally incapable. The document is simply signed by the donor in the presence of a witness; the attorney is required to sign also to say that they realize that, when the donor has become mentally incapable, they are under a duty to apply to the court for registration of the power of attorney under the Enduring Powers of Attorney Act. As and when the donor of the power becomes, or is thought to be becoming, mentally incapable, the power is registered with the Court of Protection.

Since the attorney appointed is chosen by the elderly person themselves there is not the difficulty and formality that used to be experienced with the appointment of a receiver by the Court of Protection. The power can, of course be cancelled by the donor at any time before it has been registered.

If older people cannot manage their own affairs because of mental disorder, and where an enduring power of attorney is not in existence, it is necessary to go to the Court of Protection, which exists to safeguard older persons' interests. The Court has existed in one form or another for 600 years, but is now regulated by the Mental Health Act (1983) and the Court of Protection Rules (1984). In June 1985 there were 22 545 people under the Court of Protection. It is estimated that 75% were aged over 60, many living in residential homes, others in hospitals or nursing homes and some in relatives' homes.

The Court's responsibility is for financial matters. The office address is: Court of Protection, 24 Kingsway, London WC2 (Tel: 0171 269 7000); a letter to the chief clerk will produce guidance for relatives of those in this situation. In effect, once the case has been properly investigated and the incapacity of the older person established by written evidence from the appropriate medical practitioner, all the affairs of the older person are placed under the supervision of the Court of Protection. Property cannot then be disposed of, nor can income or assets be dealt with, unless the Court of Protection agrees. The court will usually appoint some person, known as a receiver, who is often a close relative, a friend, or professional adviser, to deal, under its instruction, with the older person's property. All transactions in the financial affairs of the person concerned must be dealt with in this way. To avoid frequent applications to the Court, an order is normally made for weekly payments of the benefits of the older person, but any disposal of assets, such as a house or investments, will need the specific sanction of the Court of Protection. The legal costs of obtaining such an order and of administering it are normally dealt with out of the estate of the person concerned.

Diabetes Mellitus

The prevalence of diabetes amongst older people is between 3% and 6%[15,16]. They may have long established insulin dependent diabetes, but it is the non insulin dependent variety which is the most common. It is generally agreed that diabetes is indicated by either a fasting blood sugar of over 7.2 mmol/l, or, in a glucose tolerance test, a blood sugar level, two hours after 75 gm of glucose by mouth has been administered, of 11.1 mmol/l or more. If a patient presents with symptoms or complications of diabetes, a simple random blood sugar test is usually sufficient to make a diagnosis.

Up to one quarter of the population of patients over 75 years old have abnormal tolerance tests, but many of these are without glycosuria. Diabetes mellitus has been shown to be a frequent undiagnosed condition in older people, and, in a survey of patients of aged over 75 in general practice, the prevalence of diabetes was 5%, of which half was previously unreported[17]. It has also been shown that diabetes is a neglected area in older people and many patients are denied specialist care until a medical crisis occurs[18]. Other studies have shown that diabetes is associated with inadequate and unstructured care, severe disability and many unmet needs[15,19].

The classical symptoms of thirst and polyuria occur in older people but are less urgent than in younger people; a careful history is necessary to ascertain their presence. Weight loss and pruritus vulvae or balanitis may give the first hint of developing diabetes. A patient developing incontinence or bed-wetting should be suspected of the condition; again these are often early symptoms. Nocturia may be a presenting symptom, but this is often put down to prostatism in an older man. Diabetes may also present as one of its complications. These include vascular disease due to arteriosclerosis, either as coronary thrombosis or ischaemic disease of the lower limb. This latter, when combined with diabetic neuropathy, which often causes loss of sensation in the feet, can cause infected ulcers and eventually gangrene; this is a serious complication. Older persons with a predisposition to certain infections (eg those due to fungi, usually candidiasis, and staphylococci) should be suspected of having diabetes.

Another complication that sometimes presents is renal failure. Ketoacidosis is rare in older people, but any confused or comatose older patient should be suspected of having the disease, particularly if dehydrated. A case of late onset diabetes is sometimes found at health checks for age 75 and over patients by the finding of glycosuria. The simplest way of testing for diabetes is a stick urine test, which is easy to carry out, and, considering how common diabetes is in older people, it should always be done. Because not all elderly diabetics have glycosuria, the safest way of screening elderly people for diabetes is to do a single fasting laboratory blood sugar.

Diabetes in older people is not a mild disease. Many have complications, even at the time of diagnosis, and their development is common and serious. Morbidity is consistently underestimated in official statistics because it is underreported by about 60% on the death certificates of older people with cardiac or cerebral vascular disease or multiple chronic conditions[18]. The major cause of death in non-insulin dependent diabetes mellitus are myocardial infarction and stroke. A community study in Oxfordshire emphasized the extensive morbidity amongst diabetic patients over the age of 60 and the fact that complications were not confined to a single subgroup[20]. Only 20% were free from complications of diabetes; 75% were also suffering from at least one other disease. Management is made more difficult by the presence of other pathology, which can include arthritis, arteriosclerotic disease and dementia.

Once diagnosed, the problem facing the doctor in the management of late onset diabetes is how enthusiastically to treat the condition. Drugs should be kept as simple as possible because difficulties can arise from the patient's inability to adhere to complicated table regimens and the necessity for regular urine and blood sugar testing. Many older people, for economic reasons, live on a high carbohydrate diet and there are sometimes problems with adjustment. Many over 75-year-old diabetic patients are generally fit and well able to manage their own treatment. Sometimes, however, it is necessary to recruit the help of some responsible relative or friend to supervise this. A general discussion will be necessary to explain the nature of the problem and possible dangers, particularly hypoglycaemia and other complications of the disease.

It is important to assess the impact of the coexisting disease and the patient's quality of life, so that an adequate therapeutic package can be constructed. Many cases of non-insulin dependent diabetes mellitus can be controlled by dietary measures. The diet should be simple, even if not quite correct, so that the patient can keep to it. It is easy to lose heart coping with a detailed and complicated regimen. The diet should be in the region of 100–200 g of carbohydrate daily, a good starting point for most older patients being about 140g. The need to specify the amount of carbohydrate, however, is not really essential and nearly all diabetics need only a 'no sugar' or ordinary reducing diet. The modern tendency is to restrict fats and cholesterol a little because diabetes is associated with raised serum cholesterol and diabetic patients have enough trouble with their arteries without encouraging atheroma. A very strict low cholesterol diet is probably unnecessary, but perhaps the patient should know which foods contain most cholesterol so that they can avoid eating more than a reasonable 'small normal' amount of such things as eggs and cream. High fibre diets are also recommended. Many of the patients are also obese and the total calorie intake should be restricted.

Dieticians are very helpful in advising about these problems, but a practice nurse can often supervise the diet. When monitoring non-insulin dependent diabetic patients, regular weighing is important as well as regular measurement of fasting blood sugar.

Hypoglycaemic agents are now an established part of the treatment of non-insulin dependent diabetes in older age. Apart from having different durations of action, the sulphonylureas are all similar, but probably the safest for older people are tolbutamide and gliclazide, both of which are relatively short-acting. The main disadvantage of tolbutamide is that the tablets are rather large and really have to be taken 3–4 times per day. All sulphonylureas can cause severe, and potentially fatal, hypoglycaemia. The worst offenders are undoubtedly the longer-acting drugs chlorpropamide and glibenclamide. Patients should, however, need to be warned of the possibility and specifically told to stop the tablets if they are not eating. Apart from this, however, sulphonylureas are remarkably free from side-effects. They should always be started with the minimum possible dose, for example 40 mg (half a tablet) of gliclazide or 1.25 mg (again, half a tablet) of glibenclamide.

Patients with liver and kidney failure should not be given oral hypoglycaemic agents. It would for instance be dangerous (because of the risk of lactic acidosis) to give metformin to a patient with a raised creatinine or anyone with severe heart failure. Congestive heart failure is a special problem and the question is sometimes raised of whether hypoglycaemic agents should be used with thiazine diuretics. In practice, if the patient is in a stable situation it is probably safe, providing special caution is taken when starting treatment or changing the dose, and providing there is a constant awareness of the possibility that changes in the degree of failure, or reduction in liver or kidney sufficiency, may change the diabetic state.

Probably a relatively low proportion of older patients require insulin. Insulin dependent diabetes arising for the first time in this age group is not particularly uncommon. Management is usually straightforward and the dividend in terms of improved health is quite remarkable. Stabilization is carried out at home by a diabetic specialist nurse and it is perfectly safe providing that a start is made with low doses with a gradual build-up. The nurse can also teach the patient to monitor their own blood glucose. Most older people can manage to inject themselves and understand protocols for increasing the dose. The use of a pen injector is now becoming the norm. Non-insulin dependent diabetic patients who do best on insulin are those who are thinnest and most insulin deficient. The main disadvantage of insulin in non-insulin dependent diabetes is weight gain.

Because of the importance of the complications in older diabetic patients, these need special attention whatever the type of diabetes. Ophthalmic, renal, vascular and neurological complications should be carefully monitored; their treatment is along the usual lines described in text-books of medicine. At the earliest signs of difficulty, expert help should be sought and when hypoglycaemic attacks occur these should be treated in hospital especially for those patients who were on sylphonylureas. Chronic hypoglycaemia can easily be overlooked in older people, since the only obvious symptoms are mild confusion, shivering or sweating, which occur frequently in older age from other causes.

There is now a shift to more care of older diabetic patients in the community. This has necessitated the creation of separate diabetic clinics in health centres where GPs can look after their own older diabetic patients. There are also some health visitors who have special training in diabetes, and special liaison diabetic nurses who maintain contact with hospital diabetic clinics. Practice nurses are now being trained specifically to monitor these patients within practices. Regular follow-up is necessary to check the control of the diabetes and to detect complications early. Foot problems can be avoided by regular visits to a chiropodist.

There is also the problem of older diabetics who hold driving licences. The risks of hypoglycaemia are such that it is very important that advice should be given about eating before driving for any distance, and stopping frequently for snacks to step up the blood sugar level. If the patient finds that he/she does not have any warning of the onset of hypoglycaemia, it is probably best to advise avoiding driving altogether.

Usually a long established diabetic will not require any alteration in treatment with advancing age, but again it is important that the patient's condition is monitored. Each practice should have a check-list of actions that should be undertaken at a follow-up clinic. This would include a review of the drugs, a check of blood sugar, glycated haemoglobin, and blood urea, a test of albumin in the urine, and checks on the fundi, foot reflexes, and body weight. The identification of diabetic retinopathy is becoming increasingly important because of the successful treatment of this condition by ophthalmic surgeons using laser therapy. There is also a need at diabetic clinics to interview relatives and carers, if possible, so that any problems can be fully discussed and general support given.

Of great importance is the glycaemic control of the diabetic patient; there has been interest in the variables which might affect this in general practice. A study looking at control as measured by random glycated haemoglobin A1 estimation used multiple regression analysis to identify factors that might affect this control[21]. Women had significantly worse control than men. Other patient factors, such as age, social class, life-style, attitudes, satisfaction and knowledge, had no association with glycaemic control. Of all the doctor factors examined, only doctors who professed a special interest in diabetes achieved significantly better glycaemic control. Bigger and better equipped practices and those with diabetic mini-clinics had patients with significantly better glycaemic control, as did those with access to dietetic advice. Patients attending hospital clinics had worse glycaemic control, but this seemed to be attributable to the case-mix and practice characteristics. Shared care did not contribute to the multiple linear regression model. It was concluded that glycaemic control among diabetic patients in the community is related to such factors as treatment group, number of diabetic related clinical events, sex, and years since diagnosis; it is also related to the organization and process of care. The findings supported a policy of concentrating diabetic care on doctors with a special interest in diabetes in well equipped practices with adequate dietetic support[21].

Mobility

Assessment of mobility is a very important aspect of the examination of an older person. Loss of mobility can be partial or complete. The prevalence of totally bed-fast older people is not high, but it increases with advancing age. Relative mobility, which often means that the person is housefast, is a common cause of reduced effective health. Functional ability is all important and, before examination of the limbs and joints, it is necessary to find out what the old person can actually do. Can the patient do the following things: walk unaided or only with a frame, tripod or support from furniture; get out of bed or a chair; stoop to pick things up from the floor; or undertake basic personal tasks? It is also helpful to know whether the patient can use public transport, shop and enjoy hobbies and social contact.

If diminished mobility has been established by functional assessment, possible causes should be sought by examination. Pain, stiffness and swelling of the joints, and weakness, wasting, tremor or rigidity of the limbs, if present, are obvious; a patient's stance may also be awkward and unsteady. Movements may lack co-ordination A weak grip may interfere with the efficient use of walking aids. Examination of the feet sometimes reveals gnarled toenails and twisted joints that hinder walking. Improperly fitting shoes sometimes also contribute to immobility.

Immobility is always a feature of a disorder; by itself it does not constitute a diagnosis. Pain and weakness are the main reasons for difficulty in movement, with perhaps mental apathy contributing to the overall inertia. Pain, which must never be accepted as normal in older age, may arise from bones, muscles, tendons or joints. Bone causes include osteoporosis osteomalacia, Paget's disease and malignancy. Joint causes include osteoarthritis, rheumatoid arthritis and, less frequently, gout. Many minor muscular conditions, such as fibrositis, can cause pain and immobility. An illness that affect older people in particular is polymyalgia rheumatica. This is more common in women and is associated with pain and stiffness in the neck, spreading to the shoulder muscles and also occasionally to the gluteal and thigh muscles. The patient may also have generalized symptoms such as headaches, sweating and anorexia. This condition is sometimes associated with temporal arteritis and, in both, the ESR is raised. The illness lasts for a few months and is likely to be recurrent. The treatment is by using steroids, often initially in large doses; the dose is then reduced according to the level of the ESR and the relief of symptoms.

The condition of the feet of older people is important, as disorders easily impede mobility. Bunions associated with hallux valgus may be extremely painful, as are corns and callouses. Toe-nail deformity may make walking extremely difficult. The prevalence of fungal infection of the feet is probably high and may need treating.

Neurological disease can produce actual muscle wasting and lack of co-ordination. Two examples of this are motor neurone disease and Parkinson's disease.

Parkinson's disease is characterized by slowness of movement, rigidity and tremor; the face shows a mask-like appearance and dementia may be an associated condition. A shuffling gait, consisting of a few small steps and a tendency to lean forward, with difficulty in stopping, is frequently seen. Generalized clumsiness is often present, with difficulty in dressing and undressing a marked feature. The rigidity may be severe and the cogwheel effect of a series of small jerks when moving the elbow may be demonstrated. The tremor starts in the hand and is coarse, becoming increased when a voluntary movement is undertaken; it disappears during sleep.

Motor neurone disease is characterized by wasting of the muscles of all four limbs. Fasciculations or fine movements in the muscles can be seen and the reflexes are brisk. The weakness associated with the muscle wasting can sometimes become severe and can lead to considerable difficulty. This can be particularly burdensome when the mental state remains unimpaired. Patients who have previously been able to look after themselves, and even drive a car, find it extremely frustrating to be limited by muscular weakness. The tongue and throat muscles can be affected, giving rise to difficulties with salivation, swallowing and nutrition.

Disorders of the heart and lungs can contribute to immobility by causing breathlessness, ankle swelling, chest pain or pain in the legs on walking. General debility may result from endocrine, renal and blood diseases, reducing a patient's ability to move around. A patient's mental state, if impaired, can also contribute to inertia, and visual and hearing difficulties can have the same effect. Oversedation and the side-effects of some drugs not infrequently limit mobility. Occasionally older people can suddenly go 'off their feet' and, for no obvious reason, become bedfast. These cases are analogous to the 'failure to thrive' syndrome in infants, and the cause may be equally difficult to find. Sometimes diseases such as chest infection are responsible. More than one pathology may contribute to immobility, and such conditions as obesity and anaemia often exacerbate the problem. Extreme old age itself can influence movements (disuse atrophy), although it is often surprising how spry many 90-year-olds can be.

It can be seen that there are many causes of immobility. There must be motivation to move out of the house or at least out of the chair. Sometimes an inconveniently placed house can psychologically deter an older person from making the effort to venture outside. Management has to take all these aspects into account. However, it is important that full medical examination is carried out in order to detect underlying conditions. Physical illnesses must be treated. Chiropody may be all that is necessary in some circumstances, but occasionally full rehabilitation services may be needed to mobilize the patient. Provision of aids, appliances and modifications to the house are often helpful, particularly as part of a general programme of physiotherapy. Stimulating an older person mentally by encouraging interest in an outside activity or hobby can change a housefast isolate into a more active member of the community. Transfer to ground-floor accommodation near a shopping precinct may enable an older person once more to undertake independent shopping. In all this, the role of the community physiotherapist is very important. Help from him/her can be obtained during the initial assessment and also when planning management. Physiotherapy in the home plays a crucial part in returning an older person to full mobility or achieving the best possible result. The effect that a good physiotherapist can have on the morale and confidence of an older person is impressive to see.

Falls

Falls are a major hazard of older age and a common cause of injury and sometimes death. Morris[22] points out that in England each year 300 000 older people present following accidents to their local accident and emergency departments; 59% of these accidents occur in the home, usually as a result of a fall. As a result of accidents 4626 people age 65 and over die each year. Falls are a major cause of avoidable ill health and death of older people, particularly in extreme old age. Clarke[23], when studying falls, found that nearly three-quarters of them occurred in or near the patient's home and about one-fifth further afield. These latter take place almost exclusively near roads, particularly on pavements, kerbs and pedestrian crossings, where distraction by traffic or uneven surfaces are commonly causal factors. Getting on and off buses can also be a hazard. The remainder of falls usually take place in welfare homes or hospital; it is less common for them to occur in such places as churches, shops and places of work.

Hip fractures are the commonest major sequelae of falls, and over the last 20 years the incidence has doubled. They are twice as common in women as in men and at any age are associated with a high mortality and morbidity. At present there are 54 028 cases of hip fracture in England per year, but, with an ageing population, this figure will continue to rise. Between 28% and 34% of older people sustain a fall each year[24]. The prevalence of falls is greater in women. Not all will result in serious injury. The prevalence and frequency also tends to be much higher in the residential and nursing home sector, because of the residents' greater frailty.

Causes of Falls

Clarke[23] describes three main types of fall mechanism:

- *Accidental falls:* here the event is determined by environmental factors only, for example, slipping on an icy surface or tripping over a rug or a mat.
- *Symptomatic falls:* here the cause is due to factors within the patient and can result from either fits or faints. In this group are also falls caused by dizziness or light-headedness.
- *Mixed-type falls:* here both environmental and patient factors are combined.

Of the accidental variety, there are many possible causes; they include trips, slips and being knocked over by a vehicle or another person. Symptomatic falls can be caused, as stated above, by fits or faints. Grand mal-type epileptic fits might be due to pre-existing idiopathic epilepsy or to cerebrovascular disease, intracranial tumour, trauma or hypoglycaemia. Fainting attacks without the characteristics of a fit may be due to TIA, cardiac infarction, a Stokes–Adams attack or postural hypotension. Another cause is the so-called 'drop attack', whose nature is still rather obscure. Characteristically, in these attacks, the patient, most commonly a woman, falls suddenly because, without warning, the legs go weak and flaccid. There is no loss of consciousness but the unsteadiness of the legs often persists for some time. Falls also occur at night; these may be due to postural hypotension occurring when a person gets out of bed quickly, following a sudden urge to pass urine. A patient may be confused at night because of too heavy sedation, or restless because of too little sedation. Both circumstances can lead to nocturnal wanderings and resultant falls. Overuse of alcohol by older people, a problem that is perhaps increasing, can also be contributory. Patients with general debility and frailness are more likely to fall, particularly if they also suffer from Parkinson's disease, especially when this is combined with poor vision. Arthritis is also a common cause, and falls are also more likely after a period in bed because of illness. Many patients with progressive acquired gait disturbance, loss of balance and falling may be found who do not fit in any of the categories described above. The condition may in these circumstances be gait dyspraxia. The patient reports a sensation of extreme instability amounting to a conviction that they will fall unless they are supported either by hanging on to something secure or being helped; the feeling of instability is immediately relieved by sitting down. Gait dyspraxia probably arises from any condition causing dysfunction in the frontal lobes, including the motor associated areas. Patients presenting with gait dyspraxia should be carefully assessed and investigated because, although treatment may not be possible, help can be provided by occupational therapy, appliances and physiotherapy[25].

Management

Management of an acute fall depends of course on the injuries sustained. Ideally, an eye-witness account of the episode should be obtained so that, if there is a possibility that the fall was due to a fit, investigation can be undertaken. This could be very extensive if all the causes of a fit in an older person are to be eliminated, and common sense is necessary when deciding what tests to undertake. Help from a consultant geriatrician is usually recommended. Again, when the cause of the fall has been a faint of some type, a search for disease causes should be made; this is important as some of these conditions can be treated.

It is also important to look at the patient's social circumstances. Safety in the home must be assessed; the arrangement of the patient's living area may need adjustment. Sometimes it is necessary, where a person is having frequent falls and is living alone, to arrange transfer to welfare accommodation or to warden-supervised housing.

Prevention of Falls

The aim should be, if possible, to prevent falls. Clarke[24] lists simple ways of approaching the problem and these are summarized here:

- *Removal of hazards in the home.* In many instances these are obvious, but particular attention should be paid to loose rugs, carpets with holes and uneven surfaces. A good standard of lighting is essential and high wattage bulbs should be used. Handrails may be fitted to aid the older person's movement. All fires should be protected by fire-guards.

- *Preservation of good health and confidence.* When a patient has had a fall, assessment is necessary so that treatable conditions can be remedied. Poor vision should be corrected. Careful rehabilitation after illness or injury should reduce the possibility of further accident.

- *Wearing of appropriate footwear.* Rubber and crepe soles are unsatisfactory in wet and icy conditions. Non-slip or leather soles are preferable.

- *Special care outdoors.* In winter, when conditions are bad, high-risk persons should remain indoors. If it is necessary to go out, they should be accompanied and routes should be chosen where there is likely to be the least danger from distraction by traffic. They should cross busy roads on pedestrian crossings if at all possible, and carry shopping in a wheeled container. Care should be taken when boarding and alighting from public transport. A careful watch should be kept for uneven surfaces and care taken at kerbs.

- *Awareness of the danger of sudden changes in posture.* Patients should be careful when getting in and out of bed or chairs, and instructed to do this slowly.

- *Monitoring of night sedation.* Careful attention is needed to the level of night sedation prescribed for an older person, since this may be more a cause of falls than a help. Indeed, all drug therapy for patients with falls should be reviewed. Night sedation should, however, be adequate so that nocturnal wanderings are avoided.

It is obviously essential to identify patients who are at risk of falling. Health checks on older people can help and a note made of patients with a history of falling. Preventive measures can then be instituted and the patients educated about the various safety precautions.

Vision Failure

Over the past 20 years there has been a change in the age prevalence of blindness. These days, most severely defective vision occurs amongst older people. Visual failure can be an important cause of loss of independence and result in social isolation. With increasing blindness, mobility becomes more difficult and an older person is deprived of hobbies such as gardening, watching television and visiting the cinema. Vision can be quickly and simply assessed by asking patients if they can read a newspaper, watch television or recognize the details of a photograph or picture.

Comparatively few people become blind suddenly and there is likely to be a gradual deterioration of vision over several years. This is always due to disease and older age alone is not a cause of blindness. The commonest diseases leading to failing vision are cataract, macular degeneration and chronic glaucoma. Sudden loss of vision, when it occurs, is usually due to acute glaucoma, occlusion of the central retinal artery or vein, or a detached retina. Chronic open-angle glaucoma produces gradual loss of vision. Many of these conditions are treatable.

Cataracts, which may originate much earlier in life, develop slowly and are often symmetrical. Successful extraction and the insertion of an optical implant is now the rule and can be performed in all age groups. The operation enables the patient to achieve good vision without the use of thick spectacles.

Senile macular degeneration with pigmentation of the macula is difficult to treat, although, as the periphery is not affected, complete blindness does not occur. Many cases of macular degeneration are helped by low-vision aids, for example telescopic glasses or simple hand magnifiers.

Diabetic retinopathy can be halted to a certain extent by careful control of the disease. Partial ablation of the affected portion of the retina, either by light coagulation or laser therapy, is useful in many cases as it delays retinopathy by cutting down the oxygen needs, hence allowing the ailing vasculature to maintain the important central area.

Acute glaucoma is not very common and usually presents as an emergency. The angle is closed in these cases and the second eye is invariably at risk, hence the need for prophylactic peripheral iridectomy. Early symptoms include blurring of vision and the perception of 'halo' effects round the lights. Glaucomatous haloes are specifically rainbow-lined, the so-called 'rainbow rings' (monochromic haloes around lights are common and may indicate cataract). Vision is subsequently lost and symptoms vary from ache to severe pain. The intraocular tension is increased and the pupil is usually fixed, oval and dilated, rather than distorted. The chronic, open angle type of glaucoma that occurs in older people is more common and much more insidious in onset. The visual field is lost, often to a remarkable extent, before the situation is recognized. It is important that this loss should be appreciated as it may be highly dangerous to old people, for example, when crossing roads. Apart from field loss and raised intraocular pressure, cupping of the optic disc is present. When examining older people, it is useful to check the ocular tension and to do a simple visual field test. The condition is genetically determined and relatives of patients with glaucoma should be examined. Treatment is specialized, and surgery is recommended for acute glaucoma. Timolol maleate 0.25% is the treatment of choice in chronic open angle glaucoma, though early surgery is sometimes needed.

Despite the efficiency of eye drops, and often because of poor compliance in older people, many patients with these conditions become permanently partially sighted or blind. Even in these patients, much can be done to help. The first essential is to place the patient's name on the Blind Register. A certificate of registration (BD8 in England and Wales and BP1 in Scotland) must first be completed by a consultant ophthalmologist and forwarded to the local social services department. A social worker then interviews the person to explain the voluntary nature of registration and the benefits available. For registration, it is necessary to define the degree of blindness or partial-sightedness. These special criteria are fully set out in Form BD8.

Registration in working adults has a considerable effect on the help to which they are entitled for jobs and training, but this is rarely applicable to older people. Social services departments are responsible for social care of older people on the register. General support and counselling are available, as is help with travel, supply of white canes and 'talking books'. Rehabilitation centres sometimes cater for newly blind older people. Some voluntary organizations are particularly interested in the blind and their assistance should be sought.

Despite this help, many older people with failing vision find it difficult to cope. There is a limit to what can be achieved by re-education and perhaps it is wiser to aim at realistic objectives only. First, the newly blind older person should be encouraged to walk around the house, making sure that no dangerous objects are in the way. The furniture should remain in the same place so that they can learn the way around and gain confidence. Dressing and undressing can be made easier by using clothes that have few buttons and making use of zip fasteners. Shoes should be slip-on rather than laced. Shaving should be undertaken by an electric razor, and eating and drinking can be helped by special utensils. New interests can be encouraged, such as radio, records and tape recordings. Talking books are helpful and, for the partially sighted, books with large print can be obtained from most libraries. Good lighting is essential.

It is perhaps too late for most older people to learn Braille, but there are simpler types of tactile reading, such as the Moon system, that may be possible. There is much sympathy in society generally for the blind and an older person so affected should be encouraged to persist in social activities and remain a part of the community.

Deafness

The prevalence of deafness increases with age. In a survey of over 75-year olds, 9% were effectively totally deaf and many more could hear only the shouted voice[17]. Often they were prepared to tolerate the disability without seeking help. Unlike blindness, deafness attracts little sympathy. This adds to the sufferer's problems and, because of embarrassment, they may become socially isolated and even develop paranoid symptoms.

Very simple tests will assess an older person's hearing ability. The responses to a ticking watch, and a whispered, normal and shouted voice, give an adequate estimate of hearing. The four-inch whispered test[26] is described in Chapter 14. The basic types of hearing loss are conductive deafness, nerve deafness and a combination of the two, mixed deafness. The Rinne test distinguishes between conductive and nerve deafness. This is carried out by holding a vibrating 512 Hz tuning fork close to the aural canal and then immediately pressing the base of the fork on the bone behind. It is heard better via the bone in conductive deafness; the opposite is the case in nerve deafness (and the normal ear). A false negative Rinne, in which a tuning fork placed on the mastoid process is heard better by air conduction, occurs in severe sensoryneural loss and is attributed to sound being conducted across the skull to the opposite cochlea.

Wax may only muffle otherwise good hearing, but can considerably aggravate poor hearing. Good benefit is obtained by syringing away the wax, which, if hard, should be previously softened by a few days' use of olive oil. When syringing, it is necessary to be sure that the water is at approximate body temperature; if too hot or cold it can cause troublesome temporary unsteadiness.

Hearing is dependent on sound vibrations being collected by the eardrums and transmitted by the three small bones (ossicles) of the middle ear to the cochlea, which contains the nerve endings of the hearing nerve. Conductive hearing loss is due to a disorder of the drum or the ossicles. Two common causes are a perforated drum or ossicular adhesions, both legacies of infection. Conductive hearing loss may also be due to disease of the aural canal; another cause is otosclerosis, an inherited tendency to new bone formation, which interferes with the stapes, the innermost ossicle. This, however, is uncommon in older people and usually present earlier in life. Nerve deafness in older people is usually due to presbycousis (a word meaning gradual degeneration of the cochlea). Noise-induced hearing loss from previous noisy work commonly adds to presbycousis. Less common causes are trauma, other inherited disorders, Menière's disease and Paget's disease of the skull.

Noises in the ears and head (tinnitus) may accompany any type of deafness. In older people, while this cannot be cured, it may be treated with appropriate advice and indeed a hearing aid may be an effective way of helping to control tinnitus by providing more sound for the patient with this condition. Occasionally in older people, provision of a tinnitus masker may be of benefit. Explanation and reassurance concerning its benign nature may help patients to come to terms with the condition.

Very substantial help is given to most deaf people by hearing aids but normal hearing can never be restored. There are two type available: those worn behind the ear and the body-worn aids that may be necessary when severe deafness is present. Both are available to older people on the National Health Service. Conductive deafness responds rather better than nerve deafness. It is essential to make sure that the person knows how to use the device and a certain degree of teaching is necessary to bring maximum benefit. This is normally given at the hospital hearing-aid clinics. When talking to a deaf person it is important to speak clearly and it is preferable to face the listener. Many people, even though they have not been formally instructed in lip-reading skills, are able to utilize lip and facial information in what is being said.

A new development has been direct referrals from GPs for hearing aid provision. This is increasingly becoming the practice in departments of otorhinolaryngology and the majority are offering it to patients aged 65 and over. The GP assumes the clinical responsibility.

References

1. Thompson MK. (1986) The case for developmental gerontology - Thompson's octad. *J R Coll Gen Pract* **39**: 29–32.

2. Sandercock PA, Lindley RI. (1993) Management of acute stroke. *Prescriber's J* **33**: 196–205.

3. Folstein MF, Folstein SE, McHugh PR. (1975) Mini-Mental State: a practical method for grading the cognitive state of patients for the clinician. *J Psychiatr Res* **12**: 189–98.

4. Antiplatelet Trialists Collaboration. (1988) Secondary prevention of vascular disease by prolonged antiplatelet treatment. *Br Med J* **296**: 320–31.

5. SALT Collaborative Group. (1991) The Swedish aspirin low dose trial (SALT) of 75 mg aspirin as secondary prophylaxis after cerebo-vascular ischaemic events. *Lancet* **338**: 1345–9.

6. Levin E, Sinclair I, Gorbach P. (1989) *Families, services and confusion in old age.* Aldershot, Avebury.

7. Williams EI. (1988) Crisis management of acute confusion. *MIMS Magazine* (**1 March**): 87–93.

8. Arie T. (1973) Dementia in the elderly: diagnosis and assessment. *Br Med J* iv: 540–3.

9. Wright AF. (1992) *Depression: recognition and management in general practice.* Royal College of General Practitioners, London.

10. Goldberg DP, Steele JJ, Johnson A, *et al.* (1982) Ability of primary care physicians to make accurate ratings of psychiatric symptoms. *Arch Gen Psychiatry* **39**: 829–33.

11. Freeling P, Rao BM, Paykel ES, *et al.* (1985) Unrecognised depression in general practice. *Br Med J* **290**: 1880–3.

12. Shelk JI, Yesavage JA. (1986) Geriatric depression scale (GDS): recent evidence and development of a shorter version. In: Brink TL, editor. *Clinical gerontology: a guide to assessment and intervention.* Haworth Press, New York.

13. Anderson WF. (1971) *Practical management of the elderly.* Blackwell Scientific, Oxford.

14. Greengross S, chair. (1986) *The law and vulnerable elderly people.* Age Concern England, Mitcham, Surrey.

15. Neil HAW, Gatling W, Mather HM, *et al.* (1987) The Oxford Community Diabetes Study: evidence for an increase in the prevalence of known diabetes. *Diabetic Med* **4**: 539–43.

16. Croxson SCM, Burden AC, Boddington M, *et al.* (1991) The prevalence of diabetes in elderly people, *Diabetic Med* **8**: 28–31.

17. Williams EI, Bennett FM, Nixon JV, *et al.* (1972) Socio-medical survey of patients over 75 in general practice. *Br Med J* **2**: 445–8.

18. Tattersall RB. (1984) Diabetes in the elderly: a neglected area? *Diabetologia* **27**: 167–73.

19. Dornan TL, Petchey M, Dow JDC, *et al.* (1992) A community survey of diabetes in the elderly. *Diabetic Med* **9**: 860–5.

20. Neil HAW, Thomson AV, Thorogood M, Fowler GH, Mann JI. (1989) Diabetes in the elderly: the Oxford Community Diabetes Study. *Diabetic Med* 6: 608–13.

21. Pringle M, Stewart-Evans C, Coupland C, *et al.* (1993) Influences on control in diabetes mellitus: patient, doctor, practice, or delivery of care? *Br Med J* 306: 630–34.

22. Morris J. (1994) Falls in older people [editorial]. *J R Soc Med* 87: 435–6.

23. Clarke ANG. (1972) Falls in old age. *Modern Geriatr* 2: 332–6.

24. Cwikel J. (1992) Falls among elderly people living at home: medical and social factors in a national sample: *J Med Sci* 28: 446–53.

25. Godwin-Austin R, Bendall J. (1992) *The neurology of the elderly*. Springer-Verlag, London, 49–51.

26. Swan IRC, Browning GG. (1985) The whispered voice as a screening test for hearing impairment. *J R Coll Gen Pract* 35: 197.

19
Nutrition and Hypothermia

Nutrition

Both health and social workers need to be interested in the nutritional state of older people; it is sometimes necessary to assess whether they are getting an adequate diet and to advise on proper food and intake. This is particularly true of those who may be too apathetic to cook meals, those who are much older and those living alone, who may have difficulty with shopping. It is useful therefore to have some idea of how to assess a person's nutritional level and to understand the causes of poor food intake, so that they may be identified and the situation avoided.

It is not easy to be dogmatic about the ideal level of nutrition and there are considerable differences in the needs of people in general for energy and nutrients. These variations persist into older age. Body size, sex and physical activity are all factors that influence need. The quality of the food and the ease with which it is absorbed are also relevant. With increasing age, there tends to be a gradual decrease in physical activity and a decline in metabolism at rest. It is to be expected, therefore, that older people will eat less. If this reduction is evenly distributed throughout the diet, malnutrition should not occur unless there are circumstances such as those mentioned above where faulty nutrition is present.

How prevalent is malnutrition? Early surveys tended to find a fair amount of inadequate food intake and established cases of vitamin C deficiency were sometimes encountered. Many of these studies were on patients admitted to hospital and perhaps were not typical of the older population in the community. Studies, such as those of Exton-Smith and Stanton[1], found that, although food intake decreased with advancing age, many of the older subjects managed to eat a varied diet. A nutritional survey of older people carried out by the DHSS in 1972 found some overt malnutrition, but not much; the report stresses, however, that many are vulnerable and the margin of safety may be slight[2]. Similar findings were reported in 1979[3], but other studies have noted that the nutritional needs of older people are not simple and, for example, that the provision of Meals on Wheels will not automatically increase the food intake in those who are ill or neglecting their diet[4]. Little subsequent research has been done on the subject, but a nutritional survey of older people is at present being planned.

Clinical Assessment of Nutrition

Assessment of the nutritional status of an older person is important, but can be difficult. A health worker needs to find out whether a person is getting enough food and the methods available for doing this are often unreliable. Under these circumstances, it is necessary to rely on physical examination to determine whether the patient is well nourished. This may present difficulties, as specific signs of malnutrition may be totally lacking. Weight loss is an important feature, but examples of serious undernutrition with severe weight loss are rarely encountered, apart from in some patients with senile dementia. Weight is possibly the most single useful investigation in older people, although there are difficulties in determining what is normal weight. Ageing itself results in reduction in muscle mass, which tends to be replaced by fat. Concomitant disease can also influence weight.

Clinically, poor nutrition can show itself in general apathy and lassitude. Unexplained anaemia may point to an inadequate diet. Some of the factors likely to lead to subnutrition may be present and these will be discussed shortly. Reduction in subcutaneous fat and skinfold thickness is sometimes regarded as a sign of poor nutrition. There may be, apart from a reduction in calorie and protein intake, an inadequate supply of vitamins in the diet. Where there are signs of frank deficiency these are usually due to several different food factors being absent; this is rare. Older men living alone may sometimes show signs of vitamin C deficiency; small haemorrhages may be the only sign and these may be seen particularly in the gums and under the tongue. Confirmation can be obtained by assessing the level of ascorbic acid within the white blood cells and platelets. Early diagnosis of osteomalacia caused by vitamin D deficiency should be made biochemically since, when changes detectable by radiography have occurred, it is often too late. Osteomalacia may also tend to increase fracture rates in older people.

Factors Affecting Nutrition

Physical changes occur in older age that can contribute to a reduction in food intake. The teeth are often lost, and, although chewing is possible without them, it becomes more difficult. Dentures may be unsatisfactory and might limit the choice of foods. Loss of taste and smell can reduce the appetite. The flow of saliva decreases as age advances, and this may make chewing more difficult. Oesophageal and gastric mobility may be impaired and gastric secretion reduced. This may affect food absorption, as may the presence of a partial gastrectomy.

General physical debility is an important cause of undernutrition. The presence of such diseases as heart failure, chronic infection and arthritis can decrease an older person's interest in food. Some drugs may interfere with the absorption of certain vitamins, notably folic acid; these include phenytoin, phenylbutazone and nitrofurantoin. The mental state of an older person may also influence dietary intake. It is likely to be reduced in patients with depression or early dementia. Sometimes dietary fads persist and are exaggerated in older age. A gastric diet may be maintained for far longer than is necessary and may actually contribute to undernutrition. On the other hand, diet may well be maintained despite quite severe behaviour disorder. Alcoholism or excessive smoking may be responsible for loss of appetite, a fact that is often hidden from the doctor and relatives. A bereaved person is also likely to lose interest in food.

Various environmental factors can influence food intake. Preparing food may be difficult. Kitchen layouts and cooking facilities may be unsuitable for the frail and disabled. Regular shopping for fresh supplies may not be undertaken because of reduced mobility. The author assessed the diet of 207 over 75-year-old people[5]. One cooked meal per day was considered to be the lowest acceptable level of food intake and 28 were found to be below this level. The numbers were relatively small, but it was found that inadequate diet was commonest in socio-economic groups IV and V and amongst women aged between 80 and 90 years. Those living alone, particularly men, were also more likely to be poorly fed. It was found that the effective health of those on a poor diet was often diminished and, as an interesting footnote, that the mean haemoglobin level of patients on an inadequate diet was less that the group as a whole. These patients were not clinically malnourished, but were obviously very vulnerable. How much was cause and effect is difficult to determine; a vicious circle can be established where patients in poor health or with a low haemoglobin level become apathetic about food and reduced intake makes the condition worse.

Nutritional Requirements of Older People

The estimated average requirements for energy decline with age. While men aged 19–49 with a sedentary life-style need 2550 kcal/day, men over 75 years need 2100 kcal/day; women aged 19–49 need 1940 kcal/day, while women over 75 years need 1810 kcal/day. These are only average requirements for those with sedentary life-styles; an active older person could need more energy than a sedentary younger person. There is a danger that when elderly people are inactive, their food intake may be so low that they do not reach the minimum requirements for some nutrients. They may need encouragement to be more physically active and at the same time take in more energy-giving foods[6].

The recommended amounts of important nutrients for people above and below 50 years of age are shown in Table 19.1.

Table 19.1: Recommended daily amounts of nutrients.

Age (years)	Protein (g)	Thiamin (mg)	Ribo-flavin (mg)	Nicotinic acid equivalents (mg)	Ascorbic acid (mg)	Vitamin A retinol equivalents (µg)	Calcium (mg)	Iron (mg)
Men (19–50)	55.5	1.0	1.3	17	40	700	700	8.7
Women (19–50)	45.0	0.8	1.1	13	40	600	700	14.8
Men (50+)	53.3	0.9	1.3	16	40	700	700	8.7
Women (50+)	46.5	0.8	1.1	12	40	600	700	8.7

Source: Department of Health, 1991[6].

Nutritional Help for Older People

Good dietary habits should start at an early age; hopefully these will be continued into advanced years. When inadequate diet is a possibility, its early detection is important. It can easily be overlooked and doctors, health visitors and social workers should be constantly alert to the possibility. Certain groups already mentioned are vulnerable and need special attention. Routine health checks on those aged 75 and over are helpful for recognizing those at risk. Making sure that older people have adequate dentures can reduce subnutrition and anaemia. Those who provide Meals on Wheels and supervise lunch clubs can recognize those whose appetites are poor or whose interest in food is deteriorating. Home helps are also valuable in helping older people to receive adequate nutrition. Education in the principles of nutrition should be part of the primary health care team's role, particularly in advocating the necessity to eat fresh fruit or fruit juice and food such as oily fish, rich in vitamins A and D.

Advances in technology have meant better packaging of food and much of it is now easy to prepare. Refrigerators and freezers have meant that storage is now possible for much longer periods and this may be invaluable when patients are incapacitated for a short period. Unfortunately, some older people do not have these facilities. The wisdom of adding extra vitamins to the diet, as either pills or by fortifying foodstuffs, is debatable. Excess of vitamins A and D can be a hazard and, in general, with a well balanced diet, additional vitamins should be unnecessary, except perhaps in winter time for the housebound.

Older people with low incomes tend to buy cheaper foods and sometimes they may have to choose whether to spend on food or on other essentials such as fuel and clothing. Pensioners with special dietary needs are advised to seek Income Support and should consult social security officers. To overcome any unsuitable domestic arrangements for cooking, it is sometimes helpful for social workers to advise on alterations and special utensils. Easy access to ovens, shelves and storage units can enable a disabled person to cook, when previously this was proving difficult. Teaching an older person to use these facilities is usually necessary. Meals on Wheels and lunch clubs are, of course, very important and great care is usually given to nutritional content. Those living alone should be encouraged to use these facilities, especially if they can arrange to eat with others, as this is often a stimulus to the appetite. There is also the problem of obesity; this often shortens life expectancy and can aggravate many other problems. Patients with diabetes need special dietary advice; this is discussed in Chapter 18.

The help of dieticians is invaluable. Their role is to assess and advise on implementation of dietary regimens appropriate to the individual patient's needs. Most health authorities have dietetic and nutrition services. Referral may be for dietary assessment and such conditions as diabetes, swallowing or feeding difficulties (particularly after stroke or surgery), weight loss, and suspected deficiencies of minerals and vitamins through factors such as prolonged poor eating or poor dentition. Help from hospital or community dieticians is often necessary to construct suitable diets.

Hypothermia

Hypothermia is said to occur when the temperature of the body core (that is, deep internal temperature) is less than 35 °C (95 °F.) The condition was first described by Duguid and her colleagues in 1962[7]. Of the 23 cases she described in her Scottish study, 22 were older people. The Royal College of Physicians[8], in a study involving 10 British hospitals, found a temperature of less than 35 °C in 0.68% of admissions. Although it is perhaps dangerous to extrapolate from these figures, it could be that several thousand people are admitted to hospital each year with hypothermia. What the current true incidence of the condition is in the community is unknown, but it is probable that in winter it is not uncommon. There were over 1057 hypothermia related deaths in Great Britain in 1985[9]. Nearly all these were of people aged over 65 and over.

Temperature

There are two aspects of body temperature. There is deep temperature, sometimes known as core temperature, around the vital organs, which is maintained constantly, despite variations in external conditions. There is also the temperature of skin and subcutaneous tissues, sometimes described as shell temperature, which varies with external temperature. In older people, deep body temperature is about half a degree lower than in young people and this difference tends to increase as age advances.

Accurate recording of temperature is important when the possibility of hypothermia is present. Most clinical thermometers have 35 °C as their lower reading. Special thermometers are therefore necessary to record low temperatures in older people. Care is needed to shake down the level of mercury sufficiently, for, if this is not done, the temperature of the body may be lower than the reading. The usual method of oral measurement gives only shell temperature. For assessment of core temperature, rectal measurement is necessary. Sometimes this is inconvenient, and some surveys have overcome this difficulty by measuring temperature of the urine immediately after it has been passed. This is, however, outside the scope of normal clinical practice.

Heat Regulation

Maintenance of body temperature involves a fine balance between heat gain and heat loss. Physiologically, a point is set within the body that indicates the temperature required and any difference is registered by the hypothalamus, which sets off appropriate mechanisms for heat loss or gain. When the body is exposed to cold or it overheats, as for example in response to pyrogens being released during infection, both central and peripheral mechanisms come into play to control temperature. Many factors affect these delicate mechanisms and an important one as far as older people are concerned is the relationship of mass to body surface. Any human being or animal with a large body mass, but a small body surface area, will have more difficulty in losing heat and there are mechanisms to deal with this. A thin older person, with a high ratio of surface area to body mass, may have difficulty in conserving body heat and this may sometimes prove to be impossible. This may account partially for the impairment of temperature control that is seen in some older people. The hypothalamus, which is the centre in the brain that controls temperature, has a higher threshold of sensitivity in older people, who also cannot respond to hypothalmic stimuli, as, for example, by shivering.

Causes of Hypothermia

Although hypothermia is principally a condition of older age, it can also be found in babies and infants. Young people, such as climbers, potholers and yachtsmen who find themselves exposed for long periods to cold, wet conditions can also suffer from hypothermia. The cause is exposure to cold, but there are factors that exaggerate this effect. Impaired physiological maintenance of body temperature seems to be present in some people and this may make them more vulnerable. Many illnesses may be associated with impaired thermoregulatory mechanisms (eg myxoedema, hypopituitarism, diabetes, stroke, myocardial infarction, infection and extensive skin lesions). Immobility produced by conditions such as arthritis, parkinsonism and mental impairment can also be associated with hypothermia. Certain drugs, such as chlorpromazine, diazepam and, of course, alcohol, can also be contributory. This is important when dealing with confused older people, because sometimes the confusion may be due to hypothermia, and the use of phenothiazine tranquillizers (eg chlorpromazine) may aggravate the hypothermic condition. The environment is also important. People living in cold draughty houses, particularly those in high or exposed conditions, may be particularly vulnerable.

Clinical Manifestations

In an established case of hypothermia, the patient is obviously cold; this applies particularly to the abdomen and trunk. Strangely enough, he or she may not complain of cold. The skin may be of a pale or pinkish colour, and sometimes puffy with a resemblance to myxoedema. The voice may have a deeper tone than normal. The muscles may be rigid and the reflexes sluggish. Consciousness may be clouded and the patient may be drowsy. The pulse is usually slow and the blood pressure reduced. Breathing may be shallow and there may be signs of bronchopneumonia, although hypothermia can mask this condition, and it is only when the patient is warmed that it becomes apparent. A situation seen in the community that can be associated with hypothermia is where the older person has for some reason fallen out of bed. There may also be a fracture, particularly of the femur. The patient is usually unable to get back into bed and lies all night, scantily clad, in a cold bedroom. Discovery may not be for several hours and this type of exposure can lead rapidly to hypothermia. Hypothermia developing insidiously in old people is very common and much more difficult to identify.

Treatment

All cases of suspected hypothermia should be admitted to hospital, as the condition is associated with a high and unpredictable mortality. The basic principle of treatment is slow rewarming; this is done best by nursing the patient in a bed at a room temperature of about 25 °C (70 °F) so that deep body temperature can be allowed to rise gradually. This means insulating the whole body, especially the head, and giving warm drinks to raise the temperature of the core. Other methods, such as rapid rewarming by immersion in a warm bath, although effective in young people, are not to be recommended when dealing with older patients. The vasodilation caused by this quick surface heating may lead to a drop in core temperature and to disastrous circulatory collapse. The disadvantages of the slow method of rewarming the patient are that the hypothermia is prolonged and irreversible changes in the tissues may take place. With mild hypothermia, this is unlikely. In more severe cases, although conservative treatment is still indicated, precautions such as barrier nursing, isolation and broad spectrum antibiotic therapy can be instituted. Hypothermia demands specialist treatment and often admission to an intensive care unit. The outlook for patients suffering from severe hypothermia is not very good. Where the initial temperature is below 30 °C, mortality is high.

Prevention

Hypothermia is basically preventable. Colder countries, such as Sweden, rarely experience the condition. Economic factors in the UK are clearly important in contributing to low temperatures in the houses of older people, who should live in warm surroundings; this should include not only downstairs rooms but bedrooms also. The ideal temperature is between 65 °F and 70 °F or about 20 °C. The cost of fuel is often a problem. Central heating, of course, is ideal, particularly when it is automatically controlled. Electric heating is satisfactory but expensive. The work associated with coal fires and the danger of paraffin heaters make these two fuels unsuitable for older people. Windows should be closed at night and special attention should be paid to insulation. Double glazing, draught exclusion and roof insulation not only help to reduce the size of the fuel bill but add greatly to comfort. If it is impossible to heat the whole house in the winter it is better for the older person to live in one room, bringing the bed downstairs, to a room which can then be kept at a reasonable temperature. People should be well clothed in bed; night caps and bed socks are recommended. Electric blankets are useful, but may be dangerous if the patient is incontinent. Specially waterproofed electric blankets and low voltage over blankets, which use very little electricity and are safe, are now available.

Medical and social workers should be alert to the possibility of hypothermia and be aware of the people especially at risk. This could include all those aged over 75 and those living alone. There seems to be a certain section of the older community who have an idiopathic reduction in the body temperature stabilizing mechanism. The problem is recognizing these people. Perhaps wider use of the low reading thermometer might help. Doctors should always be alert to the possibility of hypothermia and be careful in prescribing drugs, particularly tranquillizers, to those at risk.

References

1. Exton-Smith AN, Stanton BR. (1965) Report of investigation into the diets of elderly women living alone. King Edward's Hospital Fund, London.

2. Department of Health and Social Security Panel of Nutrition of the Elderly. (1972) *Nutritional survey of the elderly*. (Report on Health and Social Subjects, No. 3.) HMSO, London.

3. Department of Health and Social Security, Committee on Medical Aspects of Food Policy. (1979) *Recommended daily amounts of food energy and nutrients for groups of people in the UK*. (Report on Health and Social Subject, No. 15.) HMSO, London.

4. Davies L. (1981) *Three score years ... and then?* Heinemann, London.

5. Williams EI, Bennett FM, Nixon JV, *et al.* (1972) Socio-medical survey of patients over 75 in general practice. *Br Med J* ii: 445–8.

6. Department of Health. (1991) *Dietary reference values for food energy and nutrients for the United Kingdom*. (Report on Health and Social Subjects, No. 41.) HMSO, London.

7. Duguid H, Simpson RG, Stowers BR. (1962) Accidental hypothermia. *Lancet* ii: 1213.

8. Royal College of Physicians. (1966) *Report of committee on accidental hypothermia*. RCP, London.

9. *Population Trends*. (1986) (Series No. 44, Summer) HMSO, London.

20
Rehabilitation

Rehabilitation of sick older people at home has been, until recently, a fairly neglected activity. Lack of appropriate therapists and poor co-operation between family doctors and other workers has been the main cause for this deficiency. However, with increasing availability of therapists and a greater understanding of their value, rehabilitation has become an important part of community care. The aim is to restore the patient from a state of dependence back to independence and the ability to live a normal life. In the community, there are two types of situation demanding rehabilitation. The first is when the patient has been discharged from hospital and where procedures to restore function have been started but need to be continued at home. It is sometimes tragic to see the effects of the hard and dedicated work done in the hospital, which has enabled the person to return home, being rapidly reversed by failure to maintain the process when he/she is back in the community. The second situation is where the person is initially treated at home, and where rehabilitation is needed to enable him/her once more to lead a normal life. In older people, this is particularly important because even minor illness can reduce the capacity for self-care; unless this is realized, full recovery may never take place.

Illnesses such as stroke may lead to major disablement and demand considerable rehabilitation, but conditions such as heart failure, pneumonia, bronchitis and urinary tract infection, where the patient may be confined to bed for even a very short time, may also run the risk of the patient developing muscular weakness, joint stiffness and general loss of mobility. It is important at the outset of an illness to get some idea of what the future holds. The way the illness can affect the ability to self-care must be remembered and an assessment of the physical, mental, psychological and socioenvironmental condition of the patient must be made with restoration of previous functional ability in mind. It is useful in this respect if the patient's previous state and circumstances are known. Physical assessment involves general examination to determine functional ability and is concerned with such activities as feeding, washing and bathing. The patient's mental state also needs assessment. Intellectual impairment following stroke or concomitant senile dementia may reduce functional ability. Depression or anxiety may be present and many older people react to illness by losing self confidence and respond with despair to the thought of losing their independence. It is also important to discover changes in perception of body image, as deterioration in this can affect functional performance. A careful look needs to be taken at the patient's home environment; the type of house he or she lives in may determine how they are to cope. Will it suit the patient's new needs and if not can it be adapted? The attitude of family and neighbours is also important. Some relatives are unwilling to accept the burden of looking after a disabled older person and it might be that such antagonism will reduce the chance of effective rehabilitation.

These are the types of question that will need to be asked in order to plan rehabilitation. Factors need identifying that might interfere with this. Realism is essential when assessing the prospects of an older person, and only attainable goals should be pursued. Many tasks are physically possible, but the patient may be unable to cope because of poor understanding, failing vision or lack of motivation. Cooking, for example, may be dangerous. Rehabilitation services must therefore aim to achieve only what is feasible and consistent with the patient's abilities. To this end assessment should be an ongoing exercise and the team should monitor progress critically and be aware of changes in the general condition of the patient. Fluctuation of the degree of disability means that what can be done today may not be possible tomorrow.

Simple Rehabilitation at Home

Most rehabilitation needs to be undertaken by skilled and qualified workers; these include physiotherapists, occupational therapists and speech therapists. However, sometimes these services are not available, or the condition is not considered serious. The family is then faced with undertaking the patient's rehabilitation alone or with the help of the community nurse. The rehabilitation process should start as early in the illness as possible and will usually begin when the patient is still in bed. Simple passive exercises for an affected limb should be undertaken with the aim of avoiding contractures. Gentle massage will help the patient to feel more comfortable. Unaffected limbs and muscles must also be exercised to prevent disuse atrophy. Special care must be taken of the shoulder of a hemiplegic stroke sufferer; it can very easily be deranged by relatives or other helpers when lifting the patient with either the hand in the axilla or holding the paralysed arm.

Speech therapy, where necessary, can also begin at this stage and the patient can be encouraged to speak. It may be possible to arrange for him/her to start reading or at least listening to the radio. As part of early occupational therapy, such things as knitting or jigsaw puzzles may be introduced. As soon as it is practicable the patient should be encouraged to sit in a chair; this is feasible when he/she is able to sit without falling. Special attention should be given to the chair. It should be upright with a seat with a surface parallel to the ground, about 46 cm (18 inches) from the floor, a firm back capable of support and it must have arms. The chair must, of course, be stable. At home it is probably better that it should not have castors and trays are best avoided. The front legs should not have a connecting bar as this prevents the older person putting his/her feet back when rising. A sprung seat may help to gain the first degrees of lift in rising.

Once the patient can sit in the chair, passive movements should be continued and he/she can start to learn how to dress. Movements of the hands and fingers should be encouraged. The patient can sit on the edge of the bed or chair to move the feet up and down. The next stage is standing; this is sometimes diffi-cult if balance is impaired. If it is, expert physiotherapist help is usually required, but sometimes the relatives, with advice, can teach the patient how to stand, using perhaps the bed rail if this is secure, and then proceed to help with walk-ing. The use of walking aids such as a Zimmer frame or tripod is often useful in helping older people to gain confidence. Gradually, and with encouragement, the patient should be able to achieve some mobility, and eventually be able to manage for themselves the tasks of general care. Where there are more complicated prob-lems, such as contractures or movement being severely restricted, expert help should be obtained and, if necessary, admission into a hospital rehabilitation unit should be arranged.

Aids and Appliances

The patient may need various aids and appliances to help him/her to regain independence, and, if full recovery is impossible, these may become permanent features of the patient's life. Rehabilitation involves assessing which aids will be needed, and also teaching people how to use them. Aids are usually small, easily handled items. If the device is larger and non-portable, it is usually described as a piece of equipment. The word 'appliance' is used to describe an aid that is pur-posely made for the individual. A series of articles by Mulley in the *British Medical Journal* in 1988 gives a comprehensive overview of aids and appliances (see Further reading).

The idea of these aids is to enable a person to do something that would other-wise be difficult or impossible. Their function is to enable the person to over-come the effects of a disability, and to become more independent. The aids themselves must be of the best design possible and they should be efficient. They should be cheap, but this does not mean shoddy or unattractive. Robust equip-ment is important because anything that is likely to break will quickly lose the user's confidence. Avoid having too many aids, as the confusion brought about by too much technology can be dangerous.

The number of aids that have been devised is endless. Many are home-made and involve considerable ingenuity. Some useful aids are described under each basic care heading.

Toileting

To be able to use the toilet is important to a patient's self respect. If the toilet is too low this can be raised with a plastic seat. Rails can be placed on either side to help with sitting and standing. If it is impossible for a person to use a pedestal toilet, a commode, bedpan or bottle may be necessary.

Washing

Washing the upper part of the body is usually no great problem, but reaching the back and feet may be difficult; long handled brushes and sponges can help. Getting in and out of the bath may be quite impossible, but some older people can manage with bath rails and a bath seat. Non-slip baths are essential; a shower is often useful.

Shaving and Grooming

Shaving can be a problem for an older man and an electric razor with a long handle may help. For women, application of make-up is easier with a long-handled lipstick holder. Similarly combs and brushes can also be attached to long handles.

Dressing

It is obvious that disabled older persons should wear suitable clothes, avoiding buttons, preferably using zips and having everything fastening at the front. Tights and trousers are easier for women to put on and have the added advantage of extra protection and warmth; they may also hide artificial limbs or callipers. Shoes should be of the non-laced type. Various aids are also available for picking up items from the floor and also for putting on stockings.

Feeding

When feeding is a problem because of poor grip or lack of co-ordination of hand movements, cutlery with large handles may help; drinking is easier using a straw or a special cup that cannot be knocked over. Plates with stable wide bases may make things easier and there are many devices for dealing with jugs and teapots. Non-slip table mats are also useful. Modified 'sporks' and plate rims can enable a hemiplegic to feed him/herself.

Mobility

Many aids are available to help with mobility. For support there are simple walking sticks, Zimmer frames, tripods and quadrapods. Wheelchairs are available, either through the social services department or directly through a GP, using form no. AOF 5G. There are two types of wheelchair available: the transit pushchair and the self-propelled. Special designs also exist for amputees. Accessories are also available, such as cushions, base boards and harnesses. Occasionally, it is necessary to adapt the house by providing extra ramps, widening doors, installing support rails and levelling out steps. Walking can also be assisted by shoe raises, surgical shoes, and callipers with toe-raising springs or inside irons and T-straps. Hoists are also occasionally provided to help older people out of bed and into a wheelchair.

Household Duties

There are many specially adapted cooking utensils. Split-level cookers are helpful, and electrical sockets should be at appropriate heights. A device may be attached to taps to make them easier to turn on. Long-handled brushes and dusters can aid cleaning.

Communication

There is a range of devices to help communication. If a person is unable to speak clearly, a pencil and pad should be nearby. There are aids to help with writing, including, a typewriter. Reading can be helped by book-rests and books with large type. A telephone may be necessary; if this is needed to summon medical help urgently, the social services department may finance this. British Telecom can also advise on special telephones for the disabled; details can be found in the telephone directory. Alarm-call systems of various types may also be helpful. These can be two-way communication alarms, but occasionally the older person can have an alarm in the form of a wrist watch or pendant.

Hobbies

Many disabled older people like to continue with their hobbies. Help may be available from voluntary organizations. Gardening, for example, may be possible using specially adapted tools.

Armchairs

Armchairs for older people should be suitable for them. Ideally, they are comfortable, easy to get in and out of, safe and stable. It is easier for an older person to rise if the seat is reasonably high. Horizontal seats are uncomfortable and it is better to have a gentle backwards slope. The material should not be too hard and should not involve a fire risk. Cushions may give added comfort. Arm rests should not be too high and it is possibly better if they are filled. Legs need to have a wide base for increased stability. Avoid the so-called 'easy chair': deep, low and acting as a foam trap.

Additional Points

As well as requiring rehabilitation for the effects of major illness and short-term problems that temporarily reduce the ability to function effectively, older people also have small ongoing problems that need occasional attention and regular watching. These are often concerned with feet, vision, hearing, teeth and the skin. An older person's feet are of extreme importance and good foot care is essential to maintain mobility. Regular visits to a chiropodist are of course helpful, but most look after their own feet or get help from relatives. Toe-nails need regular cutting, using effective cutters. Nails can get deformed and very hard in older age and more professional help is often required. Watch must be kept for infections; fungal lesions can become very troublesome. Calluses, corns and bunions need special attention.

A check on vision is an integral part of a health check on older people. Glasses may have been unchanged for many years and need replacing. Important problems like cataract need to be identified, but older people also suffer from minor irritations and infections, which, if left untreated, can become extremely troublesome. Hearing is also important and can deteriorate gradually; this may be caused by wax which is simple to remove. Hearing aids do help, but they may not be working at maximum efficiency and an older person may not understand the various adjustments. Hearing aids need to be kept clean. Otitis externa is not uncommon in older age and can be easily treated. Skin lesions also trouble older people, such as intertrigo, eczema, varicose ulcers etc. Many of these conditions are quite treatable; most of these so called minor problems deter older persons from active social life, and attempts at their relief are therefore worthwhile.

A check should therefore be made on hearing aids and spectacles. These are important aids and so also are walking sticks, walking frames, wheelchairs, toilet aids and bath aids, all of which should also be checked. The length of a walking stick should be equal to the distance of the proximal wrist crease from the ground. A rubber ferrule should be in place and must not be worn. A wheelchair should be in working order and the right size for the person and the house; the brakes are important and must be checked. Toilet aids need to fit properly, be secure and be at the right height. Non-slip flooring in the bathroom is important; rails need to be secure. A check on whether a wheelchair-bound patient can adequately use the toilet and washing facilities is sometimes illuminating.

More older people are now retaining their own teeth and regular dental checks are needed. Ill-fitting dentures can be a deterrent to effective chewing and can reduce appetite. After a serious illness, for example stroke, dentures may become loose and need replacing.

After successfully rehabilitating an older person or dealing with relatively minor problems, it is absolutely essential to maintain some supervision, especially if aids have been introduced. There is considerable risk of deterioration if the stimulus of a professional worker is withdrawn too quickly. The work of several months can be lost in a few weeks if the patient becomes apathetic. Some form of general supervision is therefore vital, so that any difficulties can be spotted early and the cause found and corrected.

Further Reading

Mulley G, editor. (1988) Everyday aids and appliances (series.) *Br Med J* **296**: issues 6614—6632.

21
Nursing an Older Person in the Community

Modern medical practice relies heavily on nursing help, both in hospital and the community, to provide comprehensive care for the sick. In the community, the traditional nursing role has been reactive rather than proactive. Thus, a patient with a problem who needs nursing care presents to the primary medical care service, which then acts in its gatekeeper role by referring him or her to the nursing care team. In the community it is of great importance that this referral is made early so that relationships built on mutual trust, respect and partnership can be built up, thus providing a holistic package where the client is central and a full and equal partner.

Both community nursing and nursing care of older people have, over the last decade, made dramatic advances in providing the specialist service required of each. This is also true when the two specialisms come together when caring for older people in the community. This has been helped by several factors, including government legislation, which has been aimed at providing patients with more effective access to a mixed economy of care. The new thinking in the caring professions in relation to multidisciplinary care, and the understanding that the client is central to that care are also important. The corporate image commended to primary health care providers has made teamwork much more realistic.

There are special challenges for the nurse working with the older person in their own home. Demographic changes have meant that there are relatively more much older people in the population, which means more frail elderly patients to nurse. The dilemma about whether to provide a paternalistic type of care, giving the patient little chance to contribute to decision-taking, or providing space for individuality, risk-taking and choice, is a real one for those providing community nursing for older people. These days, when older age often means social isolation, the community nurse may be the only visitor a person has; therefore it is necessary to include a large element of motivation into the visit and often a therapeutic cup of tea.

In the community, nurses are usually called on to care in four types of situations. First, there is the acutely ill person with, for example bronchitis, or perhaps the individual discharged from hospital postoperatively. The overall aim in providing care in these circumstances is to restore the person to full health and their normal place in the community. The nurse's role in caring for this type of patient will involve a full range of basic nursing skills in collaboration with the care provided by other members of the primary health care team. Nursing care is usually only for a limited time.

Secondly, the nursing services are often involved in the care of patients with long-term problems, such as multiple sclerosis or stroke. Here the patient may be ambulant, but nevertheless require some nursing care for contractures or pressure sores. However, the patient may be bedfast and this will entail more regular nursing care.

Thirdly, community nurses often provide considerable support for the family of an individual who is receiving palliative care. The entails not only carrying out nursing tasks, but also offering spiritual, social and psychological support to all family members.

Fourthly, the community nurse often remains in contact with individuals and families after the need for 'traditional' nursing skills has diminished. Here the nurse is providing supportive or maintenance care, which is essentially proactive and initiated by the nurse.

Basic Principles of Nursing an Individual at Home

As has been previously mentioned, it is essential for the nurse to arrive early on the scene. Nurses should educate doctors to alert them at the beginning of an illness, and not leave it until it is obvious to all that nursing care is imperative.

The room where the patient is to be nursed needs to be adequately heated and lighted. It is sometimes more convenient to nurse an older person downstairs than in a cramped bedroom. This is also easier for the family and facilitates earlier rehabilitation. It will, however, involve some furniture moving and disruption to the usual running of the house. This can cause distress to an older person, who will not like to see the sitting room turned into a bedroom; there may also be difficulties with managing stairs to go to the toilet and a commode may be necessary. The nurse will need sensitivity to help the patient to see that this is a temporary measure and make every effort to ensure that they have as much dignity as possible.

At home the bed is often too low, but it can be raised with blocks. It must be at a height that is safe for the patient to get in and out. Ideally, when the patient sits on the edge of the bed, the feet should be flat on the floor. Occasionally safety sides are necessary when there is a danger of the patient falling out of bed. It is possible to obtain hospital beds with sides for use in the home and these should be installed if necessary, as makeshift arrangements are seldom satisfactory. A bed table is also helpful, especially of the cantilever type with adjustable height and angle. Bedding needs to be light and warm. Linen is not provided, but some health authorities have laundry services that collect soiled linen and return it laundered to the patient's home. Some people prefer duvets, but they can be difficult to keep clean. Sheepskins are available and many find them very comfortable. Older people slip down the bed easily and at home ingenious relatives have sometimes been able to fix overhead handles for the patient to clasp. A rope ladder to the end of the bed can also help in some situations. In general older people should be encouraged to stay in bed for as little time as possible. This minimizing of bed rest is a fundamental precept of nursing at home. As a person recovers, the relatives will need instructing on how best to get them in and out of bed. There are special gadgets such as hoists, available for moving a very disabled person at home, although for advice the physiotherapist must be consulted. Usually a patient can be helped to swing his/her legs over the side of the bed until they are sitting upright. After a pause, they should be able to stand. The patient will also need help with dressing and undressing at this stage.

Dehydration can occur all too easily in elderly people and adequate fluid intake is necessary. The diet also needs supervising with special care to ensure that sufficient vitamins are taken. Toileting arrangements are important and the nurse may well have to resort to certain aids such as the use of a commode so that toileting is easy and comfortable. General attention to personal care, such as washing, bathing, shaving and hair-brushing is necessary. This helps the patient to preserve his or her self-respect. It is important that older people are treated as individuals; if possible, bed bathing should be kept to a minimum and they should be encouraged to wash themselves and allowed to use their own bath or shower. Clothes, too, should be kept clean and changed frequently. Community nurses are also involved in some very useful preventive work. This includes the avoidance of pressure sores, minimizing the effect of both urinary and faecal incontinence, and avoiding contractures.

Community nurses have a very special responsibility in supervising treatment. Tablets need to be taken regularly and a watch kept for side-effects. This is much more difficult at home than in the hospital, where there is the traditional drug round and total nursing supervision for the whole 24 hours of the day. At home this is impractical and the nurse has to rely on members of the family or neighbours to undertake general supervision. This involves the task of educating these helpers in what needs to be done and how to recognize relevant improvement or deterioration. If these extra helpers are not available when a patient lives alone, night sitting and home help service may be possible, but if not, it is sometimes better for the patient to be admitted to hospital. The part played by district nurses in co-ordinating other services is, however, very important in avoiding such admissions.

In the community, the nurse might find other tasks, apart from straightforward nursing, assume great importance. The nurse may well be asked to undertake simple physiotherapy under the guidance of the physiotherapist, including training a patient to use aids. Occupational and speech therapy may also be necessary, particularly for those suffering from stroke. This general rehabilitation role of the community nurse is very important and can be the critical factor that leads the patient successfully through acute illness back to independence.

Very often an older person's perception of the environment is retained, even when bedfast, and recovery may be helped by bright and cheerful surroundings, as well as the general encouragement of those giving nursing care. Some may become very dependent on the nurse and this applies even more so in the community than in hospital. There is sometimes a dilemma about how firm to be in insisting that patients undertake certain tasks themselves. It is very easy for the nurse to do more than is necessary just to save time. The hospital geriatric liaison nursing team can often help if this is a problem.

The social services department will provide aids and appliances to make nursing at home easier. These include chemical toilets, commodes, tripods, Zimmer frames, monkey chains to make moving up the bed easier, high chairs, bath seats, handrails and ramps. A community occupational therapist will be helpful in discussing the needs of an older person for such aids. The community nursing services will provide equipment for the comfort of the patient in bed, including disposable sheets and pads. Incontinence aids are also provided. In general, the social services departments provide aids to living and the nursing services provide aids to nursing, but there is some overlap. The Marie Curie Foundation makes financial allowances to patients suffering from cancer for extra diet and other comforts; it is also very helpful in providing night sitters.

Communication is better if nursing records are left at the patient's home. Temperature charts are unnecessary, but notes made of temperature and pulse rate in acutely ill patients are useful. The doctor should also record changes in medical treatment. Messages can be left on the record sheets, but there is no real substitute for direct verbal communication between doctor and nurse.

Geriatric community nursing teams are available in some areas. They co-ordinate discharge into the community and offer support and advice to relatives. Their duties are to liaise with hospital, medical, nursing and social staff, and their counterparts in the community. They also make special visits to those on the waiting list for admission to hospital. Supervision of continuing rehabilitation of discharged hospital patients may also be part of their duties.

The practice nurse usually works from the surgery and ideally has a treatment room at her disposal, so that she can treat ambulant older people. The range of care might include giving injections, dressing ulcers and dealing with injuries. General supervision of treatment may also be undertaken for patients with hypertension or diabetes. An older person may be referred for specific treatment, such as ear syringing or for eye infections.

There are four different areas in which community nursing care is very important. These are the management of pressure sores, incontinence, contracture and restless patients; they will now be described briefly.

Pressure Sores

Pressure sores can be either superficial or deep. Superficial sores are usually due to small injuries of the skin caused by sheering forces and friction as a result of moving a patient up the bed. They are the most common form of ulcer and may account for up to 90% of the total. They may become infected; this is particularly liable to occur where there is urinary incontinence. Deep sores, which are sometimes called decubitus ulcers, are more serious and occur when the skin over a bony prominence is compressed for any length of time. This causes the blood supply to be cut off with resulting tissue destruction. They may occur without the skin surface actually being broken, and discoloration may not appear immediately. Nevertheless, extensive damage may have occurred to the underlying tissues. Areas particularly vulnerable to developing this type of sore are over the main bony prominences such as the pelvis, the buttocks and the lower part of the back; they can also occur over the shoulder blades and elbows. The resultant sore is usually deep and can sometimes be covered by a hard scab hiding the necrotic changes that have taken place underneath. Other factors also contribute to the development of ulcers. Incontinence can cause skin sogginess. Unconscious and paralysed patients are vulnerable as well as those who are thin and emaciated. Arteriosclerosis can reduce the blood supply to the skin and make ulceration more likely. Fever, dehydration and poor nutrition may also be contributory. A hot water bottle may sometimes cause a burn that may become infected and ulcerated.

Nurses assess the risk of pressure sores forming by using the 'Norton score', which considers the patient's physical and mental activity, morbidity and incontinence status. These factors are individually scored from 1 to 4 and patients with a total score of 14 or less are liable to develop sores[1].

Prevention of Sores

Bed sores, both superficial and deep, are in many ways a tragic occurrence and, as they are difficult to treat, prevention is of prime importance when nursing older people. Damage can often be done in the first week of illness, or even overnight, and therefore prevention should be instituted early. The position of an older person should be changed as frequently as possible and the period of bed rest reduced to a minimum. The change in position may have to be as often as every two hours in an unconscious paralysed patient. This movement also helps to prevent chest infection. Sheepskins are regularly used; some are specially shaped to protect heels and ankles. There may be a danger of developing a pressure sore on the buttock if the patient sits out of bed too soon and remains immobile in a chair. Special care should be taken to keep the skin clean; soap and water is probably the best method. The traditional methylated spirits and powder applications are now no longer advocated. Barrier creams such as Vasogen and Conotrane may be used to protect vulnerable areas. The same effect can also be achieved conveniently by using an aerosol spray, of which Sprilon is a popular example, especially when there is early reddening, although it is expensive to use continually. Opsite spray is often used for superficial sores and is very effective. The general condition of the patient needs attention, with a special watch kept for dehydration. A diet rich in protein and with added vitamins is helpful. If incontinence is a problem, an indwelling catheter may become necessary. Sedation should be avoided so that the patient is capable of moving naturally. Skin areas that are vulnerable should be inspected, especially for early changes in colour. Heel sores can develop when the patient finds it difficult to move his/her legs because of tight sheets, and a cradle may prevent this.

Many special mattresses have been developed to help in the prevention of sores; they are considerably more sophisticated than the original sheepskins. Few, however, are of much value in the home. Ripple or alternative pressure mattresses can be used, but, although they might save nurses' time, they do need careful supervision and a reliable electricity supply. New technical developments are producing beds that may eventually solve the problem, ranging from hammock types to a continuously inflated air mattress. They are expensive and it will possibly be a long time before they are seen in the patients' homes.

Treatment

Superficial sores should be cleaned with soap and water or a non-irritant lotion such as cetrimide 1% and, after being allowed to dry, sprayed with Sprilon or Opsite. Healing usually takes place slowly, although sometimes infection may be present, when a swab should be taken for bacteriological assessment. However, antibiotics are not usually necessary.

Deep sores need to be cleaned and necrotic tissue removed. This can usually be done using forceps and scissors but powders are available, such as Debrisan, to soften the slough. Sometimes it is helpful to dissolve the powder in a little glycerine. Debrisan is expensive and cheaper products include Aserbine and Malatex. Surgical treatment is rarely needed in older age, but if the ulcer is extensive and the patient's condition is good, surgical advice about the possibility of grafting may be justified.

Urinary Incontinence

In recent years a much better understanding has been gained of the causes of urinary continence, which has led to improvement in its management. A full account of the changes associated with ageing and the anatomical and physiological background to the mechanisms can be found in textbooks of geriatric medicine. From the practical point of view, however, incontinence may be due to diseases of the brain or spinal cord (neuropathic), or to local abnormalities in the bladder and urinary tract (focal). These produce different types of bladder abnormality. Cases of neuropathic urinary incontinence characteristically have a hypersensitive bladder that empties frequently without the patient being aware of this taking place. The bladder is not usually palpable as its capacity is reduced, being small and contracted. Focal lesions, which interfere with the emptying, are usually associated with a full bladder and overflow incontinence. The patient wets him/herself, but, on examination, a full bladder is found. Causes can include such things as urethral caruncle, urinary infection, prolapse in the female and prostatic hypertrophy in the male. Constipation may be a cause in both sexes. There may be overlying emotional and environmental problems. It sometimes happens that a patient in an acute period of stress may be incontinent but, once this has passed, full continence returns. Some environmental changes, such as going to hospital or sleeping in a strange bed, can precipitate incontinence, often causing great embarrassment. Severe illness of any sort can also be a cause. Diabetes mellitus maybe an associated finding. There is increased frequency and reduced bladder capacity in older age, with immobility as a potent background cause of incontinence. This may, for instance, occur after an operation.

Nursing management first requires an assessment to establish the cause and decide on the best way to alleviate the problem. This means determining the type of incontinence, its frequency and pattern, and also any precipating causes. The patient's mental and mobility state also need to be assessed. Close co-operation between the doctor and nurse is very important at this stage. Treatment of any cause found should be instituted. If there is a local lesion present, help from a urological or gynaecological surgeon may be necessary. Rectal examination may reveal that faecal impaction is causing the condition; sometimes chronic constipation needs to be treated. Infections, if present, should be remedied, and bacterial examination of the urine is necessary to determine causal bacteria. Glycosuria should also be excluded. Sometimes a full urological examination may be necessary, including intravenous pyleography and cystocopy.

It may prove impossible to control the incontinence by formal treatment, and this is when nursing management becomes important. There is little joy in dealing with an incontinent older patient, and it may be tempting to show distaste and annoyance at the continual unclean wet state. Some older people even give the impression that they are incontinent on purpose as an attention-seeking device. This is rarely the case and much can be achieved by understanding the problem and urging the patient to keep as active as possible. In the first place, therefore, the patient should be treated sympathetically and with general reassurance, remembering that they are often extremely embarrassed by their problem. Aids to mobility, regular toileting and an alarm clock to act as a reminder may be all that is necessary. The bladder should always be emptied before retiring. It is helpful to make sure that the patient has adequate recourse to a bedside commode or bottle, particularly at night. Sedatives are best kept to a minimum and restriction of fluid in the evening may be valuable for patients suffering from nocturnal incontinence. Diuretics sometimes produce incontinence and careful timing of the dosage is important.

There are a number of drugs used in the treatment of incontinence. Anticholinergic drugs permit increased relaxation of the bladder and an increased volume. The side-effects are retention of urine, blurring of vision and dryness of the mouth. It is helpful if an incontinence chart is kept, so that the pattern of micturation can be anticipated and the drugs prescribed accordingly: the dosage may need to be changed from time to time. If there is no progress, the treatment should be discontinued. When depression is present, incontinence may be helped by antidepressant drugs.

Despite these measures, the condition is often persistent and recourse has to be made to incontinence aids. Disposable incontinence pads are very useful for the patient while in bed and they can absorb up to 300 ml of urine. The person should sit directly on them without intervening clothes. For this reason they are not suitable for use when patients are sitting in a chair. Disposable napkins or pants are available and a variety very popular with patients are Kanga pants. They ingeniously hold the pad in a waterproof pouch outside the pants, which are made of a one-way water repellent fabric that allows the urine through into the disposable pad. About 400 ml of urine can be held and there is no need to remove the pants to change the pad. Some local authorities arrange for the disposable pads to be collected from the house at intervals.

In the male, penile clamps or condom drainage is sometimes helpful. Special care of the skin and scrupulous hygiene is always needed in these cases.

Permanent catheterization is sometimes necessary. The plastic balloon catheter is the one usually used; the balloon is usually filled with sterile water using a 20 ml syringe. Infection is always a risk with this type of catheter and, even with an inflated balloon, patients can sometimes pull it out. Noxyflex solution should be instilled into the bladder if infection is present, either weekly or on alternate days. Long-term antibiotic therapy is not used routinely with older patients. A Foley balloon catheter needs changing monthly, but the Silastic or Dover's catheters need only to be changed every three months and are a great improvement. Although always a difficult task, nursing this type of patient at home is now much more feasible because of the new improved catheters. Carers and relatives need considerable support when nursing incontinent patients. Tolerance of the problem is low and full explanation and help is needed. Extra laundry can produce a financial burden and an attendance allowance should be applied for. In some areas a nursing adviser on incontinence is available.

Faecal Incontinence

This is a distressing condition that often occurs in bedfast demented patients. It is commonly due to faecal impaction and produces spurious diarrhoea. Neoplasm of the bowel is another possible cause. Short-term incontinence may be associated with an attack of diarrhoea caused by infection of the bowel or dietary disturbance. Any serious illness may be associated with faecal incontinence. Some drugs, such as antibiotics and iron, may cause diarrhoea in an older person and precipitate incontinence. Self-prescribed large doses of laxatives are not uncommon in older people and may produce diarrhoea. Nursing treatment involves attention to any predisposing causes and relief of the impaction if present. This usually involves enemas or a rectal washout, and sometimes manual removal. Suppositories, such as glycerine, may be helpful. It may also be useful to increase the volume of faeces by using a high residue diet containing bran. Certain foods cause diarrhoea in some patients; if these can be recognized, they should be avoided. If diarrhoea is persistent once infection or neoplasm have been excluded, a kaolin mixture may help to harden the stools. General attention to training and suitable clothing should be instituted as outlined in the section on urinary incontinence. Faecal incontinence is usually preventable and reversible. Diet and fluid are important, so are privacy, comfort and time to promote normal defecation.

Avoiding Contractures

When nursing a bedfast or partially bedfast older person, it is important to realize how easily contractures may develop. A stroke patient may be discharged home and, without careful supervision, may very quickly develop a contracture. They are usually associated with prolonged stay in bed, and when this is inevitable, active and passive movements of the limbs that are at risk should be encouraged. If the joints are painful, analgesics should be given to allow them to move more freely. Bedclothes should not be pulled tightly around the legs, as restriction of movement can sometimes cause knee stiffening or foot drop.

Nursing a Restless Patient

There are many causes of restlessness in an older person. Infections, particularly pneumonia, or any acute illness, and also such conditions as heart failure and anaemia, may make an older person sleepless. Impairment of consciousness, often associated with cerebral deterioration or developing cerebral thrombosis, can aggravate the condition. Uraemic patients may be particularly fretful and disorientated at night. Certain drugs used in sedation may give rise to agitation; this is particularly true of bromides and barbiturates. Other drugs may also be responsible and therapy should be reviewed when restlessness is present. Pain and discomfort may contribute and may result from a full bladder or faecal impaction. Older persons who will not settle at night are well known to nurses. They may be reasonably co-operative through the day, but, once the evening arrives, they may wander around noisily, upsetting everyone by their disorientation. Tranquillizers are helpful and the most usual ones used are promazine and chlorpromazine, both in syrup form. General measures, such as keeping the person up during the day and ensuring some activity, not allowing them to go to bed too soon, and providing a bedtime milky drink may, however, be all that is necessary.

Conclusion

Nursing older people at home is a task that demands the full resources of nursing skill. There are special difficulties involved and this demands understanding on the part of the community nursing team to achieve success. Apart from nursing, the tasks undertaken by the community team involve rehabilitation, health education, attention to diet and keeping an eye on the general social state of the individual. Supporting relatives and carers is an important part of the nurse's role and this may continue long after traditionally viewed nursing skill is no longer required.

Finally, the nursing team should, of course, be an integral part of the primary health care team and work closely with all other members.

Reference

1. Norton D, McLaren R, Exton-Smith AN. (1962) *An investigation of geriatric nursing problems in hospital.* Churchill Livingstone, Edinburgh.

22
Palliative and Terminal Care in the Community

The greater part of the care given to a person in the last few weeks or months of their life will take place at home, regardless of where the person is at the time of death. The aim of good palliative and terminal care is to allow a person to live life as fully as possible and to die with as much dignity and autonomy as can be attained, in the place of their choosing, and looked after by trusted carers. In order for this to happen:

- The patient and carers need to be as fully informed about the illness as they wish.
- They need opportunities to express their feelings about what is happening.
- The patient and family need to be encouraged to live life as normally as possible.
- They need to be aware of the range of options for care.
- The patient needs good symptom control.

In addition, support for the family needs to be continued after the death of the patient.

Communication

Many older people are prepared for, and have discussed, death with their spouse or family. However, this is not universal and there are those who are so afraid of dying, or the effect that it will have on the surviving family members, that they cannot bring themselves to face the subject. There may also be particular fears associated with cancer, especially for those who have known a relative or friend die in pain or distress.

One of the most devastating parts of having a terminal illness can be the isolation from family and friends as a result of being unable to share feelings and fears. This lack of communication is often related to the inadequacy of the patient's knowledge of the illness and/or its prognosis, and to the degree to which the patient was able to talk about how they felt at the time of the diagnosis.

Although communication with patients is improving, there are still many people who are discharged from hospital wards or clinics unclear about their diagnosis or prognosis, or about what their relatives have been told. This may be because it is a worsening of a pre-existing condition that has not previously been seen as life threatening, or it may be as a result of a new diagnosis of a terminal condition, such as cancer. It may be that the patient was not told at the time of diagnosis or, that they were told at such a time or in such a way that they could not take in the news, or that their coping mechanism at that time was denial. Whether told directly or not, most people know within themselves when they are dying. They guess from how they are feeling, from the fact that they are losing weight, from their lack of strength, and in particular from the way other people behave towards them: 'I knew it must be cancer when the doctor went to talk to all the other patients after their operations but missed me out.' They may not wish to discuss it because they are afraid to face the thought of death, because they sense others are embarrassed to talk about dying; they may be afraid to be thought foolish or morbid, or to have their fears swept aside with false reassurance: 'Don't be silly, of course you're going to get better.' Above all, they do not want their family to be upset.

For the most part, however, close relatives are told the truth in more detail, but frequently do not know how to talk with the patient. They are afraid of upsetting the patient or fear that if they know the truth they will go to pieces. The result of this is a conspiracy of silence, with a barrier set up between patient and family, leading to a feeling of extreme isolation for the patient. Some have described it as being shut out or, 'I might as well be dead already'.

An important aspect of caring for the terminally ill is therefore to facilitate communication between the patient and family. A first step is to ascertain the patient's current state of knowledge about their condition. This can only be done accurately by sensitively exploring with the patient what they already know and how much they want to know. Relying on what the hospital letters or family say about what the patient has been told is no real guide to what the patient has heard or accepted.

Gentle enquiry such as, 'What did they tell you at the hospital about your illness', or 'Is there anything you would like me to explain?', may enable the patient to open up. If the patient has already had experience of sensing that professionals are unwilling to be honest with them it may take more than one occasion for them to find the courage to ask questions. If the patient is clearly not ready to discuss the illness then that needs to be respected, but an open statement such as, 'If you do want to know any more at a later date then I will be happy to come and talk to you', will give the message that there is someone who is prepared to listen and be honest.

A common difficulty is when relatives do not want the patient to be told what is wrong: 'He doesn't know; you won't tell him, will you, doctor?' Very often this reaction is because the relatives do not know how to cope with either the patient's emotion or their own if the subject is out in the open. It is important that the relatives are reassured that the doctor will not go and blurt out the news to the patient that they are dying. It is also valuable to explore how the relatives are feeling and let them express some of their anger or sadness, as this will then enable them to cope better with the thought of the patient's reaction. It is helpful to explain that the patient may already know and may be feeling worse for not being able to talk about it, and also that it is a person's right to know the truth if that is what they want. It is also important to point out that the doctor will not lie to the patient if the patient asks a direct question. The vast majority of relatives will accept this approach, although there will still be a few who insist that the patient should not know and may try to inhibit real communication between the doctor and the patient by interrupting or changing the subject.

For this reason, and because a patient may be reluctant to talk about the illness in front of relatives in order to protect them, it may be advisable to try to see the patient alone. After some discussion has taken place it may then be helpful to get the relatives in to talk together. Sometimes there is resistance to this from other family members, children for instance, again because they are concerned about their parents being made upset.

An approach that may be helpful here is to explore whether they are the sort of family who have always shared things. To encourage them to remember the difficult times they have experienced over the years and how sharing those times helped each other, may enable them to see how they are denying themselves comfort by not sharing now.

There will always be some people who do not want to talk about dying and this may be the right course for them. The crucial question is whether lack of discussion is helping or hindering their emotional process. Signs of hindrance may include agitation, insomnia and uncontrolled symptoms, especially nausea and pain. If the patient appears peaceful and content then they have probably found the right personal balance.

In order to help others to explore their emotions and face dying, I believe that it is important that we, as professional carers, are prepared to do our own exploration of our thoughts and feelings about death and accept that our own personal experiences influence the way in which we relate to others. We need to acknowledge the necessity for support for ourselves whilst we are caring for those who are dying.

Emotional and Spiritual Care

Patients and relatives will experience a whole range of emotions from the time they receive a diagnosis, through the duration of the illness, and, for the family, after the death.

Patients may be clearly in one of the five stages of dying described by Kubler Ross; denial and isolation, anger, bargaining, depression and acceptance. More often there may be a jumble of emotions that may be hard for the person to identify and express and they may appear totally accepting one day and denying the next.

People often need to tell their story and, by doing so, try to make some sort of sense out of their experience. As they describe the history of the illness there are often questions they wish to ask or points they need clarifying. There may be anger directed at a doctor who missed the diagnosis, at those who are not able to effect a cure, or at God for allowing it to happen. Anger may not be overtly expressed, indeed sometimes it presents as depression or withdrawal, sometimes as irritability and incessant demand-making.

There are many fears someone may have when dying, often based on their previous experience. It is therefore valuable to ask about their previous experience of death and establish whether there are any particular worries. Frequent concerns are fear of choking, screaming out or going mad. Many fear what will happen to their family once they have gone and whether a surviving spouse will be able to cope. It is important to acknowledge and accept these emotions and encourage the person to express them openly, as suppressed emotion can lead to worsening of somatic symptoms, further depression, confusion and even paranoia. Being given an opportunity to talk through practical issues, such as making a will or planning the funeral service, and getting reassurance that there will be support for the family, will help to relieve anxiety.

The knowledge of impending death stimulates people to take stock of their life and its meaning. What has it all been about? What have I achieved? Why is this happening to me? As mentioned earlier, it can be a very isolating time if family and friends feel at a distance, with the patient feeling excluded from the life that is continuing around them. The message 'there is nothing more we can do' has often been heard, even if not actually said. 'Thrown on the scrap heap' is the feeling many describe. For some, the loss of role, whether it be breadwinner, cook, chauffeur, gardener, lover or friend, means that their self-esteem is very low. Facing life without a future makes it hard to look forward to anything, and to try to achieve anything may seem futile.

As a person retreats further and further into despair and hopelessness, this is not only hard for that person but very tiring and depressing for the carers at home. The professional carers can serve as a good role model here by including the patient in discussion and planning, by being interested in the patient's hopes and fears, and encouraging them to do as much as possible for themselves.

The need for hope is one of the greatest of human needs, and research has shown that there are many things which encourage people to have hope: the presence of meaningful shared relationships, recalling happy memories, or achieving an aim such as going out for the day. For some, their faith may be greatly comforting; saying prayers or listening to spiritual music may increase their sense of hope. Many people may want to think through and talk about spiritual issues with someone less overtly religious than a priest or minister. After initial discussion it may be appropriate to offer for a member of the clergy to visit, something the patient may be reluctant to ask for if they have not had regular contact with the church. Time spent with the patient exploring any of these hopes or fears enables the patient to feel valued as a human being.

Services for the Terminally Ill

The majority of people express a wish to die at home, yet many do not achieve this. There can be several reasons, but one may be that they are not prepared and are frightened of how they will cope. Successful terminal care at home depends largely on good forward planning.

If there has been open discussion about the illness, then it is possible to talk about the options for terminal care: home, hospital, nursing home or palliative care unit/hospice. There is often an expectation that people have to be looked after in some kind of institution and many people have no idea of the range of services available in the community.

It is good to involve the district nurse at an early stage even if there is no 'hands on' nursing required. Regular contact is helpful to enable a relationship to be built, to allow the nurse to assess when further help is needed, and to monitor bowel care and prevent constipation. The nurse can explain the nursing services available, including the evening and night services and the Marie Curie service, and the type of aids such as commodes, pressure-relieving mattresses and wheel-chairs, that can be provided. A home visit by the community physiotherapist or occupational therapist may be helpful in providing specialized equipment to improve mobility. There may also need to be referral to social services for domestic help or Meals on Wheels. There may be financial difficulties and the patient or family should be encouraged to apply for an attendance allowance under the special rules for the terminally ill (DS1500 Report Form). The Cancer Relief Macmillan Fund offers special grants to patients with cancer to help with bills or other special needs. The necessary forms can be obtained from Macmillan nurses or social workers. Day care provision or respite care in the local care unit for older people or hospice may give a valuable rest to carers and enable patients to stay at home for longer. Local hospice or palliative care units vary in the type of support they can offer and the diseases that come under their remit. Some will only see patients with advanced cancer whilst others will see a broader spectrum of patients. Most will offer domiciliary advice, respite care, admission for symptom control, terminal care and day care. Macmillan nurses will see patients at home to offer advice on symptom control and to give support for their choice as they are likely to receive conflicting advice and even condemnation from other family members and neighbours. It is also important to keep the options open, as the situation may change, and it is important to avoid if possible relatives feeling guilty if the patient has to be admitted, for example, to a hospital.

Assessment of the Patient's Condition and Treatment

It is helpful to reassess the need for further treatment and follow-up. Routine follow-up at several outpatients clinics may be unnecessary and the patient may want advice about whether or not to cancel an appointment. Others may find it comforting to know that they are under regular review at the hospital and find it distressing to be discharged. There are some treatments that are valuable to consider to improve quality of life. These include palliative radiotherapy for painful bony metastases, blood transfusion for symptomatic anaemia, tapping pleural effusions or ascites, and treating hypercalcaemia.

As the person becomes less well it is helpful to review medication. A common complaint from patients is about the number of tablets they have to take; these can often be minimized. For example, as the person loses weight and becomes less active antihypertensive or antianginal drugs may no longer be necessary. It is important to give an explanation to the patient and family about why these can be stopped, as the message that they need to take these the rest of their lives may be deeply ingrained and they may consider the suggestion to stop medication as an indication that their life is over.

Symptom Control

There is not space here to cover symptom control in detail, but this section attempts to give a basic approach to some of the commonly occurring problems. Suggested reading is listed at the end of the chapter. Further advice can be sought from local palliative care/hospice units or Macmillan nursing teams.

Pain is a common, though not invariable, problem for people who have a terminal illness. To manage pain successfully it is necessary to define its cause and treat it appropriately. The pain may be:

* directly due to the illness (eg due to a primary or secondary cancer)
* associated with concurrent problems such as angina or arthritis
* iatrogenic (eg dyspepsia secondary to treatment with non-steroidal anti-inflammatory drugs)
* related to general debility (eg muscle spasm from immobility, painful pressure sores).

Oral medication is the preferred route for all patients who can swallow. For pain that should respond to analgesics, the approach of the analgesic staircase should be considered, by first using simple non-opioid analgesics (eg paracetamol or non-steroidal anti-inflammatory drugs), followed by weak opioids (eg co-proxamol or dihydrocodeine); if these are not effective, then strong opioids such as oral morphine should be used. For older patients who have not been on opioids before, a starting dose of four-hourly oral morphine sulphate 2.5–5 mg (Oramorph elixir or Sevredol tablets) or 12-hourly slow release morphine sulphate 10 mg (MST or SRM-Rhotard) should be used and the dose escalated in increments of 30–50% until the pain is controlled. There may be no need for a dose of four-hourly morphine during the night, but if pain is a problem in the early hours a 50% higher dose can be given at night, perhaps allowing the patient to sleep through.

Clear instructions are needed about medication for breakthrough pain. Between

50% and 100% of the four-hourly dose of oral morphine should be adequate for breakthrough pain. An alternative is dextromoramide (Palfium), which lasts for two or three hours in cancer pain. Dextromoramide given in a dose of 5 mg is equivalent to 10 mg of morphine and can be given either orally or sublingually. Slow release morphine is not sufficiently quick acting to be useful for break-through pain. If several doses of breakthrough medication are required during 24 hours the regular dose should be adjusted accordingly. The patient may have reservations about being started on morphine and need to discuss these. They may need reassurance that they will not become addicted or be rendered uncon-scious or die more quickly because they are on morphine. Side-effects of opiates may include:

- *Drowsiness* may occur with the first few doses. This should resolve quickly and patients are usually prepared to tolerate it if they are given an explanation. If it does not resolve, this is an indication that the opiate dose is too high and needs to be reduced. It is also worth remembering that many patients blame their tiredness on the drugs, when it is more likely to be due to the illness.

- *Confusion* due to opiates used correctly is relatively rare and other causes for confusion should be ruled out.

- *Nausea and vomiting* may occur when opiates are first prescribed and a regular anti-emetic prescribed with the opiate may be beneficial (eg haloperidol 3–5 mg. daily). Other causes for nausea and vomiting should be considered.

- *Constipation* is the commonest, almost invariable, side-effect of opiates and tol-erance does not occur. Laxatives need to be prescribed routinely and a full explanation given to the patient and family about the need to take them. A combination of a stimulant and a stool softener such as co-danthrusate (Normax) or senna and lactulose is to be preferred to bulking agents.

Not all pain, particularly nerve pain, is totally opiate responsive, and coanal-gesics may need to be considered as well as other treatments such as radiothera-py, nerve blocks and transcutaneous electrical nerve stimulation. Coanalgesics frequently used in pain control include non-steroidal anti-inflammatory drugs, antidepressants, anticonvulsants and antiarrhythmics.

Nausea and Vomiting

Causes include:

- constipation
- subacute intestinal obstruction
- gastric stasis (usually due to drugs, especially opiates)
- 'squashed stomach' from hepatomegaly or ascites
- gastric irritation

- hypercalcaemia
- uraemia
- toxicity from cancer or infection
- drugs
- raised intracranial pressure
- anxiety.

Toxic, metabolic and drug-induced nausea usually responds best to an antiemetic acting on the chemoreceptor trigger zone such as haloperidol (Serenace, Haldol, Dozic) or prochlorperazine (Stemetil). Gastric stasis may be helped by metoclopramide (Maxolon) or domperidone (Motilium). Nausea due to constipation, intestinal obstruction, enlarged liver or raised intracranial pressure will respond best to cyclizine (Valoid), which acts directly on the vomiting centre. If one antiemetic alone does not work, a combination of two acting at different sites should be tried (eg cyclizine and haloperidol). For patients who are very anxious, a benzodiazepine such as diazepam or the phenothiazine, methotrimeprazine (Nozinan) may be helpful. Methotrimeprazine can be very sedative, especially in the older people and a small dose of 12.5 mg (half a tablet) twice daily should be the starting dose.

Anorexia and Weight Loss

These can be a great cause of distress, sometimes more for the family than the patient. Simple measures are helpful, such as good mouth care, treating oral candidiasis, encouraging the patient to eat small meals more frequently and providing nutritional drinks. Specific appetite stimulants may include alcohol or corticosteroids. Explanation that the patient does not need as much food as previously and that they will not get better however much they eat is important. The family need to know that it is alright for the person to eat what they like, and that refusal of food is not a rejection of themselves. Dehydration in the terminally ill does not usually cause distressing symptoms apart from a dry mouth, which is best treated by local measures. Generally it is inappropriate to admit a terminally ill patient to hospital for treatment with intravenous fluids.

Confusion

Causes of confusion include infection, constipation, urinary retention, cerebral involvement, hypercalcaemia and drugs. Haloperidol is useful for treating hallucinations and anxiety without being too sedative. Thioridazine (Melleril) can be used if a sedative effect is desirable.

Breathlessness

If appropriate, specific treatment should be tried (eg blood transfusion, pleural tap). Bronchodilators and nebulized normal saline often help the expectoration of mucus and secretions. Regular doses of morphine, benzodiazepines or chlorpromazine help to relieve the distress of dyspnoea.

Depression

Depression in the terminally ill may be overlooked, as many of the physical symptoms associated with it also occur with advanced cancer, and it is normal for someone facing their death to have a period of low mood. However, if this persists, particularly if accompanied by feelings of worthlessness, then treatment with an antidepressant should be considered.

Management of the Patient in the Last Few Days

As the patient's condition deteriorates, oral medication may no longer be possible; alternatives include the rectal and subcutaneous routes. Although morphine and oxycodone and some antiemetics are available in suppository form, the duration of action usually means using several suppositories a day; continuous subcutaneous infusion via a syringe driver is the preferred route for most patients. The majority of practices and district nurses have access to these, and, if necessary, advice on their use can be obtained from the Macmillan service or a hospice. Diamorphine is preferred to morphine in the syringe drive as it is more soluble than morphine. The conversion from oral morphine to subcutaneous diamorphine is to divide the total daily dose by three; thus a patient whose pain had been controlled on MST 30 mg bd would require diamorphine 20 mg in the syringe driver over 24 hours. An antiemetic may need to be continued if nausea and vomiting are a problem. Several antiemetics can be mixed with diamorphine (eg cyclizine, haloperidol, methotrimeprazine and metoclopramide), as can midazolam (Hypnovel) and hyoscine hydrobromide.

Midazolam is useful to control fits, ease muscle spasm and reduce restlessness. The starting dose is 5–10 mg over 24 hours, but this may be increased to 60–80 mg. Hyoscine hydrobromide will dry up pharyngeal secretions; an initial dose of 0.4–0.6 mg subcutaneously, followed by 1.2–2.4 mg over 24 hours, should prevent the distressing 'death rattle'. It is normally recommended that no more than two drugs are mixed together in the syringe. (Three can be used, but this increases the chance of the drugs being precipitated out in the syringe.)

The following drugs should not be used in a syringe driver as they are too irritant to the subcutaneous tissues: chlorpromazine (Largactil), prochlorperazine (Stemetil) and diazepam (Valium). These can be used in suppository form if indicated.

The last few days of the patient's life may be particularly stressful for the family, but also very precious if they manage to keep the person at home until the end. Regular visits from nurses and the GP give vital moral, as well as practical support. It is important that the family know when to expect the next visit from the GP and how to obtain help if they need it. If possible, it is better for the family to have a contact number for a doctor they know from the practice rather than a deputizing service who does not know the patient and may feel obliged to admit them. Some GPs give their own home telephone number, which is always greatly appreciated and rarely abused.

The contribution of the community nurse is important in the management of terminally ill patients, particularly so in the last few days. Help may be needed in the prevention of pressure sores and the management of problems such as incontinence. Supervision of pain relief and the treatment of other symptoms is also a significant nursing task. Practical issues, however, come to the fore in the late stages, for example, disposal of soiled dressings, which is mostly done by burning or wrapping in a polythene bag and putting in the dustbin. Special arrangements can be made with local authority cleansing departments for this type of disposal. Offensive smells are sometimes a problem, but can be overcome by deodorants and air fresheners. Once the patient has died, the nurse usually attends to the body and disposes of soiled linen. Any unused drugs should be destroyed and equipment removed.

Bereavement

Follow-up for the surviving relatives or friends is an important aspect of good terminal care. Bereaved people, perhaps especially those who are older, can feel very lonely, with much of the previous support given to them during the course of the person's illness having disappeared. In addition, if they had focused all their time and energy on nursing the ill person, they may now be at a complete loss. Contact with the professionals who were involved may provide a useful link between the old life and the new. It also gives an opportunity to assess whether the person is in need of more formalized bereavement counselling offered by national bodies such as CRUSE or by local groups run by a hospice or local church.

It needs to be recognised that the physical, emotional and spiritual dimensions of dying overlap. A GP engaged in the day to day care of a dying patient and the family over a period of time can come to share some of the frustrations of the situation. Help from a specialist in palliative care is useful, particularly if the question of admission to a hospice or terminal care unit has been raised.

An example of the multidisciplinary aspect of caring for the dying and help that can be given by a skilled colleague is illustrated by the following case history.

Mr Jones was terminally ill with cancer of the prostate. He had pain and was having very disturbed nights; his wife was very tired and did not think she could cope any longer. The question of admission to a consultant unit was raised. The consultant in question was asked to do a domiciliary visit. She records:

> I visited on Friday afternoon and spoke first to his wife who did not know if her husband knew his diagnosis. I then talked to the patient alone and for about half an hour we talked all round the houses about his illness. He was adamant he was getting better. Then he said, almost as an aside, 'I'm worried about what will happen to my wife when I'm gone.' 'It sounds as if you're saying you're not going to get better.' 'No, I know I'm not. I know I'm dying.' We talked further about what might be wrong with him and he still denied he knew. Then he talked about his wife having had cancer and eventually said 'I'm worried that that is what I have got. Is it cancer?' I agreed that it was and asked him whether he would feel happier if he could talk with his wife about it. He said 'yes', but didn't know how to. I offered to fetch his wife so that the three of us might talk together. She came in and sat on the bed beside him and they both began to cry. I left them together for a few minutes and then went back. They obviously did not need me there and I left, saying that I would ring them after the weekend to see how things were going. When I rang on Monday morning his wife said, 'It's alright now. We've had a good talk, his pain has gone and we're both getting enough sleep. I want to keep him at home.'

He died at home a few days later.

Further Reading

Buckman R. (1985) *I don't know what to say*. Papermac, London.

Haines A, Booroff A. (1986) Terminal care at home: perspective from general practice. *Br Med J* 292: 1051–53.

Herd EB. (1990) Terminal care in a semi-rural area. *Br J Gen Pract* 40: 248–51.

Herth K. (1990) Fostering hope in terminally-ill people. *J Adv Nurs* 15: 1250–9.

Kubler-Ross E. (1969) *On death and dying*. Tavistock, London.

Penson J, Fisher R, editors. (1991) *Palliative care for people with cancer*. Edward Arnold, London.

Regnard C, Tempest S. (1992) *A guide to symptom relief in advanced cancer*. Haigh and Hochland, Manchester.

Townsend J, Frank AD, Fermont D, *et al*. (1990) Terminal cancer care and patients' preference for place of death: a prospective study. *Br Med J* 301: 415–7.

Twycross R, Lack S. (1990) Therapeutics in terminal cancer. 2nd ed. Churchill Livingstone, Edinburgh.

23
Ethical Issues in
the Community

A greater understanding of the problems of caring for older people in the community has highlighted some ethical problems that may occur. Many of these centre around such issues as respect for the person, degrees of acceptable risk, confidentiality and matters of life and death. This chapter will examine these particularly in relation to the family doctor working in the community, but they may confront any health or social worker. Instead of analysing the problems individually, they will be discussed in relation to actual patients whose histories will be described and the ethical problems identified. Each of the cases is intended to demonstrate a particular problem, but, as always in medicine, there is a considerable amount of overlap and often two or three ethical dilemmas are confronted in the same situation. Nine cases will now be described and the underlying ethical problems and common features will be discussed at the end of the chapter. The names have, of course, been changed.

1 The Lomax Couple – through whose eyes are we looking?

Mrs Lomax is aged 84 and her husband is six years her junior. They have been married for over 50 years. They had two sons, both of whom were married and have died within the last 10 years. The only relative they have any contact with is a grandson who lives 10 miles away. The health of both is bad. Mrs Lomax has chronic heart failure, generalized osteoarthritis and an irritating skin rash. Her arthritis makes her immobile and she is only able to shuffle around the house using either a Zimmer frame or a walking stick. Mr Lomax is virtually blind, but otherwise fairly mobile and in reasonable physical health. He suffers from early senile dementia and is forgetful and occasionally confused. They live in a ground floor flat in a block built purposely for older people. Unfortunately they have few contacts with their neighbours. They have help from social services in the form of Meals on Wheels and home help.

A central feature of their life is their constant quarrelling. This seems to have been present for many years, but is, in old age, particularly distressing to those around. They both, however, manage to deal with this and it may be an important part of their relationship. In effect, Mrs Lomax acts as the brain and the eyes and Mr Lomax as the hands and the mobility. The two are in a state of brittle equilibrium and just able to attend to their domestic and personal requirements.

Comment

This case presents a number of awkward dilemmas for the doctor. Neither of the patients is receiving adequate medical care. Treatment is unreliable as tablets are not taken regularly despite daily visits by the district nurse. This non-compliance is due to a combination of apathy, forgetfulness, poor vision and confusion. Outside observers would say that both patients should be in hospital or at least in residential accommodation where treatment can be properly supervised. Nevertheless, they are just coping and the question arises of what should be the aim of medical care: therapeutic perfection, or patient satisfaction with the present state? Outsiders would also say that the pair are unhappy. One only needs to listen to their constant complaints and incessant quarrelling. This, however, may be absolutely necessary to their well-being and in no way detracts from their state of happiness. Without this stimulus, life may lack its spice and hence not be worth living.

Even more difficult is the social aspect. The house is dirty, untidy and a minefield of hazards. Cooking facilities are basic and potentially dangerous. If it were not for Meals on Wheels, nutrition would be totally inadequate. These are all very strong reasons to move the pair into some form of supervised care.

Yet through whose eyes do we observe their predicament? To the much younger eyes of the doctor, nurse and social worker, the conditions under which the Lomax couple live are wholly unacceptable. How could anyone live in such chaos it might be asked? Especially as one is immobile and the other is blind. Yet to these people this is the accepted norm, the environment that is understood. They support each other after a fashion and they have survived. How much should one meddle with such a situation? Would interference really be in the best interests of these two older people, or would a move be purely to satisfy the anxieties of the professional carers who experience a sense of unease when observing what might be described as neglect? Is it reasonable, ethically, to carry such a burden of responsibility, realizing that the best is not being achieved for these patients? Who judges what is best? How far is collusion allowable? The apathy of old age, along with the blunted understanding of early dementia, denies reality. Doctors have built into their value systems a duty to respect the person they are treating, to share with the patient a knowledge of the problems, the possibilities, the decisions and their implications; but who is the person the doctor must respect? Is it the person the doctor knew ten or 20 years ago, articulate and well integrated, or is it the person he/she now sees?

In the case of the Lomax couple, the problem can become compounded when one of them develops an illness that makes him/her unable to fulfil their part of the partnership arrangement. If, for instance, Mrs Lomax goes into heart failure and needs bed rest, it means that she becomes unable to supervise Mr Lomax in the tasks of general housework. Does the doctor admit her to hospital and leave him to manage alone, or admit him to a residential home where he would be unhappy? Alternatively, can he treat her at home and risk disaster?

What are the priorities in this situation? Is it the equilibrium that they have and that would be broken if either of them was taken away from their home for any length of time, or is it the health of Mrs Lomax? Would Mr Lomax in fact survive if he were admitted to a residential home? Unfortunately, the answers to these questions are not predictable at the time when decisions have to be made. Whatever happens, it is likely that decisions taken in favour of one will not benefit the other. Doctors are, however, expected to make the decisions. The general principle has always been to preserve life, but the dilemma sometimes arises, and it does so particularly in this case, about whose life it is best to preserve.

2 Mr Barlow – defeat

Mr Barlow is a widower aged 88. He lives alone in a state of some personal neglect. His condition is dirty and that of his house squalid. He lives in a downstairs room, where he sleeps, eats and attends to his toilet. There are no visible carers, but it is probable that there are relatives in the district who refuse to have anything to do with him because of his condition. The only contact Mr Barlow has with the outside world is through a neighbour who visits on a very irregular basis. His main diet is baked beans. He will not have a home help or Meals on Wheels service, although both have been offered by social workers on several occasions. In fact, he is averse to any type of external assistance and certainly does not want to move from his house. He is ill with chronic bronchitis and heart failure, and has been offered hospital admission. He refuses to take tablets except on a very irregular basis. His compliance with any type of therapeutic plan is almost non-existent. He is, however, in other ways quite rational and in no way demented. Medically, he has serious illnesses and socially, there is a breakdown of his domestic and personal care.

Comment

This case has similarities with that of the Lomax couple but with certain crucial differences. In their case there was a certain medical and social equilibrium, albeit fragile and they were prepared to accept medical and social help. Furthermore, there was no real antagonism from their neighbours or remaining relatives, merely a degree of non-interest. Mr Barlow, however, firmly refuses help. He lives in squalor that he accepts, but that results in his being rejected by both relatives and neighbours alike. The situation is one that, by normal standards, is unacceptable.

Herein lies the dilemma. Respect for Mr Barlow as a person requires that he lives his own life in his own way and is allowed to die his own death; but how far can this be taken? He is doing this within a community, particularly the community of his immediate neighbours. The stale food, the dirt, the smell and the vermin affect all who live around. How far can the sensibility and tolerance of his neighbours be offended before it is necessary to balance his freedom against theirs? Who takes these sort of decisions? There are legal provisions for dealing with this type of situation, where persons are a danger to themselves or others, but these are not often implemented. It is often not clear where the doctor's duty lies. At what point does he/she take action? How can the relatives be included in the decision-making? By this stage they have often withdrawn completely, or at least lost interest, perhaps because of old family feuds with resultant rancour. If the family doctor continues to attend, but fails to persuade Mr Barlow to take treatment, what happens if the patient dies? Is this suicide by self-neglect, or even death by medical neglect? What sort of responsibilities does the doctor have for this? An inquest would no doubt ensue.

Ethically, should the doctor tolerate a situation where an apparently rational man is, of his own choice, slowly dying, or should the doctor countermand the patient's wishes and bring in the law, with its powers of removal to a hospital or other place of safety? The situation is a reverse of the normally accepted aim of the doctor, which is to cure illness; here that opportunity is denied. In these circumstances must the GP's next duty be to others around who are affected by the patient's intransigence? What duty do doctors have to themselves to forestall allegations of allowing the patient to die, albeit slowly and naturally, because of lack of treatment? It might be that the patient is right and that treatment will make little difference; yet accepted wisdom is that treatment should be given and the doctors would normally accept this. Not to do so would possibly imperil their professional reputations, but should doctors be expected to impose their own wishes over those of their patients?

3 Mrs Williamson – to interfere or not to interfere?

Mrs Williamson is 89 and a widow. She lives alone in a pleasant, well cared for, semi-detached bungalow. She has good neighbours who help her through any difficulty. Medically, she has only minor problems that she copes with herself and she is mentally alert. One morning her GP is called because she has been suffering abdominal pain through the night and feels dizzy. When the doctor examines her, her pulse is weak and rapid and her blood pressure lower than previously recorded. Abdominal examination shows her to have a swelling in the upper part of her abdomen that could be an aortic aneurysm (ie a ballooning of the main artery taking blood from the heart into the abdomen and on to the lower limbs). The doctor arranges a joint home visit with a surgeon. The surgeon confirms the GP's suspicion that the patient is suffering from a leak of blood from the aneurysm and is bleeding to death. Under normal circumstances the treatment for this condition would be immediate surgery to repair the leak in the arterial wall. The surgeon, however, states that at the advanced age of 89 the operation would be extremely difficult and success would be unlikely. The operation, moreover, is a major one and, even if she survived, the result would be a long period in hospital and discomfort. Mrs Williamson has no relatives apart from a sister two years older than herself who lives abroad. Her real carers and closest friends are her neighbours. The surgeon, however, leaves the decision about what to do to the GP, on the grounds that it is the doctor who has the best understanding of the patient.

Comment

The doctor here is faced with a very difficult decision. The patient is articulate and, at this stage, fully mentally alert. Under normal circumstances the first thing to do would be to discuss the situation with relatives, but it is clearly impractical to contact the older sister and probably also unwise to involve her in a burden of this kind. Moreover, how far is it right and fair to involve neighbours? The only person with whom the GP can talk is, therefore, the patient herself, and normally this would be the right and proper thing to do. It is, after all, her life, but looking at the situation in a humane way there is a dilemma; should the patient be told the full implications of her illness and of the options open to her, or should he say very little and allow the patient to die peacefully? Can the doctor really explain the fact that she is internally bleeding to death, that the treatment is an immediate operation that she is unlikely to survive and that, even if she did so, recovery would be long and arduous? How honest could the doctor be? Is it fair to give her these options and ask her to make a decision about her own life and death?

In this case the decision is particularly pressing because the patient is becoming weaker by the hour. It is often said that GPs are the best people to make this sort of decision because they know their patients. Very often, however, it is almost impossible to know how a patient would react, especially at such critical moments when time is short.

Alternatively, should GPs make decisions about life and death on behalf of their patients? A GP is often the only one who can do so. Fortunately, in this case there is the aid of the surgeon's opinion, but can they act as a pair in this way? Removal of the disease, in this case the leaking blood vessel, could be seen to be the doctor's clear responsibility, but this is not necessarily so. Such value judgements are as important as clinical adjustments. How do doctors react to them? Do they advocate risk taking? Do they leave the decisions to patients and if so, is this humane? Should they take the decisions themselves for other human beings and face the judgements of their own consciences? It may be asked what preparation doctors have for dealing with this type of dilemma and if they are at all well equipped to do so.

4 Mrs Jones – conflicting interests

Grandma Jones (this is how she is known to everybody) is aged 70 and a widow. She is a strong matriarchal type of person who has enjoyed good health all her life and is well for her age. She is mentally alert and still continues to live life to the full. She gave up her home several years ago to live with her son and daughter-in-law in a pleasant detached house in a suburb. There are three children and, with Grandma's capital, they were able to move into a bigger house. There has always been some unease between Grandma Jones and her daughter-in-law. Many of the problems between the two have been associated with the younger woman's handling of her children and, in particular, Grandma's outspoken criticisms of it.

A crisis is precipitated in the household by the news that an unplanned fourth child is on the way. Grandma, now slightly incontinent and very embarrassed about it, is becoming an increasing burden to young Mrs Jones. Moreover, an extra room is required for the new baby, therefore pressure is placed on Grandma to move, hopefully to sheltered housing. Naturally, the elder Mrs Jones is very aggressively against this, thinking that the family house is her home and is the place where most of her capital is invested. Both women are patients of the same GP and both turn to the doctor for help, who is forced into a dilemma: to take the side of the young Mrs Jones with the problems of pregnancy and a new baby, or that of old Mrs Jones with her problems of pride and mild incontinence?

Comment

This dilemma is not uncommon for a GP. Two patients, with equal rights to care, concern, advice and support have potentially conflicting interests. The issue is complicated because it is not easy to separate primarily medical aspects from social, housing and interpersonal problems. Dilemmas exist about how far the doctor's role should go. One way out would be just to treat the older person's incontinence and ignore the effects that the domestic anxieties and unpleasantness are having on her mental state and general health. Much is made in modern general practice about whole-person medicine: seeing the patient as a complete human being and taking into account environmental, social and psychological aspects.

The younger Mrs Jones confronts the GP with a similar dilemma. She must also be considered as a total person, but both exist within a family and in some ways it can be argued that the doctor's responsibility is towards the whole family; after all GPs are also called *family* doctors. However, does this confer the authority to act as an arbitrator? In a straightforward medical case, where there are decisions to take, the doctor's responsibilities are clear and accepted. For example, the advice to have an inflamed appendix removed is almost always given and taken, but what about people in families? Does the doctor say, 'I think, Grandma, you are the lowest priority here and that you should go', and would this be accepted? Would society see this as the doctor's role? The answer is almost certainly not.

Wise doctors, of course, would perceive these pitfalls, deal with the medical aspects and then reflect their problems back onto the family. It would be hoped that, by listening and facilitating discussion, they would eventually enable the family to formulate their own list of solutions and come to a decision. It would then be their responsibility.

This example illustrates those aspects of medicine where decisions must be taken by those actually involved, with the doctor taking no decisive part. They lead sometimes to other ethical problems. A course of action may be agreed within a family that might, in fact, be disadvantageous to one of the members. An arrangement might be made, for example, for Grandma Jones to move into a small flat with the son financing the mortgage. This may seem to be fair, but the accommodation might be isolated, draughty, and away from friends and contacts. The doctor sees the risks but is faced with a family that is obviously turning a blind eye to them. Grandma, meanwhile, is not consulted and finds herself very much worse off. Should the doctor intervene?

5 Mrs Harding – to condone or not to condone

Mrs Harding is aged 75 and an ex-schoolteacher. She has always supported the idea of voluntary euthanasia and has spoken to her GP about this. They have always been good friends and over the years have formed a relationship of trust and respect. Sadly, Mrs Harding fell and fractured her femur whilst getting off a bus on a winter's day. She was admitted to hospital, survived an operation and made a reasonable recovery. She was discharged from the hospital, went home and the doctor was very pleased to see her progress. Within a week, however, she had the further misfortune to suffer a stroke. This resulted in Mrs Harding being confined to bed. The opinion of the consultant was sought and it was decided that she could be nursed at home. Despite making some initial progress, Mrs Harding gradually deteriorated until she became completely bedfast. Her mental state, however, remained alert. One day she asked the doctor for a supply of sleeping tablets. Because she had not required these previously the doctor suspected that her intent was to take the entire supply in an act of voluntary euthanasia and was somewhat taken aback. Should the GP go along with this and prescribe the tablets, or refuse to co-operate and risk destroying the relationship?

Comment

There are many ethical difficulties for the doctor here. In many ways, the fact that the patient was known well was more of a hindrance than a help. In good times they had been able to communicate easily and effectively. They had talked about death and dying and made a tacit assumption about each other's position, but, when the patient was faced with the reality of death and the discomfort of dying, the earlier easy communication had ceased. Neither felt able to talk about it and they resorted to subterfuge. Both, however, understood the implications. The doctor was not being asked to switch off a machine, as in the case of someone already dead, or mercifully withhold treatment in the case of a moribund patient. Neither was it a case of gradually increasing the dose of a powerful narcotic in a terminal illness, knowing that the patient would be helped to a painless death. Mrs Harding was mentally alert, not nearing death and certainly not in pain, but life was becoming burdensome and meaningless and she wanted to die earlier than she would do if the illness ran its normal course. Although the decision, if taken, would be entirely her own, and effectively be suicide, was the doctor aiding her unethically by providing the means? Would the GP be involved in the act or merely an innocent bystander? The legal situation is also difficult. The doctor could quite legitimately say that the sedatives were prescribed in good faith and that nothing unusual was suspected. What the patient then does with the tablets is her responsibility. If Mrs Harding had swallowed the entire supply and been found dead the next morning with an empty bottle beside the bed, would the doctor feel obliged to report the matter to the coroner, so opening the possibility of a verdict of suicide, or would a blind eye be cast on the bottle and a death certificate issued indicating a final fatal stroke? If the death is reported as suicide, has the doctor let his/her patient down, or perhaps, would the patient have been prepared to accept the verdict of suicide because this was her real intention?

Finally, what would be the situation if the doctor had refused to prescribe the sedatives? Although no contract had previously been made, the doctor, by refusing, was changing the terms of the relationship, saying in effect, 'I do not think you are the person to take decisions about your life. I am the one who decides for you and you must trust me.' This would destroy trust and might lead Mrs Harding to seek death by other methods. Whose decision is it, if it is not the patient's? One ethical point remains; the doctor could have supplied only a small quantity of relatively harmless pills, or given the prescription to a carer with instructions about only giving the correct dose each night. This, however, would be casuistry and does not solve the essential dilemma.

6 Mr Nuttall – risk taking

Mr Nuttall is aged 80 and a widower. He lives alone. His mental health is slightly failing, but he is physically in a stable condition apart from blackouts that result in occasional falls. None of these has been serious. He has had some bruises and on one occasion sustained a cut to his head that required two stitches. He is forgetful and once left his gas fire on through the night. He smokes a pipe and has had minor accidents with lighted matches. There has, however, been nothing tragic, as yet, to report. He is fundamentally contented and happy. He is seen occasionally by both his GP and the health visitor. He has Meals on Wheels three times a week and a good caring family.

His daughter has, however, become concerned and one day consults the doctor about the state of her father. She considers that there are dangers in his handling of electricity and gas, as well as with his smoking habits and falls. All these could be potentially serious. She asserts, 'It hasn't happened yet, but perhaps it will not be very long before there is an accident.' The daughter thinks that it is time that something is done. The doctor listens to all of this, is sympathetic and agrees to visit Mr Nuttall with the health visitor. They find the patient in good shape. He does not know why they have come to see him because he feels well, is content in his house and sees no dangers. The doctor and health visitor examine the hazards, look at the state of the house and decide that really there is no case for advising that the old man be moved to a residential home or sheltered housing. This is discussed with the daughter, who is not satisfied and places the responsibility for her father's safety very heavily upon the doctor.

Comment

The ethical dilemma here is: what level of risk is acceptable when dealing with older persons living at home? Is it reasonable to allow the patient to live happily despite some danger? At what point do these risks become significant enough for something to be done and the patient moved to safer surroundings, even against his will? Overprotection needs to be guarded against, as well as the possibility of allowing too high a level of risk to prevail. How much should an older person's life be changed just to satisfy the anxieties of relatives? Who are the responsible persons in this situation, the relatives and the carers, or the professional advisers? Who should take the decisions?

Can relatives be overruled, and what is the position of the doctor if something goes wrong? This is probably one of the most common ethical dilemmas to confront those working in the community and revolves round the question of who, in the last analysis, are the risk takers? Is it the patient, the relatives, or the professional advisers? This question is unanswerable and probably decides itself in practice according to the level of anxiety that each of the parties can tolerate. In any event, it is often the patient who has the least say in the eventual outcome.

7 Mrs Bagshaw – the dilemmas of screening

Mrs Bagshaw is aged 78. One day she is invited to attend a screening session that aims to provide a general check-up of her health and that perhaps will detect any unmet or unreported need. She turns up cheerfully, says that she is feeling well and has no complaints to make. When the doctor examines her, however, he finds a small discharging ulcer on her breast. She says that this has been present for some years and is not getting any bigger. 'I manage it myself, it is perfectly all right', she says. The doctor says that something needs to be done, and would, therefore, like to refer her to a surgeon. To the doctor it is obviously a carcinoma, albeit growing very slowly. She adamantly refuses to see a hospital specialist and, furthermore, makes the doctor promise not to tell her husband about it.

Comment

This raises the ethical issues of preventive and anticipatory care. As discussed earlier, preventive care is of three types (*see* Chapter 12), and it is the tertiary type that mainly concerns older people. Screening of older people to identify established treatable illness requires intervention on the part of the doctor and is therefore in contrast to the usual patient-initiated entry into medical care. This means that extra responsibilities are placed on the doctor. The screening must be reliable in identifying the conditions it sets out to discover. It must be possible to do something positive when these conditions are found.

Screening however, raises ethical problems. If something incurable is discovered, how far does the doctor carry investigation and treatment, especially if the patient was previously unaware of the problem? Obviously, treatable conditions such as diabetes mellitus and heart failure need attention, but what of Mrs Bagshaw, the patient with cancer of the breast? Should the doctor comply with her request to do nothing and, furthermore, not discuss the situation with her husband or relatives? Should the doctor communicate with all these people secretly and break the contract of confidentiality that the patient has presumed? Is it lacking in care not to give the patient the benefit of referral and the prospect of treatment? The question, to some extent, rests on the mandate that the patient gave the doctor when permission was given to carry out a screening procedure; but a patient does not always understand the full implications of this mandate. Does is imply acceptance of treatment and advice, or is this a different mandate that needs renegotiation? Clearly in Mrs Bagshaw's case, renegotiation was needed in the light of circumstances. The doctor who conducts the screen must recognize that this is a possibility and respect the patient's wishes. It, nevertheless, can result in dilemmas to which there are no straightforward solutions.

8 Mr and Mrs Fletcher – captive spouse

Mr and Mrs Fletcher live in a terraced house in an area that has 'seen better days'; she is aged 69 and he is 72. Mrs Fletcher has suffered from multiple sclerosis for the past 20 years, is now bedfast and becoming increasingly dependent. As time has passed she has developed heart failure and increased forgetfulness. Mr Fletcher is doing all the housework and shopping, as well as nursing his wife. His health is holding, but only just. His social life is non-existent and he has become totally captive to his house and task.

Mrs Fletcher develops pneumonia. The doctor advises that she be admitted to hospital, but her husband refuses, insists that he can cope and, moreover, provide better nursing. His wife supports him in this decision. The doctor is reluctant to agree because he perceives that Mr Fletcher's health is beginning to fail and that it would be risky to expose him to the extra strain. However, Mr and Mrs Fletcher's wishes are respected and full nursing services are arranged. Initially, the patient responds to treatment, but after three weeks of arduous and painstaking care by her husband, she relapses. Hospital admission is still rejected by Mr Fletcher. The doctor now seriously asks himself whether or not he should continue to treat Mrs Fletcher's bronchopneumonia or allow events to take their natural course.

Comment

This is a real dilemma. Withholding antibiotics would probably allow her a peaceful death in her own home, nursed by her husband. For his part, Mr Fletcher would feel that he had done his duty and cared for his wife to the best of his ability. The doctor might feel that, of the two lives, the more valuable one to save is that of Mr Fletcher. Mrs Fletcher could be admitted to hospital, but totally against the wishes of both. Obviously a high level of help in the house can be arranged, but what about the antibiotics? The usual action taken by a doctor would be to prescribe, with the intention of coping with the husband as and when it became necessary. How much, however, is the decision the doctor's and how far should he/she discuss the possible courses of action with both the patient and her husband? Mr Fletcher undoubtedly realizes the consequences for his own health of nursing his wife in this way. Is he implying that he too wants to die? The doctor may sense this and find him/herself colluding in a situation of considerable human significance.

9 Mr Fairweather – help or no help

Mr Fairweather, a widower, is aged 80 and lives in sheltered accommodation. He enjoys the company of other residents and is visited occasionally by relatives. He suffered from a stroke several years ago and is left with a partial paralysis of his right side. Despite this he walks reasonably well with a Zimmer frame, although he does not go out. Mr Fairweather also has severe osteoarthritis of his left hip, which compounds his mobility problems and causes him a considerable amount of pain. His doctor treats this symptomatically with pain-relieving tablets. The patient, however, desperately wants to have a hip replacement, which he considers would relieve his pain and improve his mobility. His doctor and the orthopaedic surgeon to whom he is referred were against this on the grounds of the previous stroke and the dangers of an anaesthetic. These problems are discussed fully with both the patient and his relatives. However, because of Mr Fairweather's persistence, the operation is eventually performed. He is discharged from hospital six weeks later, is bedfast, with pressure sores and urinary incontinence. His doctor is horrified.

Comment

There are two problems here. At what point should the doctor intervene when a patient is subjected, or in this case subjects himself, to procedures or treatment that carry the risk of causing further harm to his health? Can the doctor say 'no' when the risk is obviously considerable, or is the patient to be allowed to proceed? In this case, the risks of the operation were clear and it was obviously an extreme step to take if the aim was only pain relief. The surgeon needed to balance the risks with the possible benefits. In this case, pressure from the patient and relatives probably influenced the decision and the risk was taken. Was it ethical for the GP to refer the patient in the first place when there were severe doubts about the advisability of surgery?

The second problem is the doctor's reaction to the patient's condition on return from hospital. Were the bedsores a result of poor and careless nursing? Should the GP make a fuss, or quietly work to improve the patient's condition now that he has returned home? At all events the doctor might well ask the question, 'How much real help have I been to the patient?'

Discussion

Six ethical dilemmas are illustrated by these case histories. They concern: responsibility, priorities, information, confidentiality, collusion and intervention. They will be dealt with separately, though there is inevitable interlinkage. Few situations in medicine are as simple as first appears and often several ethical problems impinge on each other.

Responsibility

The problem with responsibility is: where does it finally rest? As has been seen, it is possible for an older couple (Case 1) to be living in conditions that an outsider would describe as intolerable and yet are perfectly acceptable to them. It can be argued that the responsibility for how an older person lives rests with that person, but, once the doctor enters the situation it could also be argued that he/she, by accepting it, may also share some of the responsibility. (The doctor is also colluding in these circumstances, but this will be considered later.) Similarly, relatives sometimes complain about the risks taken by an older man living alone

(Case 6). Who should accept responsibility for these risks? The relatives want the professional carers to do so, whereas the latter put the onus on the relatives. The patient's feeling may not even be considered.

The risks to professional workers who exercise these responsibilities are obvious and much fudging of the issues often takes place. In the final analysis, the actions of reasonable people having the skills normally possessed by members of their profession are seen as the norm. If too much weight is placed on autonomy, the patient may be exposed to unacceptable risks. By accepting the patient's view, is the doctor acting unreasonably in allowing potential hazards to develop?

Thus, ethical issues can impinge on legal issues and the resultant dilemmas are hard to resolve.

Priorities

The next dilemma concerns priorities. They can concern balancing the priorities of one patient against those of another, or of a patient against those of relatives, neighbours and society itself. The conflicting needs of the old lady and her daughter-in-law (Case 4) were very starkly presented to the family doctor. How far should the doctor interfere when decisions, taken quite justifiably by the family, are ethically unfair or medically detrimental to one of the parties? Again, the patient who chooses to live in neglect and refuse treatment (Case 2) has theoretically every right to do so; but what are the rights of the neighbours? Should the doctor bring in the law and have the patient removed to a place of care, or turn a blind eye and leave the neighbours, who are perhaps not the doctor's concern, to make complaints and demand action for themselves?

Furthermore, at what point do doctors need to consider their own positions? Do they need to safeguard their reputations in the neighbourhood and secure themselves against possible action in the courts (thereby relieving themselves of the burden of unacceptable anxiety)? Fortunately these situations are rare and the task of solving them can be shared with others who do not have the same clinical responsibilities. Nevertheless, in borderline cases the dilemma can be real.

Information

The question of information is usually concerned with how much should be told. The dilemma of Mrs Williamson was of this type (Case 3).

What is the ethical position of the doctor when informing patients that they are about to die? Stark situations like the one described are probably rare, but, when an urgent decision needs taking that involves assessment of risk, what factors influence the degree of involvement of the patient? Communication is the keystone of medical practice and involves giving information, but how far should this be withheld to preserve other important matters such as a patient's dignity and peace of mind? Is it right for a doctor to take crucial decisions on a patient's behalf without fully informing the patient about all the facts, even if these are very distressing? The question often poses itself of whether to interfere or not, the wisest course often being the latter. In practice, the patient, and, if present, the relatives, often want the doctor to take the decisions anyway. They place themselves in a physician's hands to relieve themselves of decision, responsibility and perhaps possible future guilt.

Confidentiality

How far confidentiality should be taken is a major issue and involves all age groups. A poignant case was that of the patient who wanted to take her own life as an act of voluntary euthanasia, when life had become intolerable to her (Case 5). If the doctor had colluded, how ethical would this have been, and how far should the doctor have gone in respecting her confidentiality? Making a false declaration on a death certificate is unlawful, but could there be instances in which the doctor might consider it a duty to the deceased patient?

The lady who had breast cancer and wanted nobody to know about it also presented an example of the dilemma of confidentiality (Case 7). Would it be ethically wrong for the doctor to inform her husband against her consent, when there were overwhelming reasons for doing it? At what point is confidentiality broken and information passed? When is it ethical to break a confidence? These are unresolved questions. Guidelines may be available, but in the end the health worker is often alone when taking such decisions.

Collusion

The problems of collusion have already been touched upon. The most obvious example is colluding with a patient who wishes to accept the unacceptable, as in the case of Mr Barlow (Case 2), but collusion is also possible in relation to information. Relatives often ask a health worker not to tell a patient about the true nature of an illness. What if the patient wants to know and asks outright? Should the member of the professional team respect the collusion sought by the relatives or is it an ethical duty to inform the patient? Very occasionally collusion between professional colleagues may occur. In the case of John Fairweather, where there may have been poor care following the operation, resulting in bedsores, should the doctor make this an issue or simply be concerned with the immediate tasks? Is the latter course unethical collusion? Where does a GP's loyalty lie in these circumstances? Again, the ethical judgement remains very much with the personal conscience of the individual.

A subtle situation also occurs when the doctor or other member of the team 'colludes' with him/herself. How often are issues avoided and actions taken that are not absolutely in the patient's best interests? Maybe the doctor's own interests of convenience, comfort or reduction in worry can result in temptation. A patient who is obviously going to prove difficult to manage can be admitted to hospital, although home care is theoretically possible and perhaps best for the patient.

Intervention

With the ever-increasing numbers of older patients, professionals in primary health care will be concerned more and more with the care of patients suffering from chronic illness. A dilemma that will arise is how active should practitioners be in the treatment and intervention? Sometimes the effect of active treatment may be more harmful than the problem itself. Many patients are admitted to hospital with iatrogenic diseases (conditions that have been brought on by the effects of treatment). An example is John Fairweather and his hip operation (Case 9). Should the patient alone decide these issues, having heard about the risks and possible outcomes? It is sometimes difficult for the doctor to be sure, despite much discussion with the patient and relatives, that a clear understanding of all the relevant issues has been achieved. How ethical is it for doctors to proceed against their own judgement? There are situations in which, obviously, they should argue strongly against certain actions, but there are also grey areas where risks are hard to evaluate and outcomes are unpredictable.

Anticipatory care is now part of normal practice; searching out previously untreated or unreported illness so that it can be alleviated. The ethical issues here also need clarification. Having found an untreated illness what then? As the case described earlier highlights, patients may not want treatment (Case 7). Is it a situation to be accepted and no help given? Ethically, should doctors accept this even though they are colluding with the patient, perhaps against what the doctor perceives as his/her better interests?

Modern general practice is aware of these ethical dilemmas and accepts the need to take them into consideration when making decisions. Consultations often give rise to ethical dilemmas, but, happily, most are resolved without too much difficulty. In the final analysis most of these issues are decided on considerations based on respect for the patient. It is only when the doctor is presented with conflicting needs that real difficulties arise.

When this chapter was first written the ethical issues described were largely seen as being those of the doctor. The increasing involvement of the whole health team in decision-making, especially with nursing colleagues, means that they too are involved in ethical issues. Social workers too face the same problems. The underlying questions described are relevant to all disciplines.

Acknowledgement

This chapter is based on one written by the author in *Medical ethics and elderly people*, edited by R. J. Elford[1]. In that work, a response to the ethical issues posed is given by Dr W. Donald Hudson, formerly Reader in Moral Philosophy, University of Exeter.

Reference

1. Williams EI. (1987) Issues in general practice. In: Elford RJ (editor) *Medical ethics and elderly people*. Churchill Livingstone, London, 199–216.

24
Audit of Care of Older People

Undertaking an audit of care of older people in a practice is a straightforward, yet very important activity. The group to be audited is easily identifiable from age/sex registers, particularly so if it is confined to the 75 and over age group. The range of possible care activities to be audited is also wide, making it possible to vary topics and maintain interest. The completed audits can help in the management of the practice and also point to ways in which care can be improved. Educational needs can also be identified.

The first thing to note, however, is that audit is a team activity, no more so than when looking at what the practice is doing for older people. All members of the team should therefore be involved at all the stages of audit. A practice plan is necessary, which will of course mean having a meeting to draw up the possibilities. Time for such meetings is at a premium and they need to be short and at times convenient to all team members. Lunch-time is often the most satisfactory. The most important matters on the agenda will be a decision about the particular aspect to be audited and who will take the lead. The lead person is crucial to the success of an audit and will be the person who will plan the details. The date of the next meeting should be fixed at the time of the first meeting.

Once the basic decisions have been taken about the need to audit care for older people, the audit process begins. There are about twelve specific stages to this, and, although it may appear complicated, an understanding of the progress through the stages can help the team to have a sense of 'where we are going' and common ownership.

The stages of the audit are as follows:

- choose the topic for audit chosen
- formulate the objectives of the audit
- decide the format of the audit
- construct criteria
- make a plan of action
- write the protocol
- assemble resources needed
- gather data
- analyse the results
- present and disseminate the findings

- consider the findings and see what changes are needed
- implement the changes
- revalue at a later date.

The first stage, therefore, is to choose which aspect of care should be audited. In general the topic should be of interest to the team, not too large, manageable and likely to produce results that will be of benefit. Sometimes, and this will happen with older people, there will be quite a number of topics that look worthwhile; it will then be necessary to prioritize. It is a mistake to do too much at once.

When carrying out audit, it is sometimes helpful to look at its structure, process, and outcome. When considering health checks for old people it might be possible to look at:

- *Structure*: identification of patients, invitations, appointments, storage of medical records etc.

- *Process:* the way in which the assessments are done; how much examination, what areas are covered, how the results are recorded.

- *Outcome:* what has been found; is it important; are the resources there to deal with the problems?

Other aspects of care can also be audited, such as influenza immunization, hospital admission and discharge, referral to social services, continuing care of specific groups (eg post-stroke patients), acute care, nursing care, repeat prescribing etc. There is a never-ending list. Coming back, however, to the concept of a team, it is vital that all members have a say in the topics chosen, because what may be of interest to one professional group may not have occurred to others.

The difference between research and audit is a fine one; many would say they are aspects of the same activity. Research tends to be on a grander scale than audit and aims to expand knowledge and deepen understanding. Audit is more concerned with achieving quality and better standards. Nevertheless, both activities must have carefully formulated aims and objectives. An overall audit aim would perhaps be to examine the care of patients aged 75 and over who are discharged from hospital. Within this overall statement would then be a number of specific objectives, for example, to identify the sample to be audited, and to identify the aspects of care to be reviewed (eg presence of nursing, arrangements for repeat prescribing, need for the doctor to visit etc.).

Having set the main aim and, as part of the objective-setting and construction of a plan of action, it is necessary to consider two further aspects. First, the format of the audit, and next, the question of setting the criteria for standards.

There are various technical forms in which audit can take place. It is not necessary to go into the full range of research methodology, as usually an audit is either prospective, retrospective or instantaneous. Retrospective audit is probably the most common and entails looking backwards through the record of events. It has the disadvantage of relying heavily on the quality of the record-keeping and also the tedium of searching through files. The advantage is that it describes what actually happened and is not biased by the audit itself. Prospective audit means careful data collection over time and the aggregation of results. This method can be used when there are no records available, such as when auditing the time taken to carry out health checks. The problem with this form of audit is that behaviour may alter as a result of data gathering itself. An example of instantaneous audit is a patient satisfaction study. This provides an instant test of how things are seen at the present moment. A similar instantaneous exercise occurs during a random audit of individual case notes, a process used when, for instance, auditing acute care. The key question is what form of audit is best for the particular subject.

Within all these forms of audit there can be introduced the concept of setting criteria before the audit starts. A criterion is defined as a pre-determined level of good practice that is to be used as the yardstick against which the actual level of practice is to be measured (ie a previously agreed expected standard). How are the criteria set? This is usually a group or team activity, although it is possible for one person to set criteria when doing an individual audit. There are occasionally national criteria, for example, what has to be covered when doing a health check for older people. Sometimes outside help may be used, but ultimately the criteria must be realistic (not too high or too low), attainable and related to accepted good practice. The criteria must be linked to the objectives and should be appropriate to the purpose of the exercise. All members of the team should agree the criteria and should have common ownership of them. They need to be written down and not altered during the audit; they will form the basis of the final review. Examples of criteria for doing a health check on an older person would be that:

- all the aspects designated in the contract should be covered
- specific aspects of health promotion and information should be given
- a blood pressure and urine test should be carried out
- the findings should be discussed with the patient.

There are of course many more and the practice team will construct a list of such criteria of good practice that they think will be appropriate. The concept of criterion-based audit is illustrated by the audit cycle, as shown in Figure 24.1. This is really a summary of the stages of audit that have already been described. The key exercise is reviewing the data collected against the pre-set criteria, followed by instituting changes as needed and then finally completing the cycle by reviewing the effect of these changes. The audit then becomes a continuing process.

Having thought out all these aspects, it is sometimes helpful to sit down and write a plan of action, sometimes called a protocol. The following headings are useful.

- *Introduction*: set the scene about what is to be done
- *Aims and Objectives*: describe very specifically what is to be done

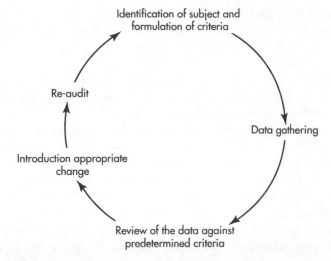

Figure 24.1: The audit cycle.

- *Criteria*: predetermined statements about what standards are to be expected
- *Methods*: how it is to be done (eg format, study group, size of sample, method of data handling, timetable etc.)
- *Analysis of results*: manual or computerized
- *Presentation of results*: decisions on the way the manuscript and tables will be arranged and who is to do this, which must be done well so that dissemination is easier
- *Plans for review*: further meetings, interim reports
- *Completing the cycle*: action and further review.

Finally, it is helpful to try out a few cases as a pilot project to test the methodology before the main audit starts, and make appropriate changes if these are found to be needed. It is essential to be absolutely clear who does what in these circumstances.

Analysing results can, of course, be time consuming and it is a good idea to have thought this out beforehand. Data that has been collected needs converting into a meaningful format. In the raw state, data usually exist on the numerous pieces of paper on which the information was first recorded. This needs dealing with as it is collected, rather than leaving the task to the end of the data collection, when it can look daunting. It is also interesting to see how things are progressing and it checks that the right information is being collected. Good audit depends on good quality information.

There are several ways of sorting out raw data; these range from simple cards to the use of a computer. For simple audits, cards are enough, but today computers are usually used. With the data in acceptable form, which means that it has been aggregated, a general look needs to be taken at the results to see if they make sense. They should then be compared with the pre-set criteria. Statistical tests are not usually needed, but may be necessary if data is being compared with a national norm or the results from another practice. Results need presenting in a 'user friendly' way, so that at a team meeting to discuss the findings they are clear and easy to read.

Finally, it is important to keep up the momentum when undertaking an audit. Faced with the tedium of data collection, enthusiasm can diminish. Common causes for this are time, people, money and criticism.

Time of course is a great problem and often the argument used against doing audit at all. Sometimes the real problem is that too much is attempted too soon. Time needs planning and it is easy to underestimate how long a task is going to take. Having too much time, though, can result in boredom. People can also cause problems. There may be too many involved or too few; there may be those around who are not interested, or who actively oppose any idea of audit, and this sometimes results in hostility. Money is also needed, maybe for buying equipment or employing additional help, and some members of the team may be against spending practice money in this way.

It is a useful audit in itself to see how much carrying out health checks costs a practice. Criticism can of course be of benefit, but it also can be destructive. Sometimes it is best to get on with things and meet problems as they arise. It is easy to get distracted at the best of times. Nevertheless, to think out some of the problems in advance is a good idea and this will avoid disappointments later.

How then is it possible to cope with all these problems and avoid pitfalls? Here are some tips:

- do not try to do too much

- plan ahead and make a realistic timetable

- set short-term targets to be achieved before going on to the next stage

- aim to finish the audit in a reasonable time (weeks rather than months)

- audit something which is interesting and useful

- allocate specific time for audit work

- if the audit is likely to take some time, produce interim results

- have regular meetings

- produce the results as rapidly as possible and share them with everybody

- make adjustments to the plan as you go along, if this proves necessary

- work with interested people

- think about motivating others; communication and involvement are important factors.

An Example of an Audit in Practice: Audit of 1990-1 Screening Programme

Background

This example concerns a practice with a list of 12 000 patients and an equivalent of six partners. The practice is situated in a suburban area with a high percentage of patients aged 75 years and over. In 1980, the practice introduced a policy of visiting patients in this age group. This was undertaken in the first place by a practice nurse. The intention was that the patients would be visited annually, friendly contact would be maintained with appropriate agencies, an attempt would be made to keep up with all the available financial allowances and to develop a working knowledge of local residential and nursing homes.

In 1987, the practice nurse retired, and, on review, it was clear that she had done much valuable work. She had screened 1538 patients over the years, and in the process had uncovered a significant degree of disease and done much to improve the living standards of many inadequately cared for and poorly housed people. The screening programme was, however, opportunistic and, as time passed, her rate of new screening and follow-up declined, as the demands of a group of 'regulars' took up increasing amounts of time.

It was obvious that the objectives of the screening programme had not been clearly enough defined at the outset. A new programme was therefore planned and a new part-time practice nurse appointed. By this time the requirements for health checks on older people in the new contract for GPs were known; this meant that more nurse time would be needed. A second part-time nurse was therefore employed in 1990. In addition to their work in geriatric screening, both nurses were required to spend some of their time in the treatment room as practice nurses. A total of 48 hours nursing time was available weekly for screening purposes. A new programme was set in hand and introduced with the new contract on 1 April 1990. At the end of the first year this was audited.

The total number of patients aged 75 and over was 1003, which was 8.49% of the total practice population of 11 811. The age distribution was as follows (Table 24.1).

Table 24.1: Age distribution.

Age range (years)	No.	% of total practice no.
75–79	488	4.13
80–84	319	2.70
85–89	142	1.20
90–94	43	0.36
95–99	11	0.09

Of these patients, 116 were in some form of residential care: 53 in sheltered housing, 35 in residential homes and 28 in nursing homes. A standard card was used for recording information, and two receptionists spent a total of two hours a week entering results into a computer. The letters of invitation were issued in batches spread over the year, with a slack period in the summer holidays and during the influenza vaccination season. Invitations were sent to all the eligible patients; 870 accepted (87%), 63 (6%) replied declining the invitation, the rest did not reply.

The objectives of the audit were to determine:

- the number of referrals
- to where they were referred
- what further investigations were performed and on how many patients
- the cost of the screening exercise.

Criteria Setting

The type of audit undertaken in this exercise was to see what was actually happening in the health check programme; it was therefore largely a monitoring process. There were, however some criteria set which were as follows:

- achievement of an 80% uptake
- completion of all the health checks within one year
- the check to be carried out according to GP contract requirements
- a referral level of 30%
- a cost-effective exercise (it was impossible to put a figure on this).

Results

The referral rate was 21%, with 185 patients being referred out of a total 870 (Table 24.2). The proportion of referrals according to age is given in Table 24.3.

Table 24.2: Breakdown of referrals.

Type of referral	No. of referrals	% of patients screened
Chiropody	31	3.6
Day care	10	0.9
District nurse	14	1.6
Housing	6	0.7
Hearing problems	14	1.6
Optician	1	0.1
Further investigations, including GP referral	30	3.4
Occupational therapy	50	5.7
Social services	29	3.3

Table 24.3: Referrals according to age.

Age (years)	Proportion	%
75–79	1 : 5	20
80–84	1 : 5	20
85–89	1 : 6	17
90–94	1 : 1.3	77
95–100	1 : 2.2	45

Further investigations undertaken are shown in Table 24.4. Five other patients also had further investigations, but, since these patients moved or died, details were not available to the practice. The investigations yielded only four abnormal findings: two infected urine samples, one new diabetic and one severe anaemia.

Table 24.4: Further investigations.

Investigation	No.
Full blood count	15
Thyroid function tests	6
Urea and electrolytes	5
MSU	5
B$_{12}$ and folate	3
Blood sugar	2
HbA1	2
Serum phenobarbitone	1

The costs of one year's (1990–91) health check programme are shown in Table 24.5. These amounted to £58.00 per referral. The capitation fees achieved by the practice for patients aged 75 and over, at £33.50 was £33 600.

Table 24.5: Costs of one year's health check programme (1990–91).

Item	£
Share of nurses' salaries (proportional to time spent on screening)	26 616
Secretarial and receptionist time	870
Postage and telephone	270
Travel expenses	643
Total	28 399
Less FHSA contribution to salaries	17 586
Total net cost	10 813

Conclusions

Uptake was reasonable and higher than expected. Those who responded positively were all seen within the year. A review of the record cards indicated that the checks were undertaken according to GP contract requirements; indeed, more aspects were included. The number of referrals made was relatively low in comparison with other published figures. This is possibly explained by the fact that many problems had previously been identified during the screening conducted over the previous 10 years. It may indicate the level to be expected in all practices in subsequent years. It may also indicate that annual screening for all patients aged 75 years and over is excessive. There was an increased number of referrals after the age of 84. This may indicate a trend, but the numbers of course are low. The commonest referrals were to chiropody, occupational therapy and social services, which is in line with other findings. The screening programme, undertaken by two professionals with clerical support, is naturally expensive. It amounted to roughly one-third of the capitation fees attracted by the patients in the practice who were 75 years and over. Referrals were costly at £58 each.

Recent Developments and Future Prospects

If the decision had been left to the practice, screening would have continued, but in a modified form, since annual screening of all over 75-year-olds hardly seemed to be cost-effective. It was decided to monitor the results even more closely.

A new computer system was subsequently installed in the practice, which led to short-term difficulties in monitoring and recall, due to problems with the transfer of information from the old to the new system. Targets for the following year included checking the data and educating the nurses in the use of the computer, thus offloading some of the secretarial work. It is hoped to make more time available in future screening visits to screen for glaucoma. It is hoped that, by careful monitoring, the annual screening programme can be adapted to ensure that it yields the maximum results for the minimum effort and cost.

Acknowledgement

This audit is published by permission of Dr Brown and Partners, Manor Surgery, Beeston, Nottinghamshire.

25
Conclusions

The impact of demographic changes on the numbers of older people, in particular the much older, over the next 20 years has now become very apparent. Older people are the fastest growing section of the population. By the year 2000 there will be a rise of around 32% in the number of people aged over 85. The increasing numbers of disabled amongst this group will mean additional demands on community services. Experience of the last 20 years has demonstrated what services should be available and how best to target them. The understanding that it is from the age of 75 years, or even 80 years, that special needs exist should enable health and social services to look realistically at provision of services. Whether adequate resources and effective planning will materialize is of course uncertain. The part played by primary care is obviously central to effective community care. On any given date, 95% of those aged 75 and over are in the care of a GP at home and most older people never see a geriatrician throughout their lives[1].

The basic philosophy underlying the care of older people in the community is also now established. It entails an understanding of the dangers of ageism and a recognition of the importance of personal autonomy in older age. A positive approach to effective health, with its emphasis on functional ability rather than absence of disease, has helped to reduce previous nihilistic attitudes towards older people.

The importance of education and training is also recognized. For medical students, it is important to demonstrate the continuum of care provided by primary and secondary services for older people. This means an understanding of the management of care at the interfaces between, not only hospital and home, but also at the point of entry into residential care. It is essential for medical schools to encourage students to take an interest in the care of older people. In vocational training too, a similar approach needs to be maintained. There is also the need for carefully planned continuing medical education to update the knowledge, skills and attitudes of both primary care and secondary care doctors. Over and above the training needs of doctors, however, is the urgent necessity to provide training for general practice staff and other health workers in the community. Practice nurses do a great deal of work amongst older people; in particular they are actively involved in the provision of health checks.

Looking to the future, there could be yet further changes. If there has been any lesson learned from the past two decades, it is that change is inevitable. The intended creation of new health authorities to replace the district health authorities and FHSAs is likely to be a beneficial move. The new authorities will have very new responsibilities, including the purchase of secondary care services, general medical services and planning. It is hoped that the care of older people will be looked at in a comprehensive way. We should at least see effective collaboration between primary and secondary care services. There may eventually be a better system of providing integrated health and social care in the community. The collaboration between one single health authority and a social services department, providing the borders are reasonably adjacent, can be its beginning. A more fundamental reform would, however, be needed to provide full integration.

A new-look public health facility, enabled to collect data from general practice, and so gain a fuller understanding of the health needs of a community, would benefit the planning process. The need for this is urgent. Fundholding practices, which have some of the functions of health authorities in purchasing and providing local services, need themselves to have public health advice about the needs of the communities they serve. Older people are high users of services and are very dependent on appropriate resources being available.

Primary health care teams will inevitably take on more responsibilities and be expected to have a wider range of skills. Many of these will relate to older person care. The part played by the hospital geriatric services may change. Already, continuing medical care in residential and nursing homes is provided by general practitioners. It is likely that this will extend to the provision of community geriatric hospitals in the community, staffed by general practitioners. Much research needs to be done before a full understanding is gained about the relationship of disability to handicap. What are the factors which affect the development of dependency and how can these be effectively minimized? What questions are yet to be answered? The aim of adding quality to years has not yet been achieved. Because of the change in the balance of care of older people between hospital and community, more teaching will inevitably be done in general practice. Members of the primary care team will have to have a clear understanding of the basic principles of care in the community if this is to be done effectively.

Finally, care of older people in the community now has an international perspective. All developed countries face a situation where more older people are requiring care, resulting in extra demand on services. Governments are interested in ways of preventing dependency, which essentially means a tertiary prevention programme. Very quickly, less developed countries will face the same challenges.

This book aims to demonstrate some of the basic principles on which community care of older people is based. It describes the UK response to some of the demographic changes and has described specific programmes of care. It is becoming obvious that many of the services introduced can be adapted to local needs in other areas of the world. This is an exciting new challenge.

Reference

1. Pereira Gray D. (1994) Health in old age. *J R Soc Med* **87**: 474–6.

26
Postscript

In this postscript I have allowed myself an indulgence. I have been interested in the care of older people in the community now for 25 years. The first edition encapsulated my experience during the first 10 of these years and it was a further 10 years before there was a need for a second edition. The need for another edition within five years has been due to far-reaching changes in the National Health Service and community social services, most of which have affected the care of older people in the community. To achieve a sense of these changes, I though it might be interesting to reprint the prefaces and conclusions of the two earlier editions.

Preface for the First Edition 1979

My interest in old people began in 1968. By that time I had already been in general practice for over ten years. Wherever I had worked, I inherited or quickly acquired what was called a chronic visiting list, which consisted in the main of persons over 65 years. Some were housebound and had a chronic illness which needed supervision; but others I had visited came to expect and even demand their monthly call. Over the years I slowly became aware of a number of things: first, that many of the patients I visited routinely were quite mobile and went out for almost all of their other requirements (indeed often went straight to the chemist's shop after my visit); secondly, that I was coming across patients with acute problems, whom I had not previously seen and who ought to have been visited earlier; thirdly I was impressed by the high incidence of anaemia in the old people. I therefore decided with the help of my partners to see every patient over 75 years and test their blood for anaemia. When planning this exercise we became aware of the work of James Williamson and his colleagues in Edinburgh on unreported need amongst the elderly. Their now classic article had been published four years previously. The work they did had been carried out on patients of 65 years and over who were partly selected from three general practices. We therefore decided to extend our own survey to a full medical and social assessment of our very old patients and to attempt to see each one in the practice and assess unreported need. The first surprise was the number of very old people we were responsible for. From a list of 7,200 patients we had 340 who were over 75 years old. I had been battling manfully to see about 40 of these a month (or at least 40 of the much larger number of over-65s). A major research exercise developed and was supported by a DHSS grant. The subsequent story has been told in many published papers, and much of the technical information gathered was written up by me as part of an MD thesis in 1973.

The study changed my attitude to the care of old people. The tedious chore of a chronic visiting list disappeared and a much more positive and interesting idea replaced it. By screening, I discover those old people who are at risk and need surveillance by either myself or the health visitor. Those who can come to the surgery are encouraged to do so and although I still visit many old people regularly, I am much happier that my visits are really necessary. I also know much more about the lives of my old patients and what they themselves want and expect from the medical and social services. A high percentage are happy, fully integrated members of society who live interesting lives. Indeed, I have enjoyed listening to and learning from the many remarkable characters who have turned up at our screening clinics. Their philosophy, considering some of the events which have happened to them during their long lives, has often been deeply moving. I was impressed by the successful living many were achieving even in advanced old age.

I therefore became interested in the quality of life after the age of 75 and felt convinced that I should be contributing to it. I rejected the nihilistic attitude adopted by many which asserts that nothing can be done to help old age and that to intervene is worthless. As one doctor put it: 'Why bother to wake a hungry man to tell him that there is no food available?' I maintain, however, that much can be done. A great deal has been learned about the ageing process and the difficulties experienced by the elderly; and it is now realised that help is possible to overcome many of these problems. These can be medical or social and sometimes a combination of both. It has been clear for some time that helping people through these situations involves a team of workers. The primary health care team comes into its own when looking after the elderly, but really needs extending to include social workers. The aim should really be to have a community care team to provide a comprehensive service.

Having said this, it is however necessary to introduce a caveat. The provision of services must not in a sense be the principal objective when considering care for the elderly. The main aim must be to keep old people self-supportive and independent. It would be wrong if as a result of intervention self-reliance were lost. Obviously, help will sometimes be necessary and may be on a long-term basis, but wherever possible a return to self-sufficiency should be the aim. The wishes of the aged themselves must always be respected and they must be consulted about their needs. Undoubtedly the independence I have just described is high on their list of priorities.

The aim of this book is therefore to describe domiciliary care in its widest sense for old people. I am not advocating a special geriatric community service, or producing a textbook of geriatrics. The care I visualise is given by the team who also look after the rest of society. Indeed, it is a basic principle that old people should be regarded as part of the community and not segregated and treated as different. The should do the shopping, collect the pension, attend the surgery and so on. But for the over-75s particularly, there are opportunities for prevention, maintenance and rehabilitation which can realistically improve the quality of their lives. This is the aim of care, and will be the major theme of this book.

Another feature which was very apparent in our original studies was the part played by the family in providing care for the elderly. This might be the husband and wife for each other, or often daughters and, occasionally, sisters and brothers. The importance of this care for the type of life lived by old people cannot be over-stressed and there is unfortunately some evidence that this availability may be diminishing. Nevertheless, the family will continue to provide most of the care needed in the community. I had originally thought of writing this book for members of the community care team, but considering the importance of the family I have tried to make it readable and informative to someone who might be looking after an elderly relative. There are therefore three different types of reader - the professional carers (doctors, nurses, social workers, physiotherapists, occupational therapists, speech therapists and, indeed all members of the team); the students of these professions; and family members and other interested lay people such as voluntary workers and reception staff at surgeries or health centres. I realise in aiming it at so wide a group of readers, I may not satisfy any one of them. The danger is obvious but as so many people are involved in looking after the aged, I thought the risk worth taking. As medical terms sometimes cause difficulty, a glossary has been included.

I have adopted throughout a practical approach to the subject and the topics chosen will, I hope, be helpful to the those engaged in looking after old people outside hospital and are based very much on my own experience. I have occasionally over-simplified, but where this has happened, I have suggested some further reading at the end of the chapter. I have also inevitably had to be selective. Some chapters are more technical than others but even so, it is hoped that they will be of interest to lay readers. The chapters on the social status of old people and the social problems they experience are not meant to be a full account of the subject, but rather an introduction that can be followed up in more detailed textbooks.

Conclusions for the First Edition 1979

The aim of this book has been to describe the problems of caring for old people in the community and to outline the facilities which should be available to help in their solution. In discussing the characteristics of illness in the elderly, and the special social and medical difficulties experienced by them, together with the problems of the caring services, it has become obvious that a new look needs to be taken at the pattern of care which is given to old people. It has been argued that a clinic for the elderly will do this and solve many of the inherent problems. It is essential to have efficient day to day care of acute problems, both medical and social, but the clinic can take this a stage further. It is fundamentally preventive and can help with such problems as unreported need, but it can also contribute to supervision of treatment, rehabilitation, resettlement and the care of special 'at risk' groups. Health education can also be undertaken. Above all, the co-ordination of activities to help the elderly and the attainment of successful co-operation between health and social workers in both the hospital and the community can be achieved. This is the central theme of the book. The clinic will not solve all the problems – nothing ever will – but it will contribute significantly to improving the standard of care for old people. Hopefully, it will help in reducing disability and in keeping old people in the community for as long a period as possible in a healthy and active state. This is going to be vital when the numbers of old people grow even larger.

There is no reason why clinics of this nature should not become widespread, preferably based on general practice and an integral part of the function of the primary health care team (as for instance are antenatal clinics). It is essential that care given to old people should be the same as that available for the whole community, and not segregated off into a specialised domiciliary geriatric service. The schemes outlined in the book are practical and, hopefully, realistic. Idealism is bound to creep in, but even under today's conditions in the community, the principles underlying the clinic should be achievable. The clinic might also be a focus for the development of new ideas about care, for undoubtedly these are necessary. The aim must be to preserve the best of what is already being achieved in the community and to extend it to include new concepts.

It is necessary to undertake research to improve the understanding of the problems of old age. For instance, it would be helpful to have further evaluation of the housing needs of old people, particularly the place and scope of sheltered housing. Communications need to be improved and it would be a useful study to find out how this can be done. Transport and maintenance of mobility are also areas which need investigating. Screening the elderly as a method of solving the problems of unreported need and vicious circle effects needs evaluation. Studies should be undertaken into the effect which screening has on specific populations, using control groups and also long-term longitudinal surveys.

The economic and financial implications of providing services for the elderly in the community also need further study. Projects are already being undertaken which are designed to gain information on the comparative costs of different forms of care for old people with defined levels of dependency in different situations. Further work on the effectiveness of alternative types of care should follow.

The modern dilemma of the diminishing availability of the family as a provider of care is probably one of the most serious aspects of the whole subject. The reasons why this should be are likely to remain for a considerable time and, if anything, become greater. Yet the family is vital and every effort will probably have to be made politically to help the families to fulfil their responsibilities towards their elderly. Society must understand that it must help and be in partnership with those providing professional help.

Having outlined the practical situation and made proposals for improving services, perhaps it is also necessary to mention some of the deeper aspects of providing care for old people. It is most important, for instance, to know how they themselves feel about their own needs as there is a danger of younger people having preconceived ideas about these. There may be a discrepancy between how old people see their requirements and the ideas about these advocated by professional carers.

The quality of life anticipated in old age is subjective in nature and is particularly affected by the expectations and satisfactions of particular generations. These will change in the future and no doubt are changing now. There may well be mismatches between the services provided and those which people actually want. It is important, therefore, to know what society expects of old people and to relate services to how old people see their own needs. Many of the attitudes expressed by doctors and social workers are reflections of their own middle-class attitudes and may perhaps be unrealistic for a large section of the population. Certainly, old people today often want to be left alone and they value their privacy and independence. Obviously *adequate* resources for help are needed when acute situations develop and physical, mental and environmental comfort is important, but choice must remain if only to help old people maintain their self-esteem and sense of purpose. Many fear disengagement and yet society seems to encourage this. Continuing work and leisure activities are sometimes difficult to achieve and yet these are often vital in promoting healthy living in old age. How this is to be fitted into the modern dilemma of reduction of work due to labour-saving machinery needs clarifying. It would be helpful to have an idea as to how old people fill their time and to attempt to identify ways in which they could be usefully employed.

Above all, problems need to be seen in context. It must be continually asked, 'Who is this a problem for?' It may not exist at all except in the mind of the observer and is merely a phenomenon inherent to old age. However, on a national level, where real problems do exist, is it likely that they will be solved, and in particular will the challenge posed by the population explosion of elderly people be met? In some ways the situation is encouraging, but some doubts remain. On the bright side, it is true that services for the elderly are developing and expanding, especially in some areas, and there is evidence that changes in the pattern of care provided have reflected changes in real need. The expansion in the residential and domiciliary provisions which have occurred over the past few years has concentrated particularly on the over-75s and a greater proportion of elderly people now receive more than one service. The meals on wheels service is currently providing a more extensive provision to those who need it. General practitioners are becoming interested in screening their elderly patients and clinics are beginning to be established.

However, attitudes must change. Professional workers must fully realise the special problems which affect the elderly. Families and society must accept the responsibility for care. Old people themselves must integrate and not segregate. Retirement must not mean disengagement. The period between 65 and 75 must not be regarded as old age but rather as a golden opportunity for fulfilment and positive living.

Finally, the care of the elderly must not be regarded as the Cinderella of the Health and Social Services. Money and intelligence must be used to ensure the real needs of the elderly are understood and satisfied. In the community, the full resources of the medical and social team must be integrated and so organised that the lessons learned over the past few years are fully utilised to improve the standard of care given to our old people.

Preface for the Second Edition 1989

The first edition of this book was based on my experiences of twenty years as a family doctor. In part, it traced my developing understanding of the natural history of ageing in the community and the real needs of old people living at home. Out of this grew a strategy of preventive medicine which, at that time, essentially meant screening entire practice populations of over-75-year olds. The emphasis has now changed and widened. Throughout the world there is an increasing recognition of the special needs of old people and to meet these, many countries are developing programmes with a specific focus on care in the community. This has meant that in the past decade there have been many developments in community and family care and these are incorporated into this new edition. The basic objectives of such care remain, however, very much as they were; the main one being to keep old people self-supportive and independent. The need to preserve functional ability has if anything become more important. Maintaining quality of life has always been a prime objective of the professional services and to achieve this it has been necessary to encourage positive attitudes towards old age and reject a nihilistic approach. The need to take account of the wishes of elderly people themselves has also been important. These basic principles of caring for the elders remain valid and contribute to the underlying philosophy of this book.

Despite some attempts at institutional care for sick and destitute old people, some dating back to the Middle Ages, most of the care provided for elderly persons has always taken place in the home. The responsibility for this care has rested with the family and medical attention has usually been provided by the general practitioner or family physician together with domiciliary nurses. In the UK this pattern of medical care was perpetuated By the National Health Service when health visiting, district nursing and general practitioner care were made freely available to all, including old people in their homes. By the 1950s when departments of geriatric medicine were being established in hospitals, it also became clear that nursing of many chronically ill old persons was taking place within the community itself. An early pioneer, J.H. Sheldon, when calling for changes in the care of old people in hospital, also drew attention to the plight of old people in their own homes (Sheldon, 1971). He thought it might be necessary to provide a special community geriatric medical service and pointed to the severe strain imposed on younger generations in caring for elderly people. He did not mention the general practitioner and other members of the community-care team as possible providers of care and it is significant that his comments were made at a time when community services were at a low point in the UK – shortly after the introduction of the National Health Service. However, since then the importance of community care complementary to, and in partnership with, hospital care has been appreciated and developed. This book does not advocate a specific geriatric service operating in the community, but a primary care service, which regards old people as normal members of the community and not medically segregated to be treated differently. It also recognises that particularly for the over-75-year-olds, there are opportunities for prevention, maintenance and rehabilitation, which can realistically improve the quality of life.

Despite the development of professional care, the family continues to provide most of the care needed in the community. This means increasingly heavy demands on husbands, wives, brothers, sisters, children and even more distant relatives and friends. Many studies have shown the intensity of the strain on carers and it is clear that they too demand special consideration and support within the community. Their needs will be discussed at various points throughout this book.

The purpose of this book is therefore to describe domiciliary care for elderly people in its widest sense. It is not a textbook of geriatric medicine, but rather a complementary work that concerns itself with what happens outside the domain of secondary care. Chapters 2–5 set the scene with an up-to-date description of the demographic, social, economic and health status of elderly people in the community. This provides information about the background to life in old age and a database for planning family-care initiatives. Chapters 6 and 7 describe the dynamics of health in association with ageing and the very important social interactions involved. Chapters 8 and 9 outline health and social care provisions in the community. This includes a careful definition of objectives. New initiatives are examined and special attention is given to the importance of the family as carers. Chapters 10–13 review developments in preventive care and the options available are critically examined. Assessment of old persons has a rapidly growing international and inter-disciplinary importance. A recent working party set up by the Kellogg Foundation and the World Health Organization has clarified many of the issues that were outstanding. The guidelines laid down by this working party are closely followed in Chapter 14. In Chapter 15 the hospital community interface is described and new guidelines for discharging patients from hospital and receiving them back into the community are presented. This is an important new area where initiatives are urgently needed. The management of patients with long-term medical problems is linked to this important area.

Chapters 16–18 consider the old person in family practice and describe the medical and nursing responses. The principles will be of relevance to primary care in both developed and developing countries. Chapter 19 describes some of the common difficulties in the community. Using a problem-solving approach it gives a practical multi-disciplinary description of management of important conditions outside hospital. Over the past few years the ethical dilemmas confronting community workers involved with old people have also been recognised and these are described in Chapter 20. The important contribution of community care for the dying patient is reviewed in Chapter 21. Finally, in the conclusion a discussion takes place on the importance of education for all those involved in caring for elderly people. This is now recognised by the inclusion in most medical schools of experience at undergraduate level in health care of elderly people. Trainee general practitioners and family doctors are also expected to gain experience in caring for old people. In the UK the newly instituted Diploma in Geriatric Medicine of the Royal College of Physicians is an important development to stimulate educational developments. This book takes into account these educational needs.

Although this work is intended primarily for members of the community care team, it is also designed for those people caring for an old person at home. Some of the chapters are, of necessity, technical and will have more relevance for the professional reader. My experience is, however, that carers and patients themselves do want to know more about the illness and I hope that the more clinical chapters will be useful to them.

There are therefore several different types of reader: the professional carers (doctors, nurses, social workers, physiotherapists, occupational therapists, speech therapists and indeed all members of the team together with the students of these professions), family members, members of voluntary organizations and very importantly, the reception staff at surgeries and health centres. The book may be of interest to teachers who are concerned with educating children about the services available in the community. It is important that young people gain an insight into what old age is really like. Many grandchildren do become the prime carers of old people. I realise that in aiming at so wide a group of readers I may not satisfy any one of them. The danger is obvious, but as so many people are involved in looking after the aged the risk is probably worth taking.

The book will also be relevant in countries other than the UK. Experience has shown that in every society the care of old persons in their homes raises the same issues and although methods of delivering care may vary from place to place, the basic natural history and the problems presented are very similar in most countries. The recent developments in the United States of America, where family medicine is taking a fuller role in looking after old persons, are of course very relevant.

The book inevitably reflects my own philosophy towards old people and their care. I have a positive and practical approach: taking action where life can be improved or saved, but not interfering unnecessarily. I try to look at the situation through the old person's eyes. I have researched many of these areas myself and am very aware of situations that need further clarification. I do not see the care of elderly people as separate from the mainstream of medical care, particularly so in the community. I believe that there should be a close co-operation between those looking after old people in hospital and in the community. They are essentially part of the same process and should link closely together in the provision of services.

The recent government White Paper *Working for Patients* is likely to form the basis of legislation which will affect both hospital and general practitioner services. Many of the proposals concern the provision of care for old people. Comments about these changes and their possible impact are made at appropriate points in the book. However, the basic principles of care will remain the same.

Reference

Sheldon J.H. (1971) A history of British geriatrics. *Modern Geriatrics*, 1, (7), 330–5.

Conclusions for the Second Edition 1989

The concluding chapter of the first edition of this book (written ten years ago) examined future developments and possible problems in caring for elderly persons. Clinics for elderly people based on general practice were forecast, and also the increasing burdens that would be placed on family and carers. Further research was envisaged especially on the economic implications of the expected increase in the numbers of elderly people. It was thought that changes in attitudes were necessary amongst professional carers towards elderly people, with appropriate educational input to achieve this. One sentence revealingly hinted that elderly people themselves would accept responsibilities for self-care and suggested that they should integrate and not segregate.

Looking back at the last ten years there have been some developments in these areas. Special clinics, although not a widespread feature of general practice, do exist and the idea of a practice having one is no longer outrageous. The problems of carers are much more fully appreciated. Little research, however, has been undertaken into the delivery of care for elderly people and the economic implications are still far from being understood. There are some changes in attitudes, but negativism is still a significant block to the development of better systems of care, and much still needs to be done educationally. Old people themselves probably now have a more positive approach to ageing, and the news is good about overall health status.

There have, however, been significant changes that were not foreseen. New ideas have emerged about preventive care. Comprehensive screening has, on the whole, given way to selective screening and opportunistic screening. Anticipatory care, with its emphasis on health promotion as well as disease prevention is now important and accepted. The need for interface care when patients move from one system to another is clearly identified. The ethical issues associated with community care are also now much better understood. The introduction of the Diploma in Geriatric Medicine examination is a stimulus to extending educational facilities amongst doctors. A major development has been the privatisation of nursing homes and rest homes, thus changing dramatically the provision of long-stay care. This has revolutionised the hospital-bed situation, but has also brought problems. How long it will last is a debatable point. Looking into the future, education is likely to become vitally significant. Health care of elderly people is now established as a discipline, with academic departments in most United Kingdom medical schools. All undergraduates have geriatric medicine in their curriculum. The exposure of students to care of elderly people in the community is also developing through academic departments of general practice or primary care. The mandatory three-year postgraduate vocational-training requirement before achieving principal status is producing much better equipped general practitioners. Most trainees get geriatric medicine hospital experience at senior house officer level, and this is to be encouraged. The one-year experience as a trainee in general practice has allowed the young doctor to learn about the care of old people at home. Hopefully, day-release courses supplement this learning. Continuing postgraduate education in general practice is not as well developed and there is an urgent need for this in the United Kingdom. Other disciplines, including nursing, social work and the therapies also need educational input into their training about health care of elderly people and this is developing. In all areas, attitudinal as well as technical awareness needs to be stimulated.

As this book is published, a nodal point has probably been reached in the evolution of primary care in the UK, and this will have important implications for elderly people. The White Paper on Primary Care, the Cumberlege Report, the Griffiths Report on Community Care and others all signal major changes. The wide examination of the health services currently being undertaken by Government may indicate even more fundamental changes. The White Paper supports preventive activity in primary care and this may well be helpful in the case of elderly people, but other changes, such as increasing competition between doctors, may be harmful. Neighbourhood nursing schemes may well remove from old people the benefit of a known practice-attached district nurse. The wide remit given by the Griffiths Report to local authorities for the provision of long term care of elderly people is very dependent upon financial resources and experienced management. The place of private capital in this needs to be clarified.

The indications are that there will be a shift of care for old people from the hospital- (secondary-) care system to the community. The dangers are that this will take place inappropriately and inadequately. Much is now understood about looking after old people, including the nature of their needs, especially those who are very old. Indeed it is with the very old that we should be presently concerned. The relative increase of the old old in the population over the next decade will mean an increased demand for services. Unfortunately, the organisational structure available in the community is not ideal for undertaking this task. The tripartite management system, health authority, local authority and Family Practitioner Committee, is inappropriate for providing the integrated care system that is essential when caring for old people. Sensible planning, proper communication, effective allocation of resources and efficient use of available staff all demand a unified system of management. None of the reports and papers have addressed this question. The final sentence of the 1979 edition of this book stated: 'In the community the full resources of the medical and social team must be integrated and so organised that the lessons learned over the past few years are fully utilised to improve the standards of care given to our old people.' Will it be different in the next ten years?

Glossary

Caring for older people in the Community involves workers from a wide range of disciplines and many do not have a medical background. It is hoped that relatives, carers and old people will also find this book informative and interesting. For these reasons a brief glossary of technical (and jargon) terms is included.

Agnosia	Difficulty in interpreting sensory data from the environment, or from one's own body. Seen in stroke patients.
Angiography	A radiological technique which outlines the arteries.
Aneurism	A swelling of an artery caused by dilation of the walls.
Anorexia	Loss of appetite.
Aorta	A large artery arising from the left side of the heart. The aortic area is the part of the chest wall where sounds coming from the aortic valve can best be heard using a stethoscope.
Antigens	A substance which when introduced into the body stimulates the production of antibodies which react specifically with that antigen. For example bacterial toxins.
Apex Beat	The heart beat felt over the left side of the chest and normally in the mid clavicular line in the 5th intercostal space.
Ascites	Free fluid present in the abdomen.
Atheroma	Fatty deposit in the wall of an artery.
Arrhythmia	Disordered rhythm of the heart.
Balantitis	Inflammation of the foreskin of the penis.
Bacteraemia	Bacteria in the blood stream.
Bradycardia	Slow heart rate.
Carbohydrate Intolerance	An inability by the body to deal with the breakdown of carbohydrates.
Carotid Bruit	A specific sound heard through a stethoscope over the carotid artery in the neck.
Caruncle	Small extrusion of mucosa from the female urethral orifice.
Chronic Open Angle Glaucoma	A form of glaucoma (increased pressure within the eye) occurring mainly in the elderly.
Contracture	A deformity usually of a limb.

Cystoscopy | Examination of the inside of the bladder using a flexible tube with a light at the end.

Decubitus Ulcer | A bed sore.

Deep Venous Thrombosis (DVT) | Clotting of blood in a largish non-superficial vein.

Dendrites | Nerve cell connections.

Dysphasia | Difficulty with speaking.

Dyspnoea | Breathlessness.

Dyspraxia | Inability to perform common tasks such as dressing.

Dupuytren's Contracture | Contracture of the hand causing deformity of one or more fingers.

Embolus | A small body, usually a blood clot, in the blood stream which eventually causes a blockage in an artery.

Endarterectomy | Removal of a clot from an artery.

Enteric Coated | A tablet covered with a substance with prevents breakdown in the stomach and so avoids gastric irritation.

Erythrocyte Sedimentation Rate (ESR) | Measurement of blood viscosity which is increased in certain conditions.

Extrapyramidal | Describes parts of the nervous system which are concerned with movement and posture.

Faecal impaction | Blockage of faeces in the rectum.

Fasciculation | Contractions of small bundles of muscle fibres visible under the skin.

Frontal Meningioma | A tumour arising in the frontal area of the brain.

Fundus | When referred to the eye, the back of the inside which contains the retina.

Glomerular Filtration | This describes the urine filtration mechanism in the kidney.

Haematocrit | A measure of the packed cell volume in the blood.

Haemoglobin | Red oxygen carrying pigment in red blood corpuscles.

Hallux Valgus | Deformity of the big toe.

Heberden's Nodes | Small swellings of the fingers seen in rheumatic conditions.

Hemianopia | Loss of half of the visual field.

Hemiplegia | Paralysis of one side of the body.

Hyperpara-thyroidism	Over activity of the parathyroid gland.
Hypothalamus	An area of the brain.
Intra ocular tension	The pressure of the fluid within the eyeball.
Infarction	Area of destroyed tissue resulting from blockage of a blood vessel.
Iridectomy	Surgical operation on the iris.
Ketoacidosis	Occurs in serious diabetes mellitus and causes excretion of ketones into the urine.
Kyphosis	A convex curvature of the thoracic spine.
Lymphocyte Count	A measure of lymphocytes (part of the white blood cell range) in the blood.
Macrocytic	Describes red blood cells which are larger than normal.
Macular Degeneration	This is the degeneration of part of the back of the eye called the macular. It is important because of resultant reduction of vision.
Necrosis	An area of dead tissue.
Neurotransmitter Systems	Pathways for conducting messages through the nervous system.
Normal Pressure Hydrocephalus	This is an increased level of fluid in the brain but without corresponding rise in intra-cranial pressure or spinal fluid pressure. A cause of dementia which can possibly be surgically reversed.
Oedema	Swelling due to fluid retention.
Overflow Incontinence	Inability to retain urine due to a full bladder and a weak urethral sphincter muscle.
Paget's Disease	A disease of bones resulting eventually in deformity of for instance the skull and tibia bones.
Palliative Care	Care of the terminally ill, in particular concentrating on relief of symptoms, good nursing, recognition of psychological needs and the quality of the environment.
Papilloedema	A swelling of the fundal region at the back of the eyes due to transudation of fluid. An important physical sign.
Paraplegia	Paralysis of the lower half of the body.
Parkinsonism	Symptoms of Parkinson's Disease including tremor and rigidity.
Presbyopia	Visual impairment to reduced accommodation. Affects ability to do close work.
Ptosis	Drooping of the upper eyelid.
Papilloma	Small slightly elongated skin tag.
Pituitary-Adrenal Axis	Reference to the hormonal relationship between the pituitary gland (situated in the skull) and the adrenal gland (situated near the kidney).

Platelets	Small components of the blood that are involved in the clotting mechanism.
Pleural Infusion	A collection of fluid between the lung and the chest wall.
Polyuria	The passage of large quantities of urine.
Position Sense	Ability to determine the position of the body in relation to the outside world.
Practice Patient Profile	Details of for instance the age range and sex distribution of the total number of patients in a practice.
Prolapse	The downward displacement of an organ for example the rectum or uterus.
Prostatic Hypertrophy	An enlargement of the prostate gland.
Pruritis Vulvae	Itching of the female genital area.
Pyelography	An Xray which outlines the shape of the kidneys.
Recognition Proteins	Proteins which control growth and replacement which if mutant may contribute to ageing.
Respiratory Efficiency	The ability of the lungs to provide sufficient oxygen in the blood.
Serological	Concerned with the serum, a component of the blood.
Spurious Diarrhoea	Diarrhoea due to constipation.
Subdural Haematoma	A clot of blood in the space between the skull and the brain beneath the dural lining.
Systolic Ejection	Describes the type of murmur in the heart sounds.
Temporal Arteritis	A chronic inflammatory process of the arteries and in particular the temporal arteries.
Terminal Care	Last stages of the care for a dying patient. Usually now referred to as Palliative Care.
Thyrotoxicosis	Over activity of the thyroid gland.
Uraemia	Renal failure characterised by high levels of urea in the blood.
Vertebro-basilar	Refers to arteries supplying blood to the brain.
Vibration sense	The ability to recognise vibrations.

Index

Index entries refer to older people in the UK unless otherwise noted.

Since the main subject of this book is the care of older people in the community, entries have been kept to a minimum under the keyword 'Community care' and readers are advised to seek more specific references.

Prefaces are conclusions from previous editions of this title (pages 317–326), have only been indexed very lightly. The glossary has not been indexed.